SANDRA GUSTAFSON'S

CHEAP EATS IN PARIS

SANDRA GUSTAFSON'S

CHEAP EATS IN PARIS

EIGHTH EDITION

A Traveler's Guide to the Best-Kept Secrets

SANDRA A. GUSTAFSON

CHRONICLE BOOKS
SAN FRANCISCO

Printed in the United States of America.

EIGHTH EDITION
ISBN 0-8118-1813-6
ISSN 1074-5068

Cover photograph: CROISSANT/COFFEE/SPOON, Paul Clancy/
GRAPHISTOCK
Book design: Words & Deeds
Original maps: Françoise St. Clair

Distributed in Canada by Raincoast Books,
8680 Cambie Street, Vancouver, B.C. V6P 6M9

10 9 8 7 6 5 4 3 2 1

Chronicle Books
85 Second Street
San Francisco, CA 94105

Web Site: www.chronbooks.com

For Sara

Contents

To the Reader

Paris is a feast, but the banquet has become painfully expensive.

—*Anthony Dias Blue*

Eating is a serious venture, if not a patriotic duty, in France.

—*Patricia Roberts*

Paris is famous for its fashion, acclaimed for its art, and notorious for its nightlife, but to visit Paris and ignore the endless opportunities for sampling its wonderful cuisine is absolutely unthinkable. Thus, along with the Louvre, the Eiffel Tower, and the Champs-Élysées, dining should be an integral part of any successful trip to Paris. The French know how to eat; if there is something a French person would rather do, no one has yet discovered what it is. For the French, good food is not a casual interest expressed only when eating out but a way of life and a celebration of the bounty of foods available throughout the year. As a result, French cooking has been raised to an art form; chefs with great talent and skill are awarded the Legion of Honor and given the same media attention we reserve for rock stars. One of the most well-known statements by French president Charles de Gaulle refers not to politics or war but to cheese. The ritual of Sunday lunch has almost been canonized, and even *Le Monde,* the most serious newspaper in the country, runs front-page stories about *cornichons*, as well as types of bread and the wines and cheeses that go best with them. In Paris you will find this love of good food reflected in more than twenty thousand cafés, bistros, brasseries, and restaurants that cater to every taste and budget, from haute cuisine to hole-in-the-wall.

Because the French demand a higher standard and quality of food and of preparation, they are usually willing to pay for it. It is easy, if you have unlimited funds, to dine at one of the Parisian cathedrals of cuisine and have an exquisite meal for over a thousand francs per person. Visitors determined to partake in Paris' ultimate culinary pleasures too often rush only to those restaurants with at least one Michelin star and, in so doing, overlook many up-and-coming restaurants that serve remarkable food at a fraction of the price. The ongoing worldwide recession and slumping French economy have not been able to sustain the bloated tabs of the culinary all-stars, forcing many to lower their prices or go out of business all together. At the same time, it has encouraged diners to experiment with less-expensive bistros and family-run restaurants. Hands-on newcomers, who learned their cooking craft from the masters, have branched out on their own in low-end, off-the-beaten-track establishments. Many seat diners in bare, humdrum surroundings, but the high-quality food and fair prices more than compensate for the lack of elegance. Talented regional chefs have put sizzle into the Paris dining scene with their artfully inspired dishes, giving foreign diners a chance to acquaint themselves with France's many regional cuisines . . . and all for the price of a main course in the restaurants these chefs once cooked in. Many of these places have at least a three- to five-day waiting list for a table, while the three-star shrines only dream of having such lists.

As we all know, selecting a place to eat can be frustrating and time-consuming because it is also quite possible, especially in Paris, to pay too much and then eat badly. Whether you're visiting for only a day or for several weeks, you don't want to waste time and money on a mediocre meal when you could be eating magnificently and paying less just around the corner. Where are these good-value restaurants? Here is where *Cheap Eats in Paris* comes to the rescue. It is very important to note that this book is not a listing of the cheapest eats in Paris. Those are left to books where quality and value are sacrificed for saving a franc, no matter what. *Cheap Eats in Paris* will improve the quality of your Parisian dining experiences and save you money by leading you away from the tourist-packed, high-priced restaurants and to the well-located picturesque ones serving reasonably priced meals of good value to mostly French patrons. *Cheap Eats in Paris* opens you to a world of taste and good food in a wide array of genuinely Parisian establishments: crowded, noisy cafés with a haze of pungent smoke and a coterie of colorful regulars; family-run bistros with red-and-white checked tablecloths and sawdust on the floor; sophisticated wine bars; cozy tearooms; big brasseries serving steaming platters of *choucroute;* and candlelit restaurants that inspire couples to leave more in love than when they arrived. Some of these are classics everyone has heard about. Others, until now, have been virtually unknown to foreigners. A few are Big Splurges that have been selected for special occasions, for when you want to sample an abundance of the very best.

My research trip for this edition took me to parts of Paris I otherwise would not have visited and led me to many new and exciting dining discoveries. In an effort to help you save money and, as much as possible, keep you from making mistakes, I revisited every listing in the seventh edition of *Cheap Eats in Paris,* as well as trying countless others that for some reason or another did not make the final cut. In the process, I walked 689 miles, was asked directions 46 times, wore out my umbrella and two pairs of shoes, and, of course, ate out every day. I was seated in English-speaking Siberia near the kitchen, under the fan, and behind a post; suffered through nearly inedible meals; was overcharged by condescending waiters who thought I didn't know beans when the bag was open; sat on chairs that could have been used in the Inquisition; and received a cool shoulder from apéritif to *digestif* just so you can avoid suffering the same thing. Many old favorite Cheap Eats remain. Unfortunately, some entries from past editions have been dropped. Places that were once wonderful are now sadly lacking; chefs and owners changed, quality dropped severely, and/or prices rose to a mind-numbing level. Cozy corner cafés fell victim to fast-food joints, and the age of concrete and modernization removed others.

The result of my research is the eighth edition of *Cheap Eats in Paris,* with more than two hundred cafés, bistros, brasseries, restaurants, tea-rooms, and wine bars offering good food quality and top value for your dining franc. *Cheap Eats in Paris* takes the uncertainty out of dining and shows you how, by cutting a few corners, to get on the inside track to some of the best dining deals in Paris.

In the back of the book is a page for your comments and notes. Naturally, I hope you are as enthusiastic about the restaurants you choose from *Cheap Eats in Paris* as I was in selecting them. I also hope this book will inspire you to strike out on your own and make your own dining discoveries. If you find someplace you think I should know about, or want to report a change in a restaurant I've listed, please take a few moments to write me a note telling me about your experience. I answer every letter, and I cannot emphasize enough how important your letters and comments are.

Whether for business, sightseeing, or as a stop on the way to another destination, Paris has been beckoning travelers for hundreds of years, and most visitors have treasured memories of their stay in the City of Light. One of the best souvenirs you can have of your trip to Paris is the memory of a good meal. I hope that by using *Cheap Eats in Paris* you will have some very special memories of Paris to take home with you. If I have helped you to do that, I consider my job well done. *Bon voyage,* and of course, *bon appétit!*

How to Use Cheap Eats in Paris

Each listing in *Cheap Eats in Paris* includes the following information: the name of the establishment, the address, the arrondissement (in parentheses), the telephone number, the most convenient métro stop, the days and hours it is open and closed, whether reservations are necessary, which credit cards are accepted, the average price for a three course à la carte meal, the price for a prix fixe meal, whether or not English is spoken and to what degree, and if there is a nonsmoking section. The number in the brackets to the left of the name of the restaurant indicates its location on the arrondissement map that precedes each section.

The following abbreviations are used in the restaurant listings:

To indicate annual vacation closing:	
No annual closing	NAC
(Otherwise, vacation dates are listed.)	

To indicate credit cards accepted:	
American Express	AE
Diners Club	DC
MasterCard	MC
Visa	V

To indicate if drinks are included in the prices quoted:	
Boissons compris (drinks included)	BC
Boissons non-compris (drinks *not* included)	BNC

At the end of the restaurant section are some "Quick-Reference Lists." These list restaurants in the Big Splurge category as well as *boulangeries* and *pâtisseries*, tearooms, wine bars, and those serving vegetarian fare and non-French food. Also listed are those restaurants that have some kind of no-smoking policy. Finally, there is a glossary of menu terms, an alphabetical index of the restaurants listed, and a page for reader comments.

Tips on How to Have the Best Cheap Eats in Paris

1. Eat and drink a block or two away from the main boulevards and tourist attractions. The difference in price for even a coffee can be considerable.
2. In smaller restaurants and cafés, arrive early for the best selection of seats and food. Remember that the last order is usually taken no less than fifteen minutes before closing.
3. Eat where you see a crowd of French people. If a restaurant is either empty or full of tourists, or it posts a menu outside in five languages, you can assume the locals know something you do not and move on.
4. French law states that all restaurants must post a menu outside. *Always* read it before going in to make sure the menu has something you want at a price you can afford.
5. Stay within and respect the limits of the kitchen's power. Don't expect gourmet fare from a corner café, and don't go to a fine restaurant and order only a salad.
6. The prix fixe menu or *formule* will always be the best value. The next best bet is the *plat du jour* ordered à la carte. This is always fresh and usually garnished with potatoes and a vegetable.
7. In more expensive restaurants, the Cheap Eating secret is to go for lunch and order the prix fixe menu. This usually costs a fraction of what it would for dinner and often includes wine *and* coffee.
8. Look for restaurants that offer *only* one price for everything, from a kir to start and a coffee to finish to three courses and wine in-between. These are popping up all over Paris and represent some of the best dining values for hungry Cheap Eaters.
9. Order the house wine (*vin de la maison* or *vin ordinaire*). Ask for *une carafe de l'eau ordinaire* (tap water), which is free, rather than paying for a bottle of mineral water.
10. Have your morning *café au lait* and croissant standing at the bar at the corner café. It will cost twice as much if it is served at a table, and even more at your hotel.
11. Always double-check the math on your bill. Mistakes are frequent and are usually not in your favor. By law, restaurants must include the service charge (which is the tip) in the price. No additional tip is necessary unless either the food or the service has been very special.

12. Restaurants change their hours and their annual vacations to adjust to the changing patterns of tourism and economics, so call ahead to make sure they will be open, especially if you're making a special trip. All of the information given in *Cheap Eats in Paris* was accurate at press time, but closings change frequently around holidays and during July and August.

13. For a really Cheap Eat, the street *marchés* (see "Markets" under "Food Shopping," page 26) are the perfect place to pick up fixings for a *déjeuner sur l'herbe* (lunch under a tree in the park). A piece of ripe Brie cheese, a fresh baguette, a ripe apple or pear, and a bottle of young Beaujolais wine . . . ah, that's Paris.

14. You will never get lost if you buy a copy of the *Plan de Paris par Arrondissement.* The free maps you get are worth what they cost: nothing. This invaluable and timeless map is available at most news kiosks and bookstores in Paris and at many travel bookstores in the United States. It contains a detailed map of each arrondissement, the métro stops, bus routes, and a wealth of other useful information. It is pocket size and every Parisian has one: you should, too, if you will be in Paris for more than forty-eight hours.

15. If you have particularly enjoyed a place recommended by *Cheap Eats in Paris,* be sure to tell the owner or manager where you found out about them. They are always very appreciative.

General Information about French Dining

Cafés, Bistros, Brasseries, Restaurants, Tearooms, and Wine Bars

"Is this a café, a bistro, a brasserie, or a restaurant?" This is the question many foreigners ask, and much confusion exists about the definitions of these names. In the pecking order of eateries, a bistro is a cut above a café and a notch below a restaurant, and brasseries fall somewhere between them all. The following explanations should help you know what to expect from each.

Cafés

The last time I saw Paris
Her heart was warm and gay
I heard the laughter of her heart in
Ev'ry street café.

—Oscar Hammerstein II

The French don't go to priests, doctors, or psychiatrists to talk over their problems; they sit in a café over a cup of coffee or a glass of wine and talk to each other.

—Eric Sevareid, "Town Meeting of the World," CBS Television, March 1966

For the visitor to Paris, the café is a living stage and the perfect place to feel the heartbeat and pulse of the city. The café experience lets anyone become a Parisian in the space of an hour or so, since by coming here, you are immediately cast into one of the best scenes in the city. For the French, it would be easier to change their religion than their favorite café. Depending on the area, it can be a café pouring a wake-up Calvados to workers at 4 A.M., the lunch spot for local merchants, a lively afternoon rendezvous for students, or a meeting place to have "one with the boys" on the way home from work. People who are lonely find company, foreigners find a place to write postcards, countesses rub elbows with cab drivers, and everyone finds *égalité.*

In a café, you can eat, drink, and sleep it off afterward, flirt, meet your lover, play pinball, hide from your boss, talk, listen, dream, read, write, order take-out sandwiches, make telephone calls, use the toilet, pet the lazy dog sprawled across the entrance, and sit at a table for as long as you like, engaging in prime people-watching. If the café is also a *tabac,* you can buy cigarettes, pipes, postcards, stamps, razor blades, cheap watches, lottery tickets, and *telecartes,* the wallet-size cards that take the place of coins in most public telephone booths in Paris. If the café has a PMU sign, you can place a bet on your favorite horse or political candidate. Talk about convenience! No wonder there is a café on almost every corner in Paris.

Cafés don't try to be trendy. The management will never consult a decorator and they don't listen to talk about *nouvelle cuisine,* lowering cholesterol, or controlling fat grams. You can expect cafés to be smoky inside. Even though the government is trying to curtail cigarette smoking, puffing away remains a solid fact of café life in Paris. At peak hours, the hectic, noisy, smoky ambience is part of café charm. The lunch hour is always lively, with service by acrobatic waiters who commit orders to memory, run with plates full of food, and never mix an order or spill a drop. The hearty *bonne maman* food is offered at prices that even struggling students can afford.

Parisians are masters of the art of the café. Almost any time of year, the most popular café tables are those on the sidewalk. These offer a window on contemporary life in Paris and allow you to linger for hours over a single drink and perfect the Parisian art of doing nothing while watching the world pass by. Of course, if you stand at the bar, whatever you order will cost less, but by paying the premium and occupying a table, you acquire privileges bordering on squatter's rights. If the table has a cloth or paper placemat, that means that the table is only for patrons who want to eat. If it is bare, you are welcome to sit, have a drink, and stay as long as you like. No one will rush you or ask you to pay until you are ready to leave, unless the waiters are changing shifts and need to settle their daily take or if the café is about to close. Don't complain when the bill comes; you are not paying $3.50 for a tiny, strong cup of coffee, you are paying for the privilege of sitting in a pleasant environment for as long as your heart desires.

Bistros

After the fall of Napoléon, the Russian soldiers who occupied Paris would bang on the zinc bars and shout "*bistrot!*" which means "hurry" in Russian. Many say that bistros served the world's first fast food. In the past, when bistros were all simple *maman et papa* run places, fast food was the order of the day. Today, bistros still make up the heart and soul of Parisian dining. Some are small, unpretentious, and family-run with a handwritten menu and decor that has not changed in thirty years. Others are elegant, with starched linens, formally clad waiters, and prices to match. In any bistro, the atmosphere is friendly, and the room is packed with loyalists who know every dish on the menu. When you are hungry enough to dig into a steaming platter of rib-sticking fare, head for a bistro. Farm-kitchen renditions of *pot-au-feu, boeuf bourguignon,* Lyon sausages, thick *cassoulets,* duck confit, salt cod, and the quintessential bistro dessert, *tarte Tatin,* are the once-lost and now-found dishes that salute the robust, nostalgic bistro cooking firmly rooted in the French past.

Brasseries

Open from early morning until past midnight, brasseries are big, brightly lit, and perpetually packed with a noisy, high-energy crowd enjoying service in the best long-aproned tradition. As opposed to bistros and restaurants, you can order food at almost any time of the day, delving into platters of *choucroute,* fresh shellfish, steaks, and chicory salad loaded with bacon and topped with a poached egg. Everything is washed down with bottles of Alsatian wine and cold beer. While reservations are appreciated, you can usually get a table without one.

Restaurants

To eat is a necessity; to eat well is an art.

—*Antheleme Brillat-Savarin,*
author of the 1825 gastronomic classic,
La Physiologie du Gout

With more than twenty thousand places to eat in Paris, any dining mood or whim can be met. A restaurant serves *only* full, three-course meals at set times for lunch and/or dinner. It is not the place to go if you want a quick sandwich or a big salad on the go. Restaurants offer a complete menu with impressive wine lists, and diners are expected to order accordingly. They are more formal in service, food preparation, and presentation than cafés, bistros, and brasseries. Because eating is such a serious business in France, especially in Paris, most restaurants have only one seating to allow for leisurely dining. No waiter worth his or her white apron or black tie would ever rush a French person through a meal in order to free the table for other diners. You can count on spending almost two hours for a serious lunch and at least three for a nice dinner. Do as the French do: relax, take your time, enjoy each course and the wine, and above all, be happy you are in Paris.

Tearooms

Salons de thé are hospitable places where you are encouraged to get comfortable and stay awhile. Hidden away in all corners of Paris, they are romantic and welcoming places for those looking for a relaxing lunch, a sightseeing or shopping break, or an afternoon of quiet, unhurried conversation with an old friend over a rich dessert and a pot of brewed tea. In addition, they are nice places to go for a light lunch, brunch, or late-afternoon snack if you know dinner will be very late. Almost every neighborhood has its *salon de thé,* and they are as different as their owners:

some are elegant, some quaint, and others high-tech modern. They often have a friendly cat to pet, periodicals to glance through, and an air of intellectualism.

Wine Bars

In France, wine is not a luxury, it is a necessity.

—*Anonymous*

Average life of a drinker of water: 56 years
Average life of a drinker of wine: 77 years
Choose!

—*Sign in a French railroad station*

The popularity of *bars à vin* continues in the City of Light. Most wine bar owners not only have a passion for good wine but one that goes with an interest in good food. The friendly rendezvous for Parisian pacesetters, wine bars are a smart solution for those looking for a place to relax over a glass or two of good wine while enjoying a light meal from noon until late in the evening. Ranging from rustic to futuristic, they serve fine wines as well as little-known vintages by the glass or bottle, along with simple meals of salads, *tartines* (slices of baguette or country bread spread with pâté or cheese), cold meats, cheeses, and usually hot main dishes.

The French Menu

Paris is just like any other city, only the people eat better.

—*Maurice Chevalier,*
in the film Love in the Afternoon

While dining in Paris is often anticipated as the most pleasurable aspect of any visit, sometimes it can be a very disappointing and unsettling experience if you do not know what to expect. Let's face it, whether it is neatly printed on an oversized menu in a fine restaurant, whitewashed on a bistro window, written in fading chalk on a blackboard, or handwritten on a sheet pinned to a café curtain, the French menu can be intimidating. This section will take the mystery out of the French menu, so that you will feel confident to go anyplace and order with style and ease.

All French eating establishments must, by law, post a menu outside showing the prices of the food they serve. *Cheap Eats in Paris* gives you enough information about each restaurant listed so that you will know generally what to expect before you get there. Still, when you arrive at your destination, read the posted menu *before* going in. This avoids unpleasant surprises and embarrassment in the event that what is offered that day does not appeal to your taste or budget.

When reading a menu, look at the *menu prix fixe* (sometimes called a *formule* or *menu conseille*) as well as the à la carte menu. The prix fixe menu will usually consist of a combination of two or three courses—the *entrée* (first course), the *plat* (main course), and cheese and/or dessert—all for one price. The drinks (wine, beer, or mineral water, and sometimes coffee) may or may not be included. The prix fixe is often a terrific bargain, especially in the higher priced restaurants, where it enables those on a tighter budget to dine in luxury. The choices may be limited, but the value is always there. Be careful, however, because more and more higher priced restaurants are offering the prix fixe menu for lunch *only.* If you opt for this menu, you will be expected to take all of the courses offered. If you want only one or two, and three are offered, there will be no reduction in price, but don't think that a three- or even four-course meal will be too much to eat. A good French meal is balanced, and the portions are not large. Enjoy your meal the way the French do—slowly—and you will not feel overfed.

Most restaurants also offer à la carte choices, and for those with lighter appetites, this often makes good sense because you are not paying for courses you do not want. On the à la carte menu, each course is priced separately. A word of caution: Always look very carefully at the prices of the à la carte choices because the sum of the parts may add up to a very expensive meal compared to the prix fixe meal.

Once inside and seated, do not ask for "the menu," ask for *la carte.* That way you will get the complete listing of all the foods served, from appetizers to desserts on *both* the prix fixe and à la carte menus. If you say "I'd like the menu," you could get a strange look from the waiter, cause some confusion, and possibly end up with the prix fixe meal, which is also referred to as *le menu.*

When ordering, keep in mind what is likely to be fresh and in season, and consider, too, the specialties of the chef. The specialties of the house are sometimes starred or underlined in red on the menu. You will also see the word *maison* (house) written by some choices, which means that it is made "in house," and therefore considered a specialty. The day of the week is also important. Fish is always worst on Sunday, when the wholesale food market at Rungis is closed, and on Monday, when most outdoor markets are closed. Also keep in mind where you are. If you are in a corner café, complete with pinball machines and a tabac in the corner, don't expect the chef to perform magic with wild game or to dazzle you with high-rising soufflés.

No matter what the size or scope of the eating establishment, one of the best choices for the main course is the *plat du jour* (the daily special). It usually changes every day, the ingredients are fresh and seasonal, and there is a rapid turnover because the dish has proven to be a winner with the regulars. It will not be a dish whose ingredients have been languishing in the refrigerator for several days or relegated to the freezer due to lack of interest.

Meals

Every good meal in Paris is like a *petite vacance.*

—*Ray Lampard*

Proper French meals usually consist of at least two or three courses: an *entrée* (starter), a *plat* (main course), and dessert, or only the *plat* with either the *entrée* or the dessert. At more formal restaurants, you can expect to be served additional courses, up to as many as seven. Bread, an essential part of any French meal, is served free, and you are entitled to as much as you want. Unless you are given a separate bread plate, place you bread on the table, *not* on your plate.

Here is a list of the traditional French courses:

apéritif	before-dinner drink, generally a kir
amuse bouche	a plate of little hors d'oeuvres served with your apéritif while you decide what to order
entrée	appetizer, starter
fish course	
plat	main course
salad or cheese	
dessert	
petits fours	plate of cookies served with after-dinner coffee
coffee	espresso

The best way to participate in the way of life in Paris (or in any place for that matter) is to dine the way the locals do, at the same times, on the native dishes and specialties that have become their culinary heritage. The French take dining very seriously. In most French restaurants, no matter how big or small, time is *not* of the essence. A meal is to be savored and enjoyed, not dispatched on the way to something else. This especially applies to dinner, which is often an event lasting the entire evening.

There was a time when one could honestly say, "You can't get a bad meal in Paris." With the influx of golden arches, pizza parlors, ethnic restaurants, and *le fast food,* it is definitely possible to suffer a bad Paris meal. Despite all of this, there are few cities in the world where you can consistently eat as well as you can in Paris, and if you plan carefully, you can have the gastronomic experience of a lifetime for much less than you would spend in any other major city in the world.

Just as Paris fashions change, so do the demands of restaurant patrons. Not too long ago dining before 8 P.M. was almost unheard of. Now, more and more restaurants are opening at 7 or 7:30 P.M. for dinner and staying open much later on Friday and Saturday nights. Many, too, are now staying open part of August, which a few years ago was absolutely unthinkable. Unfortunately, many of the long-standing restaurant standards regarding the waiter's dress have been dramatically relaxed. Levis, T-shirts, and jogging shoes have replaced black pants, bow ties, and long white aprons, especially in the cheaper places.

As a result of the desire for lighter meals, wine bars and tearooms continue to flourish. Formula restaurants offering either a limited two-course, rapid service menu or a three-course meal with several selections for each course and wine, but no à la carte, are booming. In order to keep the cost of the food down and still cope with rising inflation, more and more restaurants are adopting the use of paper napkins and paper table coverings, the corners of which are then used by the waiter to tally the bill. The Parisian love affair with anything American, especially food, shows no signs of diminishing. Carrot cake, banana and zucchini muffins, brunch, chocolate chip cookies, cheesecake, brownies, Tex-Mex food, chili, baby back ribs, and pizza delivered to the door continue to win daily converts.

No matter what the recipe or the time of year, a good French chef insists on the freshest ingredients, ignores frozen or, heaven forbid, canned, and does not cut corners or use artificial flavorings or preservatives. French eating establishments, from humble cafés to great temples of gastronomy, seldom have teenagers working part time in the kitchen or waiting tables between classes. From the chef on down, the employees are dedicated personnel who consider their jobs permanent, not way stations on the road to somewhere else. This makes a difference in everything from the quality of food on your plate to the service at your table.

Breakfast (*Petite Déjeuner*)

Breakfast is served from 7 to 10 A.M. in most cafés.

Parisians do not have a good grasp of what constitutes a real American breakfast, so do yourself a favor and follow the French example: start the day at the corner café with a *café au lait, grande crème,* or a *chocolat chaud* and a flaky croissant. If you are willing to eat standing at the bar, you will save significantly, and of course, you will save money eating breakfast almost any place but your hotel, where the markup can be 100 percent. If you insist on bacon and eggs or other staples of the American breakfast table, be prepared to pay dearly for them. Smart Cheap Eaters save their omelettes or ham and eggs for lunch.

Lunch (*Déjeuner*)

The midday meal is served from noon to 2:30 P.M., with the last order taken about thirty minutes before closing.

If you face a deadline, or do not want a full-blown meal at lunch, go to a café, wine bar, tearoom, brasserie, or put together *le snack*. Do not try to rush through a meal at a restaurant, and please do not go into a restaurant and order just a salad or an appetizer. It just is not done, and you will not be regarded well by the staff, which can result in embarrassment on your part.

A surprising number of French eat their main meal at noon. Recognizing this, many places offer very good value prix fixe menus at lunch *only.*

If you are on a shoestring budget, or you like eating your main meal at noon, there are bargains in all categories of eateries. Many places have their biggest crowds at lunch, so if you do not have a reservation, keep this in mind and try to arrive early to be assured a good seat. Remember, too, that the specials often run out, yet another reason to arrive earlier rather than later.

Paris has many delightful parks—the Luxembourg Gardens, the Tuileries, Champ-de-Mars, Jardin des Plantes, and the Bois de Boulogne—not to mention the romantic banks along the Seine and the many pretty squares throughout the city. The street *marchés* and shopping streets are the perfect places to shop for a satisfying and inexpensive al fresco *piquenique* lunch (see "Markets," page 26). If you have your picnic on a warm day in the park, you will probably share your park bench with a French person on his or her lunch hour having a *piquenique,* too.

Dinner (*Dîner*)

Dinner is served from 7 or 7:30 P.M. to 10 or 10:30 P.M., with the last order being taken about 30 minutes before closing.

Dinner is a leisurely affair, with the lunchtime frenzy replaced by a quiet, more sedate mood. American tourists eat between 7 and 8 P.M. while 8:30 or 9 P.M. is still the most popular Parisian dinner time. Few cafés serve dinner, so your best bet is a brasserie, bistro, or restaurant. If you want a light meal or a rather late one, go to a wine bar.

Fast Food *à la Française* (*Le Snack*)

Not everyone wants to devote a large segment of the day to a long lunch. Sometimes we get hungry at odd hours or have children who plead starvation if they do not have something within minutes. This is where *le snack* comes in.

Fast food *à la française,* or *le snack,* means a crêpe from the corner stand, a sandwich to go (*pour emporter*) from a café, a quiche or small pizza heated at the *boulangerie*, or something from the *charcuterie* or nearby *traiteur.* There are the café standards: a *croque-monsieur* or a *croque-madame.* A *monsieur* is a toasted ham sandwich with cheese on top, and *madame* adds a fried egg over that. *Boulangeries* also sell delicious sandwiches where the classic ham-and-cheese sandwich becomes a *jambon et gruyère,* which comes on a half of a baguette without mustard or mayo. Vegetarians can order the *crudités* sandwich, which includes lettuce, hard-boiled eggs, and tomatoes. *Charcuteries* and *traiteurs* specialize in prepared salads, pâtés, terrines, whole roasted chickens, a variety of cooked dishes, and usually one or two daily specials. All items are packed to go, and sometimes you can get a plastic fork or spoon. Most large grocery stores also have a *charcuterie* section where they sell individual slices of cold meat and portions of cheese. Add a fresh baguette, yogurt, a piece or two of fruit, and a cold drink or bottle of *vin ordinaire,* and you have a cheap and filling meal for little outlay of time and money. You can also assemble your feast from the stalls of one of the colorful street *marchés* or *rues commerçants* (see "Food Shopping," page 26). The sky is the limit here for tempting gourmet meals on the run.

Types of Food

> **Cooking is about sharing pleasure. Food is only half of what is on the plate. There is also love and truth.**
>
> —*Yves Camdeborde, owner/chef of La Réglade*

Bourgeoise Cuisine

Nostalgia is "in" declare the culinary pundits in Paris. There is no doubt about it, bourgeoise cuisine *à la grand-mère* (and popularized by Julia Child) continues to enjoy tremendous popularity in Paris. This reassuring, back-burner bistro fare is traditional cooking on which the French have subsisted for years. On thousands of menus, you can expect to see its mainstays: duck, rabbit, *cassoulet, pot-au-feu, boeuf bourguignon, blanquette de veau, tarte Tatin,* and crème caramel.

Nouvelle Cuisine

Nouvelle cuisine was coined by food critics Henry Gault and Christian Millau in the 1970s and has probably been one of the most widely talked about developments in French cooking in the past fifty years. *Nouvelle cuisine* scorns the use of rich and heavy sauces. It emphasizes instead a lighter style of classic French cooking with a greater use of vegetables, an imaginative combination of ingredients, and a stylish and colorful presentation of very small servings . . . all undercooked just a little. Over time, most people have decided that many of the dishes are contrived and result in dining adventures they do not enjoy. As a result, the popularity of *nouvelle cuisine* is about over.

Regional Cuisine

Solid regional cooking from the provinces, once snubbed by food lovers as parochial and unsophisticated, has made a remarkable comeback as the French get closer to their roots and bring back old favorites. In Paris you can travel gastronomically throughout France and never leave the city limits. The finest regional cooking is to be found in the capital, and it represents some of the best food you will ever eat.

The big brasseries feature German-influenced Alsatian specialties of steaming platters of sauerkraut, sausages, and bacon, German Riesling wines, and mugs of frosty beer. If a restaurant features food from the Savoy region, next to the Swiss-Alpine border, look for a bounty of cheeses, fondues, and *raclettes.* Food from the southwest Basque area is spicy, influenced by its Spanish neighbor. Superb seafood comes from Brittany in the north and from Nice in the south. Food from Provence is heavy with herbs, garlic, olive oil, and tomatoes. You can sample bouillabaisse, *pistou* (a pungent paste of fresh basil, cheese, garlic, and olive oil), *salade niçoise,* and ratatouille made from eggplant, zucchini, garlic, sweet peppers, and tomatoes. Veal and lamb are gifts from Normandy, and hearty *cassoulets* and huge helpings signify the robust Auvergne cooking.

Bread

Bread is one of the great charms of our civilization.

—*Jacques Chirac*

Bread is definitely the staff of life in France and is served with every meal. In the morning, a baguette is split, spread with sweet butter, and eaten with, or dunked in, a big cup of *café crème.* For lunch and dinner, it is served freshly cut, without butter, nibbled on throughout the meal, and used at the end to wipe up the last few drops of juice on the plate. A fresh basket of bread is usually served with the cheese course.

In January 1997, the French government took drastic steps to protect the baguette from mass production and cost-cutting methods that included using frozen dough. A new law is in force, aimed at safeguarding baker-artisans, and it now restricts the name "bakery" (*boulangerie*) to those shops where the bakers bake their own bread on the premises. This will require an estimated five thousand shops selling bread from factory frozen dough to remove their *boulangerie* signs.

When looking for a *boulangerie,* watch for those with long lines. You can be sure the neighborhood knows where to go for the best bread and patronizes those bakers who make their own dough and bake it on the premises. There are hundreds of types of bread available. The following list just hits the high spots.

baguette: A loaf legally weighing eight ounces, this is the long, crisp bread served most often in restaurants.

bâtard: Similar to a baguette, but softer crust.

ficelle: Very thin, crusty baguette.

pain complete: A whole-grain loaf that comes in various shapes and sizes.

pain de campagne: A blend made with whole wheat, rye, and bran that is heavier in texture and comes in all sizes and shapes; it can also be a large white loaf dusted with flour.

pain au noix: Rye or wheat bread with nuts.

pain au son: With bran.

pain Poilâne: Poilâne is the most famous bakery in Paris, with outlets in Japan and mail orders sent to the United States. It is famous for its dark, sourdough blend baked in a wood-burning oven.

Though it can be found elsewhere and is served in many restaurants, the main source for *pain Poilâne* is at Poilâne, 8, rue de Cherche-Midi, sixth arrondissement (Tel: 01-45-48-42-59). Take the métro to Sèvres-Babylone or Saint-Suplice. It is open Monday to Saturday, 7:15 A.M. to 8:15 P.M.

Cheese

The French will only be united under the threat of danger. No one can simply bring together a country that has over 265 kinds of cheese.

—*Charles de Gaulle*

Actually, France produces more than four hundred varieties of cheese, and the average French person consumes between forty and fifty pounds of it per year. When dining in France, you will quickly recognize that cheese is a vital ingredient in any meal. Cheese is served after the main course, never before dinner with cocktails or a glass of wine as it is in the United States. When you are presented the cheese tray, don't be afraid to branch out and select a variety you have never tasted. And don't worry if you see some mold around the edges. For the French, runny, moldy, smelly cheeses are the best. If a cheese does not mold a little, it is too pasteurized to be worth anything. After you return home, you may wonder why the chèvre in Minneapolis does not compare to that in your favorite Parisian bistro. The answer is simple: exported cheese must be sterilized, which kills the bacteria that give it taste.

Meat

The French eat their meat cooked much less than we do. Pink chicken is the norm, and *bleu* beef (blue, or raw to most Americans) is considered the height of good eating. *Saignant* (rare) is only slightly better done, but *à point* (medium rare) approaches the edible. *Bien cuit* (well done) may still be dripping blood, but it is at least hot and most of it will be cooked. Some meats simply do not taste good when they are well cooked, and the waiter will tell you, "It cannot be done." Trust him and order something else.

To help you answer the inevitable question, *Quelle cuisson?* (How do you want that cooked?), here is a list of responses:

cru	raw
bleu	almost raw
saignant	rare, still bleeding
rosé	pink
à point	medium
bien cuit	well done
très bien cuit	very well done

Pâtisseries

French pastries, like French women, are put together with precision.

—*Anonymous*

The Gallic passion for *pâtisserie* is a national obsession and arouses cravings unknown to most foreigners. Paris pastry lovers think nothing of traveling across the city in search of the perfect *éclair au café, Chocolate charlotte,* or *forêt-noire,* a rich fudge cake with a cherry topping. American brownies, chocolate chip cookies, and layer cakes pale by comparison . . . if you would even think of comparing them. Fine *pâtisserie* is a creation using the best ingredients, made fresh each day, and meant to be eaten immediately, if not sooner. There are *pâtisseries* all over Paris, all offering an Ali Baba's cave of tempting treats. The sky is literally the limit and your waistline the only barometer of how much you will consume and enjoy.

Unusual Foods

There is nothing discreet about French food. Remnants that are discarded in the United States are here transformed into gastronomical delicacies. You will encounter *rognons* (kidneys), *cervelles* (brains), *ris de veau* (veal sweetbreads), *moutton* (mutton), *andouillettes* (chitterling sausages), *langue de boeuf* (beef tongue), and the head, ears, toes, lips, and tails of many other animals. There are butchers selling only horse meat. You can recognize them by the golden horse head hanging over their shops. Depending on the season, you will also find *pintade* (guinea fowl), *sanglier* (wild boar), *chevreuil* (deer), and *civet de lièvre* (wild hare stew). Blood is often used to thicken sauces, especially in *civet de lièvre.* Blood is also used to make sausage, as in the *boudin noir,* pork blood sausages. All of these dishes can be delicious, and the French excel in their preparation. They represent dining experiences you must try—at least once.

Vegetarian

A vegetarian in Paris need not starve. Gone are the days when one had to settle for boring meals or a plate of crudités and a cup of lukewarm tea at the corner café. While vegetarianism in France is not what it is in the United States, it is gaining ground in Paris. Those who eat some cheese and fish will have the easiest time, but there are also havens for those who eat no animal or dairy products. There are several macrobiotic restaurants, but most serve a wider range of dishes that are guaranteed to please every dedicated veggie lover as well as their carnivorous friends eager to jump on the green bandwagon, if only for one or two meals. Go to the quick reference in the back of this book to find those I recommend.

Very often, if you call ahead to better restaurants and ask if the chef can prepare something for a vegetarian, your request will be met with pleasure. This is the best way to handle the situation, rather than arriving and not giving the chef any advance notice. If the kitchen is busy, your dish may not be very inspired, or you may have to make do with a large order of the vegetable of the day and a side of rich potatoes.

Food Shopping

Markets (*Marchés*)

The French shop for the meal, not for the week, and they measure the freshness of their food in minutes, not days. If you ask the fruit merchant if the pears are ripe, he or she will ask you when that day you will eat them, and then select just the right ones. In fact, it's customary at the smaller corner markets for the clerk to serve you; at larger *marchés*, they may or may not pick your fruits and vegetables for you, and if not, they will hand you a metal pan or basket to put your selections in. Even though indoor *supermarchés* are all over Paris, every neighborhood *quartier* has its own *rue commerçante* (shopping street) or *marché volant* (roving market). These *marchés* offer an endless source of interest and insight into the hearts and minds of ordinary Parisians, and visiting one of them is a cultural experience you should not miss. Go in the morning and gather the ingredients for a picnic lunch or supper; admire the rows of produce arranged with the same care and precision as fine jewelry displays. Take your camera and a string bag, don't mind the crowds, watch your wallet, and enjoy these lively alternatives to galleries, monuments, churches, and other must-see stops on every visitor's list. When dining out, order the food you have seen in the market. You can bet the chef has been there long before you to select perfectly ripe strawberries, fat spears of asparagus, the freshest fish, and the ripest cheeses, all for that day's menu.

Roving Markets *(Marchés Volantes)*

Roving markets move from one neighborhood to another on specific days. They are open from 7 A.M. to 1 P.M. *only* on the days listed.

Carnes, 5th, place Maubert, Métro: Maubert-Mutualité; Tues, Thur, Sat.

Monge, 5th, place Monge, Métro: Monge; Wed, Fri, Sat.

Port-Royal, 5th, in front of l'hôspital du val de Grâce at rue St-Jacques, Métro: Port-Royal; Tues, Thur, Sat.

Raspail, 6th, boulevard Raspail between rue de Cherche-Midi and rue de Rennes, Métro: Rennes or Sèvres-Babylone; Tues and Fri. On Sunday this is a *marché biologique* (organic market).

Breteuil, 7th, avenue de Saxe from avenue de Ségur to Place Breteuil, Métro: Segur; Thur and Sat.

Richard-Lenoir, 11th (next to Bastille), begins at rue Amelot, Métro: Bastille; Thur and Sun.

Aligré, 12th, place d'Aligré, Métro: Ledru-Rollin; Tues through Sun.

Dupleix, 15th, between rue Lourmel and rue du Commerce, Métro: Dupleix or La Motte-Picquet; Wed, Sun.

Cours de la Rein, 16th, between rue Debrousse and Place Iéna, Métro: Alma Marceau or Iéna; Wed, Sat.

Shopping Streets (*Rue Commerçants*)

These permanent shopping streets are usually open from 8:30 or 9 A.M. to 1 P.M. and from 4 to 7 P.M. Tuesday through Saturday. Sunday they are open only in the morning. During holidays and in July and August not all merchants are open.

Rue Montorgueil, 2nd, Métro: Sentier or Étienne Marcel.

Rue Mouffetard, 5th, Métro: Monge.

Rue de Buci, 6th, Métro: Odéon.

Rue Cler, 7th, Métro: École-Militaire.

Rues des Martyres, 9th, Métro: Notre Dame-de-Lorette.

Rue Daguerre, 14th, Métro: Denfert-Rochereau; the market begins at the southern end of the street.

Rue de L'Annonciation, 16th, Métro: La Muette; the market begins at place de Passy and rue de l'Annonciation.

Rue de Levis, 17th, Métro: Villiers; the market begins at boulevard des Batignolles.

Rue Poncelet, 17th, Métro: Ternes; the market begins at avenue des Ternes.

Rue Lepic, 18th, Métro: Abbesses.

Supermarkets (*Supermarchés*)

In Paris you won't find huge supermarket chains offering weekly specials and double coupons. Food shopping requires a different line of attack. Paris department stores are home to some of the most magnificently stocked supermarkets you will ever see. Lafayette Gourmet on the first floor of Galeries Lafayette (see page 151) and La Grande Épicerie de Paris at Bon Marché (see page 129) are the two most luxurious. Marks & Spencer (see below) stocks British goodies along with the French. Most Monoprix and Prisunic stores have a basement grocery selling everything from bread and cheese to wine, beer, and frozen products. Then there are the little Arab-run stores, open every day and until late at night, selling wilted veggies and bruised fruit . . . but if you only need a bottle of mineral water or a box of tissues, they are ports in a storm.

Marks & Spencer
35, boulevard Haussmann (8th) and rue de Rivoli (1st)
Métro: rue de Rivoli-Châtelet
Métro: boulevard Haussmann, Chaussée-d'Antin, Havre-Caumartin
Open: Mon, Wed–Sat 9:30 A.M.–7 P.M., Tues 10 A.M.–7 P.M.
Closed: Sun
Credit Cards: MC, V

Drinks

Apéritifs, Between-Meal Drinks, and *Digestifs*

The French prefer not to anesthetize their taste buds with American-style cocktails before a meal. Instead of your usual dry martini or a double scotch on the rocks, try one of the mildly alcoholic wine apéritifs such as a kir or kir royale. A kir is made from crème de cassis and chilled white wine. A kir royale substitutes champagne for the wine. The slightly bitter Campari and soda is also a good choice.

If you are hot and thirsty in the afternoon, try a *Vittel menthe:* a shot of crème de menthe diluted with Vittel mineral water and served icy cold. It is one of the cheapest and most refreshing between-meal drinks. For a nonalcoholic beverage, a good choice is *l'orange pressé* (fresh orange juice) or *le citron pressé* (lemonade). Coca Cola (*Coka*) and Orangina, a carbonated orange drink, are popular soft drinks, as are any of the mineral waters served with a twist of lemon or lime.

France is not known for beer, but if you do want a beer, don't say so. There is a French product, *Byrrh,* that sounds the same but is a bitter quinine-based wine apéritif, and this is what you are likely to get if you order "a beer." If you want a draft beer, ask for *un demi* or *une bière à la pression.* They come in three sizes: *demi* (eight ounces), *sérieux* (sixteen ounces), and *formidable* (one quart). Remember, it is pronounced "beair," not "beer." If you ask for *une bière,* you will be asked what kind because you will have ordered a bottle of beer. The best, and usually the cheapest, bottled beer in France is Kronenbourg.

After-dinner drinks (*digestifs*) are popular in Paris. The most common are cognac and various brandies. Measures are generous, but they are generally not bargains.

Coffee

Good coffee should be black like the devil, hot like hell, and sweet like a kiss.

—*Hungarian proverb*

If you order *un café s'il vous plaît* (a coffee, please), you will be served a small cup of very strong espresso with lumps of sugar on the side. The French consider it barbaric to drink coffee *with* a meal. Coffee is drunk after a meal or by itself in a café, but never, *never* with the meal and, after dinner, certainly not with milk or cream. It *may* be drunk with dessert, but you will receive an arched eyebrow from the waiter and be considered a rank tourist if you insist on it.

French coffee is wonderful. It comes in various bewildering forms, all of which are stronger and more flavorful than American coffee. All coffee is served by the cup, and there are no free refills. The following glossary of coffees should help you get what you want.

Café express, or *café noir,* is espresso coffee made by forcing hot steam through freshly ground beans. If you prefer it weaker, ask for *café allongé,* and you will be given a small pitcher of hot water to dilute it.

Café crème is espresso coffee made with steamed milk, and *café au lait* is espresso with warmed milk. Neither of these is ordered after lunch or dinner. They are strictly breakfast or between-meal *boissons.*

Café filtre is filtered coffee that is the closest to American in taste, but it is often available only in more expensive restaurants, and very seldom in a basic café.

Déca or *café décaféine* is decaffeinated espresso coffee. It bears the same resemblance to the tasteless U.S. version as a Rolls-Royce does to a bicycle.

Double and *grand* are terms used to request a double-sized cup of any of the above.

Tea

Tea is considered a breakfast or between-meal beverage, not a drink to have with a meal or after it. Outside a fancy tearoom, the tea you will be served will usually be the tea-bag variety, and the water will often be tepid. *Tisanes* or *infusions* are the terms used for herb teas. Every café serves them. They are very nice to order when you have overeaten or feel stressed. The most common infusions are *verveine* (verbena), *menthe* (mint), chamomile, and *tileul* (linden). Iced tea is almost unheard of.

Water

You could almost die of thirst before getting a simple glass of water in Paris, let alone a glass of ice water. You will not automatically be served water the minute you sit down. If you want water, you must ask for it. If you are a purist, order bottled water, which is very popular and available everywhere. You will, however, be just as well off and money ahead by ordering tap water (*une carafe d'eau*), which is one of the few free things you will get in Paris. Favorite bottled mineral waters are Evian and Vittel, which are noncarbonated (*plat* or *non-gazeuse*), and Badoit and Perrier, which are sparkling (*gazeuse).* Perrier is usually a between-meal drink because the French consider it too gaseous to be drunk with meals. If you want ice cubes, ask for *glaçons,* but don't always expect to get them.

Wine

Ask any well-fed French person and they will tell you that a meal without wine is like a kiss without the squeeze. Wine (*vin*) is drunk at almost every meal, including before breakfast for some. Red is *rouge,* white is *blanc,* and rose is *rosé.* A glass of wine at a bar is *un verre de rouge* (a glass of red), which is the cheapest, or *un verre de blanc* (a glass of white). The basic wine terms are *bruit,* very dry; *sec,* dry; *demi-sec,* semisweet; *doux,* very sweet; and champagne is champagne. There are many grape varieties, but the endless complexities of that subject would require a separate book. It is beyond the scope of *Cheap Eats in Paris* to attempt a thorough discussion of French wines or to provide a formula for selecting the perfect wine for every meal. The old rule that red was drunk only with red meat and white with chicken or fish is out—drink what you want. If you are interested in saving money, order the house wine (*vin de la maison*) or a pitcher of table wine (*un pichet du vin ordinaire*) or a bottle from the patron's own cave (*cuvée du patron*). Any of these will be perfectly drinkable and usually quite reasonably priced. The wine *carte* can be a budget killer, as most bottled vintages tend to drive up the cost of the meal inordinately. Unless you are a true wine connoisseur, it seems foolish to spend twice as much on the wine as on the food. You can bet that the Frenchperson sitting next to you won't be doing it. If you do decide to branch out and yet find the wine *carte* perplexing, don't be afraid to ask questions, state your budget, or take advice.

French Dining Manners

Crowding

When judging a restaurant, don't be put off by location, appearance, or decor. A better gauge is how crowded it is with local French, since as everyone knows, a full house is always a good sign. Crowded restaurants are an accepted fact of dining life in Paris, with the distance between tables often only one thin person wide. You can't fight this phenomenon, and besides, being comfortably wedged in along a banquette leads to some mighty interesting benchmates and conversations.

Doggie Bags + Splitting an Order = Two No-nos

The French have more dogs per capita than any other people on earth. Short of being given the vote, dogs have many rights in Paris, not the least of which is dining out with their owners. While you will seldom see anyone under eighteen in a restaurant, you will always see well-behaved dogs, especially in cafés, sitting on the seat next to their master or quietly lying at his or her feet. You would think this enormous dog population would create a demand for doggie bags, at least for the stay-at-home canines. Wrong. Half of France is on some kind of diet, and leaving food on your plate is acceptable. Asking for a doggie bag, whether for Fido or yourself, is not.

Considered just as gauche and unacceptable as the doggie bag is asking to split dishes. Despite the number of courses in a typical French meal, portions are smaller than most Americans are used to, thus diners are expected to order accordingly and do the best they can.

Mind Your Manners and Dress for Success

Good manners don't show, bad ones always do.

—*Neva C. Abernethy*

Wear black, make it tight, accessorize . . . you'll look Parisian.

—*Sandra Busby*

Good manners are international, and *la politesse* is central to all transactions in France. The French are also more formal than we are. They don't call people by their first names, and they preface statements with *Pardon Monsieur, S'il vous plaît, Madame,* or *Excusez-moi, Mademoiselle.* They will consider you to be rude if you do not do the same, or if you omit the words *monsieur, madame,* or *mademoiselle* when you speak to them. If you want good service, a *Bonjour, Monsieur* or *Merci, Mademoiselle,* along with lots of *s'il vous plaîts* and *merci beaucoups* thrown in, will go a long way toward making your dining experience better.

To get the waiter's attention, don't shout *Garçon!* Contrary to most Americans, the French consider all restaurant work to be a profession, not a filler-job while waiting for something better to come along. For best results, always refer to the waiter as *monsieur* and the waitress as *mademoiselle,* regardless of age or marital status.

It is considered very rude to eat your *frites* (french fries), chicken, or any food for that matter, with your fingers. It is not uncommon to see diners peeling a pear or other piece of fruit with a knife and fork, and eating it with a fork.

The French can spot Americans in any dining establishment without looking: they are the ones with the loud, booming voices that seem to carry out into the street. If you want to blend in and not look like a green tourist, keep your voice down.

Dressing well is part of a French person's makeup, especially in Paris. While men do not always need to wear a coat and tie and women are not always required to dress to the nines, a little conservative good judgment is in order. The French have limited tolerance for the concept of sacrificing fashion for comfort. In addition, short shorts, halter tops, T-shirts with insignias, and baseball caps in restaurants are frowned on; they will immediately brand you as a *gauche* tourist.

French etiquette demands that both hands be kept *above* the table while eating, not in the lap. And, finally, if you are full, don't look up "full" in your French dictionary and say *Je suis plein.* This is a phrase used for cows, meaning they are pregnant. Say instead, if you do not want any more to eat, *Je n'ai plus faim,* "I am not hungry any longer."

Smoking

> **The reason the French drink so much is to help them forget what they are doing to themselves by smoking.**
>
> —*Art Buchwald,* Vive la Cigarette

Cigarette stubs make up three tons of the twenty tons of trash collected *daily* in the Paris métro. There has been a lukewarm attempt to cut down on smoking in public places, but there is no French surgeon general extolling the virtues of a smoke-free environment. The antismoking law stipulates that all places serving food designate separate smoking and nonsmoking sections. Most have ignored this completely. Others have relegated nonsmokers to a table surrounded by those puffing throughout the entire meal. When the nonsmoker asks about his or her nonsmoking table, he or she will be told in no uncertain terms, "*yours* is a nonsmoking table." During the busiest times in cafés and bistros, it is nearly impossible to escape from the Gauloise-induced haze. In *Cheap Eats in Paris,* listings where smoking is prohibited or where there is a specific nonsmoking section have been boldly noted. Otherwise . . . *bonne chance.*

Reservations

To avoid disappointment, it is always better to arrive with reservations. While reservations are not necessary or accepted in a café, they are essential in most restaurants and in popular bistros and brasseries. If you arrive without a reservation, you might be told that the restaurant is *complet* (full) even when there are empty tables. The reason is that those empty tables have been reserved and are being held.

When you have a reservation, don't be late. French restaurants honor their reservation times and do not relegate patrons to the bar to wait for the present occupants to gulp down the last drop of espresso before relinquishing the table. Many places have only one seating for both lunch and dinner, so if you change your plans after booking, you should always call to cancel so that your table can be rebooked.

All entries in *Cheap Eats in Paris* state the reservation policy, so you will know exactly what to do and expect. If you do not feel comfortable making the reservation yourself, the hotel desk personnel will do it for you, possibly getting a better table than if you had tried yourself.

Closures

Very few Paris eating establishments are open every day of the year Most close at least one day a week, and sometimes for either lunch or dinner on Saturday and all day Sunday. Many close for public holidays, as well as for one week at Christmas and Easter. Some smaller family-run operations close for the school holidays in the fall and winter. The French consider their annual holiday time to be a God-given right. In fact, every working person in France is guaranteed a five-week vacation, no matter how long they have been employed in their present job. Despite government pleadings and tourist demands, many still have an annual closing (*fermeture annuelle*) for all or parts of July and August, when 75 percent of all Parisians leave the city. Closures also vary with the mood of the owner and adjust to the changing patterns of tourism and inflation. Thanks to the worldwide recession, more places are opting for a one-week closure and allowing their employees to rotate their vacation times. It is impossible to guarantee that this year's policy will carry over to the next. To avoid arriving at a restaurant only to find it closed, always call ahead to check, especially on a holiday and in July and August.

Paying the Bill

After the mysteries of the French menu, no subject is more confusing to foreigners than French restaurant bills. Your bill will not automatically be brought to your table at the end of the meal . . . you usually must ask for it (*l'addition* or *la note, s'il vous plait*).

Credit Cards

The acceptance of plastic money is second nature in Paris, and it is almost always possible to pay for most meals with a credit card. Policies often change, however, so when reserving, it is wise to double-check which cards the restaurants accepts. The most popular cards are Visa, known as *Carte Bleu,* and MasterCard, known as *Eurocard.*

The following abbreviations are used for the major credit cards:

American Express	AE
Diners Club	DC
MasterCard	MC
Visa	V

Prices

In most cases, the bottom line on your restaurant bill will depend on your choice of wine. All prices quoted in *Cheap Eats in Paris* are for one person and show whether or not drinks are included. In determining price quotations, the cheapest menu items have been avoided, including such French favorites as tripe and *andouillettes,* which do not appeal to most Americans. The prices that are quoted represent the median cost of an à la carte meal with a starter (*entrée*), main course (*plat*), and dessert. Even though every attempt has been made to ensure the accuracy of the information given, a certain margin of error in pricing exists due to fluctuating exchange rates, inflation, escalating food costs, and the whims of restaurant owners.

Service Charge

By law, all restaurants in France must include a 12- to 15-percent service charge in the price of all food and beverages served. This will be stated on the menu by the words *service compris* or *prix nets.* No additional service charge may be added to your bill. Always check your bill very carefully because mistakes are too frequent.

Important! Beware of the service charge/credit card scam. This is a deliberate gouging of the customer that should not be tolerated. If you are paying by credit card, the total should be at the bottom. If the restaurant has left the space on your credit card slip for the "tip/gratuity" blank, they are hoping you will fill in an amount, thus paying it twice. To avoid this, draw a line from the top total to the bottom total and draw an additional line through the space marked "tip/gratuity."

Tipping

Remember, the service charge *is* the tip. You do not have to leave one *sou* more . . . you have already paid it. In France you are obliged to tip the butcher, the delivery boy, the theater usher, but not the waiter, even in the finest restaurants like Jamin and Taillevent. However, if the waiter has performed some extraordinary service, or you were particularly pleased, then an additional tip may be in order. Depending on the size and type of place, anything from a few francs to 5 or 10 percent of the bill would be appreciated. In cafés, it is usually expected to leave the small change.

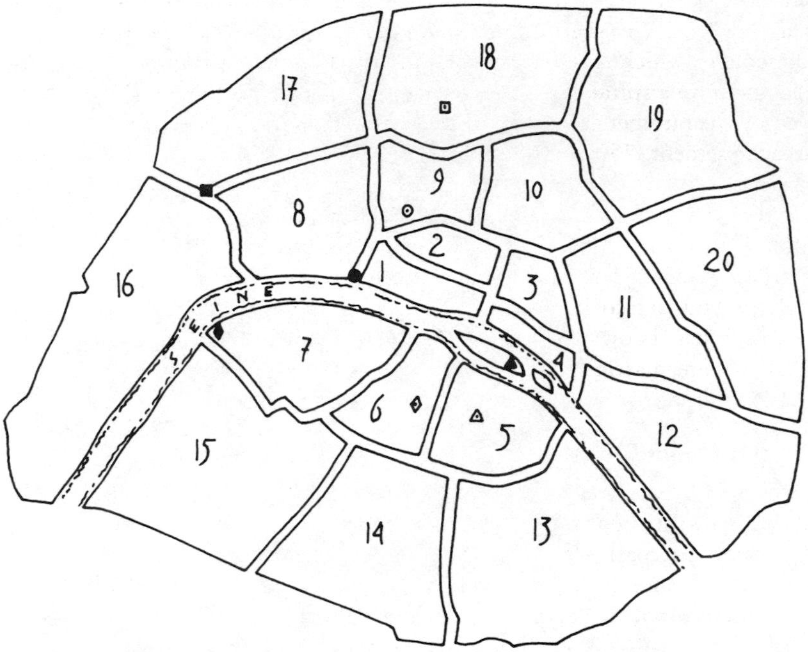

● Place de la concorde
■ Arc de Triomphe
▲ Notre Dame
◆ Tour Eiffel
⊙ Opéra
⊡ Sacré-coeur
△ Panthéon
◇ Jardin du Luxembourg

Restaurants by Arrondissement

Paris is divided into twenty districts, or zones, known as *arrondissements.* Knowing which arrondissement is which is the key to understanding Paris and quickly finding your way around. Starting with the first arrondissement, which is the district around the Louvre, the numbering goes clockwise in a spiral. The postal code, or zip code, for Paris is 750, followed by the number of the arrondissement. Thus, 75001 refers to the first arrondissement, 75004 to the fourth, and 75016 means the location is in the expensive sixteenth. The arrondissement for every restaurant is given in parentheses with each address in *Cheap Eats in Paris:* (2nd) means the second arrondissement; (18th) means the eighteenth.

An arrondissement has its own special character and feeling, so that Paris, when you get to know her, is a city of twenty neighborhood villages. Each has its own mayor, central post office, police station, and town hall, where marriages can be performed and deaths recorded. It takes a few afternoons of what the French call *flânerie,* unhurried, aimless wandering, to truly appreciate some of the more intriguing neighborhoods. When you go out, prepare to be sidetracked, diverted, and happily lost discovering all sorts of wonderful places and things.

The maps in this book are meant to help you locate the restaurants and the major landmarks, not to negotiate the city. If you are going to be in Paris for more than one or two days, your smartest and most valuable purchase will be a copy of the *Plan de Paris par Arrondissement.* It is available at all news kiosks and bookstores and contains a detailed map of every arrondissement, with a complete street index, métro and bus routes, tourist sites, and much more. Another bonus is that it is a purchase that will never go out of style or change much . . . so buy a good one.

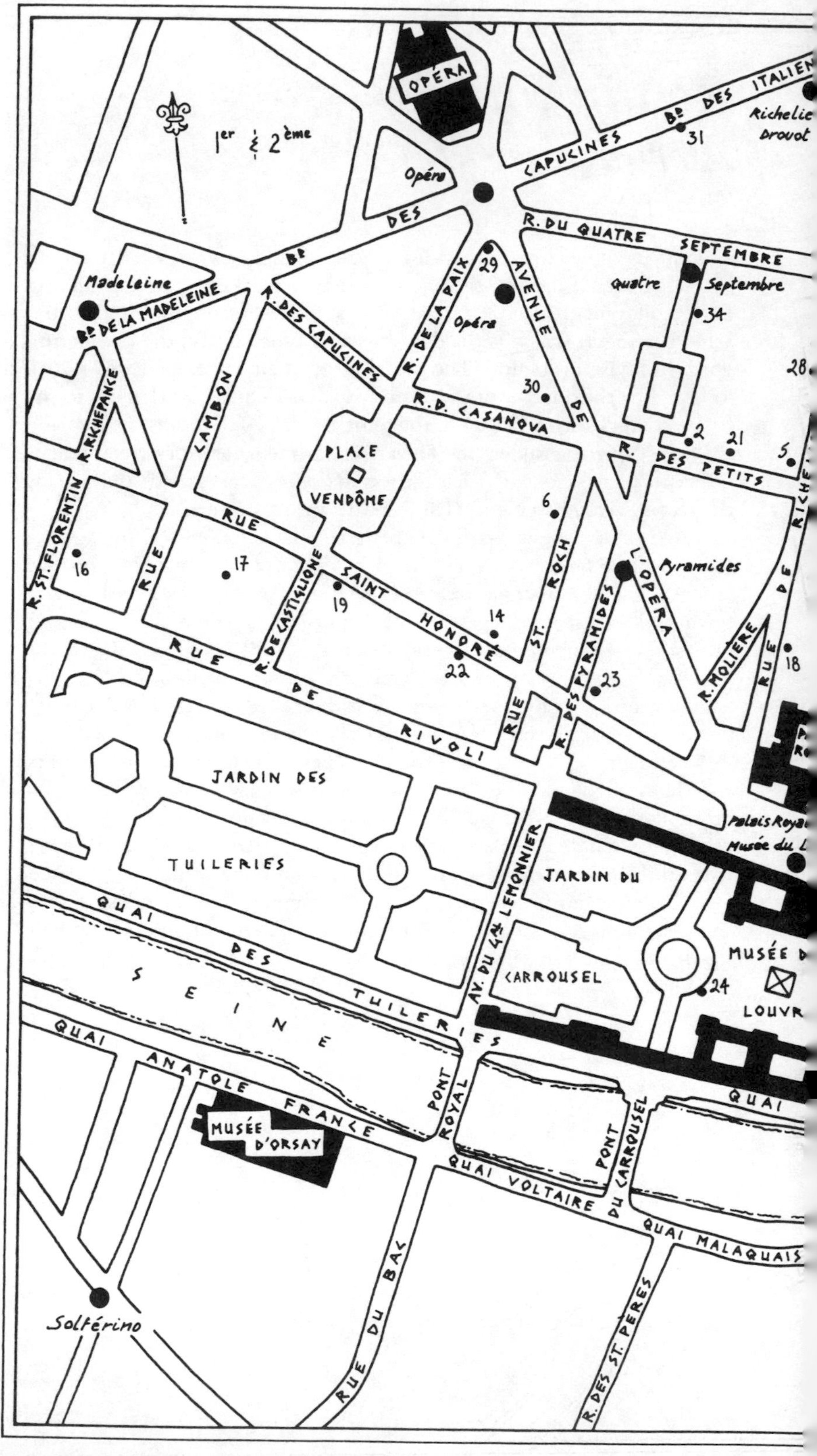
OPÉRA
1er & 2ème
B^D DES ITALIENS
Richelieu Drouot
31
CAPUCINES
Opéra
DES
R. DU QUATRE SEPTEMBRE
Madeleine
B^D DE LA MADELEINE
B^D
R. DES CAPUCINES
R. DE LA PAIX
29
AVENUE DE L'OPÉRA
Opéra
Quatre Septembre
34
28
R. RICHEPANCE
CAMBON
30
R. D. CASANOVA
PLACE VENDÔME
2
21
5
R. DES PETITS
R. ST. FLORENTIN
RUE SAINT HONORÉ
6
16
17
19
RUE
R. DE CASTIGLIONE
RUE ST. ROCH
Pyramides
14
22
RUE DE RIVOLI
R. DES PYRAMIDES
23
R. MOLIÈRE
RUE DE RICHELIEU
18
JARDIN DES TUILERIES
Palais Royal
Musée du L
AV. DU 44. LEMONNIER
JARDIN DU CARROUSEL
QUAI DES TUILERIES
SEINE
MUSÉE D
24
LOUVR
QUAI ANATOLE FRANCE
PONT ROYAL
MUSÉE D'ORSAY
PONT DU CARROUSEL
QUAI
QUAI VOLTAIRE
QUAI MALAQUAIS
RUE DU BAC
Solférino
R. DES ST. PÈRES

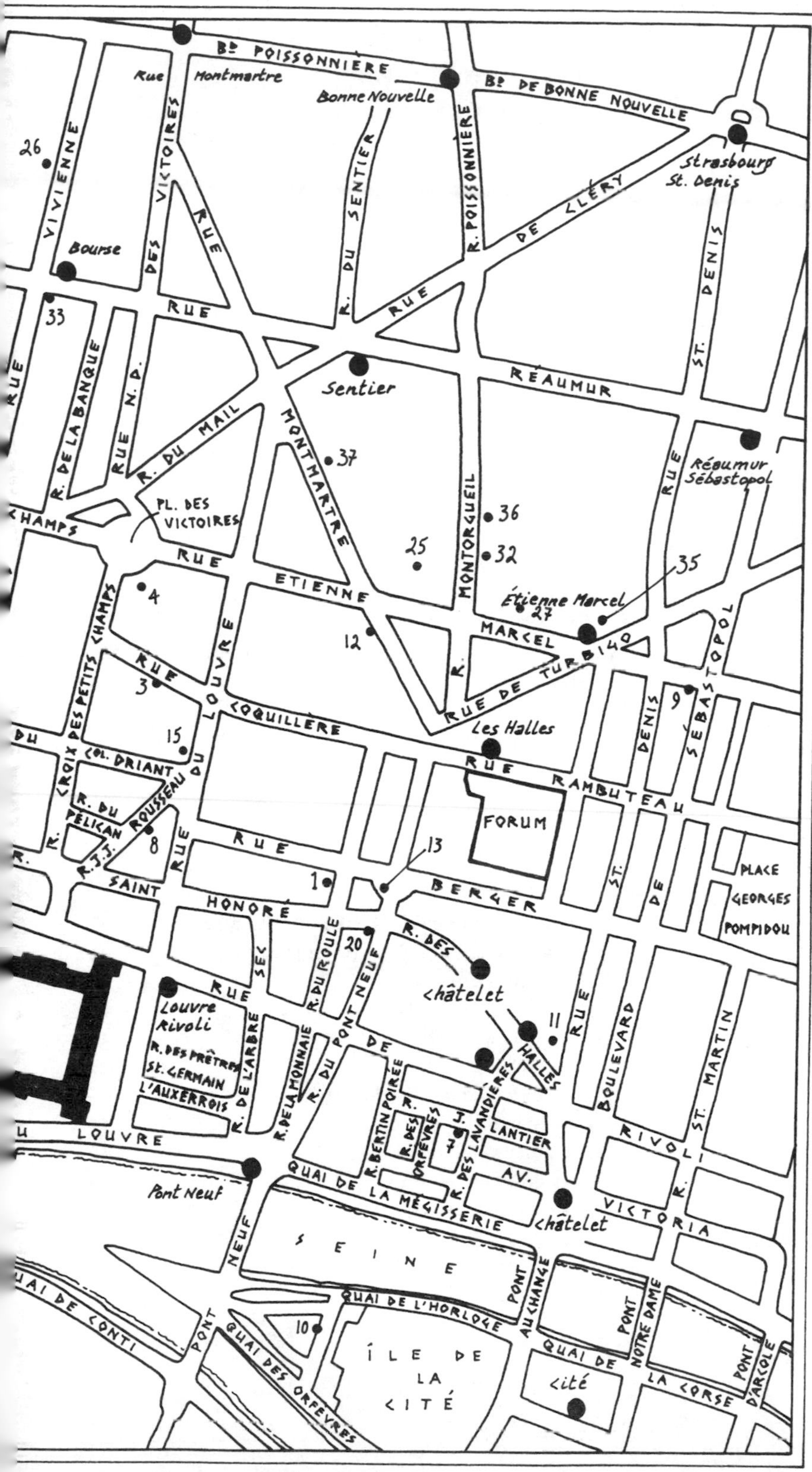

Bd POISSONNIÈRE
Rue Montmartre
Bd DE BONNE NOUVELLE
Bonne Nouvelle
Strasbourg St. Denis
26
VIVIENNE
RUE DES VICTOIRES
R. DU SENTIER
R. POISSONNIÈRE
RUE DE CLÉRY
ST. DENIS
Bourse
33
RUE
RUE
Sentier
RÉAUMUR
RUE
R. DE LA BANQUE
RUE N. D.
R. DU MAIL
MONTMARTRE
37
Réaumur Sébastopol
RUE
MONTORGUEIL
36
32
25
PL. DES VICTOIRES
CHAMPS
RUE
ETIENNE
35
Étienne Marcel
27
4
12
MARCEL
R.
RUE DE TURBIGO
SÉBASTOPOL
RUE
LOUVRE
3
RUE
COQUILLÈRE
9
DENIS
CROIX DES PETITS CHAMPS
15
Les Halles
DU
COL. DRIANT
RUE
RAMBUTEAU
R. DU PÉLICAN
ROUSSEAU
DU
8
R. J. J.
R.
RUE
FORUM
13
R.
RUE
1
BERGER
PLACE GEORGES POMPIDOU
ST.
DE
SAINT
HONORÉ
R. DU ROULE
20
R. DES
SEC
châtelet
Louvre Rivoli
RUE
R. DU PONT NEUF
DE
11
RUE
R. DES PRÊTRES ST. GERMAIN L'AUXERROIS
R. DE L'ARBRE
R. DE LA MONNAIE
HALLES
BOULEVARD
ST. MARTIN
R. BERTIN POIRÉE
R. DES ORFÈVRES
J. LANTIER
7
R. DES LAVANDIÈRES
RIVOLI
LOUVRE
AV.
R.
Pont Neuf
QUAI DE LA MÉGISSERIE
châtelet
VICTORIA
NEUF
SEINE
PONT AU CHANGE
PONT NOTRE DAME
QUAI DE CONTI
QUAI DE L'HORLOGE
PONT
10
QUAI DES ORFÈVRES
ÎLE DE LA CITÉ
QUAI DE
cité
LA CORSE
PONT D'ARCOLE

First Arrondissement

RIGHT BANK
Conciergeri (where Marie Antoinette was beheaded), Île de la Cité, Ste-Chapelle (with fifteen hundred square yards of blue-and-red stained glass), Palais de Justice, Louvre, Jardin des Tuileries, Pont Neuf (the oldest bridge in Paris), Place Vendôme, Les Halles, Palais Royal, Quai de la Mégisserie (bird, flower, and animal market)

The Île de la Cité is the historic heart of Paris. It was on this island in the middle of the Seine that a Celtic tribe of fisherman called the Parisii settled in the third century B.C. and where the Gallo-Romans later built the city they called Lutetia in the first century A.D.

The history of Les Halles parallels the growth of Paris itself over the last twenty-five or thirty years. For decades Les Halles was the central wholesale food market in Paris. Nicknamed "the belly of Paris," it was an early-morning place of meat markets, fishmongers, fruit and vegetable sellers, and cheese merchants. In 1969, the market was moved to Rungis, on the outskirts of Paris, and in its place was built the Forum des Halles, a tremendous, multilevel indoor shopping complex, housing shops and the biggest métro station in the world. Unfortunately, this is also reputed to be one of the most dangerous métro stops in the city, so be careful, especially at night. The area around the Forum des Halles now teems night and day with an inexhaustible supply of people of every size, shape, and style, providing the observer a real *tour de fashion.* While here, you can watch a fire-eating act, a sword swallower, an ascetic lying on a bed of nails, listen to all sorts of street-corner music, buy far-out fashions, observe the French *clochards* (bums) relaxing in doorways, get your hair colored or spiked, see an X-rated film, fill up on fast food, or sit in a café and almost literally watch the world parade by.

FIRST ARRONDISSEMENT RESTAURANTS

* Restaurants marked with an asterisk (*) are considered Big Splurges.

(1) À LA TOUR DE MONTLHÉRY (CHEZ DENISE)*

5, rue des Prouvaires (1st)

"It's not good, it's wonderful!" That is what the man seated one elbow away told me the first time I ate here. And he should know: he had eaten here every day for years, as have scores of other robust French. If you are looking for a colorful and authentic Les Halles bistro that has not changed in a hundred years, À la Tour de Montlhéry, or Chez Denise to the regulars, is a must, if you are willing to spend a little more. The classic spot is busy twenty-four hours a day with a colorful mixture of artists, businesspeople, and writers, all served by surefooted, white-aproned career waiters who keep running, flirting, and smiling despite the crunch. The small tables are always jam-packed, and the din of happy diners creating a blue haze of Gauloise smoke is typically French.

Eternity stands behind the almost indecipherable chalkboard menu, and no dieters need apply: this is hearty food with portions that could be considered lethal by some. To start, order the snails in garlic butter, or the *salade frisée* with crisp homemade croutons. Follow this with *tripes au Calvados, haricot de mouton,* tender rabbit in grainy mustard sauce, or the wonderful stuffed cabbage. Complement your meal with a bottle of Brouilly, the house wine. The desserts can be ignored if you insist, but I always try to save room to sample the generous cheese tray or a piece of the *gâteau Marguerite,* laden with fresh strawberries and cream.

TELEPHONE
01-42-36-21-82

MÉTRO
Les Halles, Louvre, Châtelet

OPEN
Mon–Sat morning

CLOSED
Sat afternoon–Sun, holidays, July 14–Aug 15

HOURS
Mon 7 A.M. to Sat 7 A.M., 24 hours a day, continuous service

RESERVATIONS
Essential

CREDIT CARDS
V

À LA CARTE
250-260F, BC

PRIX FIXE
None

ENGLISH SPOKEN
Enough

(2) AUX BONS CRUS
7, rue des Petits-Champs (1st)

TELEPHONE
01-42-60-06-45
MÉTRO
Bourse
OPEN
Tues–Sat lunch and dinner, Mon lunch and bar only
CLOSED
Mon dinner, Sun, one to two weeks in Aug (dates vary)
HOURS
Bar Mon–Sat 8 A.M.–11 P.M.; lunch Mon–Sat noon–3 P.M., dinner Tues–Sat 7–11 P.M.
RESERVATIONS
Not necessary
CREDIT CARDS
MC, V
À LA CARTE
50–95F, BNC
PRIX FIXE
None
ENGLISH SPOKEN
Yes

For a glass or two of good wine, a *tartine* on Poilâne bread, a hearty *plat du jour,* or just a plain omelette and a green salad, you will do well at this noisy, smoky, friendly wine bar near the Bibliothèque Nationale. The wines are sold by the glass or the bottle and start at 10F for a basic red and go all the way up to 242F for a bottle of Champagne Lancelot Wanner *Ier* Cru.

Lunchtime is a virtual mob scene, with the *plat du jour* selling out early. Casks of wine line one wall and hang over the crowded bar, where a coterie of habitués gather for their daily dose of wine and good-natured backslapping.

Stick around long enough and, who knows, maybe you will end up joining them.

(3) CHICAGO MEATPACKERS
8, rue Coquillière (1st)

TELEPHONE
01-40-28-02-33
MÉTRO
Les Halles
OPEN
Daily
CLOSED
Dec 24, NAC
HOURS
11:30 A.M.–1 P.M., continuous service; children's shows Wed, Sat, Sun 1 and 2 P.M.
RESERVATIONS
Not accepted for Fri or Sat, and not necessary otherwise
CREDIT CARDS
MC, V
À LA CARTE
100–170F, BNC
PRIX FIXE
Mon–Fri lunch only: 50F, 75F, 2 courses, BC and coffee; children's menu 60F, served continuously, BC
ENGLISH SPOKEN
Yes
MISCELLANEOUS
Nonsmoking section

The Midwestern twang of the Chicago WJMK radio disk jockey announces that it is 5:30 P.M. in Chicago and the commute is, as usual, gridlocked, then he introduces Frank Sinatra crooning, "Chicago is my kinda town." If Chicago is your kind of town, then the Chicago Meatpackers in Les Halles is your kind of restaurant. Big, bright, and fast moving, it lets you know from the minute you enter that you are in for a good time.

The American food and drinks have rapidly won the hearts and stomachs of Parisians, who come to feast on baby back ribs, prime steaks, stuffed mushrooms, buffalo wings, potato skins, corn on the cob, onion loaf, garlic bread, taco salad, five-way chili, New York cheesecake, and rich mud pie. At the huge mirror-lined bar, the friendly bartender makes one of the driest martinis in town, a lethal Singapore sling, and pours their own brew—Chicago Old Gold Beer—into ice-cold mugs. Children love the bibs, badges, and balloons; their own special menu; the clowns performing half-hour magic shows on Wednesday, Saturday, and Sunday; the model Chicago & Pacific train running and tooting overhead; and the soda machine at the front that dispenses minibottles of all their favorite drinks.

Can't finish your onion hamburger, chili cheeseburger, or Meatpakers chicken platter? Then ask for a doggie bag, probably the only one you will see in Paris. The waiters and waitresses all speak English, the restaurant is open every day, and it is all a great taste of home. Don't miss it.

(4) ENTRE CIEL ET TERRE
5, rue Hérold (1st)

What do H. G. Wells, Gandhi, Leonardo da Vinci, Tolstoy, Buddha, Voltaire, Einstein, Socrates, and Paul McCartney have in common? They are, or were, all vegetarians, and you can join their healthy ranks by eating at this attractive restaurant not far from the Paris Bourse (stock exchange).

The food here is not only good but good for you, and it's served in a 100 percent smoke-free environment, yet another reason to put it on your Cheap Eating map of Paris. Owner and chef Guillaume Botté takes his work seriously and turns out daily fare that appeals to both hard-core vegetarians and free-wheeling omnivores. *Entrées* include onion or vegetable soup, avocado mousse served with toasted *brioche,* tapenade, and tabbouleh. I would avoid the *pâté végétariale* because it is not *maison* (made here). Savory *tartes*, vegetable pancakes, lasagne, omelettes, and *gratins* round out the main courses. Botté's desserts are showcased on a large buffet. If it's here, the pear and chocolate chip cake is memorable, but if you are looking for a lighter ending, have the lemon cake with raspberry sauce.

TELEPHONE
01-45-08-49-84

MÉTRO
Louvre-Rivoli, Bourse

OPEN
Mon–Fri

CLOSED
Sat–Sun, major holidays, Aug

HOURS
Lunch noon–3 P.M., dinner 7–10 P.M.

RESERVATIONS
Advised

CREDIT CARDS
MC, V

À LA CARTE
125F, BC

PRIX FIXE
Lunch, 70F, 2 courses, 87F, 3 courses, both BNC; dinner, 90F, 3 courses, BNC

ENGLISH SPOKEN
Yes

MISCELLANEOUS
No smoking allowed

(5) JUVENILES
47, rue de Richelieu (1st)

Juveniles is a smart address to remember if you want a light meal accompanied with a glass or two of a little known but superb Spanish, French, or Australian wine. It is also a good place for those who enjoy malt whiskey or sour mash straight bourbon.

Mark Williamson of Willi's Wine Bar fame and his partner, Tim Johnston, opened Juveniles a decade ago. It was an instant hit, and it remains popular to this day, especially with readers of *Cheap Eats in Paris*. In addition to wines and spirits, Juveniles excels in serving tapas—small plates of food that can be ordered individually or as part of a prix fixe formula. Your meal might include a *tortilla d'Espagna* (a thick Spanish omelette) or warm

TELEPHONE
01-42-97-46-49

MÉTRO
Palais-Royal

OPEN
Mon–Sat

CLOSED
Sun, holidays, NAC

HOURS
Lunch noon–3 P.M., dinner 7–11 P.M.

RESERVATIONS
Not necessary

CREDIT CARDS
MC, V

À LA CARTE
45–115F, BNC

PRIX FIXE
Lunch and dinner, 98F, 2 courses, BC; 128F, 3 courses, BC

ENGLISH SPOKEN
Yes

basil-spiked ratatouille followed by a duck filet, and tiramisu with amaretto for dessert. Cheese lovers will revel in a chunk of English cheddar or Stilton blue cheese accompanied by a glass of East Indian sherry.

While you are here, be sure to notice the children's drawings hung around the room. They are all done by Tim's daughters.

(6) LA CORDONNERIE (CHEZ YVETTE & CLAUDE)
20, rue St-Roch (1st)

TELEPHONE
01-42-60-17-42

MÉTRO
Pyramides

OPEN
Mon–Fri

CLOSED
Sat–Sun, holidays, Aug

HOURS
Lunch noon–2:30 P.M., dinner 7:15–10 P.M.

RESERVATIONS
Advised

CREDIT CARDS
MC, V

À LA CARTE
150–200F, BC

PRIX FIXE
Lunch and dinner, 140F, 3 courses, BNC

ENGLISH SPOKEN
Yes

La Cordonnerie is a little restaurant made up of two dining rooms that seat just twenty-four people. One room is dominated by an open kitchen with an enviable collection of copper pots, pans, and molds; the other has a tiny bar, an antique icebox, and five tables with fresh flowers and matching red tablecloths and napkins. The restaurant was opened over thirty years ago by Claude and Yvette, with Claude in the kitchen turning out his renditions of soothing, old-fashioned French food, and Yvette acting as charming hostess and helper. The cooking is now done by their son, Hugo, and the hostess duties are shared by his wife, Valerie, and Yvette. Hugo does the shopping at Rungis, the huge wholesale food market outside Paris, and he prepares everything here, including the ice creams and sorbets. I like to start my meal with a plate of well-dressed crudités or the *terrine de foie de volaille maison,* a creamy chicken liver pâté. For my main course I always pay attention to Hugo's *plat du jour,* or whatever fresh fish he offers. For dessert, there is usually a lemon *tarte,* or my favorite, *Fondant au chocolate,* made with whipped cream and dark chocolate. It is warm on the outside, cool inside, and decadently wonderful to the last bite.

(7) LA MAISON CLÉRET
4, rue des Lavandières Ste-Opportune, at the corner of rue Jean Lantier (1st)

TELEPHONE
01-42-33-82-68

MÉTRO
Châtelet

OPEN
Tues–Sat

CLOSED
Sun, holidays, July

In my opinion, the area around Châtelet is a dining desert, populated by impersonal corner brasseries, fast-food franchises, and here-today-gone-tomorrow greasy spoons. The one star-studded exception is this *pâtisserie/ salon de thé* where four women work nonstop from 7 A.M. to 8 P.M. Tuesday to Saturday selling the best bread, pastries, and hot lunches in the *quartier.* I lived just around the corner and observed them and the never-ending stream of customers, including restaurant chefs, who bought them out on a daily basis.

It's not a fancy place, but there are tables in the back (2F extra to be served here and worth it) and a few scattered on the sidewalk when the weather permits. Your window of opportunity is large. You can start your day with a *café au lait* and a powdered sugar dusted *croissant aux amandes*, a *pain aux raisins,* or a fruit-studded *viennoiserie* (Danish). For lunch, order one of the *plats du jour* and a fresh fruit *tarte.*

In the afternoon, sip a cup of tea and treat yourself to an assortment of their cakes and pastries; later on, pick up a loaf or two of their delicious breads and a box of their own chocolates. If you are a camera buff, on Saturday mornings the shelves are lined with picture perfect goodies . . . don't miss your chance to capture it all on film.

HOURS
7 A.M.–8 P.M., continuous service for pastries; lunch noon–2 P.M.

RESERVATIONS
Not accepted

CREDIT CARDS
None

À LA CARTE
15–50F, BNC

PRIX FIXE
Not available

ENGLISH SPOKEN
No

(8) L'AMI LÉON
11, rue Jean-Jacques Rousseau (1st)

What is the magic quality that makes discriminating diners zero in on a little place and stick with it for years? Whatever it is, L'Ami Léon has it, the perfect setting and the kind of meal one hopes to find in Paris. The interior reminds me of a country restaurant somewhere in the south of France. The nicely laid tables, with their own lamps and tiny bouquets of flowers, are placed far enough apart to ensure a peacefully intimate evening.

The prix fixe menu changes monthly, and the à la carte seasonally. The choices are a bit limited, but they are nonetheless studded with treasures, all made by owner-chef Jean-Marie Léon Martin. Everything is always reliable, from the bowl of nuts placed on the table while you peruse the menu to the last drop of *café express* and the chocolates that accompany it. The restaurant's many regulars know that the velvety chicken liver terrine will always be available as an appetizer. Main courses, designed to please meat-and-potato fans, might include tender pieces of lamb in coriander, succulent rabbit with sage, or pork sautéed with olives and fresh turnips. All are garnished with fresh vegetables and roasted potatoes. The desserts are overwhelmingly tempting, especially the flaky rhubarb and strawberry *tarte.*

TELEPHONE
01-42-33-06-20

MÉTRO
Louvre

OPEN
Mon–Fri lunch and dinner, Sat dinner only

CLOSED
Sat lunch, Sun; holidays; mid-July to mid-Aug

HOURS
Lunch noon–2 P.M., dinner 8–10 P.M.

RESERVATIONS
Advised

CREDIT CARDS
V

À LA CARTE
190F, BNC

PRIX FIXE
Lunch and dinner, 98F, 3 courses, BNC

ENGLISH SPOKEN
Enough to order

MISCELLANEOUS
Nonsmoking section

(9) LA POTÉE DES HALLES
3, rue Étienne-Marcel (1st)

TELEPHONE
01-42-36-18-68
MÉTRO
Étienne-Marcel
OPEN
Mon–Fri lunch and dinner, Sat dinner only
CLOSED
Sat lunch, Sun, major holidays, Aug
HOURS
Lunch noon–2:15 P.M., dinner 7–10:30 P.M.
RESERVATIONS
Advised
CREDIT CARDS
AE, DC, MC, V
À LA CARTE
180F, BNC
PRIX FIXE
Lunch and dinner: 100F, 2 courses, BNC; 120F, 3 courses and coffee
ENGLISH SPOKEN
Yes

Book ahead . . . you won't be the only one eager to dine in this haven of Paris nostalgia, which began as a café in 1906. Classified by the French government as a national historical monument, the restaurant, with ornate hand-painted tile walls portraying the goddesses of beer and coffee, still has its original chairs, whose brass plaques bear the names of the Les Halles workers who ate here every day when the wholesale food market of Paris dominated the area. Even today, some of these chairs are occupied daily by their seventy- and eighty-year-old "owners."

Unless you are ravenous, order a light *entrée* before your *plat* and plan to go easy on dessert or skip it altogether. Instead, pay serious attention to the Auvergne specialty of the house, *la potée.* It comes in a big pot with white beans, cabbage, carrots, salt pork, ribs, smoked sausage, garlic butter, and cream. Other specialties include a pork and cabbage hot pot, duck breast in an orange sauce, and kidneys in port wine. At the end of this *grand bouffe,* you will probably stagger away a little heavier, but definitely well satisfied.

(10) LE BAR DU CAVEAU
17, Place Dauphine (1st)

TELEPHONE
01-43-54-45-95
MÉTRO
Pont-Neuf
OPEN
Mon–Fri
CLOSED
Sat–Sun, Dec 15–31, NAC
HOURS
8:30 A.M.–8 P.M., continuous service
RESERVATIONS
Not accepted
CREDIT CARDS
None
À LA CARTE
35–60F, BNC
PRIX FIXE
None
ENGLISH SPOKEN
Limited

Le Bar du Caveau occupies a prime spot on the charming Place Dauphine, which is at the tip of Île de la Cité, just after you cross the Pont-Neuf bridge. Relatively undiscovered by tourists, this lovely little square was home to Yves Montand and Simone Signoret, and it boasts a half dozen or so restaurants and a famous Cheap Sleep in Paris, the Hotel Henri IV (See *Cheap Sleeps in Paris*).

Featuring sandwiches on *pain Poilâne,* salads, egg dishes, cheese and *charcuterie* plates, and a mix of wines by the glass, *pot* (pitcher), and bottle, Le Bar du Caveau appeals to upscale regulars who arrive early and stay late, idling away a lazy Paris afternoon over wine and fellowship.

NOTE: Be sure you go to the bar, not to its sister restaurant next door, which is not designed for the budgets of most Cheap Eaters in Paris.

(11) LE BÉARN

2, place Ste-Opportune (1st)

In addition to being an earthy Cheap Eat, Le Béarn is a great place to hone your people-watching skills. In the morning, you are likely to find red-cheeked workers standing at the bar, lingering over what is obviously not their first glass of *vin rouge* of the day. A predominantly young crowd of every conceivable orientation and dress pours in at lunchtime to take advantage of the low-priced *plats du jour,* which come in pre-*nouvelle*-sized portions. These are usually overflowing plates of no-nonsense meats, accompanied by equally serious portions of homemade *frites*. Regulars know to avoid all veggies here—they are frozen. Unless it is raining or freezing cold, the outside tables on the place Ste-Opportune are *the* place to sit, front-row vantage points for watching the Les Halles fashion victims preen and prance around the *place* and the crowds surging out of the métro stop just next to it.

TELEPHONE
01-42-36-93-35

MÉTRO
Châtelet (exit place Ste-Opportune)

OPEN
Mon–Sat

CLOSED
Sun, holidays, NAC

HOURS
Lunch noon–3:30 P.M., dinner 7–10 P.M., bar 8 A.M.–11 P.M.

RESERVATIONS
Not taken

CREDIT CARDS
MC, V

À LA CARTE
40–110F, BC

PRIX FIXE
None

ENGLISH SPOKEN
Some

(12) LE COCHON À L'OREILLE

15, rue Montmartre (1st)

The business hours of this tiny bar in Les Halles will give you a hint of its clientele: by 7:30 A.M., the place is alive with local workers and red-faced tradesmen in blue coveralls drinking their early morning cognac and coffee. Lunchtime is the same, when they flock in for the daily specials and a bottle of red or a hefty sandwich on a crispy baguette and a tall beer. If getting up at the crack of dawn or rubbing elbows with the locals at lunch doesn't appeal to you, do stop by for a coffee, a drink, or a homemade pastry and admire one of the most beautiful small workingman's haunts still intact in Paris, with its original zinc bar and superbly detailed faience mural depicting Les Halles market at the turn of the century.

TELEPHONE
01-42-36-07-56

MÉTRO
Châtelet, Les Halles

OPEN
Mon–Sat

CLOSED
Sun, holidays, NAC

HOURS
Bar 7 A.M.–6 P.M., continuous service for cold food; hot lunch noon–3 P.M.

RESERVATIONS
Not necessary

CREDIT CARDS
None

À LA CARTE
70–100F, BC

PRIX FIXE
None

ENGLISH SPOKEN
The waitress told me, "I speak English with my hands. Everyone understands."

(13) LE LOUCHEBEM
31, rue Berger (1st)

TELEPHONE
01-42-33-12-99

MÉTRO
Les Halles, Châtelet

OPEN
Daily

CLOSED
Major holidays, NAC

HOURS
Lunch noon–2:30 P.M., dinner 7–11:30 P.M.

RESERVATIONS
Advised, especially on weekends and for Sunday lunch

CREDIT CARDS
AE, DC, MC, V

À LA CARTE
170F, BNC

PRIX FIXE
Lunch and dinner until 9 P.M., 90F, 3 courses, BNC; Sunday only, 190F, 3 courses, BC (kir, wine, or champagne and coffee)

ENGLISH SPOKEN
Yes

MISCELLANEOUS
Nonsmoking section

The red interior goes well with your beef and so do the many pictures of animals that line the walls at Le Louchebem, a temple of tradition in Les Halles. Despite its tourist-trap location near the Forum des Halles, it is largely unknown to outsiders. Featuring red meat in huge and satisfying portions, it has outlived dining and dietary crazes and continues to please a largely French audience that is serious about eating and drinking well.

If you go early and sit upstairs by a picture window overlooking the ornate Église St-Eustache, you will be captivated before your waiter appears with bowls of olives and pieces of ham and beef to dip into a caper sauce. When ordering your meal, throw caution, calories, and cholesterol to the winds and dig into he-man servings of steak tartare, leg of lamb, *andouillettes,* tripe, tender *cote de boeuf,* or the daunting *assiette du rotisseur*—a mixed grill displaying almost every meat on the menu. The salads are best forgotten, but not the desserts, especially the cooked to order *tarte fine*—if you can manage it at this point—a warm flaky pastry shell piled high with apples and ice cream. The wine list is limited but well priced. If you are dining with a friend, separate checks are possible without the waiter scowling. In addition, there is a nonsmoking section. And if they forget to give you the prix fixe menu, ask for it!

(14) LE MANÈGE DE L'ECUYER
6, rue de la Sourdière (angle 308, rue St-Honoré) (1st)

TELEPHONE
01-49-27-00-64

MÉTRO
Tuileries

OPEN
Mon–Fri

CLOSED
Sat–Sun, holidays, one week at Christmas, July 20–Aug 20

HOURS
Lunch noon–2:30 P.M., dinner 7:30–10 P.M.

RESERVATIONS
Advised

CREDIT CARDS
MC, V

À LA CARTE
150F, BNC

PRIX FIXE
Lunch, 79F, 2 courses, 110F, 3 courses, both BNC; dinner, 120F, 3 courses, BNC

When I walked by this place, everyone inside was smiling . . . but at the restaurant next door, the people were all scowling and talking on their cellular telephones. This was just enough for me to try Jeannine and Géorges Le Manège de l'Ecuyer, which in its previous life was a Cheap Eat in Paris known as La Providence. Now, with this couple firmly at the helm, the restaurant has greatly improved on every level.

Jeannine, with her bright smile and warm welcome, has created a place to return to night after night. The regulars who do never consider straying from Géorges's changing prix fixe blackboard menu, which features all the well-loved standbys: seasonally fresh asparagus vinaigrette, roast pork with mashed potatoes and gravy, followed by a fresh fruit strawberry *tarte.* Wines are available by the glass, *pichet,* or bottle, but those in the *pichet* are just fine to complement your exceptional Cheap Eat in Paris.

ENGLISH SPOKEN
Enough to order

(15) L'ÉPI D'OR
25, rue Jean-Jacques Rousseau (1st)

L'Épi d'Or typifies what eating in Paris is all about: waiters in black pants and long aprons serving traditional food in oversized portions to a diversified legion of habitués, who dine here regularly and until very, very late. The decor is cluttered, the place is crowded, the seats hard, and the one toilet is an antique from Turkey, but the food and atmosphere are oh, *so* French.

For the best experience of L'Épi d'Or, reserve for an 8:30 dinner and be on time, or your reservation might be given away. The best value is definitely the prix fixe menu, which is served only until 9 P.M.; the only drawback is that the *plats du jour* are not on it. You can order one of the filling servings of *jambonneau à la lyonnaise* (cured pork), *foie de veau* (liver), the *entrecôte Bordelaise avec Moelle,* or the popular steak tartare *de l'Épi d'Or.* Wines of the month always feature selections from Bordeau or the Loire Valley. Finish your feast with a slice of double-chocolate walnut cake surrounded by a rich *crème anglaise,* or a piece of their famous *tarte Tatin au Calvados,* a five-kilogram wonder that looks like a giant soufflé. If you are not up to one of these finales, at least sample a selection of the Berthillon ice cream or sorbet. A meal here is guaranteed to fill you to your toes, and you will leave happy and satisfied, probably swearing never to eat again.

TELEPHONE
01-42-36-38-12

MÉTRO
Louvre

OPEN
Mon–Fri lunch and dinner, Sat dinner only

CLOSED
Sat lunch, Sun, holidays, Aug

HOURS
Lunch noon–3 P.M., dinner 7:30 P.M.–midnight

RESERVATIONS
Advised, especially after 8:30 P.M. and Sat night

CREDIT CARDS
MC, V

À LA CARTE
200F, BNC

PRIX FIXE
Lunch and dinner (until 9 P.M.), 105F, 3 courses, BNC

ENGLISH SPOKEN
Yes

(16) LESCURE
7, rue de Mondovi (1st)

Located at the end of a short street just around the corner from place de la Concorde, the restaurant was founded in 1919 by Lèon Lescure. Today it is still owned and operated by his family, who serve simple French bourgeoise cooking at very reasonable prices.

For both lunch and dinner, diners vie for one of the sidewalk tables, or else sit elbow-to-elbow inside beneath ropes of garlic and country sausages dangling from the rafters. The service is friendly and perhaps the fastest in Paris.

If you select a dish that must be prepared that day, or better yet, cooked to order, you will be happy. Other-

TELEPHONE
01-42-60-18-91

MÉTRO
Concorde

OPEN
Mon–Fri lunch and dinner, Sat lunch only

CLOSED
Sat dinner, Sun, holidays, Aug, Dec 22–Jan 1

HOURS
Lunch noon–2:15 P.M., dinner 7–10:15 P.M.

RESERVATIONS
Not necessary

CREDIT CARDS
MC, V
À LA CARTE
145F, BNC
PRIX FIXE
Lunch and dinner, 100F, 3 courses, BC
ENGLISH SPOKEN
Yes
MISCELLANEOUS
Nonsmoking section

wise, you may run into some ingredients that are past their prime or have been reheated too much. The poached haddock is always a safe bet, and so is *la poule au riz sauce Basquaise*—chicken and rice with a tangy tomato-and-green pepper sauce (order it on the side). The most popular dessert is the special fruit *tarte*.

(17) LE SOUFFLÉ *
36, rue du Mont-Thabor (1st)

TELEPHONE
01-42-60-27-19
MÉTRO
Concorde, Tuileries
OPEN
Mon–Sat
CLOSED
Sun, holidays, NAC
HOURS
Lunch noon–2:30 P.M., dinner 7–10:30 P.M.
RESERVATIONS
Essential, several days in advance if possible
CREDIT CARDS
AE, DC, MC, V
À LA CARTE
225–250F, BNC
PRIX FIXE
Lunch and dinner: 140F, 2 courses, 180F, 3 courses, both BC (kir, wine, and coffee)
ENGLISH SPOKEN
Yes, and well
MISCELLANEOUS
Nonsmoking section in back

It is unanimous: Everyone loves Le Soufflé.

Many Parisians as well as a host of international visitors know that in this uncertain world Le Soufflé is one restaurant you can always count on for a wonderful meal. After dining here, you will feel like you are in heaven—and know that you are in Paris. The interior glows with soft lighting, pale pink walls, and fresh flowers in miniature soufflé pots on the tables, which are laid with heavy cutlery, beautiful china, and sparkling crystal. Along with polite service and discreet waiters, Le Soufflé maintains its reputation for memorable dining in Paris. After all, what could be more Parisian than a soufflé? Whether you order a fluffy cheese or spinach soufflé, a delicate smoked salmon soufflé sitting on a bed of tagliatelle, or a rich chocolate or a classic Grand Marnier soufflé—or any of the other imaginative offerings—you will enjoy dramatic dining guaranteed to please even the most jaded palate. If you want to avoid the most tourists, however, book your table for after 8:30 P.M.

In addition to the fantasia of soufflés, there are many appealing seasonal appetizers, hearty main courses, and luscious desserts. At the height of the spring season, the fat, white asparagus vinaigrette is a definite must. The fresh artichoke dressed in a tangy lemon sauce is another popular *entrée,* as is the homemade terrine or duck with green pepper and pistachios. For apple lovers, the *tarte fine aux pommes chaudes* is a dreamy dessert raising this standard French menu item to new heights. Another cloudlike choice is the *crêpe soufflé a la Marie-Brizard* . . . a puffed crêpe doused in Grand Marnier. When it arrives, covering the entire plate, you will think you can't finish it, but let me assure you that you will eat every bite and wish for more. Whatever you have at Le Soufflé will be divine and well worth the extra centimes.

(18) L'INCROYABLE

Passage between 26, rue de Richelieu, and 23, rue de Montpensier (1st)

L'Incroyable—"The Incredible"—is aptly named, with its three-course menus going for less than twenty dollars for lunch and around twenty-five dollars for dinner. It may not be the Cheap Eat it once was, and the quality can be spotty, but it is still worth considering. For this price you can't expect smoked salmon or pheasant under glass served by waiters in tuxedos, but you will get the usual basics of homestyle pâtés, chicken, beef, and pork, vegetables, creamed potatoes, simple salads, and unassuming desserts. Always stay with the prix fixe menu and the daily specials and you will rarely be disappointed.

Getting to L'Incroyable is half the fun, since it is hidden in a narrow passage running between two streets near the Palais-Royal. Either walk up rue de Richelieu or rue de Montpensier behind the Comédie Française. Once you have found it, settle into either the flower-filled courtyard adjoining the two-room restaurant or inside one of the cluttered dining rooms, and enjoy a good-natured meal in Paris.

TELEPHONE
01-42-96-24-64

MÉTRO
Palais-Royal, Musée du Louvre

OPEN
Mon–Fri May–Sept; Tues–Sat Oct–April

CLOSED
Sat–Sun May–Sept; Sun–Mon Oct–April; holidays, 15 days in July or Aug, Jan 5–Feb 1

HOURS
Lunch noon–2:15 P.M., dinner 6:30–9 P.M.

RESERVATIONS
Not necessary

CREDIT CARDS
None

À LA CARTE
Dinner only, 120F, BNC

PRIX FIXE
Lunch, 75F and 110F, 3 courses, BNC; dinner, 85F and 115F, 3 courses, BNC

ENGLISH SPOKEN
Yes

(19) LUNCHTIME

255, rue St-Honoré (1st)

Its wide variety of well-stacked sandwiches, fresh salads, and hot soups in winter have made Lunchtime a favorite haunt of secretaries, smart tourists, and cute young things around the fashionable rue St-Honoré. The inside is spacious and nicely done with murals of Cape Cod and interesting displays of big seashells, sailor's knots, and sailing artifacts.

You have a choice of at least twenty sandwiches served hot or cold on crusty *pain complete, pain de campagne,* or pita bread. The sandwiches are filled with every possible combination of chicken, cheese, egg, fish, turkey, beef, and vegetables. Six or seven salads and some rather mundane desserts complete the dining picture. Everything can be eaten here at comfortable tables (some reserved for nonsmokers) or you can have your order packed to go. They also deliver if your order is large enough. If you take your sandwich with you, it will cost a few francs less.

TELEPHONE
01-42-60-80-40

MÉTRO
Tuileries

OPEN
Mon–Fri lunch only

CLOSED
Sat–Sun, holidays, NAC

HOURS
11 A.M.–4 P.M.

RESERVATIONS
Not necessary

CREDIT CARDS
None

À LA CARTE
45–65F, BNC

PRIX FIXE
None

ENGLISH SPOKEN
Limited

MISCELLANEOUS
Nonsmoking section

(20) RESTAURANT CHEZ MAX

47, rue St-Honoré (1st floor, *ler étage*) (1st)

TELEPHONE
01-45-08-80-13
MÉTRO
Châtelet, exit St-Opportune or Les Halles
OPEN
Mon–Fri lunch and dinner, Sat dinner only
CLOSED
Sat lunch, Sun, 2 weeks in Aug (dates vary)
HOURS
Lunch noon–2 P.M., dinner 7:30–11:45 P.M.
RESERVATIONS
Advised
CREDIT CARDS
AE, MC, V
À LA CARTE
170F, BNC
PRIX FIXE
Lunch: 65F, 3 courses, BNC; 85F and 120F, 3 courses, BC; dinner: 85F and 135F, 3 courses, BC
ENGLISH SPOKEN
Yes

Max has been feeding loyal patrons in his first-floor dining room for more than two decades, and the photo gallery along the entry hall attests to the many well-known French actors, artists, and musicians who have dined here over the years. If you can look past the orange walls and the overhead lighted tree branches hung with paper bells and birds, you, too, will do well at Chez Max.

The attention-getting Cheap Eat is his daily changing, *marché*-based 65F three-course lunch menu written on a blackboard. It headlines five choices for your *entrée* and *plat* and includes house pastries or ice cream for dessert. Double your money buys you starters of homemade foie gras, escargots, spinach salad, fresh salmon, *confit* or *magret de canard,* and a wider dessert choice. *En plus*, Max throws in a carafe of drinkable house red or white wine. There's à la carte, too, but what for? Everything is already on one of the value-packed menus.

(21) RESTAURANT LA MANGERIE

17, rue des Petits-Champs (1st)

TELEPHONE
01-42-97-51-01
MÉTRO
Bourse
OPEN
Mon–Fri lunch only
CLOSED
Sat–Sun, holidays, Aug
HOURS
Lunch 12:15–2 P.M.
RESERVATIONS
Advised
CREDIT CARDS
MC, V (over 150F)
À LA CARTE
115F, BNC
PRIX FIXE
None
ENGLISH SPOKEN
Limited

La Mangerie is convenient and a good bet for traditional lunch at a reasonable price. The neighborhood folds up in the evening and on weekends, so you have to hit this one during the week. Before you go inside, notice the display of homemade desserts tempting you from the front window and be sure to plan ahead, especially if the *gâteau citron* is there. Try to avoid sitting in the front room, which serves as a passageway to the two back rooms, where the regulars congregate at bare wood tables along a wall of banquettes or at one of the oilcloth-covered tables with paper overlays. The menu plays it safe with familiar favorites such as *poireau vinaigrette, museau de boeuf* (boiled beef muzzle), *carrottes rapées,* herring with potatoes, roast chicken, lamb sautéed with vegetables, and inexpensive pitchers of basic wines. No, it is nothing gourmet foodies would line up for, but eating here gives you a good taste of what the average French professional eats for lunch, and that is more interesting to some than a meal in a stiff, high-priced *name* restaurant.

(22) RESTAURANT LE VIEIL ECU

166, rue St-Honoré (1st)

Rustic and generous are the bywords at Le Vieil Ecu, which serves mountains of basic French fare to scores of thrift-minded Cheap Eaters every day except Sunday. At lunchtime, it seems to be the favorite canteen for sturdy office workers who appreciate meat and potatoes served in trucker proportions.

On the main floor, tables are squished together under a beamed ceiling hung with copper pots, farm utensils, and lace-covered lights. Upstairs, the tone is quieter, prettier, and much less congested. The problem is that the upstairs is only open when the downstairs room is packed full. Smart lunchers know to order the 70F, two-course menu, which offers a choice from the *entrées* and the *plats du jour* and includes either wine, water, or a beer. At dinner, the two prix fixe menus are a bit more upscale, offering escargots, salmon, *confit de canard,* and even a vegetarian plate. Fine pastries and opulent desserts are not the forte here, so opt for the sorbet or the *tarte Tatin,* if it looks fresh. À la carte is available only in the evening, but I can't imagine going this route unless you only wanted a main course and nothing else. House wine is the screw-cap variety, so you may want to upgrade a notch or two.

TELEPHONE
01-42-60-21-14

MÉTRO
Palais-Royal

OPEN
Mon–Sat

CLOSED
Sun, NAC

HOURS
Lunch 11:30 A.M.–2:30 P.M., dinner 6:30–11 P.M.

RESERVATIONS
Not necessary

CREDIT CARDS
MC, V

À LA CARTE
140F, BNC

PRIX FIXE
Lunch: 70F, 2 courses, BC; 100F, 3 courses, BNC; dinner: 70F and 100F, 3 courses, BNC

ENGLISH SPOKEN
Yes, with English menu

(23) ROSE THÉ

91, rue St-Honoré (1st)

Rose Thé can be found at the end of the Village St-Honoré, a narrow alleyway filled with dealers of antiques and bric-a-brac, just minutes away from all the noise and brash glitter of the Forum des Halles and the Centre Pompidou. The inside of this napkin-sized tearoom is painted a soft yellow. Metal lights, dried flowers, or perhaps a ceramic pear sit on top of an assortment of interesting old tables, which are set with yellow placemats and green napkins. Big armchairs stress comfort and encourage long stays, making this a relaxing choice for a quiet lunch *à deux,* or a soothing cup of tea and a homemade dessert while sitting at one of the outside tables by a fountain. Everything is made fresh daily in the miniature kitchen by the owner, Chantal Leger. Sample a savory *tarte du jour,* an *assiette composée*—a one-plate meal consisting of vegetable crudités, cheese, and sliced chicken—or the hot dish of the day. For an afternoon delight, order her dense *fondant au chocolat* or

TELEPHONE
01-42-36-97-18

MÉTRO
Musée du Louvre

OPEN
Mon–Sat for lunch and afternoon tea

CLOSED
Sun, holidays, 15 days in mid-August

HOURS
Lunch noon–6:30 P.M. (or until the food runs out), tea 2–6:30 P.M.

RESERVATIONS
Not necessary

CREDIT CARDS
V

À LA CARTE
40–75F, BNC

PRIX FIXE
None

ENGLISH SPOKEN
Yes

the fruit crumble. On your way out, pay a visit to the shop on the corner of the Village St-Honoré that deals in magnificent antique silver.

(24) UNIVERSAL RESTORAMA IN THE CARROUSEL DU LOUVRE

Passage du Carrousel, under the Louvre (entrance through 99, rue de Rivoli) (1st)

TELEPHONE
01-40-20-53-17

MÉTRO
Musée du Louvre

OPEN
Daily

CLOSED
Major holidays, NAC

HOURS
8 A.M.–11 P.M., continuous service

RESERVATIONS
Not accepted

CREDIT CARDS
None

À LA CARTE
35–75F, BC

PRIX FIXE
None

ENGLISH SPOKEN
Depends on the stand

When the Carrousel du Louvre underground shopping mall opened in November 1993, the first North American–style food court opened alongside it, serving *le fast food à la française.* The self-service food stands are set on the mezzanine of the mall, just off I. M. Pei's majestic pyramid. The food certainly is not three-star gourmet, but it is filling, fresh, and inexpensive, especially when you consider the million-dollar surroundings. Judging by the crowds during lunch, the self-service concept is an unqualified hit.

Best battle plan is to walk around, survey the stands, and then decide what looks best. The food stands come and go, so it is impossible to guarantee that your favorite Middle Eastern stall will be in business the next time around. However, the round-the-world choices available during my last visit included Asian, Tex-Mex, hot and cold Spanish tapas, Italian pizza and pasta, French crêpes, a health bar (with fresh fruits, veggie plates, and juices), hamburgers and fries, Hector le Poulet (serving rotisserie chicken), and a coffee stand dispensing muffins and cookies to munch with your *café au lait*. In the late afternoon, it is relaxing to stop by the cheese bar, which offers a selection of French cheeses and wines, and then take your glass of wine to one of the tables along the edge and watch the throngs surging through below.

Second Arrondissement

(See map on pages 38–39.)

The second arrondissement can hardly be called a tourist hub in comparison to some others. It is the home of the stock market (Bourse) and some big banks. It is also dotted with *passages:* those relics of the time before department stores that were the shopping malls of the early 1900s. (See *Cheap Sleeps in Paris,* "Shopping," for a listing of the most interesting *passages.*)

RIGHT BANK
Bibliothèque Nationale, Bourse, Cognacq-Jay Museum, *passages,* Place des Victoires

SECOND ARRONDISSEMENT RESTAURANTS

* Restaurants marked with an asterisk (*) are considered Big Splurges.

(25) À LA PERDRIX
6, rue Mandar (2nd)

You can go with a slim wallet and a big appetite to À la Perdrix and find simple food served in a homey dining room, which is scrubbed and polished every day. This long-standing Cheap Eat is just off rue Montorgueil, one of the most interesting food shopping streets in Paris.

The regulars do not have to consult the menu; they just wait for the waitress to tell them what is best that day. The three prix fixe menus are bargains and include all the favorites. Even the least expensive lunch menu, which changes daily and includes a beverage, has choices for each course. Big spenders can opt for the most expensive menu and choose a half-dozen snails, crudités, or homemade rabbit terrine with tarragon for the *entrée,* and *faux filet,* stewed chicken, or *coq au vin* for the *plat.* I would avoid the fish because it's all frozen. A piece of Camembert cheese, an ice cream parfait, or the dessert of

TELEPHONE
01-42-36-83-21

MÉTRO
Sentier, Étienne-Marcel

OPEN
Mon–Fri lunch and dinner, Sat lunch only; Sat dinner by group reservation only

CLOSED
Sat dinner, Sun, holidays, 2 weeks in Aug

HOURS
Lunch noon–3 P.M., dinner 6:30–10:30 P.M.

RESERVATIONS
For more than 4; Sat dinner for large groups

CREDIT CARDS
MC, V

À LA CARTE
135–150F, BNC

PRIX FIXE
Lunch only, 60F, 3 courses, BC; lunch and dinner, 85F and 110F, 3 courses, BNC

ENGLISH SPOKEN
Yes

the day ends the meal perfectly. Smaller appetites will be pleased with the main-dish salads, which include *salad niçoise* and *salade Parisienne* (with ham, tomatoes, and hard-boiled egg).

(26) AUX LYONNAIS
32, rue St-Marc (2nd)

TELEPHONE
01-42-96-65-04

MÉTRO
Bourse

OPEN
Mon–Fri lunch and dinner, Sat dinner only

CLOSED
Sat lunch, Sun, holidays during May–Sept, NAC

HOURS
Lunch noon–2:30 P.M., dinner 7–11:30 P.M.

RESERVATIONS
Advised

CREDIT CARDS
AE, DC, MC, V

À LA CARTE
160F, BNC

PRIX FIXE
Lunch only, 95F, 2 courses, BNC

ENGLISH SPOKEN
Yes

What more can anyone ask of a bistro? Pretty surroundings, interesting people, reliable food, a pleasant owner and staff, honest prices . . . Aux Lyonnais has them all. At lunch it hums with the voices of office workers and stockbrokers from the Bourse and the matronly waitresses in black rushing to serve them. In the evening, the pace slows and the service and mood become more relaxed and refined.

The menu offers dishes that have been served here and in bistros like it for generations. The first-rate fare is well prepared, with no unpleasant surprises. You start with a basket of crispy baguettes to be spread with sweet butter. *Entrées* include a salad with warm sausage or chicken livers, a trio of spicy sausage patties covered in herbs and lightly sautéed, and a fish terrine. Chicken fixed several ways, lamb chops with fresh spinach, *confit de canard,* and a tender rabbit covered in shallots, all served with *gratin dauphinois* (potatoes baked in cream), highlight the main courses. The dessert not to miss is the *Oeuf à la Neige*—floating island served in a large sundae dish and topped with caramel glaze.

(27) AUX TROIS PETITS COCHONS
31, rue Tiquetonne (2nd)

TELEPHONE
01-42-33-39-69

MÉTRO
Étienne Marcel

OPEN
Tues–Sun dinner only

CLOSED
Mon, Aug 1-15

HOURS
Dinner 8:30–10:30 P.M.

RESERVATIONS
Essential

CREDIT CARDS
MC, V

À LA CARTE
Not available

Aux Trois Petits Cochons (the three little pigs) stands for the three very slim and slight friends who joined together to open this outstanding Cheap Eat in Paris. Open only for dinner, the place comes into its own around 9:30 P.M. when it fills with a glossy, artistic mix of patrons both straight and otherwise.

These dedicated returnees know a bargain in delicious dining when they find it, and they always book a day ahead to be assured a table. The two formula menus offer a choice of two or three courses of up-to-date food that is imaginatively prepared and artistically presented. The service is always polite, the linen and crystal table settings correct, and the bottom line on your bill reflects the talents of the exceptional chef. Its pleasures might include a springtime salad of lightly cooked onions and mushrooms with a coriander *pistou*, fresh and smoked salmon seasoned with olive oil and lemon and served with *pain Poilâne* toast, or sole terrine with a vegetable *confit* and spinach cream. The *filet de cabillaud* (cod fish) comes with lemon butter and is garnished with fresh spinach and broccoli. I also like the cider-roasted duckling paired with potatoes and cooked pears. Dessert keeps up the pace with an almond-flavored cookie basket housing a trio of fresh sorbets or flaky pastry leaves served with bourbon-spiked vanilla ice cream and caramel sauce.

PRIX FIXE
119F, 2 courses, 135F, 3 courses, both BNC

ENGLISH SPOKEN
Yes

(28) CHEZ DANIE
5, rue de Louvois (2nd)

You don't have to be down and out in Paris to eat here, but it is a good place to come if you are. It is also a useful Cheap Eat if one of you wants only a large salad and the other is ready to tackle something more substantial. The tiny cream-colored room is casual, to say the least. There are only a few tables and the menu is scribbled on a blackboard over the window of the lilliputian kitchen in the back. You can order the *plat du jour*—maybe a beef and carrot stew—or a quiche and a side salad, and for dessert, splurge on a slice of *tarte Tatin* or a plate of Danie's *beignets de poire* . . . deep-fried sweet fritters that literally melt in your mouth as if they were fresh from the cauldron. Danie does all the cooking herself and she is assisted out front by one waitress. By 12:30 or 1 P.M., every seat is taken, while next door it is half empty. This tells you the locals know something, and Cheap Eaters should pay attention.

TELEPHONE
01-42-96-64-05

MÉTRO
4-Septembre

OPEN
Mon–Fri lunch only

CLOSED
Sat–Sun, holidays, 2 weeks in Aug

HOURS
Lunch noon–2:45 P.M.

RESERVATIONS
Not necessary

CREDIT CARDS
MC, V

À LA CARTE
65F, BNC

PRIX FIXE
48–55F, 3 courses, BNC

ENGLISH SPOKEN
Some

(29) COUNTRY LIFE
6, rue Daunou (2nd)

The vegetarian tourist en route to Paris need not fear the only nourishment available will be omelettes, *frites,* and crudités at the corner café. Almost every vegetarian in Paris knows about Country Life on the rue Daunou, near the Opéra and across the street from Harry's New York Bar. Harry's advertisement, "Tell the taxi driver 'sank, roo de noo,'" will also get you to Country Life.

You enter through their natural products shop and bookstore. It is worthwhile to take a few minutes if you are into herbal and natural cosmetics. In the back, the plain white-tiled restaurant offers an expansive, all-you-

TELEPHONE
01-42-97-48-51

MÉTRO
Opéra

OPEN
Mon–Thur lunch and dinner, Fri lunch only

CLOSED
Fri dinner, Sat–Sun, holidays, NAC

HOURS
Lunch 11:30 A.M.–2:30 P.M., dinner 6:30 P.M.–10 P.M.; shop, Mon–Thur 10 A.M.–10 P.M., Fri 10 A.M.–3 P.M.

RESERVATIONS
Not taken
CREDIT CARDS
AE, DC, MC, V
À LA CARTE
None
PRIX FIXE
Lunch and dinner, 70F, all-you-can-eat buffet, BNC; desserts 15–20F extra
ENGLISH SPOKEN
Enough
MISCELLANEOUS
No smoking allowed

can-eat, self-serve, hot-and-cold buffet and varied salad bar. The daily choices always include a soup, several grain dishes, potatoes, and assorted veggies that are 80 to 90 percent organically grown. Desserts and beverages are extra.

Don't plan on ordering booze, coffee, or tea because they don't serve them. You can order fresh juice, mineral water, or a fruit shake to accompany your meal. There is a no-smoking policy for the entire restaurant.

(30) LA FERME SAINT HUBERT
17–19, rue d'Antin (2nd)

See page 144 for description. All other information is the same.

TELEPHONE: 01-42-65-42-74
MÉTRO: Opéra
OPEN: Mon–Fri lunch and dinner, Sat dinner only
CLOSED: Sat lunch, Sun, holidays, NAC
HOURS: Lunch noon–2:30 P.M., dinner 7–10:30 P.M.

(31) LA PATATA
25, boulevard des Italiens (2nd)

TELEPHONE
01-42-68-16-66
MÉTRO
Opéra
OPEN
Daily
CLOSED
Christmas day, NAC
HOURS
11 A.M.–midnight, continuous service
RESERVATIONS
Not necessary
CREDIT CARDS
V
À LA CARTE
50–90F, BNC
PRIX FIXE
94F, potato, fresh fruit, and dessert, BNC; 91–109F, potato and dessert, BC
ENGLISH SPOKEN
Limited

For more food than you can probably eat in one sitting, drop in anytime at La Patata and order a giant baked potato topped with a variety of delicious ingredients and served on platters garnished with salad and fresh fruit. There is something for every taste. Starting with a *Patata Tradition* (topped with chicken gizzards and sour cream), you can move on to the *Patata Sportive* (cucumbers, corn, tomatoes, carrots, and sour cream), or the *Patata Californienne* (hamburger, ketchup, onions, and corn slathered with cheese fondue). Mashed potato fans can order *les gratins de monsieur Parmentier;* served in its own dish, it is potato purée covered with a variety of ingredients then topped with cheese and browned in the oven. The *l'Antlantide* pairs scrambled eggs and smoked salmon under a roof of melted cheese. If you want to raise both your guilt and fat gram intake, order *le Forestier,* which is ham and mushrooms mixed with a béchamel sauce and then gratinéed. Tipping the dessert scales are huge sundaes and the amazing *Banana Patata:* a big dish overflowing with maple-walnut and vanilla ice cream, surrounded by hot chocolate and whipped cream, with an entire banana under it all.

NOTE: If you are in Paris long enough, join the *Patata club*. Members have three months (or less) to eat ten potato dishes, and then they get the eleventh one free.

(32) LE BRIN DE ZINC . . . ET MADAME
50, rue Montorgueil (2nd)

One of the best ways to discover and appreciate the real Paris is through her bistros, brasseries, and cafés. It would be hard to find a more Parisian bistro than Le Brin de Zinc . . . et Madame. The corner location is busy day and night, especially the pavement tables that provide occupants with a fine perch to watch the comings and goings along this cobblestone pedestrian walkway that serves as the *quartier's* main shopping street. The inside mixes a great Art Deco mirror and draped lights with pictures of soccer teams and one enormous athletic shoe. Fast-talking, black-clad waiters efficiently serve the loud, jolly elbow-to-elbow patrons.

The classic blackboard display of the bistro's repertoire offers twenty-three *entrées*, almost as many *plats,* and all the dessert faves we love. Lighter appetites will do very well with just a main course, which will be served not on a mere plate . . . but on a platter. It all adds up to a great evening of fun, especially if the singers make an appearance.

TELEPHONE
01-42-21-10-80

MÉTRO
Étienne Marcel, Sentier

OPEN
Mon–Sat lunch and dinner, Sun dinner only

CLOSED
Sun lunch, NAC

HOURS
Lunch noon–2 P.M., dinner 7–11:30 P.M.

RESERVATIONS
Essential

CREDIT CARDS
MC, V

À LA CARTE
150–175F, BNC

PRIX FIXE
None

ENGLISH SPOKEN
Limited

(33) LE VAUDEVILLE
29, rue Vivienne (2nd)

A polished crowd of locals and out-of-towners drifts into Jean-Paul Bucher's 1920s-style brasserie for the pleasure of meeting and eating. At lunch, you will share your meal with stockbrokers and commodity traders from the nearby Bourse (stock exchange). About 10 P.M. in the evening, the sophisticated set arrives in anything from black tie and satin to pastel pullovers and athletic shoes to take advantage of the two-course menu deal available *only* after 10 P.M. Formally clad waiters serve during the peak hours without keeping anyone waiting too long or appearing overworked.

On a warm day, the coveted terrace tables are a great place to sit and soak up the street scene as you delve into familiar dishes ordered from the vast daily changing menu. A good-value prix fixe lunch and dinner option includes not only wine but a *café*. This is the sort of place where it is easy to get carried away and spend too much, but if you choose wisely, ordering the dry house Riesling

TELEPHONE
01-40-20-04-62

MÉTRO
Richelieu-Drout, Bourse

OPEN
Daily

CLOSED
Dec 24 for dinner, NAC

HOURS
Lunch noon–3:30 P.M., dinner 7 P.M.–2 A.M.

RESERVATIONS
Advised, especially for dinner

CREDIT CARDS
AE, DC, MC, V

À LA CARTE
200F, BNC

PRIX FIXE
Lunch, 125F, 2 courses, BC; dinner: 170F, 3 courses, BC; 130F (only after 10 P.M.), 2 courses, BC

ENGLISH SPOKEN
Yes

wine if you are going à la carte, your final tab should not be too astounding.

(34) MELLIFÈRE
8, rue de Monsigny (2nd)

TELEPHONE
01-42-61-21-71

MÉTRO
4-Septembre

OPEN
Mon–Fri lunch and dinner, Sat dinner only

CLOSED
Sat lunch, Sun, NAC

HOURS
Lunch noon–2:30 P.M., dinner 7:15–11 P.M.

RESERVATIONS
Essential

CREDIT CARDS
AE, MC, V

À LA CARTE
Not available

PRIX FIXE
Lunch and dinner, 125F, 2 courses, BNC; 145F, 3 courses, BNC

ENGLISH SPOKEN
Yes

For Paris restaurateurs still in the grip of the economic crisis, maintaining *le business* is what counts. At Mellifère, *le business* is booming, and after eating here just once it is easy to see why the locals create an SRO situation for both lunch and dinner. The food stands out not only for its quality and value but for its preparation of selections from the two *formules* featuring either a two- or three-course meal with wine by the pitcher (good) or bottle (both cost extra). When reserving, ask for a table along the mirrored wall of banquettes and try to avoid those close to the bar and upright piano, or you will be watching the kitchen action and in the line of fire of the amazing waiter. If I ever open a restaurant, I am going to hire this young man, whose hair stands on end . . . and no wonder. He *never* stops moving. My dinner companion equated him to a ballet dancer as he glided through the traditional room never missing a step, ignoring a table, or failing to negotiate a sharp turn.

Your meal will get off to a good start with one of the vegetable terrines, the artichoke heart topped with a poached egg, or the simple endive salad liberally served with Roquefort cheese. You can safely forget the only dud on the menu . . . the *chévre chaude* sitting on a bed of frisée, masked by heavy dressing. Noteworthy main courses include a delicate sole *meunière*, poached turbot with Hollandaise, and a sensational, herb-crusted, tender pink rack of lamb served with a tomato-zucchini gratin. Dessert classics tempt with crème brûlée, a fruit crumble with crème fraîche, and my very favorite . . . *profiteroles* blanketed with rich, warm chocolate sauce.

(35) RESTAURANT CHEZ PEIRROT*
18, rue Étienne Marcel (2nd)

TELEPHONE
01-45-08-17-64, 01-45-08-05-48

MÉTRO
Étienne Marcel

OPEN
Mon–Sat

"Oh, this is perfect! Just what I imagined eating in Paris was all about," crooned my hometown friend who joined me here for dinner one night. She is right . . . this *is* the perfect place to appreciate the art of dining that is so much a part of Paris.

Frankly, I have wanted to include it in this book for years, but until recently, no prix fixe menu was available to offset the over-the-top à la carte prices. Now, with a very generous prix fixe menu, Cheap Eaters in Paris can experience this timeless choice in a reasonable way.

Tradition reigns supreme from the moment you enter the yellow room with its lacy curtains and plants lining the windows. A zinc bar, aging mirrored walls, globe lights, and serious waiters wearing black aprons complete the picture. With the set menu, you will start with a kir and a bowl of radishes spread with sweet butter. Following that are choices of a dozen escargots, *poireaux, vinaigrette* (leeks), their own *fois gras de canard,* or *jambon persillé* (ham molded in aspic). Main courses are nicely garnished with a choice of potatoes and include salmon, pepper steak, lamb, duck, or kidneys. In the spring, desserts revolve around fresh strawberries, allowing you to sample a slice of strawberry *tarte* or their creamy layer cake called a . . . *fraisier*. Wine is included and so is the after-dinner coffee. It all adds up to a wonderful meal that never lets you forget for a minute that this *is* Paris.

CLOSED
Sun, holidays, Dec 24–Jan 1, NAC

HOURS
Lunch noon–2:30 P.M., dinner 8–10:30 P.M.

RESERVATIONS
Essential

CREDIT CARDS
AE, MC, V

À LA CARTE
255F, BNC

PRIX FIXE
Lunch and dinner, 195F, 3 courses, BC (kir, wine, and coffee)

ENGLISH SPOKEN
Limited

(36) STOHRER
51, rue Montorgueil (2nd)

Parisian pastry lovers think nothing of crossing their city in search of the perfect croissant, the richest chocolate mousse cake, or the best lemon *tarte.* At Stohrer's they come for the *Puits d'Amour* (wells of love)—individual, cream-filled, flaky puff pastries lightly caramelized with a hot iron. Others come for the famous seven-fruit tart made up of picture-perfect raspberries, strawberries, tangerines, peaches, kiwi fruit, rose figs, and white pears set in almond paste in a *sablé* crust. I like to go when the doors open and buy a bag of their buttery croissants, or to go by at lunchtime and take out a picnic *extraordinaire* made up of quiche, pâtés, fresh salads, and of course, several divine desserts. In the afternoon, schoolchildren line up outside by the cart selling homemade ice creams and sorbet.

The shop has a long and interesting history. It was opened in 1730 by one of Louis XV's pastry chefs and named for Marie Antoinette's private *patissier*. It is now classified as a historical monument. Inside, the beautiful painted walls and ceiling depicting nymphs holding trays of pastries were painted by Paul Baudry, who is famous for his paintings on the Opéra.

TELEPHONE
01-42-33-38-20

MÉTRO
Étienne Marcel, Sentier

OPEN
Daily

CLOSED
First 3 weeks of Aug

HOURS
7:30 A.M.–8:30 P.M., continuous service

RESERVATIONS
Not taken

CREDIT CARDS
MC, V (over 100F)

À LA CARTE
10–85F, BNC

PRIX FIXE
None

ENGLISH SPOKEN
Some

(37) THÉ AU FIL
80, rue Montmartre (2nd)

TELEPHONE
01-42-36-95-49

MÉTRO
Sentier

OPEN
Mon–Fri lunch and tea only

CLOSED
Sat–Sun, holidays, Aug (dates vary)

HOURS
Lunch noon–3 P.M., teatime 3–6:30 P.M., continuous service

RESERVATIONS
Not necessary

CREDIT CARDS
V (over 150F)

À LA CARTE
50–100F, BC

PRIX FIXE
None

ENGLISH SPOKEN
Yes

Rue Montmartre and the surrounding streets have been reset with cobblestones and are now designated pedestrian walkways. The result is impressive, and so are the crowds sitting at the cafés and filling the many restaurants. The bright green Thé Au Fil is just a block or so away from the hustle, thus attracting knowing local patrons who sit inside around green-and-white cloth covered tables, or on a sunny day, at one of the four tables outside. The food appeals to diners who are watching what they eat and want wholesome food presented in sensible servings. Everything is made here, using fresh ingredients. From noon until 3:00 P.M. blackboard listed dishes are served. There will always be a hot dish of the day in addition to *tartes,* flans, steamed veggie plates, covered baked potatoes, pastas, filled bagels, and tartines, but a warning is in order . . . don't arrive at 2:30 or 3:00 P.M. and expect all the hot dishes to be available. Quantity is limited and when they sell out . . . that's it. From 3:00 P.M. on it is teatime, which features a host of their homey desserts headlined by rice pudding with caramel sauce, apricot, pear, or apple crumbles, *fondant* chocolate with *crème Anglaise,* and cheesecake with raspberry sauce. The wines merit attention: they are all directly bottled by the producer and offered by the glass, *pichet,* or bottle.

Third Arrondissement

Marais means "swamp" in French, and this area was just that until the fourteenth century when it became a royal park. Today, a walk through this area is a lesson in the history of French domestic architecture. The area has been redeveloped with panache, and many of the seventeenth- and eighteenth-century buildings have been made into museums or returned to their former glory as sumptuous apartments. This heaven for walkers and wanderers of all types is full of shops, boutiques, appealing restaurants, and fascinating history.

RIGHT BANK
Carnavalet Museum (the museum of the city of Paris), French National Archive, part of the Marais, Picasso Museum

THIRD ARRONDISSEMENT RESTAURANTS

* Restaurants marked with an asterisk (*) are considered Big Splurges.

(1) AU BASCOU*
38, rue de Réaumur (3rd)

If you can't go to the Basque region of France, Au Bascou will at least put you in a southwestern frame of mind with its modern Basque food and sensibly priced wines, served by Jean-Guy Lousteau. The 1930s bistro, which was voted Bistro of the Year in 1995, is not near the usual tourist track. The area is full of wholesale clothing merchants, cheap Chinese restaurants, and older Parisians carrying little dogs and feeding the ravenous pigeons. Don't let this slice of local color discourage you. The restaurant is less than a two-minute walk from the métro, and remember, you are here for the food, which is not only rich and full-flavored but extremely well made and presented. The menu is seasonally based, but there are some standards that always appear. Such starters are the duck terrine, *piperade basquaise* (sweet peppers and tomatoes flavored with onion and garlic and served with scrambled eggs and cured ham) and their own foie gras.

TELEPHONE
01-42-72-69-25

MÉTRO
Arts-et-Métiers

OPEN
Mon–Fri lunch and dinner, Sat dinner only

CLOSED
Sat lunch, Sun, holidays, 1 week at Christmas, Aug

HOURS
Lunch noon–2 P.M., dinner 8–10:15 P.M.

RESERVATIONS
Essential

CREDIT CARDS
AE, DC, MC, V

À LA CARTE
200–225F, BNC

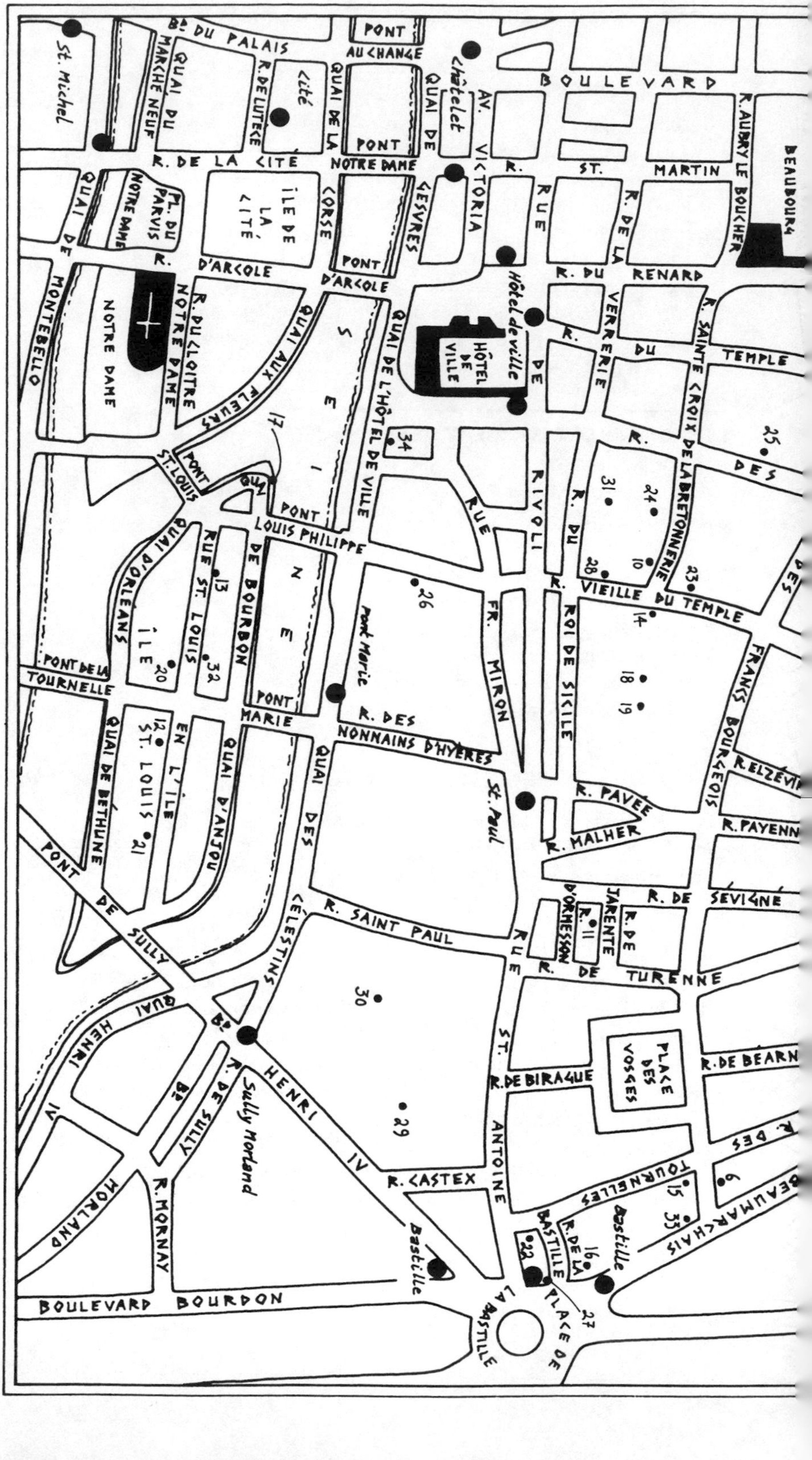
St. Michel
Bd DU PALAIS
QUAI DU MARCHÉ NEUF
R. DE LUTÈCE
Cité
PONT AU CHANGE
QUAI DE LA CORSE
Châtelet
QUAI DE GESVRES
AV. VICTORIA
BOULEVARD
R. AUBRY LE BOUCHER
BEAUBOURG
R. DE LA CITÉ
PONT NOTRE DAME
R. ST. MARTIN
QUAI DE MONTEBELLO
NOTRE DAME
PL. DU PARVIS NOTRE DAME
ÎLE DE LA CITÉ
R. D'ARCOLE
PONT D'ARCOLE
RUE
R. DE LA VERRERIE
R. DU RENARD
Hôtel de ville
HÔTEL DE VILLE
R. SAINTE CROIX DE LA BRETONNERIE
R. DU TEMPLE
R. DU CLOÎTRE NOTRE DAME
QUAI AUX FLEURS
SEINE
QUAI DE L'HÔTEL DE VILLE
RUE DE RIVOLI
R. DES
PONT ST. LOUIS
QUAI
17
34
PONT LOUIS PHILIPPE
RUE
R. DU ROI DE SICILE
VIEILLE DU TEMPLE
31
24
25
28
10
23
14
26
13
QUAI D'ORLÉANS
RUE ST. LOUIS
QUAI DE BOURBON
ÎLE
20
32
Pont Marie
FR. MIRON
18 19
FRANCS BOURGEOIS
PONT DE LA TOURNELLE
PONT MARIE
R. DES NONNAINS D'HYÈRES
R. ELZÉVIR
QUAI DE BÉTHUNE
12
ST. LOUIS EN L'ÎLE
QUAI D'ANJOU
QUAI DES CÉLESTINS
St. Paul
R. PAVÉE
R. MALHER
R. PAYENNE
21
PONT DE SULLY
R. SAINT PAUL
R. D'ORMESSON
R. JARENTE
11
R. DE SÉVIGNÉ
RUE ST. ANTOINE
R. DE TURENNE
30
QUAI HENRI IV
Bd HENRI IV
PLACE DES VOSGES
R. DE BÉARN
R. DE SULLY
Sully Morland
Bd
R. DE BIRAGUE
29
R. DES TOURNELLES
R. DES
BEAUMARCHAIS
6
15
33
Bastille
16
R. DE LA BASTILLE
22
27
R. CASTEX
MORLAND
R. MORNAY
Bastille
BOULEVARD BOURDON
PLACE DE LA BASTILLE

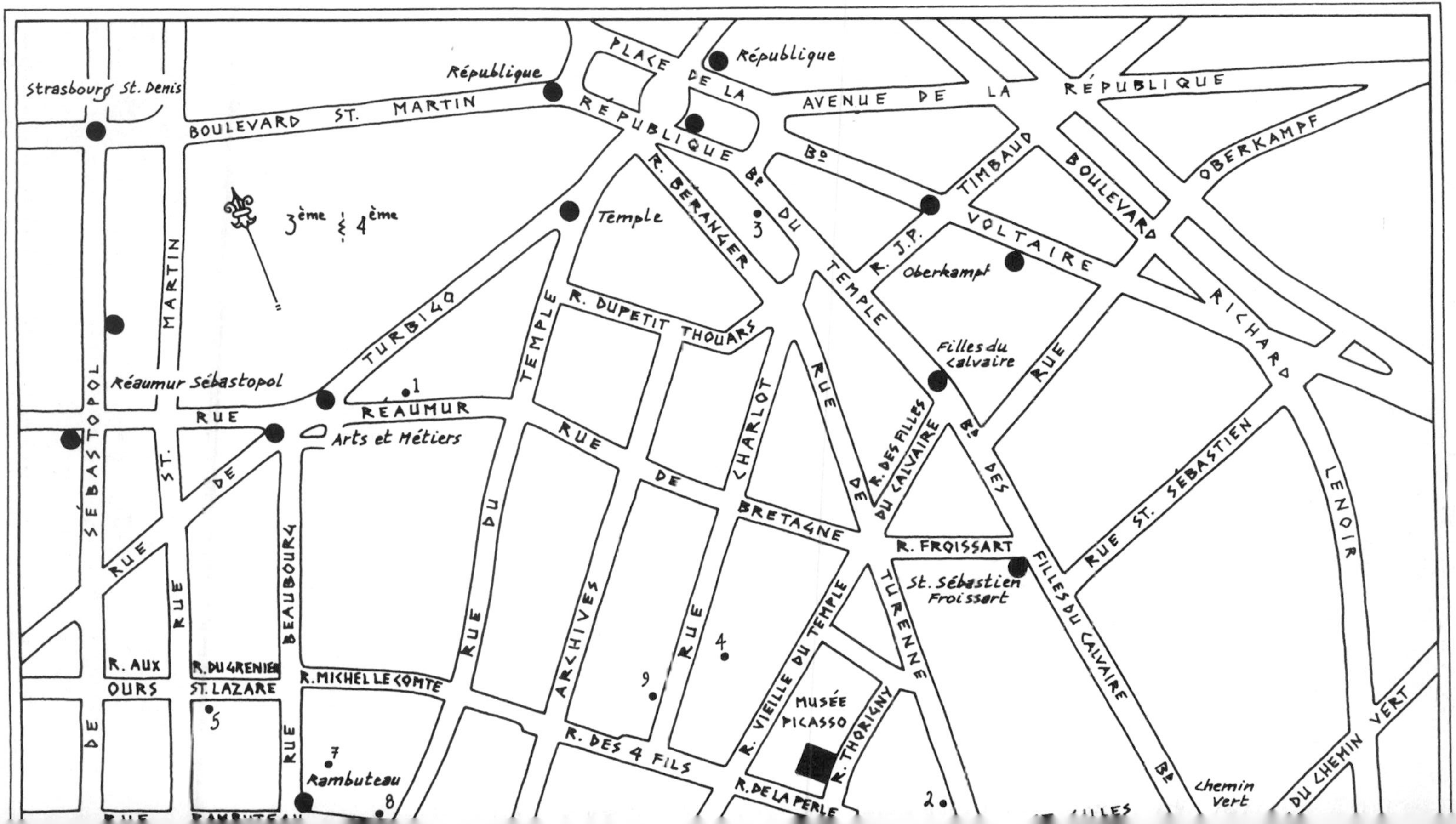

Strasbourg St. Denis
BOULEVARD ST. MARTIN
République
PLACE DE LA RÉPUBLIQUE
République
AVENUE DE LA RÉPUBLIQUE
OBERKAMPF
3ème & 4ème
Temple
R. BERANGER
3
Bd DU TEMPLE
Bd TIMBAUD
R. J.P.
VOLTAIRE
Oberkampf
BOULEVARD
RICHARD
MARTIN
Réaumur Sébastopol
TURBIGO
1
REAUMUR
RUE
Arts et Métiers
R. DUPETIT THOUARS
TEMPLE
Filles du Calvaire
RUE
SÉBASTOPOL
DE
RUE ST.
RUE DE
RUE DE BRETAGNE
CHARLOT
RUE
R. DES FILLES DU CALVAIRE
Bd DES FILLES DU CALVAIRE
RUE ST. SÉBASTIEN
LENOIR
R. FROISSART
St. Sébastien Froissart
TURENNE
RUE DU
ARCHIVES
RUE
4
9
R. VIEILLE DU TEMPLE
MUSÉE PICASSO
R. THORIGNY
BEAUBOURG
R. AUX OURS
R. DU GRENIER ST. LAZARE
R. MICHEL LE COMTE
5
7
Rambuteau
8
R. DES 4 FILS
R. DE LA PERLE
2
Bd Chemin Vert
DU CHEMIN VERT

PRIX FIXE
Lunch only, 95F, 2 courses, BNC
ENGLISH SPOKEN
Yes

Morue (salted codfish) is the steady fish staple, but if you love abundance, order the roast leg of lamb served with fresh vegetables. Desserts and cheeses do not quite measure up to the rest of the meal. I would skip the small and dry cheese offerings and order instead the *duo de gâteaux basques* or the chocolate terrine with an orange sauce.

(2) CAFÉ DES MUSÉES
49, rue de Turenne (3rd)

TELEPHONE
01-42-72-96-17, 01-44-59-86-16
MÉTRO
Chemin-Vert, St-Paul
OPEN
Daily
CLOSED
Sun night after 8 P.M., holidays, Aug
HOURS
Mon–Sat breakfast 7–8 A.M., lunch noon–2:30 P.M., dinner 7–11 P.M.; Sun breakfast 9–11 A.M., lunch noon–2:30 P.M., light snacks 2:30–8 P.M.
RESERVATIONS
Not accepted
CREDIT CARDS
None
À LA CARTE
110–130F, BNC
PRIX FIXE
None
ENGLISH SPOKEN
Some

Café des Musées is a well-worn corner café that plays to a packed house of contented regulars. For lunch, it is best to go early to nab one of the prize tables on the sidewalk; otherwise you will be crowded inside where it can get hot and smoky, not to mention very noisy with the din of the happy crowd.

Don't come here for fancy garnishes or the latest food fad. Go instead with an appetite and an eye toward a satisfying meal quickly served by hardworking waitresses. Check the blackboard specials, and if the steak tartare, cold poached salmon, or lamb sautéed with potatoes and onions doesn't speak to you, perhaps a mushroom and cheese omelette or a *tarte provençale* with a green salad will. The patron bottles his own Côtes de Lyonnais house wine and features a wide selection of beers. Desserts? You can safely save the guilt for someplace else.

(3) CHEZ JENNY
39, boulevard du Temple (3rd)

TELEPHONE
01-42-74-75-75
MÉTRO
République
OPEN
Daily
CLOSED
July 18–Aug 12
HOURS
11:30 A.M.–1 A.M., continuous service
RESERVATIONS
Advised
CREDIT CARDS
AE, DC, MC, V
À LA CARTE
200F, BNC

Chez Jenny celebrates the food and wine of Alsace, served in a magnificent old brasserie full of fabulous regional artwork. Rosy-cheeked waitresses wearing starched headdresses and dirndls serve the brimming plates with speed and, unfortunately, very little good cheer. However, if you are looking for some of the best *choucroute* in Paris, look no farther. For the uninitiated, *choucroute* is a steaming platter combination of smoked slab bacon, bratwurst, plump white veal sausages, lean smoked pork loin, and savory sauerkraut and potatoes; a stein of golden beer is the perfect accompaniment. For a lighter supper, order the assorted *charcuterie* of mild Alsatian sausages or a *plat* of iced oysters and shellfish with a glass of chilled Reisling wine. Warning: The fish *choucroute* makes for a strange combination.

The cavernous interior is as impressive as the food: carved wall plaques, life-sized wooden figures in native Alsatian dress, and lovely murals depicting life in this colorful region along the German border. For the best overall atmosphere, reserve a table on the ground floor.

PRIX FIXE
Lunch "express menu," 70F, garnished main course, BNC; lunch and dinner, 140F, 2 courses, 170F, 3 courses, both BC; Mon–Fri 3–6 P.M., all *choucroutes* 20 percent off

ENGLISH SPOKEN
Yes

(4) CHEZ NENESSE
17, rue de Saintonge, angle de Poitou (3rd)

There is nothing glamorous about the decor or service at this homey hideaway near the Picasso Museum, but the food is enough on target to lure the regulars back on a day-to-day basis. The gray corner site houses a large room with an old heating stove in the middle and live green plants in the window. In the evening, white cloths and napkins dress up the atmosphere from the bare table, paper napkin lunch trade. The *marché* food at lunch is more Cheap Eater friendly, but at dinner the choices expand and the dishes are a bit more sophisticated. The chef/owner M. Le Meur uses his Brittany heritage in the kitchen to prepare seasonally fresh fish plus most of the familiar bistro dishes everyone recognizes. You will start with escargots, *gratinée à l'oignon* (onion soup), or a *fondant de legumes et coulis de tomates* (a vegetable cake dressed with tomato purée). Veal medallions in a honey and celery sauce, chicken fricasée with morille mushrooms, or lamb with mint sauce are a few of the main course options. Best desserts by a long shot are the two you must order ahead: *feuilleté de pommes sauce caramel* (flaky pastry covered with cooked apples and caramel sauce) or *tartelette des fruits* (fruit tart with cold sabayon sauce).

TELEPHONE
01-42-78-46-49

MÉTRO
Files-du-Calvaire

OPEN
Mon–Fri

CLOSED
Sat–Sun, holidays, 1 week in Feb, Aug

HOURS
Lunch noon–2 P.M., dinner 7:45–10 P.M.

RESERVATIONS
Advised

CREDIT CARDS
MC, V

À LA CARTE
Lunch 70–85F, dinner 150–165F, both BNC

PRIX FIXE
None

ENGLISH SPOKEN
Some, with English menu

(5) L'AMBASSADE D'AUVERGNE*
22, rue du Grenier-St-Lazare (3rd)

The long-standing owners of L'Ambassade d'Auvergne regard themselves as culinary representatives of their native region. Over the years, their restaurant has remained true to its heritage and is today one of the finest regional restaurants in Paris. Over the many times I have eaten here, I have always found all the elements of the restaurant working together to create a satisfying dining experience. There are six dining rooms and a clientele that includes prominent political figures. For the most authentic and beautiful atmosphere,

TELEPHONE
01-42-72-31-22

MÉTRO
Rambuteau, rue du Grenier-St-Lazare exit

OPEN
Daily

CLOSED
Never

HOURS
Lunch noon–2 P.M., dinner 7:30–10 P.M.

RESERVATIONS
Yes
CREDIT CARDS
AE, MC, V
À LA CARTE
250F, BNC
PRIX FIXE
Lunch and dinner, 185F, 3 courses, BNC
ENGLISH SPOKEN
Yes

reserve a table downstairs, which has an open fireplace and massive beams from which hang hundreds of Auvergne hams.

Country abundance is evident in every delicious dish, from the specials that remain the same each day of the week to the monthly and seasonal offerings. A variety of excellent, little-known regional wines are available to accompany your feast. Wonderful *entrées* anytime are the cabbage soup with white beans, ham chunks, potatoes, carrots, and Roquefort cheese and the warm *lentilles du puy* salad. Tempting main dishes are the spicy Auvergne sausages with lentils, *la falette* (a stuffed, boned breast of veal in an herb sauce), and for the adventurous, the *tripous à l'estragon* (tripe). An absolute *must* with whatever you order is *l'aligot,* a masterful blend of puréed potatoes and melted Cantal cheese, whipped at your table and served from copper pans. Trying to save room for dessert is next to impossible, but if you can, the creamy chocolate mousse served nonstop from a crystal bowl is worth the overload. If you can't do dessert, consider ordering one of their ten prune digestives as a grand finale.

(6) LA MULE DU PAPE
8, rue du Pas de la Mule (3rd)

TELEPHONE
01-42-74-55-80
MÉTRO
Chemin-Vert
OPEN
Mon–Sat lunch and dinner, Sun brunch and lunch
CLOSED
Sun dinner, weekend of Aug 15, 3 days at Christmas, Easter, NAC
HOURS
Mon–Fri lunch 11 A.M.–4 P.M., dinner 7–10:30 P.M.; Sat 11 A.M.–10:30 P.M., continuous service; Sun 11 A.M.–7 P.M., continuous service
RESERVATIONS
Suggested
CREDIT CARDS
AE, MC, V
À LA CARTE
85–120F, BNC
PRIX FIXE
Sun brunch, 135F, BC
ENGLISH SPOKEN
Yes

La Mule du Pape has everything a good Cheap Eat in Paris should: comfortable, flower-filled surroundings, good food, fair prices, and Ursule, an adorable long-haired dachshund who comes for lunch with her owner, Mme. André. The menu offers enticing choices that make dining here a pleasure worth repeating. The emphasis is on light lunches, dinners, weekend afternoon tea, and Sunday brunch. Beautiful main-dish salads come with a basket of fresh toast. Habit-forming egg creations include *oeufs florentine* (eggs resting on a bed of creamed spinach topped with parmesan), scrambled eggs with smoked salmon, and a cheese, bacon, and chive omelette garnished with a side salad and toast. For dinner, you might try poached haddock, pork medallions with an onion *confiture,* or a roast veal with sautéed cumin-spiked carrots. All the lovely desserts are displayed for your selection. The fruit crumbles are always popular and so is the chocolate *tarte* served with a pistachio ice cream. If you are visiting the Picasso Museum or the place des Vosges just down the street, this is definitely one to remember.

(7) LE HANGAR
12, impasse Berthaud (3rd)

TELEPHONE
01-42-74-55-44

MÉTRO
Rambuteau

OPEN
Mon dinner only, Tues–Sat for lunch and dinner

CLOSED
Mon lunch, Sun, holidays, Aug

HOURS
Lunch noon–3 P.M., dinner 7:30 P.M.–midnight

RESERVATIONS
Advised

CREDIT CARDS
None

À LA CARTE
130–160F, BNC

PRIX FIXE
None

ENGLISH SPOKEN
Some

Le Hangar, on a hidden impasse just steps from the Beaubourg, Forum des Halles, and the little-known Musée de la Poupée (doll museum), attracts a well-heeled clientele who value the chef's sophisticated interpretations of familiar favorites and the smiling welcome extended by the owner, Sylvie Ciercuel. On a warm day, it is very pleasant to sit on the covered terrace, which is free from dust, birds, dirt, and automobile fumes. The mood inside is rather modern, with linens, crystal, green plants, and an efficient waitstaff changing the silver and crumbing the tables between courses. The prices are as attractive as the setting, with imaginative choices for each course and appropriate wines suggested to enhance them.

You start by spreading rich *tapenade* on toast as you decide your order. Cold *entrées* feature a salmon tartare, barely cooked green beans drizzled with olive oil, and a lusty lentil salad. If you love *chèvre chaud,* it comes in three roasted mounds resting on a bed of designer greens. Another delicious hot *entrée* is the ravioli in an eggplant cream sauce. Carnivores will love the meaty servings of *blanquette de veau,* the beef filet with morille sauce, and the mouth-watering duck liver served with creamy mashed potatoes. Depending on the season, fish fanciers can look for *daurade* (white sea bream) with steamed potatoes, scallops in a parsley cream sauce, or a delicate sole. Save room for dessert, especially the orange crêpes with Grand Marnier sauce, fresh fruit *clafoutis* cooked to order, or the chocolate creation filled with warm chocolate sauce that melts over two little scoops of vanilla ice cream. A plate of their own cookies and an espresso will end your truly wonderful meal.

(8) RESTAURANT DE LA CITÉ
22, rue Rambuteau (3rd)

TELEPHONE
01-48-04-30-74

MÉTRO
Rambuteau

OPEN
Daily

CLOSED
Never, NAC

HOURS
Lunch noon–4 P.M., dinner 7:30 P.M.–midnight

You will find this narrow Cheap Eat discovery on one of the few remaining *marché* streets in the area, just minutes away from all the hoopla around Beaubourg and Les Halles. With its daily specials carefully handwritten on blackboards hanging both inside and outside, this little hole-in-the-wall café always packs them in, especially at lunch, when all the seats are taken by 12:15 P.M. and the crowd often overflows onto the sidewalk and into the street.

RESERVATIONS Not necessary
CREDIT CARDS V (over 150F)
À LA CARTE 50–90F, BNC
PRIX FIXE Dinner only, 70F, 2 courses, BNC, desserts 20–25F extra
ENGLISH SPOKEN Limited

The food is not sophisticated and you will not be sampling exotic sauces or wild game. You will, however, be eating old-fashioned, back-burner-style French cooking and plenty of it, all for a great low price, along with coveralled construction workers, young professionals, local artists, and neighborhood regulars who are doing the same.

(9) RESTAURANT LA FONTAINE GOURMANDE
11, rue Charlot (3rd)

TELEPHONE 01-42-78-72-40
MÉTRO Filles-du-Calvaire, République
OPEN Mon–Fri lunch and dinner, Sat dinner only
CLOSED Sat lunch, Sun, holidays, Aug
HOURS Lunch noon–2 P.M., dinner 7:30–10:30 P.M.
RESERVATIONS Suggested
CREDIT CARDS MC, V
À LA CARTE 160–170F, BNC
PRIX FIXE Lunch only, 49F, 1 course, BNC; 75F, 3 courses, BC
ENGLISH SPOKEN Yes

When I want dependably wonderful food, superb value, and pleasant service in a nontouristy corner of Paris, I reserve a table at La Fontaine Gourmande, where generous helpings of sure-to-please bistro dishes are served by owner/chef Thierry Odiot. At noontime, you will find well-dressed diners sitting in the small stone-walled room ordering the three-course bargain lunch, which includes several choices and a glass of wine. At dinner, the regulars are back at the candle-lit tables ordering à la carte classics such as warm leek vinaigrette; fat spring asparagus, lightly poached and topped with fresh parsley and green onions; the rich foie gras *maison;* or the tangy *chiffonnade d'endives* with blue cheese and *pleurottes* (oyster mushrooms). The nearly impossible to decipher chalkboard menu lists rich, full-flavored lamb, salmon, tender rabbit, *confit de canard,* and several beef preparations. Garnishes are seasonal vegetables and potato *galettes.* For dessert, order the fresh fruit on a *sablé* (cookie crust) smothered in whipped cream. Your coffee will come with Thierry's madeleines, and the final bill will be as reassuring as the entire meal.

NOTE: Wednesday nights feature specialties *à la broche* (spit-roasted meats).

Fourth Arrondissement

(See map on pages 64–65.)

RIGHT BANK
Notre Dame, Île St-Louis, Centre Georges Pompidou (Beaubourg), Hôtel-de-Ville (City Hall), Jewish Quarter, continuation of the Marais, Maison de Victor Hugo, Place des Vosges

Point zero is a compass rose set in the pavement in front of the Notre Dame Cathedral. This is the spot from which all distances are measured in France, but more than that, the cathedral serves as the spiritual and emotional heart of France.

Île St-Louis was developed by Henri IV in the seventeenth century. It has been home to Voltaire, Baudelaire, Colette, and George Sand. Today it is one of the most expensive plots of real estate in Paris. Full of atmosphere, the narrow streets house beautiful *hôtel particulières* (private mansions) occupied by film stars, authors, the Rothschilds, and six thousand other lucky people. In the Marais, the place des Vosges is considered the most beautiful square in Paris. It was an up-and-coming area some years ago—now it has *arrived!* Young fashion designers fight for shop space and rents are astronomical. The famous fashion houses on the rue de Faubourg St-Honoré and avenue Montaigne are for affluent clientele; stylish French men and women shop in the Marais for the last word in clothes. The area is also the center of the Parisian Jewish community. Take a stroll down rue des Rosiers and discover marvelous kosher delicatessens, bakeries, and restaurants.

While you are in the fourth arrondissement you can visit the museum of modern art, better known as the Centre Georges Pompidou, or the Beaubourg, and now the number-one tourist attraction in Paris, surpassing the Eiffel Tower and the Louvre Museum in its number of visitors per year.

FOURTH ARRONDISSEMENT RESTAURANTS

* Restaurants marked with an asterisk (*) are considered Big Splurges.

(10) AQUARIUS
54, rue Ste-Croix-de-la-Bretonnerie (4th)

TELEPHONE
01-48-87-48-71
MÉTRO
Hôtel-de-Ville
OPEN
Mon–Sat
CLOSED
Sun, holidays, Aug (dates vary)
HOURS
Noon–10:15 P.M., continuous service
RESERVATIONS
Not necessary
CREDIT CARDS
MC, V (over 100F)
À LA CARTE
65–100F, BNC
PRIX FIXE
Lunch only, 59F, *plat du jour* and dessert, BNC; lunch and dinner, 90F, 3 courses, BNC
ENGLISH SPOKEN
Yes
MISCELLANEOUS
No smoking allowed

For a healthy, low-cost vegetarian lunch or dinner, Parisians head for one of the two Aquarius locations. The choices range from colorful salads, *tartes,* quiches, and homemade soups to large *plats du jour* designed around grains and cooked veggies. Fruit desserts seem to be more popular than the plain yogurt and dishes of prunes. The nondescript decor leans toward the ascetic, as do most of the diners, who seem to be engrossed in books or magazines even when they are sharing a table. A nice feature is that you can order as little or as much as you want . . . and not feel out of place doing so. Keep this one in mind when the budget is in trouble because you can always have a satisfying, healthy Cheap Eat here with a glass of organic wine or designer water for under 100F. Other location: 40, rue de Gergovie, in the fourteenth arrondissement (see page 179).

(11) AUBERGE DE JARENTE
7, rue de Jarente (4th)

TELEPHONE
01-42-77-49-35
MÉTRO
St-Paul, Bastille
OPEN
Tues–Sat
CLOSED
Sun–Mon, holidays, one week from Aug 15

It is not much from the outside, but what counts is the food, and it is *good.* This two-room, family-owned *auberge* on the edge of the Marais specializes in Basque dishes from southwestern France. If you order either prix fixe menus, you will have some difficult dining decisions ahead. Should you start with the *pipérade,* a mixture of sweet red peppers, tomatoes, onions, and garlic mixed with scrambled eggs and topped with spicy sausage? Or would a bowl of fish soup or the frog's legs be a better beginning? For the main course, will it be the *cassoulet* or the *confit de canard,* both for two people, or the *cailles à la façon du chef:* two highly flavored quail served with sautéed potatoes? For dessert, far and away the two best choices are their versions of *gâteau Basque,* a plain cream-filled cake. For the nicest experience of the restaurant, arrive about 9 or 9:30 P.M. when the French do, order a bottle of the Madrian red wine, and settle into a full-flavored meal that will not put a major strain on your budget.

HOURS
Lunch noon–2:30 P.M., dinner 7:30–10:30 P.M.

RESERVATIONS
For lunch and after 9 P.M.

CREDIT CARDS
AE, MC, V

À LA CARTE
175–190F, BNC

PRIX FIXE
Lunch and dinner: 117F, 3 courses, BNC; 134F, 3 courses, BC; 185F, 4 courses, BC

ENGLISH SPOKEN
Yes

(12) AU GOURMET DE L'ÎLE
42, rue St-Louis-en-l'Île (4th)

One of the more interesting meals in Paris can be found at this rustic seventeenth-century restaurant on the Île St-Louis, where diners can be assured of finding expert versions of French country classics served in a friendly, crowded, candlelit atmosphere. On Sunday, the lunch crowd is heavy with portly locals who have made this a family tradition. When reserving, especially on Sunday, be sure to request a table on the ground floor, not in the cramped, stuffy subterranean room below.

A warning is in order: The food here is not for the faint-hearted or those with tame tastes. In the window is a sign reading, "A.A.A.A.A.," which stands for the Amiable Association of Amateurs of the Authentic Andouillette. If you would like to but have never tried one of these French soul-food sausages made with chitterlings, now is the time. This is also the place to sample such French standards as *boudin* (blood sausage) and *ris d'agneau* (lamb kidneys).

Those with less adventurous palates will enjoy the other house specialties of grilled guinea hen with lentils and the filling *la carbonnée de l'Île,* a robust pork stew in red wine with bacon, onions, potatoes, and croutons. For the wine accompaniment, try a bottle of Marcillac, a Chinon, or a red Saumur from the Loire Valley.

Everyone will agree on the delicious desserts, especially the *crème limousine,* a caramel custard swimming in warm chocolate sauce, the poached pear in red wine, or the rich *profiteroles* filled with ice cream.

TELEPHONE
01 43-26-79-27

MÉTRO
Pont-Marie

OPEN
Wed–Sun

CLOSED
Mon–Tues, NAC

HOURS
Lunch noon–2 P.M., dinner 7–10 P.M.

RESERVATIONS
Advised for Sunday lunch and dinner on weekends

CREDIT CARDS
MC, V

À LA CARTE
160F, BNC

PRIX FIXE
Lunch and dinner: 135F, 4 courses, BNC; 175F, 4 courses, BC (kir, wine, and coffee)

ENGLISH SPOKEN
Yes, with English menu

MISCELLANEOUS
Nonsmoking section

(13) AU LYS D'ARGENT
90, rue St-Louis-en-l'Île (4th)

TELEPHONE
01-46-33-65-13
MÉTRO
Pont-Marie
OPEN
Daily
CLOSED
Never
HOURS
Winter: noon–3:30 P.M., 6–10:30 P.M.; summer: 11:30 A.M.–10:30 P.M., continuous service
RESERVATIONS
Not necessary
CREDIT CARDS
MC, V (minimum 100F)
À LA CARTE
40–75F, BNC
PRIX FIXE
Lunch and dinner, 59F and 79F, 3 courses, BNC
ENGLISH SPOKEN
Limited, with English menu

Forty varieties of tea, light meals based around quiches, *tartes*, salads, and crêpes, plus homemade pastries keep visitors well fed here when they are on the Île St-Louis—an island in the middle of the River Seine that is a picturesque microslice of Paris. On weekends and holidays, the waves of tourists, browsers, and occasional natives can be *very* discouraging. For those looking for a bit of sustenance while here, the Au Lys d'Argent provides something on its menu for just about everyone.

Not to be forgotten are their rich chocolate drinks made to order from melted bars of pure chocolate, whole milk and cream (allow ten minutes please and don't tell your cardiologist). For a complete chocolate blow out, and why not, order a slice of their dark chocolate cake to go with your *chocolat à l'ancienne.*

(14) AU PETIT FER À CHEVAL
30, rue Vieille du Temple (4th)

TELEPHONE
01-42-72-47-47
MÉTRO
Hôtel-de-Ville, St-Paul
OPEN
Daily
CLOSED
Never
HOURS
Noon–1 A.M., continuous service
RESERVATIONS
Not necessary
CREDIT CARDS
None
À LA CARTE
65–100F, BNC
PRIX FIXE
None
ENGLISH SPOKEN
Yes

Cheap, cheerful, and truly French—that's Au Petit Fer à Cheval, a popular meeting place for everyone from shopkeepers and stray tourists to New Wave patrons just in from Pluto.

The slightly seedy Marais landmark has been in operation since 1903 and consists of sidewalk tables and a marble-topped horseshoe *(fer à cheval)* bar in the front room. In back, there is a larger room with booths made from old wooden métro seats. For Flash Gordon and Mr. Marvel fans, the stainless-steel WCs are not to be missed. The nice thing about this place is that you can come in anytime for a quick *café* standing at the bar, or sit down and consume a home-cooked lunch or dinner. While the food doesn't inspire rave reviews, it is filling and typical native grub consisting of salads, daily *plats,* and the dessert standards of chocolate mousse and floating island.

(15) BARACANE-BISTROT DE L'OULETTE*
38, rue des Tournelles (4th)

TELEPHONE
01-42-71-43-33
MÉTRO
Bastille

For one of the best bistro meals going, book a table at Bistrot de l'Oulette on the edge of the Marais. Owner and chef Marcel Baudis opened here a few years ago and was an instant hit with his impeccable dishes from Quercy in southwestern France. Now he has moved to a larger location in the Bercy area near the Gare de Lyon (see L'Oulette, page 174). Baudis still oversees the kitchen, which maintains his standards of excellence in every dish served. His partner, Alain Fontaine, monitors the business end of the narrow dining room, which has also lost nothing in the transition.

The real appeal of this bistro lies in its consistently fresh foods complemented by an excellent wine list, with most bottles selling for under 120F. The *formule* menus—available for either lunch or dinner—offer a wide selection from the seasonal menu. Some favorites do remain, at the insistence of loyal patrons. For starters, you can count on a bountiful salad bursting with preserved chicken gizzards or the satiny-smooth duck foie gras spread on pieces of whole-grain bread. For the main course, the *cassoulet, confit de canard* with parsleyed potatoes, or the grilled *magret de canard* are sure-fire winners everyone loves. Seasonal specialties and fresh fish round out the choices. Sweet endings no one wants to miss include a chocolate cake flavored with orange, a refreshing prune ice cream with Armagnac, and the satisfying *croustillant aux pommes* (apple crumble).

OPEN
Mon–Fri lunch and dinner, Sat dinner only

CLOSED
Sat lunch, Sun, holidays, NAC

HOURS
Lunch noon–2:30 P.M., dinner 7 P.M.–midnight

RESERVATIONS
Essential

CREDIT CARDS
MC, V

À LA CARTE
215F, BNC

PRIX FIXE
Lunch only, 55F, 2 courses and coffee; lunch and dinner: 82F, 2 courses, BNC; 128F, 3 courses, BC; 215F, 3 courses, BC (apértif, wine, and coffee)

ENGLISH SPOKEN
Yes

(16) BRASSERIE BOFINGER
5–7, rue de la Bastille (4th)

What better way to spend the evening than in the company of friends, enjoying good food and wine in the oldest and most handsome brasserie in Paris, located only a few minutes from the new opera house at place de la Bastille? While not the place for a romantic tête-à-tête, you can't help feeling glamorous and festive when dining at Bofinger. The magnificent Belle Epoque decor on two floors, with its maze of mirrors, brass, stained glass, and flowers, provides the perfect backdrop for the see-and-be-seen crowds of fashionable French who flock here every night. Do not even *think* of arriving without a reservation, and when booking, request a seat under the stained-glass dome, the most beautiful part of the restaurant, which is also the nonsmoking section. While culinary fireworks are not the order of the day, the food is dependable, and the copious servings cater to healthy, meat-loving appetites. Platters of oysters, traditional *choucroutes,* and grilled meats lead the list of the best dining choices. The house Riesling is a good wine

TELEPHONE
01-42-72-87-82

MÉTRO
Bastille

OPEN
Daily

CLOSED
Never, NAC

HOURS
Lunch noon–3 P.M., dinner 6:30 P.M.–1 A.M.

RESERVATIONS
Essential

CREDIT CARDS
AE, DC, MC, V

À LA CARTE
180–200F, BNC

PRIX FIXE
Lunch and dinner, 169F, 3 courses, BC

ENGLISH SPOKEN
Yes

MISCELLANEOUS
Nonsmoking section

selection. The service by black-tied waiters, who sometimes ferry plates over the heads of diners, is swift and accurate.

NOTE: Women should not miss seeing the opulent ladies room. See page 81 for information on the new Le Petit Bofinger.

(17) BRASSERIE DE L'ÎLE ST-LOUIS
55, quai de Bourbon (4th)

TELEPHONE 01-43-54-02-59
MÉTRO Pont-Marie
OPEN Thur–Tues
CLOSED Wed, Aug
HOURS Fri–Tues 11 A.M.–2 A.M., Thur 6:30 P.M.–2 A.M., continuous service
RESERVATIONS No
CREDIT CARDS MC, V
À LA CARTE 150–170F, BC
PRIX FIXE None
ENGLISH SPOKEN Yes

A stroll over the pedestrian bridge behind Notre-Dame to the Île St-Louis brings you right to the doorstep of this picturesque old *auberge,* which is the favorite watering hole and gathering place for many of the writers, entertainers, and expatriates who live on the island. Its outdoor terrace is prime seating for a lazy afternoon spent with friends, admiring the beautiful people passing by or just celebrating your visit to Paris. Inside the atmosphere is bustling, colorful, and friendly, making it impossible to feel lonely here for long.

The food . . . well, in all honesty that is not this place's *raison d'etre.* It is the camaraderie that counts; eating is secondary. What to expect? The menu features typical brasserie dishes as well as Alsatian specialties of tripes in Riesling wine, pigs knuckles, omelettes, terrines, pâtés, *cassoulet,* and onion *tarte* served with pitchers of house wine or mugs of frothy beer. Desserts tend to be uninspiring. Instead walk down the center of the island to any one of the ice cream shops—or go straight to the renowned Berthillon itself (31, rue St-Louis-en-l'Île) and treat yourself to several scoops of their famous ice cream or sorbet, with equally famous prices and long queues.

FINKELSZTAJN: FLORENCE AND SACHA
(18) Florence Finkelsztajn : 24, rue des Ècouffes, corner of rue des Rosiers (4th)
(19) Sacha Finkelsztajn: 27, rue des Rosiers (4th)

TELEPHONE Florence: 01-48-87-92-85, Sacha: 01-42-72-78-91
MÉTRO St-Paul
OPEN Florence: Thur-Tues, Sacha: Wed-Mon
CLOSED Florence: Wed, Aug, Sacha: Tues, July
HOURS Florence and Sacha: 10 A.M.–1 P.M., 3–7 P.M.

The two Finkelsztajn bakery/*traiteur* shops sell treats not to be missed in Paris. For over five decades, they have been household names in the Jewish quarter of Paris, where they dish out daily supplies of sweet and savory Russian and eastern European Jewish foods. At Florence's, nicknamed "The Blue Bakery," prepare yourself for authentic recipes of borscht, blini, Polish almond *babkes*, strudels, and a dozen or more homestyle breads either plain or bursting with seeds and dried fruits.

Walk into Sacha's yellow location a few doors away on rue des Rosiers and try the traditional Russian cheesecake, *tarama*, latkes, or herring. At both sites, plan to take your food with you because the two or three corner stools in each are always full.

RESERVATIONS
Not taken
CREDIT CARDS
None
À LA CARTE
15–70F, BNC
PRIX FIXE
None
ENGLISH SPOKEN
Generally

(20) LA CASTAFIORE
51, rue St-Louis-en-l'Île (4th)

La Castafiore has had many lives. When I lived on l'Île St-Louis, it was a family-owned bistro and one of my favorite Cheap Eats. Since then, it has had a series of owners, but nothing seemed to make it until Gerrard and Edward took over and began serving wonderful Italian dishes. There is room for only eleven small, closely packed tables, and to make sure you are sitting at one of them, reservations are essential.

If your budget is tight, remember the 65F, two-course lunch menu, which comes with a bowl of onion soup or mozzarella on toast followed by a plate of gnocci with basil sauce, turkey marsala, or steak and grilled onions. Desserts are 25F extra, but frankly, the main course portions are so big you won't be able to consider anything extra. The two-course dinner menu allows you to select from any of the *entrées* (except the snails) and any of the pastas on the menu. This Cheap Eat, good until 8 P.M., draws many of the visitors staying in the several charming hotels on the island (see *Cheap Sleeps in Paris*), creating an unfortunately hot, stuffy, sardinelike atmosphere. Later, around 9 P.M., when the rush is over, the mood is much more peaceful and romantic in the candlelit room. When ordering, start with the traditional mozzarella and tomato salad or the lusty stuffed mushrooms, filled with spinach and cream cheese, in a tomato sauce. Eight vegetarian pastas, five or six meat or seafood pastas, meat dishes that win praise from the carnivores among us, flowing house wine, and a wicked tiramisu add up to terrific dining. I wish I still lived in the neighborhood.

TELEPHONE
01-43-54-78-62
MÉTRO
Pont-Marie
OPEN
Daily
CLOSED
Never, NAC
HOURS
Lunch noon–2:30 P.M., dinner 6:30–11 P.M.
RESERVATIONS
Absolutely, especially for dinner
CREDIT CARDS
AE, DC, MC, V
À LA CARTE
180F, BNC
PRIX FIXE
Lunch only, 65F, 2 courses, BNC; lunch and dinner, 160F, 3 courses, BNC; dinner only (before 8 P.M.), 90F, 2 courses, BNC
ENGLISH SPOKEN
Yes

(21) LA CHARLOTTE DE L'ÎLE
24, rue St-Louis-en-l'Île (4th)

Sylvie Langlet is the owner and mother superior of this quarter-century-old Paris tearoom that specializes in her own rich chocolate pastries and candies, poetry

TELEPHONE
01-43-54-25-83
MÉTRO
Pont-Marie, Sully-Morland

OPEN
Thur–Sun
CLOSED
Mon–Wed, most holidays, July and Aug
HOURS
Tearoom 2–8 P.M., continuous service; puppet shows, Wed only at 2:30 and 4 P.M.; live piano music Fri 6–8 P.M.
RESERVATIONS
Required for puppet shows (minimum 12 children)
CREDIT CARDS
MC, V
À LA CARTE
50–70F, BC
PRIX FIXE
None
ENGLISH SPOKEN
Yes

readings, puppet shows, live piano music, and most importantly, warm, fuzzy good cheer. Just being in her cluttered two-room shop, filled with a whimsical collection of baskets, children's drawings, chocolate sculptures of children and animals, old teapots, and painted plates, makes you feel like you are having tea with *grand-mère.* For its regular customers, it obviously is an ideal oasis for meeting friends for a good dose of gossip, milk flirtation, listening to music, or treating a child to sweets before a puppet performance. When you go, order a hot chocolate made from melted bars of pure chocolate (thinned with milk, if you must dilute it) or her bittersweet chocolate *tarte de tantie,* a baked chocolate mousse with a chocolate glaze. Don't overlook her pure fruit lollipops, which grown men have been known to buy by the bagful. A small handwritten sign in the window says it all: "Here we sell happiness." How true.

(22) LE BISTROT DU DÔME*
2, rue de la Bastille (4th)

TELEPHONE
01-48-04-88-44
MÉTRO
Bastille
OPEN
Daily
CLOSED
Never, NAC
HOURS
Lunch 12:30–2:30 P.M., dinner 7:30–11:30 P.M.
RESERVATIONS
Advised
CREDIT CARDS
AE, MC, V
À LA CARTE
195–250F, BNC
PRIX FIXE
None
ENGLISH SPOKEN
Yes

Good tips often come from readers, and this is one of them. However, if you do not like fish, move on . . . because fish is the *only* thing you can order here. The sunny, yellow interiors by noted restaurant designer Philippe Slavik are casually elegant, creating a sleek and contemporary look that gives diners a feeling of space in uncluttered surroundings.

As everyone knows, fish is never cheap in Paris, whether you buy it at the market or order it in a restaurant. Prices here are not for budgeteers counting every penny, but they are certainly competitive. Depending on the main course, you may want to vary your starter. The *fricassée de langoustines au curry* (curried prawns), the *soupe de pistou* (fish soup laden with vegetables), or the *palourdes sautées à la fleur de thyme* (cherrystone clams sautéed with shallots and thyme) are hearty and delicious beginnings. Popular *plats* are the *filets de racasse,* white rock fish in a fresh tomato sauce served with garlic-laced mashed potatoes, and the *gigot de lotte braisé aux choux,* monk fish with cabbage. For something unadorned, try the grilled tuna (*pavé de thon*) or the traditional sole *meunière.* The dessert extravaganza means you must try to save a little space for the *crêpe exotique,* crepes filled with mangoes, coconut, and other fruits, topped with a caramel-and-honey sauce, or the *gratin de poire, aux glace cannelle,* warm pears filled with cinnamon ice cream.

NOTE: Second location: 1, rue Delambre in the fourteenth arrondissement (see page 187).

(23) LE COLIMAÇON
44, rue Vieille-du-Temple (4th)

There is always an attractive crowd of regulars at Le Colimaçon, a charmingly unpretentious dining choice in the Marais. At lunchtime, you will dine with businessfolk and shopkeepers and on holidays with other visitors. At night, look for a more sophisticated, laid-back group of artists, writers, and neighbors who have every table filled by 9:30 P.M. The best seat in the house is up a winding staircase at the table by the open window, where you will have a grandstand seat on the world cruising by below.

It is important to arrive hungry, starved if possible, to enjoy the smartly simple, beautifully presented, consistently good food that comes in very generous portions. You could easily start with six snails or a duck salad, but why not try the mushroom and chicken liver *fricassée* or the salmon and haddock salad served with lemon, orange, and grapefruit. My dining companion said, "The *magret de canard aux fruits de saison* is by far the best I have ever had. I could eat it three times a week!" Other dishes worth repeating often would be the seven-hour roast leg of lamb or the *bavette* cooked with shallots. If you order the prix fixe menu, your dessert choices are limited to the fruit *tarte* or sorbet. Nice but boring, let's face it. Definitely *not* boring, and worth repeating as often as possible, is the feather-light meringue, filled with rich ice cream and covered in warm chocolate sauce.

TELEPHONE
01-48-87-12-01

MÉTRO
Hôtel-de-Ville

OPEN
Mon, Wed, Thur dinner only; Fri–Sun lunch and dinner; holidays

CLOSED
Tues; Mon, Wed, Thur for lunch; 3 weeks in Aug

HOURS
Lunch noon–2:30 P.M., dinner 7:30 P.M.–1 A.M.

RESERVATIONS
Advised, especially for dinner and holidays

CREDIT CARDS
AE, MC, V

À LA CARTE
200–225F, BNC

PRIX FIXE
Dinner only, 130F, 3 courses, BNC

ENGLISH SPOKEN
Yes, with English menu

(24) LE COUDE FOU
12, rue du Bourg-Tibourg (4th)

To paraphrase an old saying, "Life is too short to drink bad or boring wine." That will never happen at Le Coude Fou, Patric Segall's appealing *bistro à vins,* which is a good, safe place to try various wines at reasonable cost while enjoying good times and good food. The locals indulge in lunchtime plates of sturdy hot meals and return in the evening for French country cheeses and *charcuteries.* Everyone stands around the bar or spills into the two rustic rooms, sitting at the bare tables made from wine casks.

TELEPHONE
01-42-77-15-16

MÉTRO
Hôtel-de-Ville

OPEN
Mon–Sat lunch and dinner, Sun lunch only

CLOSED
Sun dinner, NAC

HOURS
Lunch noon–3:15 P.M. (Sun till 4 P.M.); dinner 7:15 P.M.–midnight

RESERVATIONS
Advised on weekends
CREDIT CARDS
AE, MC, V
À LA CARTE
50–145F, BNC
PRIX FIXE
Mon–Fri lunch: 95F, 2 courses, BC; 110F, 3 courses, BC; Mon–Thur dinner, 130F, 3 courses, BNC
ENGLISH SPOKEN
Yes

The murals depicting party-goers from ancient times to caricatures of Parisian barflies adds to the lighthearted mood. As for the wines, try whatever is the special of the month, or perhaps a red Saint-Joseph from the central part of France.

(25) LE DOS DE LA BALEINE
40, rue des Blancs-Manteaux (4th)

TELEPHONE
01-42-72-38-98
MÉTRO
Hôtel-de-Ville, Rambuteau
OPEN
Tues–Fri lunch and dinner; Sat–Sun dinner only
CLOSED
Mon; Sat–Sun lunch; NAC
HOURS
Lunch noon–2:30 P.M., dinner 8–11 P.M. (till midnight on Sat)
RESERVATIONS
Advised, especially if eating late
CREDIT CARDS
MC, V (100F minimum)
À LA CARTE
Not available
PRIX FIXE
Lunch: 69F, 2 courses, BNC; 79F, 3 courses, BC; dinner: 99F, 2 courses, BNC; 134F, 3 courses, BNC
ENGLISH SPOKEN
Yes

If you want to try imaginative twists on the usual French menu standards with pleasing dishes for every course, book a table at this late-night Marais dining favorite. The stone-arched back room has plank floors dotted with oriental rugs with banquettes or setees positioned amid changing art exhibits. Waiters wearing white shirts and colorful ties provide service to the definitely mixed all-French crowd. Sometimes on the weekend as the evening builds, the service and decible levels can be stretched to their limits.

The monthly changing menu is driven by what is best at the *marché,* but it always includes a beef carpaccio with foie gras and a to-die-for chocolate cake with chocolate sauce hiding a ball of vanilla ice cream that is aptly named *suicide au chocolate.* I like the creamed bacon and prune ravioli and the fresh tomato stuffed with chèvre cheese as starters. Chicken and noodles comes in its own pot; the fish is garnished with interesting vegetables, and for nonchocolate dessert eaters, the mango *tarte* is a light way to wrap up. Red wines of the month dominate the wine card, but there are enough whites to keep everyone happy.

(26) LE GRENIER SUR L'EAU
14, rue de Pont-Louis-Philippe (4th)

TELEPHONE
01-42-77-80-96
MÉTRO
Pont-Marie
OPEN
Mon–Fri lunch and dinner, Sat dinner only
CLOSED
Sat lunch, Sun, holidays, first 3 weeks in Aug

Bernard Mauget's intimate, two-level interior with starched pink linens, classical music, and masses of Provençal dried-flower arrangements strikes a formal tone for the fashion-conscious matrons and business executives who dine here at lunch. In the evening, couples of all ages are still pouring in at 10 P.M. For a discrete lunch or dinner with someone special, reserve a corner banquette table on the ground floor.

The well-thought-out lunch and dinner *formules* make sense for most Cheap Eaters in Paris. It is reassuring to know that whatever you order will reflect well-maintained standards of good food and polite service by the pleasant waitstaff. The menus afford interesting choices for all three courses. To begin, there are four hot or cold *entrées* plus a daily special. Depending on the season, your cold choices could be tomatoes stuffed with chèvre and basil or smoked salmon with leeks. Warm beginnings include *ravioles d'escargots* in a light cream sauce and a cassoulette of *pleurottes* (mushrooms) with shallot *confite*. There are always two or three fresh fish offerings in addition to filet mignon, herb-roasted rabbit on soy tagliatelli, or rosemary flavored lamb. Desserts try your willpower, but one very nice sweet surrender is the *mousse de fromage blanc au coulis des fruits rouges*—a light cottage cheese mousse with a tangy seasonal red fruit sauce.

HOURS
Lunch noon–2 P.M., dinner 8–11:30 P.M.

RESERVATIONS
Advised

CREDIT CARDS
AE, MC, V

À LA CARTE
Not available

PRIX FIXE
Lunch, 115F, 2 courses, BC; dinner, 150F, 3 courses, BNC

ENGLISH SPOKEN
Limited

(27) LE PETIT BOFINGER
6, rue de la Bastille (4th)

The worldwide economic recession hit Paris restaurants hard, making it unfashionable to spend huge sums of money dining out. Now people don't have time to spend hours over large lunches or drawn-out dinners accompanied by expensive wines and liquors. The trend is toward lighter food, quickly prepared and consumed, all without sacrificing quality or preparation. Many two- and three-star restaurants have jumped on the bistro bandwagon and opened less expensive venues. Brasserie Bofinger, the oldest and most beautiful brasserie in Paris, has opened a spin-off, Le Petit Bofinger, right across the street. The decor is simple by comparison and evokes the old neighborhood of the Bastille with black-and-white photos of the area, an original tiled floor, and a mural along one wall. A nonsmoking section demonstrates the management's desire to please the growing number of French who find life very pleasant when *not* dining in a smoke-induced haze.

The food is not lavish, but it is reasonable and dependable. Pay attention to the daily specials and the two prix fixe menus. Two other features worth remembering are that you can order just one dish at a time and not be subjected to icy stares from a frosty waiter and today's menu lists tomorrow's specials on both the à la carte and prix fixe menus. Two excellent starters are always the *foie*

TELEPHONE
01-42-72-05-23

MÉTRO
Bastille

OPEN
Daily

CLOSED
Never, NAC

HOURS
Lunch noon–3 P.M., dinner 7 P.M.–midnight

RESERVATIONS
Advised

CREDIT CARDS
AE, MC, V

À LA CARTE
150–160F, BNC

PRIX FIXE
Lunch only Mon–Sat, 95F, 2 courses, BC; lunch and dinner, 150F, 3 courses, BNC; children's menu (under 12), 45F, 3 courses, BC

ENGLISH SPOKEN
Yes

MISCELLANEOUS
Nonsmoking section

gras de canard maison and half a dozen Brittany oysters. The kitchen has a sure hand with fish and lamb, as demonstrated by the haddock with a cucumber cream sauce and the leg of lamb garnished with colorful al dente vegetables. Dessert offers a modish vanilla-bourbon-flavored *pot de creme* and *oeufs à la neige* with *crème anglaise* and toasted almonds.

(28) LES PHILOSOPHES
28, rue Vieille-du-Temple (4th)

TELEPHONE
01-48-87-49-64
MÉTRO
St-Paul, Hôtel-de-Ville
OPEN
Mon–Sat; holidays for dinner only
CLOSED
Sun, one week at Christmas, one week late April or early May, Aug
HOURS
Lunch noon–2 P.M., dinner 7:30–11 P.M.
RESERVATIONS
Yes
CREDIT CARDS
AE, DC, MC, V
À LA CARTE
185F, BNC
PRIX FIXE
Lunch and dinner, 85F, 2 courses, 100F and 135F, 3 courses, all BNC
ENGLISH SPOKEN
Yes

It is a joy to return to this perfect little *restaurant du quartier* and find it unchanged over the years. The formal dining room, framed by lacy window curtains, displays fresh flower bouquets, starched linens on well-spaced tables, and a tiny corner bar. The traditional menu, conceived by chef Gilles Lizenart, has something to appeal to everyone; the specialties are excellent, and the prices are right—three solid reasons why residents who want to share a few hours over a nice, affordable meal with a bottle of good wine reserve tables here. The prix fixe menus display a range of classic cuisine, which is carefully prepared with the best fresh ingredients. You can expect to find such timeless favorites as duck terrine, *oeuf en gelée sur saumon fumée, confit de canard "maison,"* and a tantalizing hot apple *tarte* that must be ordered at the start of the meal. Tempting those who are more daring are a fricassée of brains and kidneys in a mushroom sauce, a fine A.A.A.A.A. *andouillette,* and liver in a light bacon and cream sauce. If you order from one of the set menus and complement your meal with an inexpensive wine, your bill should be much less than you would pay for the same meal at home . . . if indeed you could find such food at any restaurant back home.

(29) LE TEMPS DES CERISES
31, rue de la Cerisaie (4th)

TELEPHONE
01-42-72-08-63
MÉTRO
Sully-Morland, Bastille
OPEN
Mon–Fri
CLOSED
Sat–Sun, holidays, Aug
HOURS
Bar 7:30 A.M.–8 P.M., continuous service; lunch 11:30 A.M.–2:30 P.M.

Le Temps des Cerises is the place to have a cheap lunch and a beer or two while polishing your fractured French. When you arrive, you won't miss owner Gerard, with his handlebar mustache, standing behind the bar pouring drinks for the regulars and teasing all the women. Lunch is the liveliest time here, attracting a relatively young neighborhood clientele who seem to accept the crowded conditions in order to enjoy the kind of honest homecooking that Mother never has time to make anymore. The blackboard listed selections read like a café cookbook and include all the basics, from Auvergne sausage and grilled steak with a pile of sinful *frites* to a plain fruit *tarte* for dessert. Before and after the hectic lunch scene, the café is calm and only cold food is served, with old-timers standing at the bar dusting off memories about times gone by. No one speaks much English, and you might have to share a table or elbow your way to a space at the bar, but go ahead, don't be shy. Everyone is friendly, and new faces are welcome.

RESERVATIONS
Not taken

CREDIT CARDS
None

À LA CARTE
70–100F, BNC

PRIX FIXE
Lunch, 70F, 3 courses, BNC

ENGLISH SPOKEN
No

(30) L'EXCUSE*
14, rue Charles-V (4th)

There is an elegant glow to the small bar and two dining rooms, which are tastefully decorated with soft lighting, fresh flowers, and attractive framed posters. Correctly set, well-spaced tables preserve a sense of intimacy, and the strains of classical music enhance the sophisticated mood, making L'Excuse a perfect choice for *le dîner à deux.*

Owner Jean-Denis Barbet is on hand daily to make sure no details go unnoticed or unattended. Throughout the year, his chef creates four seasonally innovative à la carte menus and weekly prix fixe menus that reflect the best the *marchés* have at the moment. In the spring, the à la carte menu may list such imaginative starters as a fricassée of wild mushrooms served on a bed of fresh salad herbs, prawn or langoustine ravioli in basil cream sauce, or eggplant cannelloni. Heading the list of worthy main courses might be fresh Scottish salmon, scallops served with endive fondu, a lobster cassolette, or a *côte de boeuf* with glazed onions. Desserts are all designed to please, especially the two that must be ordered at the start of the meal: a light honey sponge cake topped with bitter cherries and thyme flavored ice cream or the warm apple caramel *tarte* with a buttery crust. In the fifteen years it has been open, L'Excuse has developed a dedicated following of readers of this book, as well as of Paris residents, making reservations essential. Whenever you go, you will have an exquisite meal and enjoy impeccable service.

TELEPHONE
42-77-98-97

MÉTRO
St-Paul, Sully-Morland

OPEN
Mon–Sat

CLOSED
Sun, holidays, 3–4 days around Aug 15

HOURS
Lunch noon–2 P.M., dinner 7:30–11 P.M.

RESERVATIONS
Essential

CREDIT CARDS
AE, MC,V

À LA CARTE
300–325F, BNC

PRIX FIXE
Lunch only, 130F, 2 courses, BNC; Lunch and dinner, 175F, 3 courses, BNC

ENGLISH SPOKEN
Yes

(31) MARIAGE FRÈRES
30–32, rue du Bourg-Tibourg (4th)

No serious tea lover can afford to miss the Tiffany of tearooms in Paris: Mariage Frères, which has been dedicated for more than 140 years to the art of tea drinking.

TELEPHONE
01-42-72-28-11

MÉTRO
Hôtel-de-Ville

OPEN
Daily
CLOSED
Major holidays, NAC
HOURS
Lunch Mon–Fri noon–4 P.M., brunch Sat–Sun noon–6 P.M., afternoon tea 3–7 P.M., store 10:30 A.M.–7:30 P.M., continuous service at all times
RESERVATIONS
Not necessary
CREDIT CARDS
AE, MC, V
À LA CARTE
100–145F, BC
PRIX FIXE
Lunch, 130F, 3 courses and tea; brunch, 130–175F, 3 courses (at least) and tea; afternoon tea, 100F, pastry or sandwich and tea
ENGLISH SPOKEN
Yes
MISCELLANEOUS
No smoking allowed

Over 350 teas from twenty-five countries are prepared in these world-famous shops by master tea makers who still do everything by hand, including carefully cutting and stitching each tea bag out of tissue or muslin.

As the menu states, "Tea is not all in the pot." The ambience is an important part of the experience of drinking tea in this civilized establishment reminiscent of colonial times. Waiters in white present the tea menu, suggesting the appropriate tea to drink with each meal with the seriousness of a sommelier. The tea is prepared with filtered water and served in an insulated pot at the temperature best suited to its taste. Many of the dishes are prepared with tea, from jams and jellies to sauces, ice creams, and sorbets. The food in general is not as remarkable as the teas, but the pastries do keep pace, so plan to go for a lovely pastry and a sublime cup of tea. However, if you arrive outside of afternoon tea hours, you must order a meal. The prices are slightly high and so are the noses of some of the management, but it's all worth it for the experience.

In conjunction with the tearoom on rue du Bourg-Tibourg, there is a wonderful tea shop, which uses the original cash box from the first tea shop, and a small tea museum. The second location on rue des Grands-Augustins (sixth arrondissement) does not have the wide range of teas and tea accessories to buy, but the resturant is the same. At both locations, patrons are requested not to smoke.

(32) NOS ANCÊTRES LES GAULOIS
39, rue St-Louis-en-l'Île (4th)

TELEPHONE
01-46-33-66-07, 01-46-33-66-12
MÉTRO
Pont-Marie
OPEN
Mon–Sat dinner only, Sun and holidays lunch and dinner
CLOSED
NAC
HOURS
Lunch Sun and holidays noon–2 P.M.; dinner daily, two seatings at 7 P.M. and 10:30 P.M.
RESERVATIONS
Advised, especially on weekends
CREDIT CARDS
AE, DC, MC, V

"Our Ancestors the Gauls" promises raucous fun and all-you-can-eat farm food in beamed and vaulted rooms at trestle tables set for two to twenty revelers. Up to 330 party animals can be served each night by the tireless, rough-hewn waiters, who wear tunic vests made from clipped brown-and-white fur and coerce guests into making gluttons of themselves. You start by munching on loaves of dark country bread, cold meats, and raw vegetables and helping yourself to the salad buffet while waiting for your chosen main dish, which might be a steak, lamb chops, or shish kebabs grilled over an open fire and accompanied by rice, ratatouille, or spinach. The main course is followed by great platters of cheese and a choice of five desserts. As much red wine as you can drink, served from a huge cask at the center of the restaurant, is included in the price of the meal. Strolling guitarists and a singer entertain during the 7 P.M. seating. While gorging yourself and drinking quantities of barrel wine do not an intimate, romantic evening make, this is a great place to unwind with a group and have a Rabelasian feast you will long remember.

À LA CARTE
None

PRIX FIXE
Lunch and dinner, 195F, all-you-can-eat, 4 courses, BC

ENGLISH SPOKEN
Yes

(33) PAUL BUGAT—PÂTISSIER À LA BASTILLE
5, boulevard Beaumarchais (4th)

The French passion for pastries can be satisfied at this beautiful shop, where a full range of traditional and sublime French sweets are made each day with the freshest ingredients. They are snapped up and eaten almost as soon as they come from the oven. Try the macaroon and chocolate mousse confection called *Le Paris,* the *fruit clafoutis* with cherries and raisins, or the glazed chestnuts, available only in winter. You can sample these creations on the spot, either downstairs in the nonsmoking section or outside under an umbrella-covered table facing the Bastille. It is also a place to remember for a fast-food lunch, Parisian-style. Why settle for a plebian Big Mac and *frites* when you can have a plate of fresh salmon or Parma ham garnished with fresh crudités, a quiche and a salad, or *filet de sole* with steamed potatoes for just about the same price? It is also a nice stop for a quick bite before attending a performance at the new Opéra de la Bastille, located just across the street.

Pâtissier Paul Bugat has very impressive credentials. Not only has he been presiding over his well-known shop since the mid-fifties, when he took it over with his parents, but he has taught the art of French pastry cooking at Yale University and is the author of three large English-language volumes on the subject. Bugat said of his coauthor, former nuclear physicist Bruce Healy, "I turned Healy into a French pastry chef, but the opposite didn't apply." Thank goodness!

TELEPHONE
01-48-87-89-88

MÉTRO
Bastille

OPEN
Tues–Sun

CLOSED
Mon, Aug

HOURS
Tues–Sat 8:30 A.M.–8 P.M., Sun 8 A.M.–7:30 P.M., continuous service

RESERVATIONS
Not taken

CREDIT CARDS
MC, V

À LA CARTE
10–110F, BNC

PRIX FIXE
None

ENGLISH SPOKEN
Very little

(34) TRUMILOU
84, quai de l'Hôtel-de-Ville (4th)

It's a bar, a bistro, or a restaurant, depending on where you sit in this Cheap Eats jewel located in a sixteenth-century building along the Seine and run by the Drumond family. For years Trumilou has been rewarding artists, writers, students, and many other devotees with low tabs, good service, and sensible food that has survived the changing times, trends, and food crazes

TELEPHONE
01-42-77-63-98

MÉTRO
Hôtel-de-Ville, Pont-Marie

OPEN
Daily

CLOSED
3–4 days at Christmas, NAC

HOURS
Lunch noon–3 P.M., dinner 7–11 P.M., bar 8 A.M.–1 A.M.

RESERVATIONS
Recommended for larger parties

CREDIT CARDS
MC, V

À LA CARTE
140F, BNC

PRIX FIXE
Lunch and dinner, 70F and 85F, 3 courses, BNC

ENGLISH SPOKEN
Yes

rolling through Paris. The place radiates authenticity. It doesn't matter whether you eat in the large main room crowded with tables for two or four and filled with farm and family memorabilia from the Drumond's ancestors; in the slightly smaller, more intimate room with vases of flowers and crystal chandeliers; next to the bar and the pinball machine; or on the sidewalk terrace. The only concern here is the food, which brings diners back time after time. The regulars know enough to go early for both lunch and dinner to avoid the inevitable crowds.

The tried-and-true *plats du jour* change for winter and summer, and in the warmer months there are rewarding meals of lamb on Monday, stuffed cabbage on Tuesday, *blanquette de veau* on Wednesday, *potée* (a stew made from pork, sausage, bacon, and vegetables) on Thursday, and on Friday, catfish with aioli (garlic mayonnaise). The 85F, three-course menu is an unchanging institution. Start with a salad or rabbit terrine, then have their famous *poulet provençal* (a quarter chicken in tomato sauce) served with boiled potatoes, and finish with *chèvre,* Camembert, fruit, or rice pudding.

Fifth Arrondissement

The Latin Quarter is named after the students who came to Paris in the Middle Ages to study at the Sorbonne. Since that time, this area has been the student *quartier* of Paris. Associated with youth, intellectuals, artists, writers, poets, and a bohemian lifestyle, the area is filled with restaurants, cafés, bars, bookstores, and movie theaters. Many of the eating places are nothing more than greasy spoons, especially along rue de la Harpe and rue de la Huchette. A visit to one of the most colorful outdoor markets in Paris, along rue Mouffetard, is a must. The *marché* is open Tuesday through Sunday from 8 A.M. to 1 P.M. and is overflowing with every kind of food imaginable, clothing boutiques, little cafés, and a fascinating parade of people. The nearby Panthéon church is where many famous French are buried, including Rousseau, Voltaire, and Emile Zola.

LEFT BANK
Cluny Museum (art of the Middle Ages and ruins of Roman Baths), Jardin des Plantes, Latin Quarter, Rue Mouffetard, Panthéon, Sorbonne

FIFTH ARRONDISSEMENT RESTAURANTS

* Restaurants marked with an asterisk (*) are considered Big Splurges.

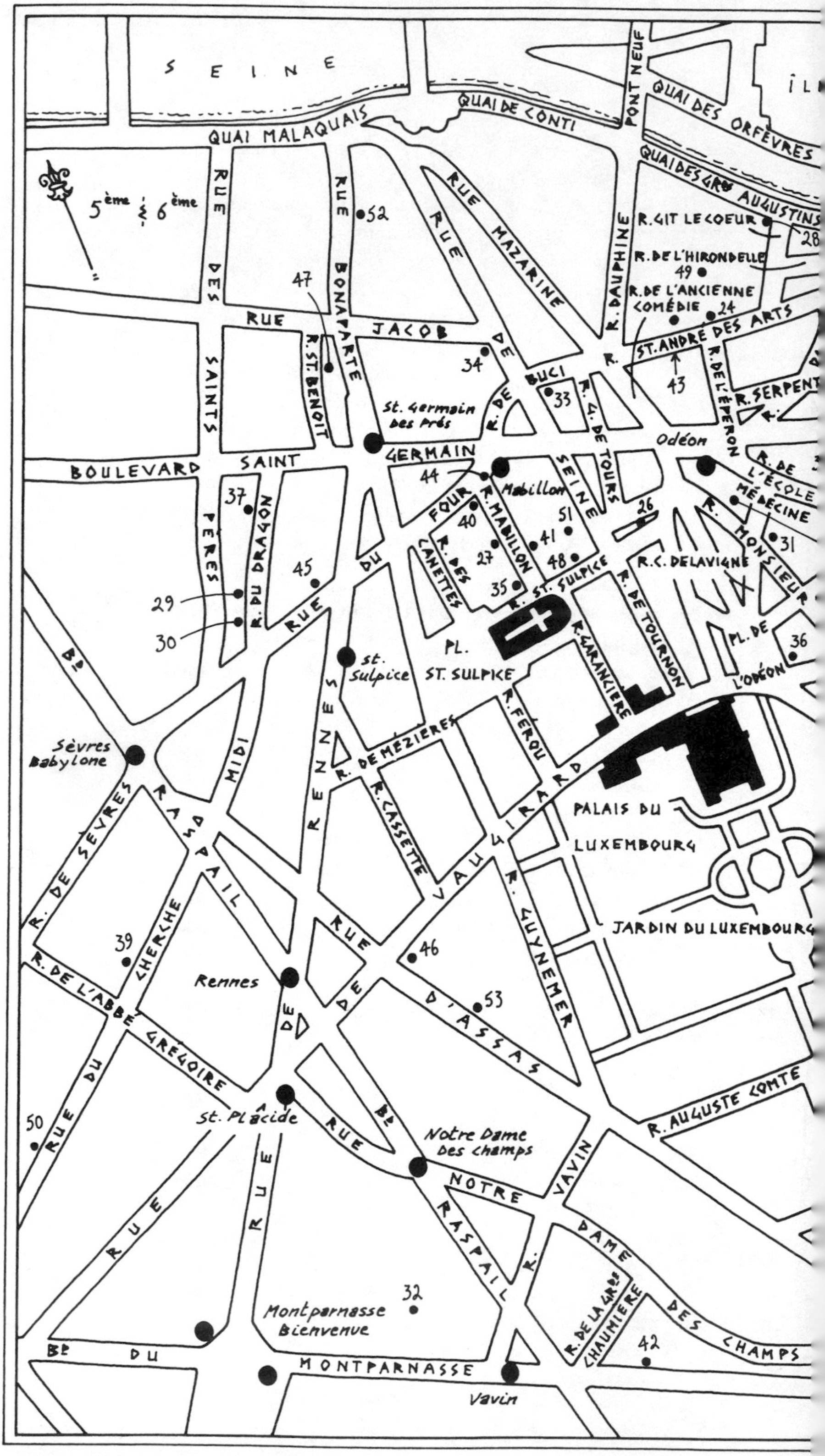
SEINE
QUAI MALAQUAIS
QUAI DE CONTI
PONT NEUF
QUAI DES ORFÈVRES
QUAI DES GRDS AUGUSTINS
5ème & 6ème
RUE DES SAINTS PÈRES
RUE BONAPARTE
RUE MAZARINE
R. DAUPHINE
R. GIT LE COEUR
R. DE L'HIRONDELLE
R. DE L'ANCIENNE COMÉDIE
ST. ANDRÉ DES ARTS
RUE JACOB
R. ST. BENOIT
RUE DE BUCI
R. DE L'ÉPERON
R. SERPENTE
St. Germain des Prés
BOULEVARD SAINT GERMAIN
Odéon
Mabillon
R. DE L'ÉCOLE MÉDECINE
R. DU DRAGON
R. DU FOUR
R. MABILLON
R. DES CANETTES
RUE DE SEINE
R. DE TOURS
R. ST. SULPICE
R. C. DELAVIGNE
R. MONSIEUR
R. DE TOURNON
PL. DE L'ODÉON
RUE DU
St. Sulpice
PL. ST. SULPICE
R. GARANCIÈRE
R. FÉROU
R. DE MÉZIÈRES
RUE DE RENNES
RUE DU MIDI
Bd. RASPAIL
Sèvres Babylone
R. DE SÈVRES
R. CASSETTE
VAUGIRARD
PALAIS DU LUXEMBOURG
R. GUYNEMER
JARDIN DU LUXEMBOURG
R. DU CHERCHE
Rennes
R. DE L'ABBÉ GRÉGOIRE
RUE DE
RUE D'ASSAS
R. AUGUSTE COMTE
St. Placide
RUE DU
Notre Dame des champs
RUE NOTRE DAME DES CHAMPS
R. VAVIN
RUE RENNES
R. RASPAIL
R. DE LA GRDE CHAUMIÈRE
Montparnasse Bienvenue
Bd. DU MONTPARNASSE
Vavin
52
47
34
33
43
24
49
28
44
37
40
51
26
31
45
27
41
48
35
29
30
36
39
46
53
50
32
42

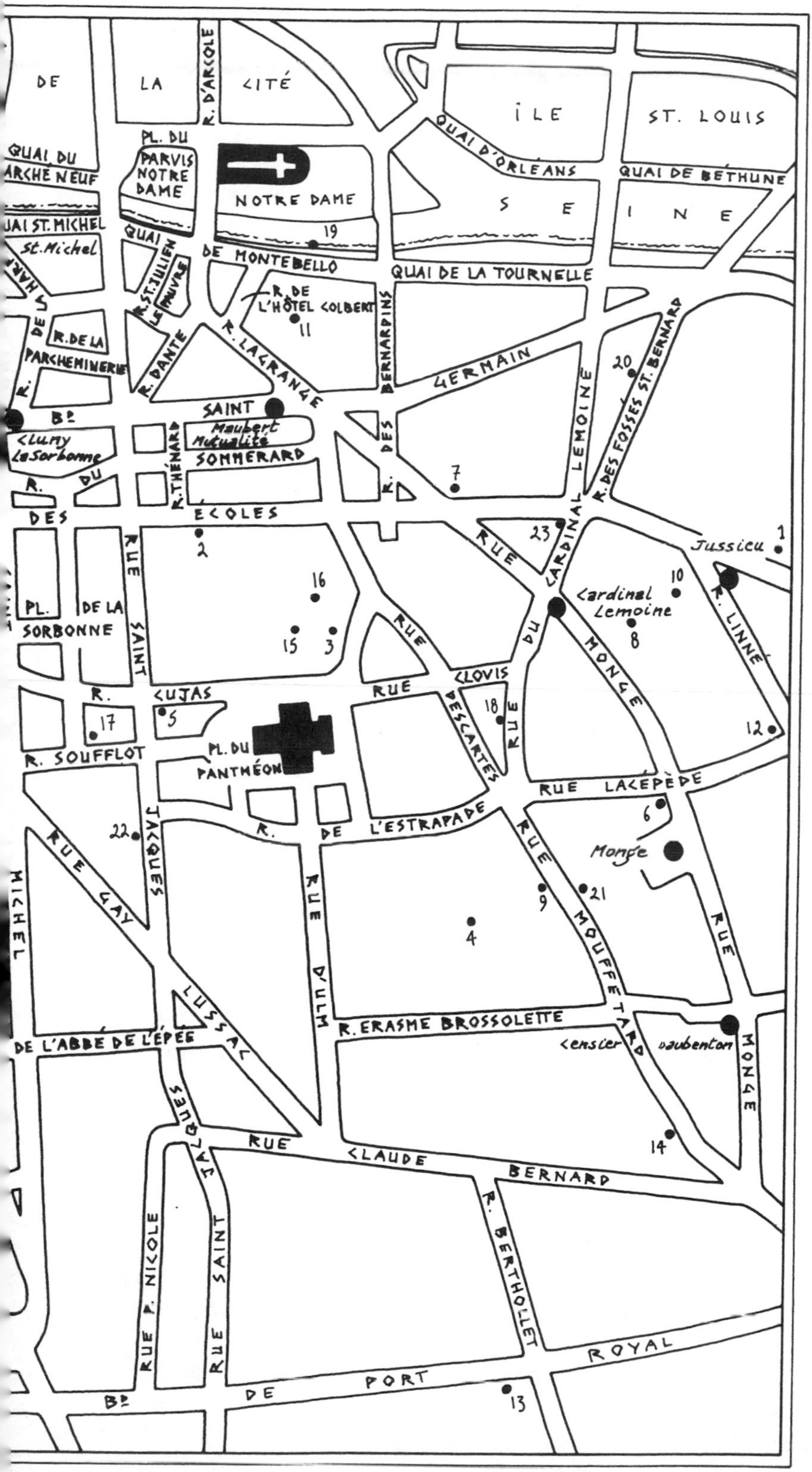
DE LA CITÉ
R. D'ARCOLE
ÎLE ST. LOUIS
PL. DU PARVIS NOTRE DAME
QUAI DU ARCHE NEUF
NOTRE DAME
QUAI D'ORLEANS
QUAI DE BETHUNE
SEINE
UAI ST. MICHEL
St. Michel
QUAI DE MONTEBELLO
19
R. ST. JULIEN LE PAUVRE
QUAI DE LA TOURNELLE
R. DE L'HÔTEL COLBERT
11
R. DE LA PARCHEMINERIE
R. DANTE
R. LAGRANGE
R. DES BERNARDINS
SAINT GERMAIN
20
R. LEMOINE
R. DES FOSSES ST. BERNARD
Bd
Cluny La Sorbonne
Maubert Mutualité
R. THÉNARD
R. DU SOMMERARD
7
R. DES ECOLES
23
RUE DU CARDINAL
1
Jussieu
2
16
10
Cardinal Lemoine
R. LINNÉ
8
PL. DE LA SORBONNE
RUE SAINT
15
3
MONGE
RUE CLOVIS
R. CUJAS
RUE DESCARTES
18
17
5
12
R. SOUFFLOT
PL. DU PANTHÉON
RUE LACEPÈDE
6
R. DE L'ESTRAPADE
22
Monge
RUE GAY LUSSAC
JACQUES
MICHEL
RUE D'ULM
9
21
4
RUE MOUFFETARD
RUE
R. ERASME BROSSOLETTE
DE L'ABBE DE L'EPÉE
Censier Daubenton
MONGE
14
RUE CLAUDE BERNARD
R. BERTHOLLET
RUE P. NICOLE
RUE SAINT JACQUES
Bd DE PORT ROYAL
13

(1) AU BUISSON ARDENT
25, rue Jussieu (5th)

TELEPHONE
01-43-54-93-02
MÉTRO
Jussieu
OPEN
Mon–Fri
CLOSED
Sat–Sun, holidays, Aug
HOURS
Lunch noon–2:30 P.M., dinner 7–10 P.M.
RESERVATIONS
Recommended (Note: reservations not accepted if you are ordering the 3-course, 75F lunch menu.)
CREDIT CARDS
MC, V
À LA CARTE
175F, BNC
PRIX FIXE
Lunch only, 75F, 3 courses, BNC; lunch and dinner, 150F, 3 courses, BNC
ENGLISH SPOKEN
Limited

This restaurant once sparked the beginning of a romance. The romance did not last too long, but my affection for this old Left Bank landmark has never wavered. As most visitors to Paris soon learn, crowded dining tables are an accepted fact of French life. Here you will experience crowding at its height, especially at lunch when the place is positively jumping. Despite the hectic scene, you can enjoy a top-quality meal for a surprisingly reasonable tab. The truly fine bourgeoise cooking, prepared with sincerity and served in warm surroundings by pleasant middle-aged waitresses, has kept the well-fed regulars coming back for years.

First-class choices on the menu always include a *salade de chèvre chaud,* leek *tarte, moules farcies, confit de canard maison,* leg of lamb, and any one of the fresh fish or *plat du jour* selections. All dishes are liberally garnished with two vegetables and some of the creamiest potatoes imaginable. Topping the desserts is the fruit *clafoutis* or, in season, the *charlotte à la framboise.* The portions are dauntingly large, so arrive hungry!

(2) BRASSERIE BALZAR
49, rue des Écoles (5th)

TELEPHONE
01-43-54-13-67
MÉTRO
Odéon, Cluny
OPEN
Daily
CLOSED
Aug
HOURS
8 A.M.–1 A.M., continuous service
RESERVATIONS
Necessary
CREDIT CARDS
AE, MC, V
À LA CARTE
165–180F, BNC
PRIX FIXE
None
ENGLISH SPOKEN
Yes

You will find sawdust on the floor and waiters in white shirts and black cutaway vests in this genuine old Left Bank brasserie, which was founded in 1890 by the same family who began Brasserie Lipp. Located close to the Sorbonne's sprawling campus, it has long been a favorite of Left Bank intellectuals and would-be bohemians of all types. Sartre and Camus were customers, and it is said they had their last argument here. During the day you will find it has a faded charm, one you will quickly learn to appreciate and enjoy as a reflection of the literary and political life of the *quartier.* In the evening, the pace picks up, and the clientele is a bright mix of pipe-smoking professors, artists, actors, and pretty young women, making this one of the liveliest places to be in the Latin Quarter. On Sunday nights, it is considered de rigueur for the neighborhood regulars to have dinner here. When you go, zero in on the succulent *poulet rôti* (roast chicken) and a basket of *pommes frites,* or try the *gratin dauphinoise* (creamed potatoes) and the *raie au beurre* (skate fish) with a bottle of the house Beaujolais.

Top it off with a piece of warm *tarte Tatin* for a good meal that will not strain your pocketbook.

(3) CHANTAIRELLE
17, rue de Laplace (5th)

If you cannot get to France's Massif Central and the area of Livradois-Forez located between Clermont-Ferrand and Lyon, then you must promise to treat yourself to a taste of the region by dining at Chantairelle in the heart of Paris. This regionally inspired restaurant offers guests a total experience of the area, not only from a food standpoint, but from a visual and aural one as well. Tapes of chirping birds and ringing church bells from owner/chef Frédéric Bethe's native village of Marsac float over the rustic, beamed dining room, where guests sit on rush-seated, ladder-backed chairs placed around bare wooden tables and look out onto a back garden filled with native trees and plants. In front, as you enter, is a boutique overflowing with products from this little Auvergne village.

The food is as authentic as the surroundings and the portions so enormous you might want to share an *entrée* of lentils with *jambon* (ham) or the blue cheese and leek *tarte*. *Les plats* feature copious servings of wonderful Auvergne *charcuteries*, stuffed cabbage, sturdy *potées* (stews), and cheeses. Dessert—if you have room—should be the *millard aux mirtilles* (blueberry/billberry) *tarte* served with a poached pear and cream or the honey-based warm apple *tarte* with Armagnac ice cream. Apéritifs, wines, and even the mineral water all come from the region, guaranteeing a total immersion in this lovely part of France, if only for a few hours.

TELEPHONE
01-46-33-18-59

MÉTRO
Cardinal-Lemoine

OPEN
Mon–Fri lunch and dinner, Sat dinner only

CLOSED
Sat lunch, Sun, major holidays, NAC

HOURS
Lunch noon–2 P.M., dinner 7–11 P.M.

RESERVATIONS
Essential

CREDIT CARDS
MC, V

À LA CARTE
190–200F, BNC

PRIX FIXE
Lunch only, 80F, 2 courses, 95F, 3 courses, both BC; children, 55F, 2 courses

ENGLISH SPOKEN
Yes

(4) CHEZ LÉNA ET MIMILE
32, rue Tourneforte (5th)

The slightly passé pink dining room—with burgundy velvet seats, an odd mixture of mediocre art, and tulip lamps on the tables—opens onto a delightful summer terrace overlooking a leafy square filled with jacaranda trees. On Thursday and Friday nights in the winter there is a piano player and a singer who are quite good.

The lunch and dinner one-price-only menus are a study in confirmed, tried-and-true French cooking. Be sure to bring your appetite. Starters include the house duck foie gras, escargots, leeks in warm vinaigrette, herring with lentils and beets, and eggs scrambled with

TELEPHONE
01-47-07-72-47

MÉTRO
Place Monge, Censir-Daubenton

OPEN
Mon–Fri lunch and dinner, Sat dinner only

CLOSED
Sat lunch, Sun, major holidays, 2 weeks in Aug

HOURS
Lunch noon–2 P.M., dinner 7:30–11 P.M.

RESERVATIONS
Advised for dinner
CREDIT CARDS
MC, V
À LA CARTE
None
PRIX FIXE
Lunch, 98F, 2 courses, BNC (desserts 30–40F extra); dinner, 185F, 3 courses, BC
ENGLISH SPOKEN
Yes

tarragon. The fish *choucroute magret de cannard* with turnips or the roast chicken are nothing fancy, but certainly satisfying main courses. Vegetarians will appreciate the sage flavored ravioli. Desserts are headlined by pears poached in wine, chocolate mousse, and the daily pastry. The nougat ice cream is best forgotten. A kir to start, wine poured throughout dinner, and a *café* to end are included with the price of the meal. Lunch is geared to those with time constraints and includes only the *entrée* and *plat* . . . all else is extra.

(5) CHEZ PENTO
9, rue Cujas (5th)

TELEPHONE
01-43-26-81-54
MÉTRO
Luxembourg, Cluny
OPEN
Mon–Fri lunch and dinner, Sat dinner only
CLOSED
Sat lunch, Sun, holidays, Dec 24–Jan 2
HOURS
Lunch noon–2 P.M., dinner 7:30–11 P.M.
RESERVATIONS
Advised
CREDIT CARDS
AE, MC, V
À LA CARTE
Two courses 125–150F, desserts 40F, BNC
PRIX FIXE
Lunch only, 90F, 3 courses (limited choices), BNC; lunch or dinner, 110F, 2 courses (unlimited choices), BNC
ENGLISH SPOKEN
Limited
MISCELLANEOUS
Nonsmoking section

If I lived in this neighborhood near the Panthéon, I could easily become a regular at the always bustling, noisy, and crowded Chez Pento, where a comfortable clientele from all walks of life descends for both lunch and dinner. Bare tables, with white paper covers and linen napkins, are sandwiched in a properly frayed room ringed with posters and banquettes in need of retying. To one side is another room reserved for nonsmoking patrons, an almost unheard-of courtesy anywhere in Paris.

The menu offers what the French call *qualité prix,* or what we call value for money. You can either select a prix fixe lunch or dinner or have exactly the same food à la carte. Desserts are extra no matter how you place your order. Every day there are three different *entrées* and *plats* along with world-class regulars of *soupe à l'oignon,* herring with warm potato salad, a dozen mussels, curried oysters, and escargot. Long-running standbys of beef tartare, *petit salé aux lentilled,* tripe, *tête de veau,* and grilled salmon hit the spot every time. Desserts are familiar servings of chocolate cake, triple chocolate mousse, crème brûlée, ice creams, and sorbets. Because the service is swift, lingering usually isn't part of the program.

(6) LA CRÊPE CARRÉE
42, rue Monge (5th)

TELEPHONE
01-43-26-99-98
MÉTRO
Place Monge, Cardinal-Lemoine
OPEN
Mon–Sat
CLOSED
Sun, holidays, NAC

A crêpe is a crêpe is a crêpe . . . but not necessarily at this little *crêperie,* which is a notch or two above the competition.

You can either order yours to go or sit at one of the twenty-eight places inside to enjoy this French fast-food treat. Owner and crêpe maker par excellence, M.

Combastel offers over one hundred versions of these filled, thin pancakes, from one simply spread with butter to the *Texane*, bursting with ground beef, cheese, onions, and béchamel sauce. Dessert selections start with a sugar-filled crêpe and go up to one filled with all the ingredients you would find in a banana split, including whipped cream and nuts. Cider, wine, or beer minimize drink options, and the prices keep Cheap Eaters in Paris within budget.

HOURS
Lunch noon–3 P.M., dinner 6:30–10 P.M.

RESERVATIONS
Not accepted

CREDIT CARDS
MC, V (100F minimum)

À LA CARTE
35–65F, BNC

PRIX FIXE
None

ENGLISH SPOKEN
Yes

(7) LA FONTAINE SAINT-VICTOR

Maison de la Mutualité, 24, rue St-Victor (off rue des Écoles) (5th)

TELEPHONE
01-40-46-12-04

MÉTRO
Cardinal-Lemoine, Maubert-Mutualité

OPEN
Daily, lunch only

CLOSED
Holidays, Aug

HOURS
11:45 A.M.–2:30 P.M.

RESERVATIONS
For groups only

CREDIT CARDS
MC, V

À LA CARTE
165F, BNC

PRIX FIXE
95F, 2 courses, 115F and 175F, 4 courses, all BNC

ENGLISH SPOKEN
Some

"Who would ever want to eat here?" I thought the first time I arrived at the unimpressive French Social Security building just off rue des Écoles. Things began to pick up as I walked up the expansive art deco staircase to the second-floor dining room. As I finished the last bite of my lemon *tarte,* I knew why this Cheap Eats sleeper is so popular with dignified French pensioners, who have been lunching here for half a century.

From the bar you can order a gin and tonic, a dry martini, or a scotch and soda, and a good bottle of wine will be less than 100F. To polish off your lunch, the only meal they serve, in grand style, an Armagnac or cognac will set you back less than 45F. Along with the booze, you will probably have something to eat, and the traditional menu is varied, the food good, and above all, it is well priced, whether you stick to the set menu or go à la carte. I like the four-course, 115F menu because it includes a large sampling of cheeses along with everything else. It is a big meal, but you can go easy on dinner. The service by white-jacketed waiters is flawless, the tables are set with linens and fresh flowers, and during your quiet and proper lunch you will be surrounded by sweet *grand-mères* and *grand-pères* who haven't forgotten how to enjoy dining well.

(8) LA PETITE LÉGUME

36, rue des Boulangers (5th)

TELEPHONE
01-40-46-06-85

MÉTRO
Cardinal Lemoine, Jussieu

OPEN
Mon–Sat

"Live well, eat sensibly" is the motto at Michel and Patricia's La Petite Légume. And they deliver: A meal here is prepared without refined sugar, salt, or meat products and is served in a smoke-free atmosphere. For

CLOSED
Sun, major holidays, NAC
HOURS
Lunch noon–2:30 P.M., dinner 7–9:30 P.M., shop 9:30 A.M.–10 P.M.
RESERVATIONS
Not taken
CREDIT CARDS
MC, V
À LA CARTE
40–85F, BC
PRIX FIXE
Lunch only: 50–65F, 3 courses, BNC; 75F, 3 courses, BC
ENGLISH SPOKEN
Yes, with English menu
MISCELLANEOUS
No smoking allowed

cash-strapped vegetarians or anyone eager to watch what they eat, this is a Cheap Eat well worth noting. For less than 60F you can walk out guilt-free and full of good food that's good for you. The menu lists something for every level of vegetarianism, from whole-cereal dishes with seaweed, miso, and tofu to salads, soups, and an overflowing *plat du jour* of *crudités,* rice or grains, vegetables, dried fruit, and nuts. Order a nonalcoholic beer, organic wine, or a tumbler of freshly pressed carrot juice, and indulge in a slice of their nonfat cheesecake or chocolate cake to round out the repast. Don't have time to stop for a meal? They will pack everything to go and even charge a bit less to do so. On your way, take a minute or two to glance through the shop, which sells macrobiotic books and natural products.

(9) L'ASSIETTE AUX FROMAGES
27, rue Mouffetard (5th)

TELEPHONE
01-45-35-14-21
MÉTRO
Place Monge
OPEN
Thur–Tues
CLOSED
Wed, one week at Christmas, NAC
HOURS
Shop 10:30 A.M.–10 P.M., restaurant noon–11 P.M., continuous service
RESERVATIONS
Not taken
CREDIT CARDS
MC, V
À LA CARTE
95–135F, BNC
PRIX FIXE
45F, 2 courses, BC
ENGLISH SPOKEN
Limited, with English menu

Smile, say "Cheese," and head for L'Assiette aux Fromages, a great place to go for lunch with a small group, order several different plates of cheese, have a couple bottles of the house red or white wine, and then walk off the consequences in the nearby Jardin des Plantes. Unfortunately, not all of the staff smile when they say "Fromage," and they could stand to brush up their customer service and satisfaction skills.

France reportedly produces over four hundred varieties of cheese, a fact that can be overwhelming to anyone used to only Roquefort, cheddar, and swiss. Now cheese-lovers of all types can taste, eat, and buy over two hundred varieties of cheese from all over France in this bright, modern *fromagerie* with its garden restaurant, not far from place de la Contrescarpe on the colorful rue Mouffetard.

The menu, which is in English and German as well as French, offers many enticing cheese-inspired dishes, from big salads and sandwiches to quiches, *tartes, raclettes,* fondues, and desserts. The smart move here is to order a *salade de saison* and one of the *plateaux des fromages,* which have five regional or specialty cheeses per plate: *doucer* (mild), *saveur* (strong), chèvre (goat), *l'avergnat* (cheese from the Auvergne), *suspens* (their selection). Or order *personnalisé,* five cheeses of your choice from a list of eleven. All cheese plates are served with pots of sweet butter, crusty baguettes, and *pain Poilâne.*

(10) LE BAPTISTE
11, rue des Boulangers (5th)

You can eat, drink, and be merry at Le Baptiste without it costing you an arm and a leg. The service is friendly, the crowd good-natured, and you are bound to have a good time, stuffing yourself along with the students and locals who have made this budget-priced spot so popular for smart Cheap Eaters. Located in an ancient building on a narrow, seven-hundred-year-old cobblestone street, this rustic restaurant has enough wooden beams and stone to build a real farm. The inside is lit by antique brass-and-ceramic lamps, and the stone walls are hung with the paintings and drawings of local artists.

The prix fixe menus offer an excellent selection of sturdy terrines and sizable salads that will spark your appetite for the main courses of beef, duck fish, lamb, or one of the daily specials, followed by an avalanche of desserts.

TELEPHONE
01-43-25-57-24

MÉTRO
Jussieu

OPEN
Mon–Fri lunch and dinner, Sat dinner only

CLOSED
Sat lunch, Sun, 1 week at Christmas, August 7–21

HOURS
Lunch noon–2 P.M., dinner 7–10 P.M. (Fri–Sat till 11 P.M.)

RESERVATIONS
Not necessary

CREDIT CARDS
AE, MC, V (100F minimum)

À LA CARTE
100–250F, BNC

PRIX FIXE
Lunch, 65F, 2 courses, 75F, 3 courses, both BNC; dinner, 75F, 135F, and 185F, 3 courses, all BNC

ENGLISH SPOKEN
Yes

(11) LE GRENIER DE NOTRE-DAME
18, rue de la Bûcherie (5th)

It's all natural, the food is imaginative, not too expensive, and the environment is smoke free. It adds up to one of the best vegetarian restaurants in Paris because it has something for everyone, from hardcore macrobiotics and habitual health nuts to dedicated dieters or those vegetarians who will eat fish. For anyone in search of a wholesome meal in pretty garden surroundings, Le Grenier de Notre-Dame is a good choice.

The long menu lists tasty soups, salads, jazzy main courses, fresh-squeezed juices, tonic drinks to set you straight, and organic wines. Each table has its own bottle of extra-virgin olive oil, soy sauce, *gomazio* (ground sesame seeds and sea salt), and a bottle of Levure de Bière, a malt substance to drizzle over soups or salads for an extra flavor kick. A bonus for many is the English menu, so you won't order tofu burgers by mistake.

TELEPHONE
01-43-29-98-29

MÉTRO
Maubert-Mutualité

OPEN
Daily

CLOSED
Never, NAC

HOURS
Lunch noon–2:30 P.M. (Sun till 3 P.M.), dinner 7–10:30 P.M. (Fri–Sat till 11 P.M.)

RESERVATIONS
Not necessary

CREDIT CARDS
AE, MC, V

À LA CARTE
85–140F, BNC

PRIX FIXE
Lunch and dinner, 80F, 85F, and 105F, 3 courses, all BNC

ENGLISH SPOKEN
Enough, with English menu

MISCELLANEOUS
Nonsmoking sections

(12) LE JARDIN DES PÂTES

4, rue Lacépède (5th)

TELEPHONE
01-43-31-50-71

MÉTRO
Jussieu, Place Monge

OPEN
Tues–Sun

CLOSED
Mon, NAC

HOURS
Lunch noon–2:30 P.M., dinner 7–11 P.M.

RESERVATIONS
Advised

CREDIT CARDS
V

À LA CARTE
95–110F, BNC

PRIX FIXE
None

ENGLISH SPOKEN
Yes

Les Jardin des Pâtes has two homes, one near the Jardin des Plantes in the fifth arrondissement and the second in the thirteenth arrondissement (see page 178). At both locations, an arty tone is set by the flowers and plants crowding the front window and the white walls hung with changing art exhibits.

Fresh food, simply served, continues to be the guarantee from Mireille and Charles Maggio at both of their Cheap Eats locales. One taste tells you that you have found something *very* good, and the crowded tables confirm it. The specialty is homemade pasta, made from rice, corn, wheat, and rye flours ground in their kitchens and topped with imaginative sauces. Everything is prepared to order and served à la carte. One of the most popular dishes is the *pâtes de chataigne* (a *chataigne* is a type of chestnut), which is a rich mix of pasta topped with duck fillet, mushrooms, crème fraîche, and just a hint of nutmeg. Another is the rice pasta topped with sautéed vegetables and chunks of tofu and seasoned with fresh ginger. Another filling and unusual combination is the omelette with pasta, served with a green salad. Soups, seasonal salads, and some rather heavy desserts fill out the rest of the menu. Worth serious thought for all who count chocolate as a daily necessity is the (calories? who's counting?) chocolate-marmalade *tarte*. Reasonable wines are served by the *pichet,* but watch out for the bottle of Chateau Haut-Marbuzet . . . it goes for 260F a pop!

(13) LE LANGUEDOC

64, boulevard du Port-Royal, at rue Berthollet (5th)

TELEPHONE
01-47-07-24-47

MÉTRO
Gobelins, Port-Royal

OPEN
Thur–Mon

CLOSED
Tues–Wed, Dec 21–Jan 5, Aug

HOURS
Lunch noon–2 P.M., dinner 7–10 P.M.

RESERVATIONS
Advised on weekends

CREDIT CARDS
MC, V (130F minimum)

À LA CARTE
135F, BNC

Le Languedoc has the relaxed feel of an old-fashioned Parisian restaurant; its contented regulars enjoy the authentic atmosphere and know to stick to the basics when ordering. Checked tie-back curtains, wooden tables covered with yellow linen and white paper overlays, three coat racks, a grandfather clock, assorted copper pots—everything has been in the same position for twenty years . . . and there is no hint of change on the horizon.

There is plenty to choose from on the purple and pink handwritten stenciled menu and really no need to stray from the bargain-priced prix fixe, which allows a wide choice from the à la carte selections. Start with bowls of herring filets or flavorful terrines brought to the table and left for you to help yourself. Follow with a good *cassoulet*, any *plat du jour,* or the grilled *entrecôte,* which comes with crispy *frites* and a side salad. Seasonal desserts or chocolate mousse put a nice ending to a very good value Cheap Eat in Paris.

PRIX FIXE
Lunch and dinner, 110F, 3 courses, BC

ENGLISH SPOKEN
Limited

(14) LE MOUFFETARD
116, rue Mouffetard (5th)

In the fifteenth century, rue Mouffetard was known as Hell Raisers' Hill because of the many taverns and brothels in the area. The steep street, which begins at place de la Contrescarp and winds down to the St-Mediard Church near the Censier-Daubenton métro stop, is still full of greasy spoons and probably a brothel or two if you look hard enough. The best reason to go there today is to wander through the colorful open-air morning street *marché* and the inexpensive clothing shops that line both sides of the long street. When you go, be sure to stop in at this little down-to-earth spot known as Le Mouffetard.

The café has been owned and run by the members of the Chartran family for years, and they get up with the chickens to serve locals on their way to work. Arrive a little later in the morning and you can indulge in the house specialties: buttery croissants and rich yeasty brioches made every day by M. and Mme. Chartran. At lunchtime, try the pork in a tangy mustard sauce or the thickly sliced ham with plum sauce and a side of pasta. With your meal will come a basket of their home-baked *pain de campagne.* Even if you are not up to sharing an eye-opening cognac with the locals at dawn, or you can't make it for lunch, at least stop by for a coffee and one of their *chaussons aux pommes* or *pruneaux*—flaky apple or prune turnovers.

TELEPHONE
01-43-31-42-50

MÉTRO
Censier-Daubenton, Place Monge

OPEN
Tues–Sun

CLOSED
Mon, July

HOURS
Tues–Sat 7 A.M.–9:30 P.M., Sun 7 A.M.– 8 P.M., continuous service

RESERVATIONS
Not taken

CREDIT CARDS
AE

À LA CARTE
45–95F, BNC

PRIX FIXE
Breakfast, 40F; lunch or dinner, 80F, 3 courses, BNC

ENGLISH SPOKEN
Not much

(15) LE RACCARD
19, rue Laplace (5th)

With a group or just one other person, Le Raccard is the place to fill up on the lip-smacking Swiss specialties of fondue and *raclette. Raclette,* for the uninitiated, is bubbling hot melted cheese served over boiled new potatoes and accompanied with tangy *cornichons* (pickles) and tiny pickled onions. I absolutely guarantee that it is as delectable as it is filling and fattening.

The Swiss-style chalet is located not far from the Panthéon, and it is worth the short climb from the métro because you definitely need a good appetite when

TELEPHONE
01-43-54-83-75, 01-43-25-27-27

MÉTRO
Maubert-Mutualité

OPEN
Tues–Sun, dinner only

CLOSED
Mon, NAC

HOURS
7:30 P.M.–12:30 A.M.

RESERVATIONS
Advised on weekends

CREDIT CARDS AE

À LA CARTE 160–180F, BNC

PRIX FIXE None

ENGLISH SPOKEN Limited

eating here. Stay with the house specialties and you won't go away unhappy. The desserts, which you will not have room for anyway, are best forgotten. The waiters can be impatient, but when pushed they do speak enough English to suggest appropriate combinations. Before leaving, be sure to notice the authentic hay crib, or *raccard,* in the back, which has been skillfully turned into a little bar.

(16) LES FÊTES GALANTES
17, rue de l'Ècole Polytechnique (5th)

TELEPHONE 01-43-26-10-40

MÉTRO Maubert-Mutualité

OPEN Mon–Sat

CLOSED Sun, Christmas day, NAC

HOURS Lunch noon–2:30 P.M.; dinner 6:30–11:30 P.M.

RESERVATIONS Advised on weekends

CREDIT CARDS MC, V

À LA CARTE 200–245F, BNC

PRIX FIXE Lunch, 60F, 2 courses, BNC; dinner, 80F (Mon–Fri until 9:30 P.M., Sat until 8:30 P.M.), 100F, and 165F, 3 courses, all BNC

ENGLISH SPOKEN Yes, with English menu

Good things often come in small packages. At Les Fêtes Galantes this is certainly true, especially if you go for their two-course lunch or arrive at the fashionably incorrect dining hours between 6:30 and 9:30 P.M. (8:30 P.M. on Saturday) to take advantage of the three-course menu for around twenty dollars. The food and welcome offered by Bibi, the owner, will make you want to return again.

A hand-painted forest mural makes a nice backdrop for the twenty-two places on pink-clad tables, each with its own glass-shaded lamp and a bouquet of fresh flowers. Forget the à la carte and zero in on one of the very affordable prix fixe menus. The well-planned presentations revolve around seasonal food. Pâtes, escargots, hot and cold soups, and salads laden with fresh asparagus, foie gras, and avocados figure among the able starters. Lamb, veal, duck, and fresh fish are featured in the vegetable garnished *plats*. Desserts delight with made to order fruit *gratinés*, a hot cinnamon spiced pear *tarte* with either vanilla ice cream or lemon sorbet, and *profiteroles* filled with coffee ice cream and covered in dark hot chocolate sauce.

(17) LES FONTAINES
9, rue Soufflot (5th)

TELEPHONE 01-43-26-42-80

MÉTRO Luxembourg

OPEN Mon–Sat

CLOSED Sun, major holidays, Aug 1–21

HOURS café drinks, 8 A.M.–11 P.M., continuous service; lunch noon–3 P.M., dinner 7–11 P.M.

You can't judge a book by its cover, and that is certainly true about Les Fontaines. Unless you knew about it ahead of time, you would never go in on the basis of looks alone. When it comes to cafés in Paris, everyone has his or her favorite. But dogs, children, pensioners, trendies, bespeckled professors, blue-haired matrons, families—everyone comes to this popular spot located in the tourist-intensive area between the Panthéon and the entrance to the Luxembourg Gardens.

No one comes for the decor or for polished ambience: the interior is a time warp of plastic, chrome, and bright neon. But the food—ahhh—that is something to come back for again and again. The menu will melt the hearts of all carnivores with time-honored dishes of foie gras, *rillettes de porc* (a coarse type of pâté), *confit de canard* (duck), *rognons de veau* (veal kidneys) in a mustard sauce, and huge steaks. The meat-based meals arrive on platters, not plates. Fish lovers will have at least seven seasonal selections, including tuna, salmon, and lobster. If you love pears and chocolate (and who doesn't?), request the *feuillete de poires au chocolate chaud* when you place your order. Otherwise, try the souffléd orange crêpes, the apple tarte, or a simple crème caramel. All of this is brought to you with speed and precision by a fleet of fast-footed servers in black pants, white shirts, and snappy ties.

RESERVATIONS
Essential

CREDIT CARDS
MC, V

À LA CARTE
180–200F, BNC

PRIX FIXE
None

ENGLISH SPOKEN
Yes

(18) LES QUATRE ET UNE SAVEURS

72, rue du Cardinal-Lemoine (5th)

Only fresh, natural ingredients are used at this appealing *macrobiotique* vegetarian restaurant near the place de la Contrescape and rue Mouffetard. The open, airy interior is dominated by four arrangements of dried grains and pastas. Framed posters remind you of the seven conditions of good health and happiness: avoid fatigue, have a good appetite, sleep well, and develop good memory, good humor, swift judgment, and a sense of justice.

Just as important are the winning combinations of food they serve, which go a long way toward promoting your health and happiness while in Paris. The menu starts off with full-bodied miso or vegetable soups and accents one-dish meals of salads or hot vegetables centered around grains, beans, tofu, or fish. Fresh fruit and vegetable juices, herbal teas, organic wine, plus the best sugar-free apple crisp you will taste add up to a healthy and delicious Cheap Eat.

TELEPHONE
01-43-26-88-80

MÉTRO
Cardinal-Lemoine, Place Monge

OPEN
Tues–Sun

CLOSED
Mon, major holidays, NAC

HOURS
Lunch noon–3 P.M., dinner 7–10:30 P.M.

RESERVATIONS
Not necessary

CREDIT CARDS
MC, V

À LA CARTE
100–130F, BNC

PRIX FIXE
Lunch and dinner, 120F, 3 courses, BC (tea or coffee)

ENGLISH SPOKEN
Yes

MISCELLANEOUS
No smoking allowed

(19) LE VER-MEER CAFÉ

19, quai de Montebello (5th)

Charlie, a black dog wearing an American flag scarf tied around his neck, welcomes guests to Margolaene and Katherine's café along the banks of the Seine. Boasting a million-dollar view of Notre-Dame Cathedral, it

TELEPHONE
01-40-46-96-50

MÉTRO
St-Michel, Maubert-Mutualité

OPEN
Daily; Mon lunch only

CLOSED
Mon dinner, NAC
HOURS
Café drinks and brunch 10 A.M.–midnight, continuous service; lunch 11 A.M.–3 P.M., dinner 7–10 P.M.
RESERVATIONS
Not necessary
CREDIT CARDS
MC, V
À LA CARTE
Hot meals, 125–155F, BNC
PRIX FIXE
Lunch only, 55F, *plat du jour,* BC
ENGLISH SPOKEN
Limited

draws a diverse clientele, who enjoy either a light meal at any time of day or a one- to three-course lunch or dinner.

Considering the location, the food is a bargain, and it's good besides. Salads, soups, meat, fish, brunch served all day, a *plat du jour,* and their own desserts should fill almost anyone's Cheap Eating needs in this tourist trafficked part of the fifth arrondissement.

(20) MOISSONNIER*

28, rue des Fossés St-Bernard (5th)

TELEPHONE
01-43-29-87-65
MÉTRO
Cardinal-Lemoine
OPEN
Tues–Sat lunch and dinner, Sun lunch only
CLOSED
Sun dinner, Mon, major holidays, Aug
HOURS
Lunch noon–2 P.M., dinner 7–10 P.M.
RESERVATIONS
Necessary
CREDIT CARDS
MC, V
À LA CARTE
225–270F, BNC
PRIX FIXE
Mon–Fri lunch and dinner, 150F, 3 courses, BNC
ENGLISH SPOKEN
Yes, with English menu

There have been some recent changes at the forty-year-old Moissonnier, but they are all positive, especially the addition of the prix fixe menu, which enables a wider audience to afford the pleasure of dining at this Left Bank landmark. M. Moissonnier has retired and turned over the reigns to M. and Mme. Mayet, who worked for him for years. They have followed in his footsteps, insuring that this will continue to be a perfect example of a French family-owned bistro. The best seating in the two-floor restaurant is on the ground floor, with its high ceiling, massive bouquet of fresh flowers, and tiny service bar along one side. The best time to go is for lunch on Sunday.

The well-rounded Lyonaise selection of dishes makes this an excellent dining choice and a good culinary value considering the quality of the food, which is prepared from scratch on the premises everyday. Look for the regional and house specialties written in red on the menu. A good *entrée* choice is the *saladier,* a large cart rolled to your table laden with salads, terrines, herring in cream, marinated vegetables, and many other tempting appetizers. This is followed by specialties such as *quenelles de brochet* (light pike dumplings in a smooth tomato sauce), *tablier de sapeur* (fried tripe), veal kidneys in mustard sauce, or an outstanding rack of lamb with potatoes au gratin. Complete the meal with an assortment of fine regional cheeses, ethereal *oeufs à la neige* (puffs of egg whites floating in vanilla custard), or a seasonally perfect *tartlette aux fraises* (strawberry tart). House wines are served in *pots,* heavy, thick glass bottles that keep the wine cool.

(21) MOUFF' TARTES

53, rue Mouffetard (5th)

When you first arrive, check out the window display of homemade quiches—both savory and sweet—then go in and sit at one of the pink cloth–coverered tables and enjoy a nice Cheap Eat in Paris. A baker's dozen of savory quiches and as many sweet ones comprise the menu along with salads and assorted beverages, including wine and beer. It is a good pit stop if you have hungry children on your hands or need a filling snack on the run. Also, they will pack any order to go. If you order a slice of their signature quiche, the chocolate dessert specialty, and a cup of tea, you will barely be out ten dollars.

TELEPHONE
01-43-37-21-89

MÉTRO
Place Monge

OPEN
Tues–Sun

CLOSED
Mon, NAC

HOURS
11:30 A.M.–midnight, continuous service

RESERVATIONS
Not accepted

CREDIT CARDS
None

À LA CARTE
45–60F, BNC

PRIX FIXE
None

ENGLISH SPOKEN
Yes

MISCELLANEOUS
Everything can be packed to go

(22) PERRAUDIN

157, rue St-Jacques (5th)

For decades, Perraudin has demonstrated the glory of substantial French cooking. Possessing a winning combination for Cheap Eaters, it serves homespun food to a packed audience for both lunch and dinner. In addition, some of the wines are exceptional, the atmosphere is authentic, the prices realistic, and children are welcome! Sitting at one of the little bistro tables, looking at the classic, daily printed menu, and watching the cast of faithfuls positioned around the room, you will soon have the feeling that nothing has changed here for years—and you will be right.

After polishing off weighty servings of smoked herring with warm potato salad or tangy onion *tartes,* well-fed diners tuck into main courses of *confit de canard,* poached salmon, grilled steaks, and popular daily specials. They top it all off with a slice of the irresistible fruit *tartes,* a *clafoutis maison* (fruit cooked in a pancakelike batter), or a wedge of Camembert cheese. Wine can be anything from a glass or pitcher of the house variety to a little-known regional *cru* seldom seen in Paris. Owner Hubert Gloaguen (who also owns Le Bistrot d'André, see page 193) and his sister, Marie-Christine Kvella, who manages Perraudin, are proud of their wine *cave* and its wide-ranging, undiscovered selections in all price ranges.

TELEPHONE
01-46-33-15-75

MÉTRO
Luxembourg

OPEN
Tues–Sat lunch and dinner, Mon dinner only

CLOSED
Mon lunch, Sun, last 15 days in Aug

HOURS
Lunch noon–2:30 P.M., dinner 7:30–10 P.M.

RESERVATIONS
Not accepted

CREDIT CARDS
None

À LA CARTE
125F, BNC

PRIX FIXE
Lunch only, 65F, 3 courses, BNC

ENGLISH SPOKEN
Yes, with English menu

(23) RESTAURANT L'ÉPOQUE
81, rue du Cardinal-Lemoine (5th)

TELEPHONE
01-46-34-15-84

MÉTRO
Cardinal-Lemoine

OPEN
Mon–Sat

CLOSED
Sun, major holidays, 1st week in May

HOURS
Lunch noon–2:30 P.M., dinner 6–11 P.M.

RESERVATIONS
Recommended on weekends

CREDIT CARDS
MC, V (over 100F)

À LA CARTE
150F, BNC

PRIX FIXE
Lunch and dinner, 75F and 118F, 3 courses, 170F, 4 courses, all BNC

ENGLISH SPOKEN
Yes

L'Époque is a reliable choice just far enough from the hype along the rue Mouffetard to escape the endless line of touristy restaurants reaching out for your wallet with loud music, gaudy fake decor, windows full of sizzling meats, and sweaty chefs serving poor fare. L'Époque is where the residents of this quarter eat, and when you are here, you should do the same. This is a Cheap Eat in Paris that doesn't put on airs. The small room's wooden bistro tables are topped with straw placemats and paper napkins. The customer profile shifts with the hour: at lunch it is workers and shopkeepers, and at night, students, couples, and just plain folks. All come for chef Ben's satisfying French cuisine.

All pocketbooks are accommodated with three well-constructed prix fixe menus. Á la carte is also available, but it's not the good value meal here. Depending on your budget and taste, start with a simple leek quiche, onion soup, or herring served with warm potatoes. Big spenders can order fois gras served with a glass of Sauterne or smoked Norwegian salmon to start, followed by a taste of lemon sorbet to cleanse the palate. The *plats* for all menus are meat based, with fresh fish costarring. Desserts are good adaptations of the usual chocolate mousse, *tartes,* floating island, and sorbets.

Sixth Arrondissement

(See map on pages 88–89.)

The sixth is a continuation of the Latin Quarter, but *plus chic.* Running from the Seine to the busy boulevard du Montparnasse, the sixth is symbolized by the trendy yet scholarly neighborhood around the church of St-Germain-des-Prés, the oldest church in Paris. The emphasis is on art galleries, antiques, fashion boutiques, and restaurants in all categories. Café society in Paris has always been epitomized by two famous cafés here: Café des Duex Magots and Café de Flore. In their glory, they were the prime haunts of the existentialists of the post-war years. While their original lustre has dimmed, they are still crowded day and night and offer some of the best people-watching in Paris.

LEFT BANK
École des Beaux-Arts, Luxembourg Gardens, Odéon National Theater, Place St-Michel, St-Germain-des-Prés Church (the oldest in Paris), St-Sulpice (murals by Delacroix)

SIXTH ARRONDISSEMENT RESTAURANTS

* Restaurants marked with an asterisk (*) are considered Big Splurges.

(24) À LA COUR DE ROHAN
59–61, rue St-André-des-Arts (enter through Cour du Commerce St-André) (6th)

TELEPHONE
01-43-25-79-67
MÉTRO
St-Michel, Odéon
OPEN
Daily for lunch and tea; June–Aug Fri–Sun for dinner also
CLOSED
Dinner daily Sept–May, Mon–Thur June–Aug; major holidays, July15–Aug 15
HOURS
Lunch and brunch noon–3 P.M., tea 3–7 P.M.; Fri–Sun (June–Aug), noon to 10 P.M., continuous service
RESERVATIONS
Advised for weekends and dinner
CREDIT CARDS
MC, V
À LA CARTE
75–125F, BC
PRIX FIXE
Sat–Sun brunch, 100F, 150F, and 170F, BC
ENGLISH SPOKEN
Limited
MISCELLANEOUS
No smoking allowed

Situated in an eighteenth-century *passage* that runs between boulevard St-Germain and rue St-André-des-Arts, À la Cour de Rohan is a cozy tearoom that's become a Left Bank fixture; it's the place to go with a friend for an intimate afternoon of gossip or romance surrounded by soft, classical music. The downstairs room overlooking the *passage* is crowded with tables and a big hutch displaying high-calorie temptations. For a cozier experience, I prefer to sit upstairs, where the frilly chintz curtains, well-worn English furniture, and aromas of tea remind me of a maiden auntie's British parlor.

Beautiful salads, pastas, creamy egg dishes, house specialties of ratatouille or *gratins,* and a host of homemade pastries are served on an eclectic mixture of flowered china. Twenty or more varieties of tea are poured from pretty China teapots into delicate teacups. Nothing quite matches, but that is part of the charm.

NOTE: Smoking is prohibited.

(25) AU PETIT PRINCE
3, rue Monsieur-le-Prince (6th)

TELEPHONE
01-43-29-74-92
MÉTRO
Odéon
OPEN
Tues–Sat lunch and dinner, Mon dinner only
CLOSED
Mon lunch, Sun, holidays, Aug
HOURS
Lunch noon–2 P.M., dinner 7:30–11 P.M.
RESERVATIONS
Advised

According to my mail, this is one of the most popular Left Bank listings in *Cheap Eats in Paris.* The tiny, two-level, very Parisian restaurant is decorated in an aviation motif with airplane posters and pictures from St-Exupery's novel *The Little Prince.* The clientele is a predominantly young crowd of businesspeople at lunch and a still young but casually attired group for dinner. Hardworking owner Pascal Seray, the very attentive host, is always on board, running the dining room and making sure every guest is pleased.

Both the lunch and dinner prix fixe menus change daily and feature whatever catches the chef's fancy that day at the market. The selections are limited but always imaginatively executed and well presented. The à la carte offers a wider variety of seasonal dishes that display the same creativity shown on the daily changing menus. On the à la carte side, I like to start with *salade du Petit Prince,* made with fresh and smoked salmon and haddock on a bed of greens and garnished with avocado. *Sole meunière* or the duck confit with sautéed potatoes are sure main course selections, and the mango mousse or oranges soaked in Grand Marnier are refreshing endings. Coffee comes with a plate of tiny cookies . . . the perfect ending to the kind of meal we all hope to find in Paris.

CREDIT CARDS
MC, V

À LA CARTE
185–200F, BNC

PRIX FIXE
Lunch, 110F, 2 courses, BC; dinner, 139F, 3 courses, BNC

ENGLISH SPOKEN
Yes

(26) AU SAVOYARD
16, rue des Quatre-Vents (6th)

Au Savoyard is a good place to arrive with an appetite since the food has a sturdy Savoie pedigree. Wall displays of antique plates, copper pots, and stuffed game hens enhance the rustic atmosphere of this representative of one of France's mountainous regions. The honorable cooking is hardly elaborate, but it is generous and very filling. You can expect huge portions of specialties such as *salade savoyard,* featuring ham, cheese, tomatoes, onions, and peppers; beef and cheese fondues; *racelette; tartiflette*, a rich cheese and potato combination; and *pierrade de boeuf,* which is beef cooked at your table on a hot stone without fat or oil. The *tarte Tatin flambée* or the light lemon mousse are the best desserts. Round out the meal with a bottle of wine from Savoie.

TELEPHONE
01-43-26-20-30

MÉTRO
Odéon

OPEN
Daily

CLOSED
A few days around Christmas, Aug

HOURS
Lunch noon–2 P.M., dinner 7–11 P.M.

RESERVATIONS
Advised

CREDIT CARDS
MC, V

À LA CARTE
150–200F, BNC

PRIX FIXE
Lunch only, 75F, 2 courses, BNC; lunch and dinner, 110F and 145F, 3 courses, both BNC

ENGLISH SPOKEN
Yes

(27) AUX CHARPENTIERS
10, rue Mabillon (6th)

Aux Charpentiers—"The Carpenters"—is the type of Parisian bistro I hope will never die, with its zinc bar, wooden floors sprinkled with sawdust, and diners straight out of central casting. The name commemorates the important role of the eighteenth-century journeyman carpenter's and cabinetmaker's guild in the politics and architecture of France. Next door is a small museum that displays scale models created by guild members in preparation for the construction of the spires and roofs of

TELEPHONE
01-43-26-30-05

MÉTRO
Mabillon

OPEN
Daily

CLOSED
Never, NAC

HOURS
Lunch noon–3 P.M., dinner 7–11:30 P.M.

RESERVATIONS
Advised
CREDIT CARDS
AE, DC, MC, V
À LA CARTE
160–180F, BNC
PRIX FIXE
Lunch only, 125F, 2 courses, BC; lunch and dinner, 155F, 3 courses, BNC
ENGLISH SPOKEN
Yes

such famous landmarks as Notre-Dame and Ste-Chapelle.

The solid, stick-to-your-ribs fare includes platters of roast duck and olives, beef fillet cooked with bone marrow, pigs feet, veal kidneys, roast Breton chicken, and blood sausage. If these do not appeal, take advantage of the Monday through Saturday specials: veal Marengo, beef with carrots, salt pork and lentils, *pot-au-feu,* cold whitefish served with a garlic sauce, and stuffed cabbage. While you will not be overwhelmed with delicate or subtle cooking, you will have polished off a typical French meal without spending a fortune.

(28) AUX GOURMETS DES ARTS
15, rue Git-le-Coeur (6th)

TELEPHONE
01-43-26-29-44
MÉTRO
St-Michel, Odéon
OPEN
Daily in summer; Mon–Sat in winter
CLOSED
Sun in winter, NAC
HOURS
Lunch noon–2 P.M., dinner 7–11 P.M.
RESERVATIONS
Not necessary
CREDIT CARDS
MC, V
À LA CARTE
Not available
PRIX FIXE
Lunch only, 75F, 2 courses, BC; lunch and dinner, 80F and 100F, 3 courses, both BNC; dinner only, 120F, 3 courses, BNC
ENGLISH SPOKEN
Yes

Put this one on your list for inexpensive, basic food served in nondiet portions when you have meat eating on your mind. The location is in a touristy corner dog-eared with tacky restaurants whose menus are in four or five languages in hopes of snagging one-time diners from the competition next door. The food at Aux Gourmets des Arts is better than most in the vicinity and served in more attractive surroundings. The beamed dining room has the requisite wainscoated, white stuccoed walls, linens and candles at night, and semi-comfortable padded seats you will encounter in many such places in Paris. The service by the owner's wife is attentive and eager to please. She brings the food on time, changes the silver when necessary, and crumbs the table between your main course and dessert.

When consulting the menu, don't pause by the wierd zodiac cocktails . . . better to get a big *pichet* of the house red or white wine to sip throughout your meal. The prix fixe menus are good Cheap Eating, especially when you can have smoked salmon blini, *confit de canard,* or *boeuf sauce cocotte* (beef in a red wine sauce flavored with chunky bacon, onions, and mushrooms), and your choice of any dessert for under 100F. Spring for the top price and you will be eating salads with smoked duck and foie gras, tournedos of beef with morille mushrooms, shrimps flambéed in whiskey, or *coquilles St-Jacques à la provençal* (scallops in a spicy tomato sauce).

(29) CHEZ CLAUDE SAINLOUIS
27, rue du Dragon (6th)

With a set formula he has followed for more than thirty-five years, Claude Sainlouis promises no surprises, just good food and plenty of it. For around twenty-five dollars you will get a three-course dinner that includes salad, a bottle of house wine, a bowl of dark chocolate mousse, an ending espresso, and only four choices for your main dish: grilled salmon or steak, lamb chops with thyme, or steak *tartare maison,* all garnished with hot potato puffs or spinach.

That's it: good, dependable, well-cooked food. It's served by red-shirted waiters in a congenial room accented with bright red linen tablecloths and napkins, and you'll be joined by scores of hungry French diners enjoying yet another well-priced meal.

TELEPHONE
01-45-48-29-68

MÉTRO
St-Germain-des-Prés

OPEN
Mon–Fri lunch and dinner, Sat lunch only

CLOSED
Sat dinner, Sun, holidays, 15 days at Easter and Christmas, all school vacations, Aug

HOURS
Lunch 12:30–2 P.M., dinner 8–11 P.M.

RESERVATIONS
Advised

CREDIT CARDS
None

À LA CARTE
None

PRIX FIXE
Lunch and dinner: 125F, 3 courses, BNC; 165F, 3 courses, BC

ENGLISH SPOKEN
No

(30) CHEZ ENZO
12, rue du Dragon (6th)

Somehow this one has slipped by the other guidebooks, probably because it is buried in a sea of Left Bank gastronomic tourist traps. In all honesty, the inside of Chez Enzo looks "touristy," especially the streetside dining room set with bright orange table linens that clash with the dated, maroon velvet chair and banquette coverings. Even though smoking is allowed, and it is windowless, the intimate room downstairs with a painted, arched ceiling is more appealing. At the foot of the stairs is a table filled with the cold antipasti that should whet your appetite for the Italian meal ahead. Professional service by jacketed waiters is attentive.

The pastas are rich and filling, never overpowered by heavy red sauces and gooey creams. All the required regulars we know and love make appearances: pasta with pesto, shrimp and garlic, lasagna, rigatoni, tortelloni, and eggplant Parmesan. Veal is the meat headliner, prepared with herbs, cheese, lemon, or tomatoes. All main courses are garnished with zucchini or pasta, or both if you can handle it all. Tiramisu and the chef's special hot apple *tarte* are the best dessert considerations. Inexpensive pitchers of Italian wine will complement any order.

TELEPHONE
01-42-22-84-87

MÉTRO
St-Germain-des-Prés

OPEN
Mon–Sat

CLOSED
Sun, NAC

HOURS
Lunch noon–2:30 P.M., dinner 7–11 P.M.

RESERVATIONS
Advised for dinner

CREDIT CARDS
AE, MC, V

À LA CARTE
125–150F, BNC

PRIX FIXE
Not available

ENGLISH SPOKEN
Limited

(31) CHEZ MÂITRE PAUL*

12, rue Monsieur-le-Prince (6th)

TELEPHONE
01-43-54-74-59
MÉTRO
Odéon, Luxembourg
OPEN
Daily in winter; Mon–Sat in summer
CLOSED
Sun in summer, May 1, Dec 25, Jan 1, NAC
HOURS
Lunch noon–2:30 P.M., dinner 7–10:30 P.M.
RESERVATIONS
Advised
CREDIT CARDS
AE, DC, MC, V
À LA CARTE
200–225F, BNC
PRIX FIXE
Lunch and dinner: 155F, 3 courses, BNC; 190F, 3 courses, BC
ENGLISH SPOKEN
Yes

Upscale patrons continue to fill this refined, comfortable restaurant presided over by Jean François Debert. The nicely spaced tables are formally set with starched linens, fresh flowers, and sparkling crystal in a soft gray room with subdued lighting and attractive artwork on the walls.

The decidedly rich, full-flavored cuisine features specialties from the France–Comté region in eastern France. Among the *entrées* you will find a *terrine maison* made with chicken livers, a plate of garlicky sausages served warm with tiny potatoes, and in the spring, fat white asparagus in warm vinaigrette. A main course must is the *poulet au vin jaune*—tender chicken in tomato, mushroom, and wine sauce. Two other award-winning chicken dishes are the *poulet sauté au vin blanc* and the *poulette à la crème gratinée* (chicken in a cream and cheese sauce). Most of the other main course dishes are served with Jura wine sauces that are perfect for mopping up with crusty baguettes. If you can still think about dessert, the crème brûlée is definitely worthwhile, and the local cheeses are interesting.

(32) CHEZ MARCEL

7, rue Stanislas (6th)

TELEPHONE
01-45-48-29-94
MÉTRO
Notre-Dame-des-Champs, Vavin
OPEN
Mon–Fri
CLOSED
Sat–Sun, holidays, NAC
HOURS
Lunch noon–2 P.M., dinner 7:30–10:30 P.M.
RESERVATIONS
Preferred
CREDIT CARDS
MC, V
À LA CARTE
190F, BNC
PRIX FIXE
Lunch only, 80F, 2 courses, BNC
ENGLISH SPOKEN
Yes

In this area of Paris, where you are likely to see more baseball caps than berets, it is hard to find an authentic neighborhood restaurant. Chez Marcel is just that—a local pick, nothing fancy or worth a taxi ride across town, but definitely worth consideration if you are nearby. It is a reliable place, the sort we all go to when we don't feel like cooking. The place could double as a set on the back lot of a Hollywood film studio: old walls hung with curling posters, two original 1936 chandeliers, an antique buffet displaying desserts, fresh flowers in a pretty vase, a table or two on the sidewalk, and a gentle owner who knows his customers by name.

The Lyonnaise food is served à la carte for lunch and dinner, and there is a bargain lunch *formule.* The food choices run from A to almost Z, beginning with artichokes vinaigrette, escargots, and pâtés to Lyonnaise sausages, lamb, beef, and veal. The *tarte au chocolate* is my dessert of choice, though a scoop or two of Berthillon ice cream is never bad, and it's the only dessert not made here.

(33) COSI

54, rue de Seine (6th)

Cosi is a chi-chi gourmet sandwich shop just off rue de Buci. Put together a delicious, hot, made-to-order-while-you-watch sandwich on warm bread, a glass of good wine, and classical opera music and you have Cosi, a new fast-food concept in Paris that has caught on big-time, keeping the little spot continually busy and crowded. The idea was developed by a New Zealander who made violins in Italy, learned how to make bread there, then moved to Paris, adapted the recipe, and voila! It's Cosi. The colorful and tasty sandwiches are made with foccacia-style bread, cooked as you watch in a wood-fired oven, then filled while still hot with an ingenious combination of tasty ingredients. You pay according to the ingredients you select, which could be anything from chèvre and cucumbers to roasted egg-plant, guacamole, tomatoes, salmon, chili, cole slaw, vinaigrette, tuna, or roast beef. Your order is placed on a tray that *you* carry to an attractive upstairs dining room, where you eat surrounded by photos of famous opera stars and listening to their famous arias. In addition to the marvelous sandwiches, there are salads served with bread on the side and desserts made with a thousand calories of butter and sugar . . . especially the chocolate treachery, otherwise known as chocolate cake. Slightly less sinful is the Italian gelato.

NOTE: Everything on the menu can be taken out.

TELEPHONE
01-46-33-35-36

MÉTRO
Odéon

OPEN
Daily

CLOSED
Dec 24–Jan 2, NAC

HOURS
Noon–midnight, continuous service

RESERVATIONS
Not taken

CREDIT CARDS
None

À LA CARTE
Sandwiches from 35–50F, desserts 25–30F, BNC

PRIX FIXE
None

ENGLISH SPOKEN
Yes

(34) GUENMAÏ

6, rue Cardinale (6th)

"What are all these fashion models, actors, and other attractive people doing milling around outside with plates of food in their hands?" I wondered the first time I strolled by this natural foods restaurant/shop. When I could get close enough to look in, I could see others sitting on tiny stools balancing plates on their knees, and still more standing behind the shop counter and sitting on the stairway. I knew that Guenmaï had to be offering something very good to attract such a crowd in a neighborhood known for having every type of restaurant imaginable. When I was finally served, my lunch was not only delicious and filling, it was reasonable. No one stands on ceremony here, and service can be distracted during the noon mob scene. The owner, Sophie Daniac, lives upstairs, and if you need to use the bathroom, she

TELEPHONE
01-43-26-03-24

MÉTRO
St-Germain-des-Prés

OPEN
Mon–Sat lunch only

CLOSED
Sun, holidays, Aug

HOURS
Shop 9 A.M.–8:30 P.M., restaurant 11:45 am.–3:30 P.M.

RESERVATIONS
Not accepted

CREDIT CARDS
V

À LA CARTE
65–95F, BNC

PRIX FIXE
None
ENGLISH SPOKEN
Yes

will tell you to use hers, which is up a wooden staircase and off a tiny landing.

The food leans toward the macrobiotic and uses no butter, sugar, milk, or eggs. Limited amounts of fish are served. The entirely à la carte menu features such creations as vegetable spring rolls, croquettes, *tartes*, and *plats du jour* based around grains, tofu, and seaweed. There are also a nice array of freshly squeezed juices, *biologique* (organic) wines, and nonalcoholic beers. For the best selection and variety, because they do run out, arrive before the hungry herd . . . by noon at the latest.

(35) J. C. GAULUPEAU-PÂTISSIER
12, rue Mabillon (6th)

TELEPHONE
01-43-54-16-93
MÉTRO
Mabillon
OPEN
Tues–Sun
CLOSED
Mon, major holidays, Aug (dates vary)
HOURS
7 A.M.–8 P.M., continuous service
RESERVATIONS
Not accepted
CREDIT CARDS
None
À LA CARTE
10–50F, BNC
PRIX FIXE
None
ENGLISH SPOKEN
Limited

The customers at this bright corner *pâtisserie* range from locals dashing in when the doors open for a takeout order of croissants to businesspeople munching a sandwich at lunch and tourists Aunt Alice and Uncle Ralph from Detroit. It's a good address for everyone to remember anytime a sweet bite is in order. If you decide to eat here (which costs an extra 2F), this is the drill: place your order at the counter, pay for it, then sit down and wait until it is brought to you. In the early morning, you may have to wait a few minutes until the second batch of buttery *pain aux raisins* comes out of the oven, but you can sip an orange juice or a bracing *café au lait* while you do. You will soon be served by one of the polite ladies—they seem to know everyone and dote on them all.

(36) LA BASTIDE ODÉON
7, rue Corneille (off place de l'Odéon) (6th)

TELEPHONE
01-43-26-03-65
MÉTRO
Odéon, RER Luxembourg
OPEN
Tues–Sat
CLOSED
Sun–Mon, holidays, July or Aug (call to check)
HOURS
Lunch 12:30–2 P.M., dinner 7:30–11 P.M.
RESERVATIONS
Essential as far in advance as possible

People always ask me about my favorite new restaurants in Paris. I have several, and La Bastide Odéon is definitely one, where a table puts you in the middle of one of Paris' most talked about culinary successes. For best effect, avoid the 7:30 P.M. tourist seating and arrive around 9 P.M. with the well-dressed French.

The Provençal cooking from chef Gilles Ajuelos, whose credentials include working under Michel Rostang, is authentic, interesting, and delicious . . . and there are very few misses. In fact, you could point blindly to anything on the menu and be pleased. I like to start with the *millefeuille tiede aux aubergines grillées* (a warm, flaky, basil-flavored pastry starring grilled eggplant, tomato, and cheese) or the carmelized endive stuffed with goat cheese. The tagliatelle with pistou and wild mushrooms is a vegetarian dream. Ajuelos's deft hand also shines in the peppered tuna with ratatouille and in the lamb, pork, and beef dishes he beautifully prepares with the seasonings and flavors of Provence. The magic continues with his desserts. If you love chocolate, you must have the dense chocolate slice, covered in ice cream and coffee sauce. It sounds rather simple, but let me tell you it is one of the best desserts I can imagine. Other favorites are the warm carmelized banana madeleine and the almond *tarte* with Armagnac ice cream.

CREDIT CARDS
MC, V

À LA CARTE
Not available

PRIX FIXE
Lunch and dinner, 139F, 2 courses, 180F, 3 courses, both BNC

ENGLISH SPOKEN
Yes

(37) LA BOULE MICHE
19, rue Dragon (6th)

After you have been in Paris for a day or so, you will realize it is almost impossible to walk more than a block without passing one or two *boulangeries* or *pâtisseries*. What is amazing is how they all manage to thrive, given the intense competition. It is clear that La Boule Miche has the formula for success down pat because since 1788 there has been a bakery at this address, and for the last forty-five years it has been run by one *very* hardworking lady, who wears some of the most uncomfortable-looking shoes imaginable. My Paris flat was located around the corner from the bakery, so I had an opportunity to get to know it well. All day long the owner and her helpers serve a constant stream of customers eager for their delicious breads. From Tuesday to Saturday a special type is featured in addition to a dozen or more of the regular varieties. Bulk bread orders are also handled. Each morning one of the flour-dusted young bakers loads warm baguettes into the bicycle-wagon parked in front and pedals off to make his delivery rounds. It looks like something right out of *Oliver Twist*!

You can either take your purchase with you or eat here, nabbing one of the two mushroom-shaped black-covered perches along the mirror-backed brass bar or sitting on one of the nursery-school-sized backless stools poised around two or three little tables, which spill onto the sidewalk in every type of weather except a driving rainstorm. There is a lunch special of a sandwich, pastry, and coffee that is a Cheap Eat steal, as well as unusual sweet treats—all made here, of course—filling the front window.

TELEPHONE
01-42-22-77-12

MÉTRO
St-Germain-des-Prés

OPEN
Mon–Sat

CLOSED
Sun, major holidays, 15 days in Aug

HOURS
7:30 A.M.–8 P.M., continuous service

RESERVATIONS
Not accepted

CREDIT CARDS
None

À LA CARTE
20–45F, BC

PRIX FIXE
Lunch only, 35F, sandwich, pastry, and coffee

ENGLISH SPOKEN
No

(38) LA LOZÈRE
4, rue Hautefeuille (6th)

TELEPHONE
01-43-54-26-64
MÉTRO
St-Michel
OPEN
Tues–Sat
CLOSED
Sun–Mon, holidays, Christmas week, Aug (dates vary)
HOURS
Lunch noon–2 P.M., dinner 7:30–10:30 P.M.
RESERVATIONS
Advised, but essential on Thursday night
CREDIT CARDS
MC, V
À LA CARTE
100–145F
PRIX FIXE
Lunch only, 95F, 3 courses, BC; lunch and dinner, 125F and 155F, 4 courses, both BNC
ENGLISH SPOKEN
Some

The menu is short, highlighting the cuisine from the rugged Lozère region in central France. Sitting at a wooden table in extremely close proximity to your neighbor, you will sample popular country hams, sausages, cheeses, omelettes, and bracing regional specialties. When you are seated, a huge loaf of dark country bread is brought to your table for you to slice as much as you can eat. Go easy, there is much more to come . . . such as *tripoux Lozère* (mutton tripe cooked with white wine and tomatoes) or *La Maoucho* (a soul-food dish of cabbage and sausage baked with potatoes). On Thursday nights, a line forms for La Lozère's potato specialty, *l'aligot,* a dish of creamy mashed potatoes mixed with melted Cantal cheese and flavored with garlic. It makes heaven out of any meal it accompanies. At Thursday lunch, you can order it ahead if you are having one of the prix fixe menus, though for lunch there is a two-person minimum. Reservations are essential for Thursday night and strongly recommended other times.

The restaurant doubles as a tourist bureau for the Lozère region and operates a boutique across the street selling handmade arts and crafts, preserves, and other gift items.

(39) LA MARLOTTE*
55, rue du Cherche-Midi (6th)

TELEPHONE
01-54-48-86-79
MÉTRO
St-Placide, Sèvres-Babylone
OPEN
Mon–Fri
CLOSED
Sat–Sun, holidays, Aug
HOURS
Lunch noon–2:30 P.M., dinner 8–11 P.M.
RESERVATIONS
Essential
CREDIT CARDS
AE, MC, V
À LA CARTE
185–250F, BNC
PRIX FIXE
None
ENGLISH SPOKEN
Yes

Dining at La Marlotte is a truly pleasurable experience. The restaurant is owned by Lucie Agaud and her husband, Michel Bouvier. They also own two of my favorite hotels in Paris—Hôtel le Saint-Grégoire, not far from La Marlotte, and Hôtel le Tourville, a four-star in the seventh arrondissement (see *Cheap Sleeps in Paris*)—so it is no surprise that their restaurant is equally as chic and sophisticated. The setting, especially at night with its subdued lighting, pretty provincial paintings, candles, and beautifully arranged vases of fresh flowers, is elegantly romantic and quietly discreet. The stylishly dressed guests have every table filled by 9 P.M., making reservations mandatory as far in advance as possible.

The cooking is the best kind: generous, fresh, and resolutely traditional. Regulars come back often for the time-honored renditions of lentil salad with shallots, *terrine de campagne maison,* and in spring, fat white asparagus dressed in a light vinaigrette. Pink lamb with perfectly roasted potatoes, tender rabbit with tarragon, and an out-of-this-world lemon tart that positively melts in your mouth are other all-time favorites. The small but very adequate wine list includes Bordeaux, Bourgogne, Beaujolais, and Loire Valley vintages. Lunch or dinner at La Marlotte is a Big Splurge . . . but then so is going to Paris. I recommend them both.

(40) LE BISTRO D'HENRI

16, rue Princesse (6th)

If you like Le Machon d'Henri, listed on page 115, chances are excellent you will add Jean-Luc Rouliere's second restaurant, just around the corner, to your preferred list of Cheap Eats in Paris. The dining room, with its black-and-white tiled floor, offers slightly more comfortable leatherette banquette seating, and the open kitchen gives it a larger feeling. The same type of bistro fare is featured, with daily changing *entrées* and *plats du jour.* There is a formula of sorts for both lunch and dinner, with all the starters, main courses, and desserts identically priced. While neither place is a temple of gastronomic art, both provide a Parisian dining experience that includes friendly waiters and many satisfied guests.

TELEPHONE
01-46-33-51-12
MÉTRO
Mabillon
OPEN
Mon–Sat
CLOSED
Sun, Christmas, New Year's Day, NAC
HOURS
Lunch noon–2:30 P.M., dinner 7:30–11:30 P.M.
RESERVATIONS
Advised
CREDIT CARDS
None
À LA CARTE
150F, BNC
PRIX FIXE
None
ENGLISH SPOKEN
Yes

(41) L'ÉCAILLE DE P.C.B.*

5, rue Mabillon (6th)

Pierre and Colette Bardèche, who own Aux Charpentiers down the street (see page 105), also own this wonderful fish restaurant. Here you might rub elbows with L'Écaille's rich-and-famous regulars, including actress Catherine Deneuve among many others. They eat here because M. Bardèche is a genius when it comes to cooking fish, and they are assured of an impeccable meal, simply but expertly prepared and served.

All the fish is fresh daily and cooked to order with the sauces served on the side. The *plats du jour* and the chef's suggestions are only a few of the many fish delicacies that await you. Dieters will be especially pleased with the *menu minceur,* which suggests three courses that add up to no more than six hundred calories in total. For those not watching their waistlines, there is an unusual trout caviar starter served with toast or lightly mixed

TELEPHONE
01-43-26-73-70
MÉTRO
Mabillon
OPEN
Mon–Fri lunch and dinner, Sat dinner only
CLOSED
Sat lunch, Sun, NAC
HOURS
Lunch noon–3 P.M., dinner 7–11 P.M.
RESERVATIONS
Essential
CREDIT CARDS
AE, DC, MC, V
À LA CARTE
290–350F, BNC

PRIX FIXE
Lunch and dinner: *menu minceur,* 225F, 3 courses, BNC; *menu affaire,* 195F, 3 courses, BNC

ENGLISH SPOKEN
Yes, with English menu

with tagliatelle. Worthy main dish options include delicious rotisserie cooked turbot, *loup* (bass), and *Saint Pierre* (John Dory). *Osso buco de lotte a l'orientale* (lobster prepared three ways) and wild salmon are others just at the tip of the iceberg. A few red meat dishes are on the menu, but frankly they are out of place. Fish is the brilliant star of the show here. Prices are definitely in the Big Splurge category, but dining at L'Écaille is a real treat for fish lovers.

(42) LE CAMÉLÉON
6, rue de Chevreuse (6th)

TELEPHONE
01-43-20-63-43

MÉTRO
Vavin

OPEN
Mon–Fri lunch and dinner, Sat dinner only

CLOSED
Sat lunch, Sun, holidays, 15 days in Aug

HOURS
Lunch noon–2 P.M., dinner 8–10:30 P.M.

RESERVATIONS
Essential

CREDIT CARDS
AE, MC, V

À LA CARTE
175–185F, BNC

PRIX FIXE
Lunch only, 120F, 2 courses, BC

ENGLISH SPOKEN
Yes

Le Caméléon is still the best kind of Parisian bistro: always noisy and packed, with all kinds of wonderful-smelling platters parading past your nose as they are borne by fast-moving waiters. Another sure sign of quality is the mixed crowd: businesspeople next to rosy-cheeked elderly husbands and wives next to young couples busy falling in love. Everyone sits along banquettes or at marble-topped tables in the center of the room, digging into steaming plates of hearty, flavorful food.

The menu changes two or three times a year, but you can always count on *courgettes marinées au citron* (raw, grated zucchini in lemon marinade), a superb *salade de haricots verts et foie gras,* and rich lobster-filled ravioli. For the main course, the veal with noodles is my favorite. During the winter the *confit de canard* (preserved duck) and braised beef cheeks in a red wine sauce with onions are dishes the faithful adore. For dessert anytime of year, you *must* try the *fondant au poires,* a pear cake/tart made from a classic recipe. When it is served, the enormous slice will seem too big to finish, but finish it you will and wish you had room for more.

(43) L'ÉCLUSE GRANDS-AUGUSTINS
15, quai des Grands-Augustins (6th)

TELEPHONE
01-46-33-58-74

MÉTRO
St-Michel

OPEN
Daily

CLOSED
December 24–25, NAC

HOURS
Noon–1:30 A.M., continuous service

L'Écluse was a trailblazer in popularizing wine bars in Paris, and it is still one of the best and most popular. Offering wines by the glass or the bottle, these trendy spots cater to those seeking food, wine, and uncomplicated meals served in agreeable surrounding by a low-key waitstaff. The final bill will depend on the modesty or the majesty of the vintages you consume and, of course, how much food you order.

Specializing in Bordeaux wines, all L'Écluse locations have the same menu, but each wine bar features a different type of Bordeaux wine. The up-market clientele drops by from noon until the wee hours to sample wines ranging from 25F for a simple glass to over 250F for a bottle of a *grand cru*. The food is selected to go well with the varieties of Bordeaux wine served. Featured are house terrines, *rillettes,* foie gras, beef tartare, grilled meats, assorted cheeses, a hot plate of the day, and their famous diet-destroying chocolate cake.

RESERVATIONS
Not accepted

CREDIT CARDS
AE, DC, MC, V

À LA CARTE
80–150F, BNC

PRIX FIXE
None

ENGLISH SPOKEN
Enough

(44) LE MACHON D'HENRI
8, rue Guisarde (6th)

Jean-Luc Rouliere's pocket-sized bistro seats twenty-six people sandwiched around twelve tiny, marble-topped tables. It is the sort of place where an up-to-date clientele comes for a good, honest meal carefully prepared with seasonal ingredients. Jean-Luc is an amazing one-man show: he greets, seats, cooks, serves, jokes, flirts, presents the bill, and then hugs and kisses everyone good-bye.

The menu is written in very tiny lettering on a blackboard. The main courses are filling, so start with the fresh green beans or beets tossed in vinaigrette. If you like liver, it is required ordering here. Cooked to pink perfection, it is served with grilled onions and creamy potatoes. Another good selection is the rich beef stew with carrots. The lamb chops can be avoided with ease. Chocolate fans will relish every bite of the chocolate cake, and traditionalists will love the lemon *tarte.* Good wines of the month are reasonably priced.

NOTE: Le Bistro d'Henri, around the corner at 16, rue Princesse, is also owned and operated by Jean-Luc Rouliere (see page 113).

TELEPHONE
01-43-29-08-70

MÉTRO
Mabillon

OPEN
Daily

CLOSED
Christmas, New Year's Day, NAC

HOURS
Lunch noon–2:30 P.M., dinner 7–11:30 P.M.

RESERVATIONS
Essential

CREDIT CARDS
None

À LA CARTE
170F, BNC

PRIX FIXE
None

ENGLISH SPOKEN
Yes

(45) LE PETIT BISTRO
2-3, rue du Sabot (6th)

No, it's hardly the haute cuisine of your dreams, but the food served at Le Petit Bistro could be encased in a shrine to everyday French cooking. It's a local spot where a cross section of regulars arrive for a filling Cheap Eat at prices that allow many repeat visits . . . almost every night for some.

Bypass the à la carte and go for one of the weekly changing menus, which list almost everything on the à la carte menu anyway. The solid grandmotherly food

TELEPHONE
01-45-48-16-65

MÉTRO
St-Germain-des-Prés, St-Sulpice

OPEN
Mon–Fri lunch and dinner, Sat dinner only

CLOSED
Sat lunch, Sun, holidays, Aug

HOURS
Lunch noon–2:30 P.M., dinner 7–10:30 P.M.

RESERVATIONS
Advised for dinner

CREDIT CARDS
MC, V

À LA CARTE
150–160F, BNC

PRIX FIXE
Lunch and dinner: 65F, 2 courses, BNC; 97F, 3 courses, BC; 175F, 3 courses, BNC

ENGLISH SPOKEN
Yes

starts you off with well-recognized dishes of terrines, warm goat cheese salad, oysters, fish soup, and escargots. Moving along, you will find *sole meunière,* lamb steaks, grilled beef . . . all garnished with *frites* unless you ask for a change of potatoes. If the *omelette Bretagne,* one of the house specialty *plats,* is not listed, ask for it. It is at least a three-egg omelette filled with mushrooms, potatoes, tomatoes, and peppers . . . and coupled with a salad, all you will probably manage. The desserts are not the restaurant's strong suit, especially the glass of four lonely prunes soaking in some sort of liqueur. If you must, go for one of the red fruit *gratins* or the rum raisin ice cream. Drinkable house red or white wines come by the glass and in various sizes of pitchers.

(46) LE PETIT LUXEMBOURG
29, rue de Vaugirard (6th)

TELEPHONE
01-42-22-12-22

MÉTRO
St-Sulpice, St-Placide

OPEN
Mon–Sat

CLOSED
Sun, holidays, one week at Christmas, Aug

HOURS
Lunch 11 A.M.–2 P.M., dinner 7:30–11:30 P.M., bar 10 A.M.–midnight

RESERVATIONS
Recommended, especially for lunch

CREDIT CARDS
MC, V

À LA CARTE
110–150F, BNC

PRIX FIXE
None

ENGLISH SPOKEN
Generally

It is a restaurant, a wine bar, and above all, a typical neighborhood hangout. Michel, the colorful *patron,* banters with the ageless, animated regulars and assorted café lizards lined up at the bar. His wife, Nicole, oversees the dining room while minding everyone's business and serving good wines with homey dishes that have been staples in French kitchens for years. The crunch is really on during the lunch hour, when it assumes its role as the neighborhood rendezvous.

The menu is wide-ranging and tries to cover too many bases. Forget the frills and stick with the specialties of the house: a *tartine* made on roasted *pain Poilâne, poulet Luxembourg* (chicken with rice and vegetables), *confit de canard* (leg and shoulder of duck cooked with potatoes in duck fat and flavored with garlic and parsley), or on Friday, *brandade de morue,* a flavorful dish that is better than it sounds. It's made with salt cod, garlic, and potatoes simmered in hot milk and cream then puréed. There is quite a list of desserts, but only three should catch your attention: a slice of either the rich chocolate or orange cake or the *tarte Tatin,* if it is available.

When you arrive at Le Petit Luxembourg, you may notice a window next door filled with all sorts of gourmet goodies. The shop is never open. You have to ask the owner, who is the restaurant *patron,* to open it for you, which he does with pleasure.

(47) LE PETIT SAINT-BENOÎT
4, rue St-Benoît (6th)

Le Petit Saint-Benoît, owned for decades by M. Gervais, is a marvelous bistro sitting smack in the heart of St-Germain-des-Prés. The interior is vintage Paris: brown walls aged by years of heavy cigarette smoke, brass hat racks, fresh white paper covering red tablecloths, and a big, lazy dog crowding the busiest aisle. Outside, several hotly fought-over sidewalk tables offer ringside seating for the passing parade. Motherly waitresses serve a cross section of intellectuals, B.C.B.G.s (*bon chic bon genre*: French yuppies), artists, and portly French men with young companions. The handwritten, mimeographed daily menu lists low-priced basics that are cooked to a T and served in portions worthy of lumberjacks. Start with a soothing vegetable soup, a plate of crisp radishes and sweet butter, or an avocado vinaigrette, and go on to a nourishing serving of roast chicken and mashed potatoes, *petit salé* (salt pork with cabbage), or cold salmon. Top it all off with a pitcher of the house wine and a bowl of chocolate mousse. Lingering over a *café express,* you will no doubt begin to seriously consider moving to Paris.

TELEPHONE
01-42-60-27-92

MÉTRO
St-Germain-des-Prés

OPEN
Mon–Sat

CLOSED
Sun, NAC

HOURS
Lunch noon–2 P.M., dinner 7–10 P.M.

RESERVATIONS
Not accepted

CREDIT CARDS
None

À LA CARTE
110–125F, BNC

PRIX FIXE
None

ENGLISH SPOKEN
Yes

(48) LE PETIT VATEL
5, rue Lobineau (6th)

Changes have taken place at Le Petit Vatel, and they are all positive. While still not a place to impress your stuffy mother-in-law, it continues to be a good choice for the hard-core Cheap Eater. Everyone sits close together on rush-seated chairs or on stools at tables set with colorful plastics from Ikea. The small room has been cleaned and painted. The large, pink 1914 cookstove that once dominated the restaurant, with the chef presiding over the hot burners, is gone. It was declared a fire hazard and replaced by a beautiful, up-to-the-minute kitchen in the back.

Fortunately, the old stove is the only thing missing; the Cheap Eats are still here. The daily menu includes seasonal soups, homemade terrines, two *plats du jour,* and a vegetarian plate. Always available is the chef's own *pamboli*, toasted wholegrain bread spread with olive oil, tomatoes, and ham and covered with a mound of cheese. It is a meal in itself and costs around 35F. For dessert there is a choice of chocolate cake, fruit, ice cream, or cheese.

TELEPHONE
01-43-54-28-49

MÉTRO
Mabillon, Odéon

OPEN
Mon–Sat

CLOSED
Sun, holidays, Aug (dates vary)

HOURS
Lunch noon–3 P.M., dinner 7 P.M.–midnight

RESERVATIONS
Not necessary

CREDIT CARDS
MC, V

À LA CARTE
110–115F, BNC

PRIX FIXE
Lunch only, 75F, 2 courses, BC

ENGLISH SPOKEN
Yes

MISCELLANEOUS
A kir will be offered to readers who show a copy of this book.

(49) MARIAGE FRÈRES
13, rue des Grands-Augustins (6th)

See Mariage Frères page 83. All other information is the same.

TELEPHONE: 01-40-51-82-50
MÉTRO: St-Michel

(50) MARIE-THÉ
102, rue du Cherche-Midi (6th)

TELEPHONE
01-42-22-50-40
MÉTRO
Sèvres-Babylone
OPEN
Daily
CLOSED
Major holidays, NAC
HOURS
9 A.M.–7 P.M., continuous service
RESERVATIONS
Recommended for lunch
CREDIT CARDS
AE, MC, V
À LA CARTE
45–80F, BC
PRIX FIXE
Four breakfast menus, 45–95F, BC
ENGLISH SPOKEN
Yes

Every Parisian neighborhood has its share of tearooms, those gentle places that nourish the body and soothe the soul, providing a peaceful place to while away an hour or two over a quiet meal or a pot of tea and dessert. This one will charm you with its fanciful collection of teapots displayed around the room, which has ceiling fans to diffuse the smoke and good lighting to promote reading.

The menu changes four times a year and always features omelettes with different fillings, seasonal salads, quiches, and cheese-, tomato-, or ham-topped *tartines* on *pain Poilâne.* There are four breakfast menus, starting with a simple serving of coffee or juice and a pastry and ending with a brunch of pancakes, scrambled eggs, toast with jam or honey, dessert, and coffee, tea, chocolate, or orange juice. Lunch is served all afternoon, and so are over thirty varieties of tea, which you can sip with a slice of chocolate cake, a fresh fruit *tarte,* or a plate of scones with butter and jam.

(51) MILLESIMES
7, rue Lobineau (6th)

TELEPHONE
01-46-34-22-15
MÉTRO
Mabillon, Odéon
OPEN
Tues–Sun
CLOSED
Mon, mid-Dec to end of Feb
HOURS
Lunch noon–3 P.M., dinner 7 P.M.–1 A.M.
RESERVATIONS
Suggested on weekends
CREDIT CARDS
MC, V
À LA CARTE
60–110F, BNC
PRIX FIXE
Lunch and dinner, 98F, 2 courses, BNC

If you are looking for something friendly, stop by this welcoming wine bar/restaurant located across the street from the glitzy Marché St-Germain, an indoor shopping mall that replaced the old covered *marché.* The kitchen is squeezed into a corner behind the bar, and it consists of an oven, two hot plates, and a toaster—but it's been turning out meals its loyalists have loved for years. Owners Max Braud and his British wife, Diana, are the host and hostess, chief cooks and bottle washers, and servers. Their wine cellar offers a selection of wines from all the wine-producing areas of France. In addition to a regular menu with omelettes, salads, *charcuterie* and cheese plates, and *tartines* made with *pain Poilâne,* there is a three-course lunch and dinner menu, plus their own desserts . . . the best of which is either the apple crumble or the chocolate cake—I still can't decide.

ENGLISH SPOKEN
Yes

(52) RESTAURANT DES BEAUX ARTS
11, rue Bonaparte (6th)

If you want to know what student life used to be like in Paris, eat at Restaurant des Beaux Arts, one of the most famous student canteens, both then and now. The dining rooms are busy and cramped but not enough to discourage the faithful. The best seating is on the main floor, where you get a full view of the steaming pots in the open kitchen, the beautiful bar, the baskets of fresh baguettes, and the murals painted by students from l'École Nationale des Beaux-Arts across the street. Upstairs the mood is more relaxed but definitely not as much fun. Although not quite the cheap thrill it once was, the menu is long and plentiful and is definitely a bargain considering the size of the portions. All the standards are here, from *oeuf dur mayonnaise* (hard-boiled egg with mayonnaise), grilled sardines, and lentil salad to *boeuf bourguignon,* lamb stew, chicken with wine, mushrooms, and tomato sauce, and veal escallope. The dessert specialty of the house is warm *tarte Tatin* with crème fraîche. With a pitcher of wine or a mug of beer, you will probably get away with spending around 120 to 125F if you select à la carte, and even less if you go with the set menu.

NOTE: The first floor is air-conditioned, so if you do not smoke, you'll probably find the clearest air here.

TELEPHONE
01-43-26-92-64

MÉTRO
St-Germain-des-Prés

OPEN
Daily

CLOSED
Christmas day, NAC

HOURS
Lunch noon–2 P.M., dinner 7–10:45 P.M.

RESERVATIONS
Preferred

CREDIT CARDS
None

À LA CARTE
120–125F, BNC

PRIX FIXE
Lunch only, 60F, 3 courses, BNC; lunch and dinner, 90F, 3 courses, BC

ENGLISH SPOKEN
Yes, with English menu

(53) RESTAURANT DU LUXEMBOURG
44, rue d'Assas, at rue de Fleurus (6th)

The regulars who live in the neighborhood consider the Luxembourg to be an extension of their own homes, a place where they can always go for a dependable variety of fresh food at affordable prices. The friendly *patron,* Sylvain Pommerau, meets and greets everyone with warmth and good cheer. Unless you arrive when they open, be prepared to wait up to an hour if you are without reservations, especially at lunch. The service is personable, even when it gets hectic. The decor is classic: walls covered with antique and reproduction posters, ceiling fans, the original tiled floors, and a bar to the right as you enter. For most visitors, it is a window on the day-to-day dining of middle-class Parisians.

TELEPHONE
01-45-48-90-22

MÉTRO
Notre-Dame-des-Champs, St-Placide

OPEN
Mon–Fri lunch and dinner, Sat lunch only

CLOSED
Sat dinner, Sun, holidays, Aug

HOURS
Lunch noon–2 P.M., dinner 7:15–9:30 P.M.

RESERVATIONS
Advised

CREDIT CARDS
MC, V

À LA CARTE
145F, BNC

PRIX FIXE
Lunch only, 95F, 3 courses, BNC

ENGLISH SPOKEN
Very little

The food is just as time-honored as the clientele. Snails, foie gras, terrines, salads, and smoked fish lead the way to prime portions of *confit de canard, bavette aux échalottes* (skirt steak with shallots), and *escalope de veau Normande* (veal in cream sauce), all liberally garnished with *pommes frites.* Desserts aimed to please are centered around homemade *tartes,* fresh fruit, *île flottante* (puffs of egg whites floating in custard), and the usual ice creams and sorbets. The wine list is satisfying, with some pleasant alternatives to the basic house variety.

Seventh Arrondissement

The right Paris zip code is 007, as it has been since the early 1700s when blue-blooded families fled Versailles and settled in this part of Paris. A sense of good living and a feeling of luxury pervade the streets of this *beau-quartier,* where fashionable people live and pay high rents and young chic meets old guard. The handsome tree-shaded avenues are lined with government offices, foreign embassies, beautiful shops, and lovely, small hotels. The seventh is also one of the most food-conscious, with outstanding restaurants and some of the city's best bakeries, *charcuteries, traiteurs, fromageries, pâtisseries,* and confectioners.

LEFT BANK
Champ-de-Mars, École Militaire, Eiffel Tower, Invalides (final resting place for Napoléon), Musée d'Orsay, National Assembly, Rodin Museum, UNESCO

SEVENTH ARRONDISSEMENT RESTAURANTS

* Restaurants marked with an asterisk (*) are considered Big Splurges.

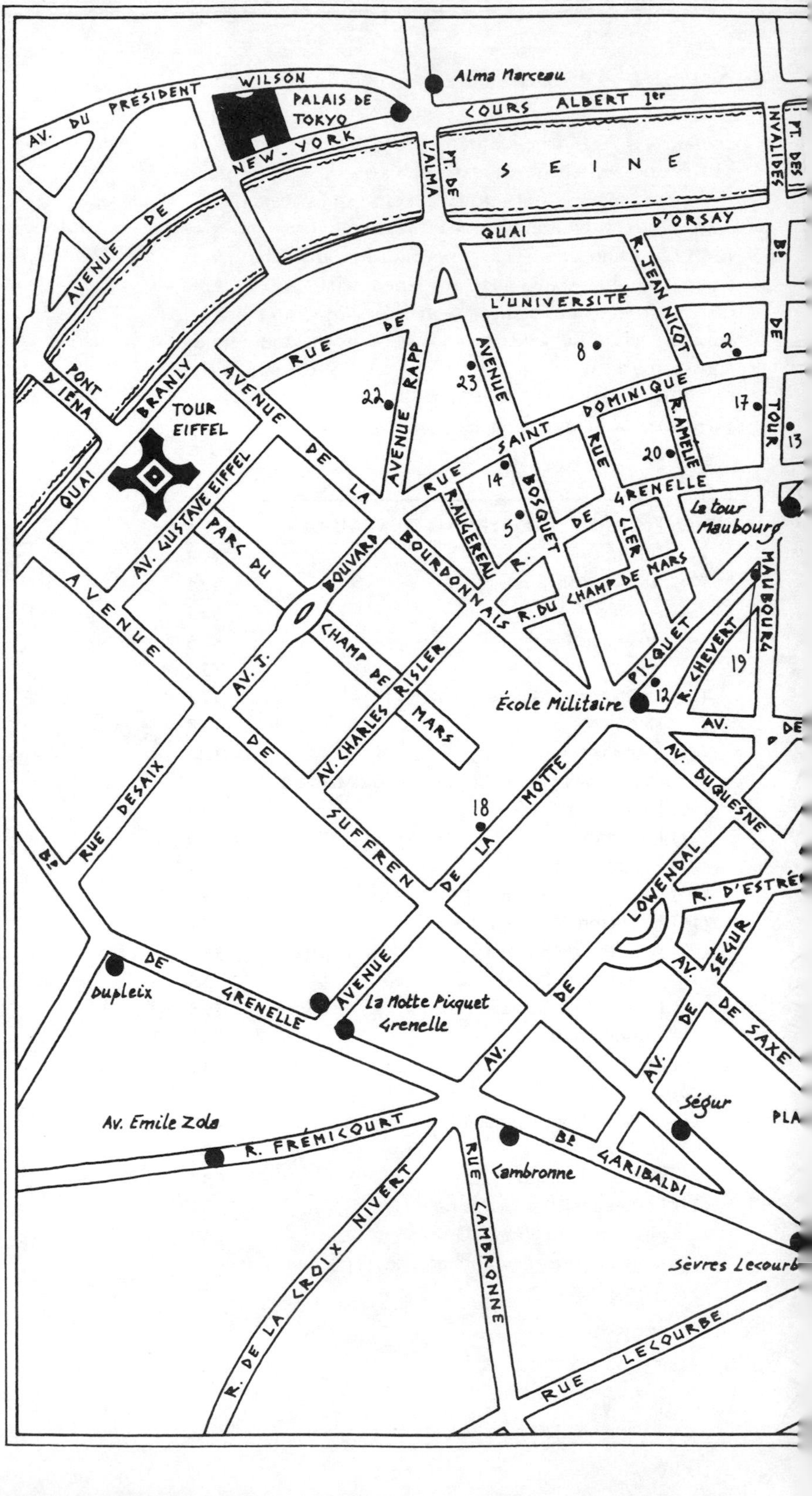
Alma Marceau
AV. DU PRÉSIDENT WILSON
PALAIS DE TOKYO
COURS ALBERT Ier
AVENUE DE NEW-YORK
PT. DE L'ALMA
SEINE
PT. DES INVALIDES
QUAI D'ORSAY
R. JEAN NICOT
RUE DE L'UNIVERSITÉ
AVENUE RAPP
AVENUE BOSQUET
PONT D'IÉNA
QUAI BRANLY
TOUR EIFFEL
AVENUE DE LA BOURDONNAIS
RUE SAINT DOMINIQUE
R. AMÉLIE
RUE DE GRENELLE
Bd DE LA TOUR MAUBOURG
La tour Maubourg
R. AUGEREAU
AV. GUSTAVE EIFFEL
PARC DU CHAMP DE MARS
AV. J. BOUVARD
R. DU CHAMP DE MARS
R. CLER
AV. CHARLES RISLER
R. CHEVERT
École Militaire
AV. DE LA MOTTE PICQUET
AVENUE DE SUFFREN
AV. DUQUESNE
RUE DESAIX
Bd DE GRENELLE
AV. DE LOWENDAL
R. D'ESTRÉ
AV. DE SÉGUR
AV. DE SAXE
Dupleix
La Motte Picquet Grenelle
Av. Emile Zola
R. FRÉMICOURT
Cambronne
Bd GARIBALDI
Ségur
PLA
Sèvres Lecourb
RUE CAMBRONNE
R. DE LA CROIX NIVERT
RUE LECOURBE
8
2
23
22
17
13
20
14
5
12
19
18

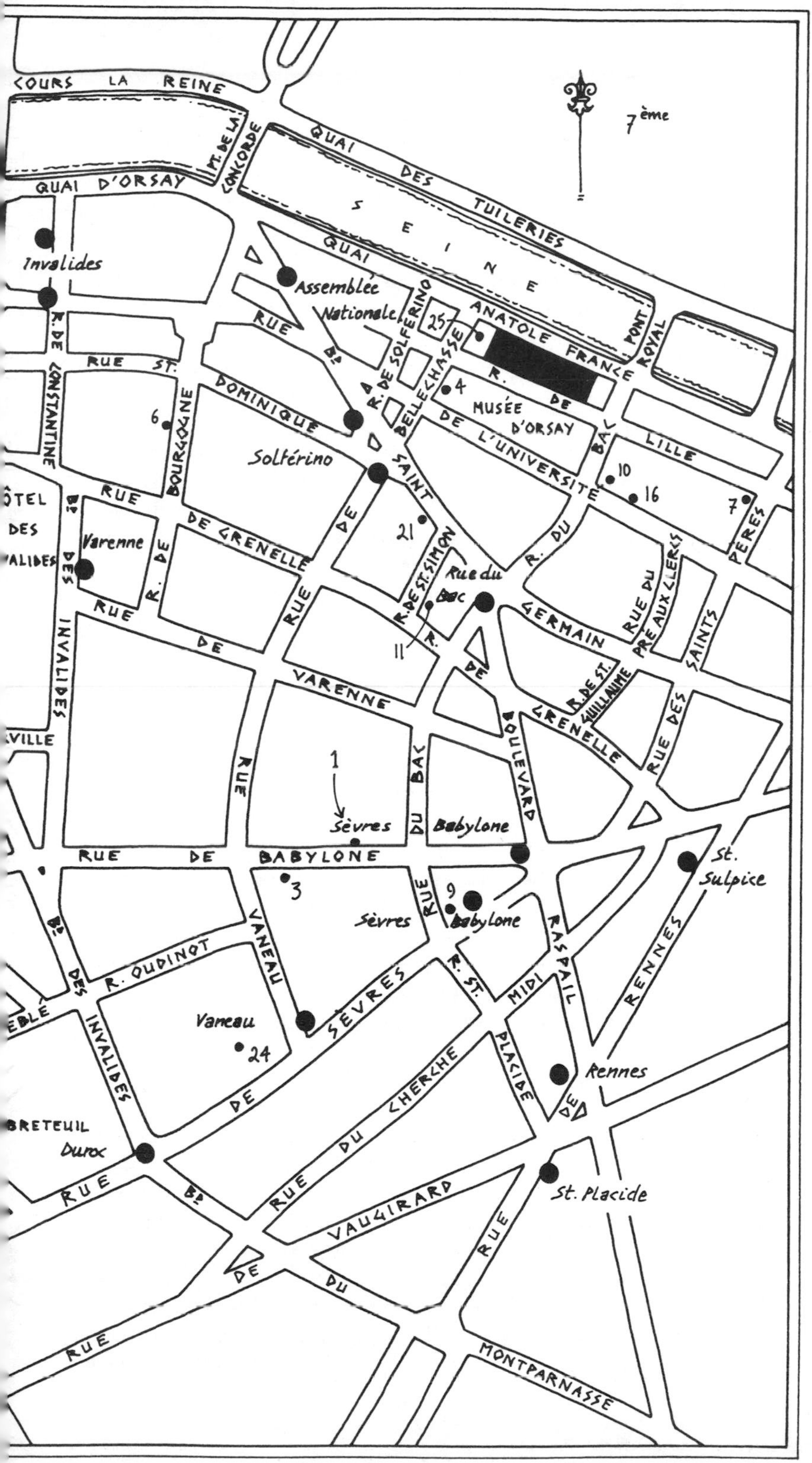
COURS LA REINE
QUAI D'ORSAY
PT. DE LA CONCORDE
QUAI DES TUILERIES
SEINE
7ème
Invalides
Assemblée Nationale
QUAI ANATOLE FRANCE
PONT ROYAL
R. DE SOLFERINO
BELLECHASSE
25
4
MUSÉE D'ORSAY
R. DE LILLE
RUE DE L'UNIVERSITÉ
R. DE CONSTANTINE
RUE ST. DOMINIQUE
BOURGOGNE
6
Solférino
BD ST. GERMAIN
RUE DU BAC
10
16
7
HÔTEL DES INVALIDES
RUE DE GRENELLE
Varenne
R. DE VARENNE
21
R. DE ST. SIMON
Rue du Bac
11
R. DU PRÉ AUX CLERCS
RUE DES SAINTS PÈRES
R. DE ST. GUILLAUME
RUE DE VARENNE
BD DES INVALIDES
BOULEVARD RASPAIL
1
Sèvres Babylone
RUE DE BABYLONE
3
9
RUE DES RENNES
St. Sulpice
R. OUDINOT
RUE VANEAU
Vaneau
24
RUE DE SÈVRES
R. ST. PLACIDE
R. DU MIDI
RUE DU CHERCHE MIDI
Rennes
BRETEUIL
Duroc
St. Placide
RUE DE VAUGIRARD
RUE DU MONTPARNASSE

(1) AU BABYLONE
13, rue de Babylone (7th)

TELEPHONE
01-45-48-72-13
MÉTRO
Sèvres-Babylone
OPEN
Mon–Sat lunch only
CLOSED
Sun, holidays, Aug
HOURS
Lunch 11:30 A.M.–2:30 P.M.
RESERVATIONS
Advised
CREDIT CARDS
None
À LA CARTE
90–100F, BNC
PRIX FIXE
100F, 3 courses, BC
ENGLISH SPOKEN
No

It is easy to spot the dining *habitués* at Au Babylone: they are the ones using red linen napkins; you will be using white paper ones. When the linen napkins are not in use, they are stored in their own numbered, pigeon-hole cupboard at the back of the restaurant.

Time has left its mark on this nostalgic old bistro not far from Bon Marché, the department store. Owner Mme. Garavana has been presiding over her flock for four decades and shows no sign of slowing down or changing anything in her yellow-walled establishment, still hung with the same mirrors, plates, and paintings as the day she opened. Serving only lunch, she sets seventy-six places, and they are always filled with a cross section of Parisians enjoying her *bonne-maman* cuisine. These predictable standards are served in amazing portions: pâté and simple salads of grated carrots, cooked beets, or sliced cucumbers paired with dishes of roast veal, lamb, chicken, *andouillettes,* and *faux filet* of steaks, with potato purée and a vegetable as the garnishes. On Saturday, *île flottante* is the dessert specialty everyone waits for. Otherwise, desserts are the usual crème caramel, chocolate mousse, and fruit compote.

(2) AU PETIT TONNEAU
20, rue Surcouf (7th)

TELEPHONE
01-47-05-09-01
MÉTRO
La Tour-Maubourg
OPEN
Daily Oct–May; Mon–Sat June–Sept
CLOSED
Sun June–Sept; Aug 15–22, some holidays
HOURS
Lunch noon–3 P.M., dinner 7–11:30 P.M.
RESERVATIONS
Advised, especially for dinner
CREDIT CARDS
AE, DC, MC, V
À LA CARTE
195F, BNC

Ginette Boyer's Au Petit Tonneau is a true gem, and it should be a required stop for anyone who wants to scratch the surface of local life. Service is slow-paced, but the regulars don't mind, since time waiting is well-spent over another bottle of their favorite wine while getting caught up on the neighborhood news. The dining room is small and typical, with smoky walls, an old tile floor, mirrored bar, and assorted paintings. Service and linen-covered tables are correct.

Ginette, a natural-born cook, was taught the basics by her grandmother. Her wonderful food is a lesson in superb simplicity, using only the best fresh ingredients, which she personally selects and buys. How do I know? Because I was lucky enough to go with her several times, along with her dog, Wattie, *before* the crack of dawn to Rungis, the wholesale food market on the edge of Paris. What a trip! It is not for the squeamish or those who blanche at the thought of enormous warehouses filled with row upon row of hanging animal parts, skinned heads, bins of toes, tails, and tongues, icy cold fowl storage halls, or pungent fish pavilions—all viewed way before breakfast. However, the food enthusiast will be rewarded with a peek at the largest, most all-encompassing food market in Europe. It is a visit you will *never* forget, if you are lucky enough to have the opportunity to go. Unfortunately, this food mecca is only open to people in the trade or by special arrangement.

What to order at Au Petit Tonneau? Find out what is fresh from the market and have that. Ginette has a way with fresh fish (especially Scottish salmon), turns out a perfect *blanquette de veau,* prepares the creamiest omelette you will eat in Paris, and creates a chicken liver terrine to remember. Her *tarte Tatin* (caramelized apple tart) ignores any dietary constraints, especially when you pile on the crème fraîche served on the side. Or, if you prefer a fresh fruit *clafoutis,* hers is heavenly.

Eating a meal here makes you feel you are in a house of plenty, not only for the food we usually only dream of, but for the friendly atmosphere created by Ginette's warm welcome, which she extends to everyone. Before you leave, Ginette, wearing her tall chef's hat and white coat, will come out of her tiny kitchen into the dining room to meet you. She is modest yet generous, with a heart of gold. She likes nothing better than to share her food with an appreciative audience. When you go, don't forget to say hello for me, and please check on Wattie and her big black cat Noee as well.

PRIX FIXE
Lunch and dinner, 150F, 3 courses, BC

ENGLISH SPOKEN
Yes

(3) AU PIED DE FOUET
45, rue de Babylone (7th)

This noisy, crowded Cheap Eat is a neighborhood gathering spot, the colorful regulars returning week after week for the belt-popping meals. The restaurant is one hundred years old, and believe me, not much has been done to it in that time. The walls are peeling artfully, the coat hooks could use some polishing, and the miniscule kitchen is an original. You definitely want to sit downstairs at one of the tables covered with red-and-white checkered bistro cloths. Upstairs is perilous quarters for anyone over five feet tall.

Lunch and dinner offer routine sustenance: grated carrot or cabbage salad, the old *oeuf dur mayonnaise* standard, roast pork with mashed spuds, and one you don't see often, calamari. If you are committed to desserts, pick the fruit tart, or as my dining neighbor wisely

TELEPHONE
01-47-05-12-27

MÉTRO
Sèvres-Babylone, Vaneau

OPEN
Mon–Fri lunch and dinner, Sat lunch only

CLOSED
Sat dinner, Sun, holidays, Aug, Dec 25–Jan 1

HOURS
Lunch noon–2:30 P.M., dinner 7–9:30 P.M.

RESERVATIONS
Not taken

CREDIT CARDS
None

À LA CARTE
80–100F, BNC

PRIX FIXE
None
ENGLISH SPOKEN
Yes

confided to me, "anything made by Monique." Coffee is only served standing at the zinc bar in order to free the tables faster for the next diners.

(4) AUX PETITS OIGNONS
20, rue de Bellechasse (7th)

TELEPHONE
01-47-05-48-77
MÉTRO
Solférino
OPEN
Mon–Sat
CLOSED
Sun, holidays, Aug
HOURS
Lunch noon–2 P.M., dinner 7:30-10:30 P.M.
RESERVATIONS
Advised
CREDIT CARDS
MC, V
À LA CARTE
175F, BNC
PRIX FIXE
Lunch only, 115F, 3 courses, BNC
ENGLISH SPOKEN
Yes
MISCELLANEOUS
Nonsmoking section

Good manners and gentility are as much at home here as the local regulars, who have made this bistro a popular neighborhood fixture. They quickly fill the nine tables in the downstairs dining room, which is simply decorated with tiny floral prints draped over white tablecloths. Upstairs is equally appealing, provided you can navigate the steep winding staircase. Trays of *pâtisserie* are on display near the entrace, and the house dog, a beautiful Lab named Cashmere, will be there to greet you along with the owner, Edith, who has been here for two decades.

There is an excellent prix fixe lunch-only menu and an imaginative à la carte section. On the à la carte side, you have a choice of ten cold and six hot *entrées.* I like to begin with the *salade Bonne Mine,* which is crudités served with *fromage blanc.* This is a light starter that leaves room for either of the two house specialties: *magret de canard à la confiture de petits onions* (duck breast with onion jam) or the *foie de veau aux avocats* (veal liver with avocados). A word of advice: Leave enough space for the famed chocolate cake or *la tarte au citron d'Edith.* If these are too much, try her other specialty, Irish coffee.

(5) BISTROT LE P'TIT TROQUET
28, rue de l'Exposition (7th)

TELEPHONE
01-47-05-80-39
MÉTRO
École-Militaire
OPEN
Tues–Sat
CLOSED
Sun–Mon, holidays, Aug 1–15
HOURS
Lunch noon–3 P.M., dinner 7–10:30 P.M.
RESERVATIONS
Essential
CREDIT CARDS
MC, V

To all Cheap Eaters in Paris: Look no farther, here it is—that perfect, romantic little Parisian restaurant hidden away on a back street that only *you* have discovered. And, once you have, you face the dilemma of whether you should tell about it or keep it to yourself, hoping no one else finds it, fearing it will become overrun with so many tourists it will be ruined. Not to worry . . . that will not happen here. Bistrot Le P'tit Troquet continually tops my short list of favorite restaurants not to miss whenever I am in Paris. Judging from what many readers have written to me—"Every course was a treat for the palate and the eyes," and "We should have saved the best for last . . . dining here has spoiled us for all that followed"—everyone seems to agree.

Inside, marble-topped bistro tables with linen cloths and vases of dried flowers fill two small rooms imaginatively decorated with assorted paintings, posters, fringed lamps, and flea-market memorabilia from the 1930s. The entire effect is one of comfortable and quiet intimacy. The food is all purchased and prepared by Patrick Vessière and nicely served by his wife, Dominique. Patrick insists on smoking his own duck and salmon, making his own *confits,* pâtés, and terrines, baking all the breads, and churning his own ice creams. When you consider the fine quality his food represents, the price tags are low. Depending on the time of year, you might start with a cold avocado and chicken liver pâté surrounded by fresh tomato sauce or a colorful summer salad filled with a mélange of fruits and vegetables. His *côte de veau, lapin à la moutarde, confit de canard,* and perfectly pink lamb are just a few samplings of the possibilities awaiting you. Of course, no self-respecting diner would forget dessert, and you should not pass up this opportunity to indulge in his expertly prepared crème brûlée, nougat ice cream, or fine pastries filled with the best fruits from the market. The wine list is as wonderful as the food. It features wines from small wineries throughout France and small *crus* from vintage years. After dinner, coffee arrives with a plate of tiny meringue cookies, winding up a leisurely Parisian meal you will remember for a long time.

À LA CARTE
Lunch, 120F; dinner, 170F; both BNC

PRIX FIXE
Lunch and dinner, 149F, 3 courses, BNC

ENGLISH SPOKEN
Yes

(6) LA BOLÉE DES MINISTÉRES
30, rue de Bourgogne (7th)

There is a new name and new owner, but the smells are still tantalizing and the servings generous at this handkerchief-size *crêperie,* with its cozy kitchen and converted-parlor atmosphere. Open only for lunch, it fills up quickly with people from the nearby French ministries and the Musée d'Orsay, often leaving some waiting outside for a seat.

The menu lists large salads and every mouthwatering buckwheat crêpe you can think of—and probably some you never imagined. All are not available every day, and there are daily specials: On Monday you can count on one featuring smoked duck. On Tuesday, the special will be filled with egg, asparagus, mushrooms, and béchamel sauce, and on Wednesday, mushrooms, garlic, parsley, gruyère cheese, and crème fraîche. Thursday it is chicken, and Friday is always a surprise. Saving room for a sweet

TELEPHONE
01-45-51-32-48

MÉTRO
Assemblée Nationale

OPEN
Mon–Fri lunch only

CLOSED
Sat–Sun, holidays, NAC

HOURS
11:30 A.M.–2:30 P.M.

RESERVATIONS
Not taken

CREDIT CARDS
MC, V

À LA CARTE
70–95F, BNC

PRIX FIXE
65F, 3 courses, BC

ENGLISH SPOKEN
Yes, with English menu

ending is not difficult when you know it will be *Le Mendiante*, with chocolate, almonds, raisins, and walnuts filling your dessert crêpe.

(7) LA CALÈCHE*

8, rue de Lille, at rue des Saints-Pères (7th)

TELEPHONE
01-42-60-24-76

MÉTRO
Rue du Bac

OPEN
Mon–Fri

CLOSED
Sat–Sun, holidays, Dec 24–Jan 4, last 3 weeks in Aug

HOURS
Lunch noon–2:30 P.M., dinner 7–10:30 P.M.

RESERVATIONS
Advised

CREDIT CARDS
AE, MC, V

À LA CARTE
190–225F, BNC

PRIX FIXE
Lunch and dinner, 100F, 130F, and 175F, 3 courses, all BNC

ENGLISH SPOKEN
Yes

The dignified ambience and excellent quality-to-value food are two good reasons to book a table at La Calèche, which has been owned for over a quarter century by M. and Mme. Pouget. The neighborhood bespeaks old money and position and the regulars mirror that image. As you enter the restaurant, look to your left to see framed pictures of several *calèches,* or carriages.

The three prix fixe menus and the à la carte menu are designed to please a variety of tastes and inspire repeat visits. Fresh bread, sweet butter, and olives in a little bowl arrive immediately as you are seated. I like to begin with the *salade des gourmets,* artichoke hearts, fresh green beans, and foie gras on a bed of perfectly dressed greens. The salmon crêpes, served bubbling hot in their own dish, is another study in simple elegance. Depending on the season, you might find veal served with wild mushrooms, *noisettes* of lamb flavored with tarragon, or fresh pasta tossed with morilles and ham. Desserts are a *must,* especially the chocolate *charlotte* and the *feuillantine aux poire et chocolat.*

(8) L'AFFRIOLÉ*

17, rue Malar (7th)

TELEPHONE
01-44-18-31-33

MÉTRO
La Tour-Maubourg

OPEN
Mon–Fri lunch and dinner, Sat dinner only

CLOSED
Sat lunch, Sun, major holidays, first 3 weeks in Aug

HOURS
Lunch noon–2:30 P.M., dinner 7:30–11 P.M. (till 11:30 P.M. Fri–Sat)

RESERVATIONS
Essential

CREDIT CARDS
MC, V

À LA CARTE
225F, BNC

Owner Alain Atebard's restaurant makes a nice first impression. Faux terra-cotta-finished accents on pillars frame yellow walls hung with assorted prints and paintings by Atebard's sister. Two rows of banquettes face perfectly set tables and stunning floral arrangements crafted by his wife, which are whimsically softened by a bowl with one goldfish in it and a copper pot that belonged to his grandmother displayed at the entrance. Shelves to one side display jars of Atebard's own preserves and terrines made from his mother's recipes, which are nice gifts you can buy to take home.

Atebard is a creative chef and his pride is more than justified in his able presentations of both humble and involved fare. The menu is seasonally based, and the offerings change often. To start, a basket of warm homemade bread and a plate of *amuse gueules* (tiny appetizers) are brought to your table. The quality of the fish is excellent; try the lobster ravioli or the red cabbage salad with haddock and quail eggs, which are served as *entrées*. A few of the unusual and delicious *plats* include tender veal accompanied by ham-stuffed endive; young turkey osso buco and potato purée sprinkled with truffles; and *dorade* (delicate white fish). A selection of cheeses leads to artfully conceived desserts, especially the warm orange soufflé served in orange shells or the honey-flavored apple *tarte*, both prepared to order. The wine prices seem a bit high, but the quality is unsurpassed, as is the charming service and the consistently imaginative food.

PRIX FIXE
Lunch, 160F, 2 courses, BC; dinner, 185F, 4 courses, BNC

ENGLISH SPOKEN
Yes

(9) LA GRANDE ÉPICERIE DE PARIS (AT BON MARCHÉ)

38, rue de Sèvres (Magasin 2, main floor) (7th)

Close your eyes and think of a supermarket in heaven; open them, and you will be in La Grande Épicerie de Paris . . . the Left Bank's answer to Fauchon (see page 143). Even if you have no intention of buying anything, a visit to this Paris market is an interesting break from the usual, almost mandatory, sightseeing and museum going. Take a few minutes and wander up and down the aisles admiring the magnificent produce, cheeses, and wines, the *pâtisserie* and *boucherie* counters, and every kind of canned, bottled, or packaged food on the planet. There is even an American section if you are suffering withdrawal pangs. If you are planning to put together a picnic, this is the perfect place to create one for the record books.

TELEPHONE
01-44-39-81-00

MÉTRO
Sèvres-Babylone

OPEN
Mon–Sat

CLOSED
Sun, major holidays, NAC

HOURS
Mon–Fri 8:30 A.M.–9 P.M., Sat 8:30 A.M.–10 P.M.

CREDIT CARDS
MC, V

ENGLISH SPOKEN
Yes

(10) LA NUIT DES THÉS

22, rue de Beaune (7th)

Paris tearooms are usually stylishly decorated places where you can relax for an hour or so over a light meal, a pastry, and a cup of good tea. Jacqueline Cédelle's tearoom near the Musée d'Orsay is just such a pleasing refuge for a quiet break from the rigors of museum going or wandering through the antique and art galleries that define this part of Paris. Her interesting collection of teapots and cups are displayed in the window and in a lighted cupboard near the back. Fresh flowers on white linens, mirrored walls, and marble floors set the rather formal tone. All the food is fresh and made here, including the jam you spread on your scones. Lunch leans heavily on salads, cold plates, and egg creations; brunch is a filling multicourse affair starting with juice and tea

TELEPHONE
01-47-03-92-07

MÉTRO
Rue du Bac

OPEN
Daily, brunch, lunch, and tea only

CLOSED
July and Aug

HOURS
Mon–Sat 11:30 A.M.–7 P.M., Sun 11 A.M.– 4 P.M., continuous service

CREDIT CARDS
MC, V

À LA CARTE
110–135F, BC

PRIX FIXE
Brunch, 150F, BC

ENGLISH SPOKEN
Yes

or coffee, scones or pancakes, eggs fixed several ways, and ending with a choice of four desserts, including chocolate brownies with cream. If you are just going for tea, her lemon meringue or chocolate *tartes* are wonderful, as are the macaroons . . . strawberry in the summer and pistacchio in the winter.

(11) LA RIVALDIÈRE
1, rue St-Simon (7th)

TELEPHONE
01-45-48-53-96

MÉTRO
Rue du Bac

OPEN
Mon–Fri lunch and dinner, Sat dinner only

CLOSED
Sat lunch, Sun, mid-July to Aug

HOURS
Lunch noon–2:30 P.M., dinner 7:15–10:30 P.M.

RESERVATIONS
Advised

CREDIT CARDS
MC, V

À LA CARTE
150F, BNC

PRIX FIXE
Lunch and dinner, 100F, 3 courses, BNC

ENGLISH SPOKEN
Yes

As I studied the menu posted outside, two satisfied diners said to me, "This is great. We eat here all the time." After just one meal, I knew why and returned as often as possible.

The set menus are hard-to-beat Cheap Eats. Both lunch and dinner on these daily changing menus offer three courses for under twenty dollars, which is cheaper than a sandwich, beer, and coffee would be in an expensive brasserie along some Parisian tourist beat. In addition to the traditional bistro food, which is prepared with care, and the above-average wines, including monthly featured vintages, there are several other things to like about La Rivaldière. First, the paintings and posters of Singapore birdcages are eye-catching, and the yellow walls bordered with grapes remind you that the owner is serious about his wines. The red velvet banquettes promote comfort, and Gaspar, the long-haired weimaraner dog who lunches here with the owner's wife each day, adds just the right French touch. I also like the cast of businesspeople at lunch and the prim, frugal diners at dinner, who tuck into such classics as chicken liver terrine, haddock salad, *coq au vin,* duck *l'orange,* veal with *gratin dauphinois* (creamy potatoes), and *fromage blanc* or smooth chocolate pudding for dessert.

(12) LA TABLE D'EIFFEL
39, avenue de la Motte Picquet (7th)

TELEPHONE
01-45-55-90-20

MÉTRO
École-Militaire

OPEN
Daily

CLOSED
Never, NAC

HOURS
Lunch noon–2:30 P.M., dinner 7–11 P.M.

The worldwide recession packed a lethal punch for Paris restaurants. People are now dining out less often, and when they do, they are not eager to threaten their children's education to do so. Enter the formula restaurant, the new wave of dining that has taken Paris by storm. Here is the deal: for one price you get a substantial three-course meal that includes wine and coffee, and often a kir to start and chocolates to finish.

La Table d'Eiffel offers an all-inclusive kir-to-chocolates dinner and a two-course lunch that is not quite the bargain dinner is. Dinner starts with flaky cheese pastries served with kir to tide you over while selecting from the ten *entrées*, *plats*, and desserts offered. Start with a block of foie gras and warm prunes, a seafood crêpe, or salmon-filled cannelloni. Veal kidneys, lamb chops, liver, seasonal fish, and a daily special are a few of the main courses. The dessert run-down is usually a pleasant dilemma, which can often be solved by convincing everyone at your table to order something different and then sharing. The menu changes three times a year, and the service by owner Jean-Jacques Amestoy and his wife is always very pleasant.

The sedate regulars book their favorite table from week to week. Best seats in the house are along the window or, if weather permits, on the umbrella-shaded sidewalk terrace set off from foot traffic by green plants.

RESERVATIONS
Preferred for dinner, weekends, and holidays

CREDIT CARDS
AE, DC, MC, V

À LA CARTE
None

PRIX FIXE
Lunch Mon–Fri only, 98F, 2 courses, BNC; lunch, dinner, and holidays, 175F, 3 courses, BC (apéritif, wine, and coffee)

ENGLISH SPOKEN
Yes, with English menu

(13) L'AUBERGE BRESSANE*
16, avenue de la Motte-Picquet (7th)

If it's a restaurant with a Parisian atmosphere you are after, they don't come any better or more packed than the wood-paneled L'Auberge Bressane, which a well-heeled crowd has made their own. At lunchtime, men in suits and blondes in black skirts predominate. In the evening, the dinner trade attracts a more jovial group, who come for a night of eating and drinking and smoking—not just cigarettes but cigars as well. To avoid the brunt of the haze, request a booth toward the front.

The loyalists know to base their meal around at least one of the ethereal soufflés, which literally melt in your mouth, especially the deep dark chocolate puff that tastes like a bar of Belgian chocolate. Beautifully presented, pleasing servings of salads piled high with fresh greens and mushrooms, marinated raw salmon served with herring and warm potatoes, roast chèvre cheese resting atop roasted red peppers, chicken in creamy morel mushroom sauce or cooked in wine, and meaty versions of kidneys and veal liver are only a few of the rich dishes awaiting you at this wonderful dining address near Les Invalides.

TELEPHONE
01-47-05-98-37

MÉTRO
La Tour-Maurbourg, École-Militaire

OPEN
Mon–Fri, Sun lunch and dinner, Sat dinner only

CLOSED
Sat lunch, Aug 15–22

HOURS
Lunch noon–2:30 P.M., dinner 7:30–11 P.M.

RESERVATIONS
Essential

CREDIT CARDS
AE, MC, V

À LA CARTE
180–225F, BNC

PRIX FIXE
Lunch only, 90F, 1 course, 130F, 2 courses, both BC

ENGLISH SPOKEN
Yes

(14) L'AUVERGNE GOURMANDE
127, rue St-Dominique (7th)

Blink twice and you will miss Christiane Miguel's tiny, four-table nook tucked snugly along rue St-Dominique, only a ten-minute walk from the Eiffel Tower.

TELEPHONE
01-47-05-60-79

MÉTRO
École-Militaire

OPEN
Mon–Fri lunch only
CLOSED
Sat–Sun, holidays, NAC
HOURS
Noon–4 P.M.
RESERVATIONS
Not taken
CREDIT CARDS
None
À LA CARTE
65–80F, BNC
PRIX FIXE
None
ENGLISH SPOKEN
Some

The setting is homey, with cooking utensils lining the walls and a radio playing in the background near the open kitchen. The cheery welcome and good food more than make up for the tiny space and the limited, lunch-only menu.

The restaurant is popular with students, shoppers, and neighborhood women, one of whom told me that it is one of her favorite lunch spots because the food is always so good. She is right . . . it *is* good. The exclusively à la carte menu suggests several nice salads, a plate of cold meats, two daily hot dishes, and homemade desserts, including a devastatingly rich chocolate fudge cake. Everything is made fresh each morning in small quantities. The daily specials and desserts sell out fast, so to avoid disappointment, go early for the best selection.

(15) LE BISTROT DE BRETEUIL
3, place de Breteuil (7th)

TELEPHONE
01-45-67-07-27
MÉTRO
Duroc, Sèvres-Lecourbe
OPEN
Daily
CLOSED
Never, NAC
HOURS
Lunch noon–2:30 P.M., dinner 7:15–10:30 P.M.
RESERVATIONS
Advised
CREDIT CARDS
MC, V
À LA CARTE
None
PRIX FIXE
Lunch and dinner: 170F, 3 courses, BNC; 182F, 3 courses, BC (aperitíf, wine, and coffee)
ENGLISH SPOKEN
Yes
MISCELLANEOUS
Nonsmoking section

Le Bistrot de Breteuil has what it takes to keep the respect of discriminating Parisian diners: great atmosphere, attentive service, reasonable prices, and reliable food . . . every time. Located not too far from Les Invalides (the final resting place of Napoléon), the restaurant has one of the most beautiful dining terraces in Paris. Wrapped around an entire corner of the place de Breteuil, the open and airy glassed-in site hosts a *branché* crowd who make elegance look easy. The tables are beautifully set with heavy, white linens and fresh flowers, and they are served with precision and aplomb by teams of traditionally outfitted waiters.

There is *only* a prix fixe menu, which includes eight seasonal choices for the *entrée, plat,* and dessert. A half bottle of house wine is included for each person. Good bets are the well-dressed mixed salad with a piece of warm goat cheese on top, the leg of lamb or *confit de canard maison,* and the apple *tarte* or dark chocolate fondant with custard sauce. By Paris standards, this is on the A-list, so plan accordingly and don't arrive without reservations.

NOTE: If you go for Saturday lunch, allow time before you eat to walk along the street *marché* along avenue de Breteuil. It's one of the best.

(16) LE BISTROT DE L'UNIVERSITÉ

40, rue de l'Université (between rue de Beaune and rue du Bac) (7th)

As you walk down rue de l'Université between rue de Beaune and rue du Bac, look for No. 40 with its bright red exterior and a chalkboard with the daily menu written on it hanging in the window. At noon, the narrow room is packed solid and rings with the satisfied buzz of people eating well. The simple warming fare might start off with a vegetable soup or *oeufs en meurette* (poached eggs in a bacon and onion flavored red wine sauce). Dishes piled with roast chicken, sausage served with sautéed potatoes, and a bowl of *fromage blanc* with raspberry sauce pay homage to classic bistro cooking.

TELEPHONE
01-42-61-26-64

MÉTRO
Rue du Bac

OPEN
Mon–Fri lunch and dinner, Sat lunch only

CLOSED
Sat dinner, Sun, holidays, 2 weeks in Aug

HOURS
Lunch noon–2:30 P.M., dinner 8–10:30 P.M.

RESERVATIONS
Advised at lunch

CREDIT CARDS
MC, V

À LA CARTE
150–165F, BNC

PRIX FIXE
Lunch only, 80F, 2 courses, BNC

ENGLISH SPOKEN
Limited

(17) LE BISTROT DU 7ÈME

56, boulevard de la Tour-Maubourg (7th)

"This meal is worth the price of your book!" exclaimed my dining companions. Indeed, M. and Mme. Beauvellet's restaurant is always consistent, and above all, it *is* a great Cheap Eat in Paris. For around sixteen dollars for lunch and twenty dollars for dinner, your choices include foie gras and pâtés; tomato, basil, and mozzarella salad; herring fillets with warm potatoes; and salads topped with chicken livers. Main courses tempt with *confit de canard,* veal in a mushroom cream sauce, fresh salmon, poached haddock, and the daily special. Ice cream and sorbets dominate the desserts. Reasonable wines allow you to stay happy during the dinner service, which can be somewhat slow when it gets busy.

TELEPHONE
01-45-51-93-08

MÉTRO
La Tour-Maubourg

OPEN
Mon–Fri lunch and dinner, Sun dinner only

CLOSED
Sun lunch, Sat, one week at Christmas and in Aug

HOURS
Lunch noon–2:30 P.M., dinner 7–11 P.M.

RESERVATIONS
Advised

CREDIT CARDS
MC, V

À LA CARTE
150F, BNC

PRIX FIXE
Lunch, 80F, 3 courses, BNC; dinner, 95F, 3 courses, BNC

ENGLISH SPOKEN
Yes

(18) LE FLORIMOND*

19, avenue de la Motte-Picquet (7th)

TELEPHONE
01-45-55-40-38
MÉTRO
Ècole-Militaire
OPEN
Mon–Fri lunch and dinner, Sat dinner only
CLOSED
Sat lunch, Sun, major holidays, one week in Aug
HOURS
Lunch noon–2:30 P.M., dinner 7–10 P.M.
RESERVATIONS
Advised
CREDIT CARDS
MC, V
À LA CARTE
185–225F, BNC
PRIX FIXE
Lunch only, 110F, 2 courses, BNC; lunch and dinner, 155F, 3 courses, BNC
ENGLISH SPOKEN
Yes

White linens in a burgundy interior set off by lacy window curtains and a small sidewalk terrace form the background for dining at Le Florimond, Pascal Guillaumin's twenty-eight-seat restaurant not too far from the Eiffel Tower. People in the neighborhood eat here, hotels listed in *Cheap Sleeps in Paris* recommend it, and after one meal, you, too, are bound to become a fan. It is the perfect choice if you are looking for something geared for a little romance or some serious conversation.

Le Florimond has both seasonal and daily changing menus of delicious pleasures derived from creatively updated humble ingredients. In addition, there are some dishes you can always count on, such as the lobster ravioli to start, followed by Guillaumin's grandmother's recipe for slow-cooked stuffed cabbage, and a beef *onglet* served in a tangy mustard sauce. Desserts will leave you with sweet memories of a wonderful meal, especially the brown-sugar-crusted crème brûlée or the vanilla *mille feuille*.

(19) LE MAUPERTU*

94, boulevard de la Tour Maubourg (7th)

TELEPHONE
01-45-51-37-96
MÉTRO
La Tour-Maubourg
OPEN
Mon–Fri
CLOSED
Sat–Sun, Aug 10–31
HOURS
Lunch noon–2:30 P.M., dinner 7–10 P.M.
RESERVATIONS
Advised
CREDIT CARDS
MC, V
À LA CARTE
220–225F, BNC
PRIX FIXE
Lunch and dinner, 140F, 3 courses, BNC
ENGLISH SPOKEN
Yes

At another restaurant not too far away, I knew even before the arrival of my main course that it was destined for the pile of rejects. Then as I spoke to two diners sitting next to me, they asked if I had been to Le Maupertu, which opened in 1990. "Sophie Canton and Alain Deguest know how to keep their customers happily returning on a regular basis. Alain does it with the food . . . Sophie with her affable, charming attention to each guest," they said. Of course, I had to try it, and the result is that I can now recommend Le Maupertu to you. I hope you will be as pleased with it as I am.

The setting, especially at night, couldn't be more beautiful, with floor-length windows and a small terrace overlooking the beautifully lighted dome of Les Invalides. By all means, reserve one of these window tables under the glass roof and you will know what I mean.

The presentation of the remarkable prix fixe menu is exceptional, and the portions are balanced to allow you to enjoy three courses without feeling stuffed. The food is all seasonal, and in the early spring, you may see such starters as a salmon-herb *roulade* or a citrus-shrimp salad. The veal scallops surrounded by pasta lightly dressed with tomatoes and the chicken fricassée in sherry vinegar are winning food combinations. A generous cheese board is brought to your table, or you can end with a velvety chocolate mousse or an assortment of ice creams or sorbets served with a Florentine cookie. The monthly featured wines are good buys and are available by the glass, pitcher, or bottle.

(20) LE PETIT NIÇOIS*
10, rue Amélie (7th)

Over and over again, neighborhood residents will tell you that Le Petit Niçois is one of the best *restaurants du quartier.* I agree, and so do the many readers who have written to me after eating here.

Le Petit Niçois is a tiny, two-level, family-run restaurant that is filled to the brim with a noisy, mixed crowd. If you want meat, delicate soufflés, or *nouvelle cuisine,* look elsewhere. The specialty here is fish, fish, and more fish. Owner-chef Rolan Rulos makes some of the best bouillabaise served on the banks of the Seine, and his paella (which takes thirty minutes to prepare) is worth a special trip. For perfectly grilled jumbo shrimp or sardines, fresh lobster, or an exquisitely poached piece of turbot, eat here. To start, there are several tempting appetizers, but the hands-down winner is the *beignets aubergines* (eggplant fritters). The desserts always look good, but after the gargantuan main course and starter, no one has much room for anything more than a cool sorbet or chocolate mousse.

TELEPHONE
01-45-51-83-65
MÉTRO
La Tour-Maubourg
OPEN
Tues–Fri lunch and dinner, Sat and Mon dinner only
CLOSED
Sun; Mon and Sat lunch; major holidays; NAC
HOURS
Lunch noon–2:30 P.M., dinner 7–10:30 P.M.
RESERVATIONS
Advised
CREDIT CARDS
AE, MC, V
À LA CARTE
180–225F, BNC
PRIX FIXE
Lunch only: 100F, 3 courses, BNC; 130F, 2 courses, BC; lunch and dinner: 155F, 3 courses, BNC
ENGLISH SPOKEN
Yes, with English menu and food terms

(21) LE RELAIS SAINT-GERMAIN
190, boulevard St-Germain (7th)

Offering a menu of great variety and imagination, Le Relais Saint-Germain has been a success since the day it opened as one of the first upscale restaurants serving a prix fixe menu *only.* Recognizing the impressive food value offered, Parisians return often for the enlightened cooking served with professional *savoir faire* in air-conditioned surroundings.

The four-course menu, complete with house red or white wine, headlines at least ten *entrées,* including fresh asparagus, escargots, rich fois gras served on toast points,

TELEPHONE
01-42-22-21-35,
01-45-48-11-73
MÉTRO
St-Germain-des-Prés, Rue du Bac
OPEN
Daily
CLOSED
Never, NAC
HOURS
Lunch 12:30–2:30 P.M., dinner 7:30–11 P.M.

RESERVATIONS
Yes
CREDIT CARDS
MC, V
À LA CARTE
None
PRIX FIXE
Lunch and dinner, 200F, 4 courses, BC
ENGLISH SPOKEN
Yes

and ravioli stuffed with baby scallops in a saffron sauce. There are twelve main-dish offerings, including the favorite *foie de veau au vinaigre de miel* (liver), *aiguillettes de boeuf à la moutard de Meaux* (thin slices of tender beef in a mustard sauce, served with fresh pasta), and a *panaché* (mixed plate) of steamed fish. After a selection of Brie or chèvre cheese and an irresistibly rich dessert, you will agree with your fellow diners: *C'est magnifique!*

(22) LE SANCERRE
22, avenue Rapp (7th)

TELEPHONE
01-45-51-75-91
MÉTRO
Alma-Marceau, École-Militaire
OPEN
Mon–Sat
CLOSED
Sun, holidays, Aug 15–Sept 1
HOURS
Mon–Fri 8 A.M.–9:30 P.M., Sat 8 A.M.–5 P.M., continuous service
RESERVATIONS
Suggested for lunch
CREDIT CARDS
MC, V
À LA CARTE
80–110F, BNC
PRIX FIXE
None
ENGLISH SPOKEN
Some
MISCELLANEOUS
Nonsmoking section

The only thing that has changed since the first time I ate here in 1977 is that the back room is now designated for nonsmokers. Other than that, this venerable Parisian wine bar has not really changed at all in the forty-plus years it has been in operation.

The menu is short, but the food and wine always rate an A+ with the nonstop flow of regulars, who have made it one of the most popular lunch spots in this part of the seventh arrondissement. Past the somber exterior is a pleasant, rustic interior filled with the comforting sounds and smells of the busy kitchen. This is the place for a creamy herb or cheese omelette with a side of golden pan-fried potatoes and a crisp green salad, or for the more adventurous, a spicy *andouillette* made with Sancerre wine. A light choice is to order a *crotin de Chavignol,* the sharp goat cheese that goes perfectly with a glass or two of Sancerre. While waiting for your meal, baskets of Poilâne bread and crocks of sweet butter are brought to the table. Your wine, of course, will be Sancerre, and your dessert should be a piece of the gorgeous *tarte Tatin.* Ask to have it heated.

NOTE: If you appreciate Art Nouveau architecture, check out the facade of the building directly across the street at 29, avenue Rapp, constructed in 1901 by the architect Lavirotle. Then turn right and walk to the post office at No. 37. At the end of the dead end street by the post office are more lovely doorways and latticework.

(23) LE 6 BOSQUET*
6, avenue Bosquet (7th)

TELEPHONE
01-45-56-97-26
MÉTRO
Alma-Marceau

Everyone is talking about—and trying to book a table at—Le 6 Bosquet, a stylish address that once housed a Michelin two-star restaurant, which fell by the wayside due to its dated food and service philosophies. The new owners, Chef Emmanuel Joinville and his wife, Christine, changed the name, lightened the ambience and the food, and reduced the prices by more than half. As a result, they fill every table with well-dressed Parisians feasting on one of the best values in the *quartier*.

The Parisian atmosphere of the dining room is echoed by the kitchen's classic offerings, which have been artfully updated. Depending on the time of year, the chef's culinary repertoire might include such dishes as smoked salmon accompanied by haddock mousse, ravioli with foie gras, or a rabbit terrine with onion *confit*. I loved the long-cooked lamb served with spring vegetables and the pink beef filet with corn pancakes. The pear and kiwi gratin or the caramel sauced dense chocolate fondant served with vanilla ice cream rate dessert awards.

OPEN
Mon–Fri lunch and dinner, Sat dinner only

CLOSED
Sat lunch, Sun, holidays, Aug (dates vary)

HOURS
Lunch noon–2:30 P.M., dinner 8–11 P.M.

RESERVATIONS
Essential

CREDIT CARDS
AE, MC, V

À LA CARTE
185–225F, BNC

PRIX FIXE
Lunch, 125F, 2 courses, BC; dinner, 165F, 3 courses, BNC

ENGLISH SPOKEN
Yes

(24) RESTAURANT CHEZ GERMAINE
30, rue Pierre-Leroux (7th)

I first learned about Germaine's from a fellow passenger while we were stranded in the Jakarta airport waiting for a monsoon to let up. Naturally, the minute I got to Paris, I could not wait to try it, and when I did, it lived up to all of its advanced billing: Germaine's is an unsung place that serves homespun food at almost philanthropic prices, especially if you stick to one of the set menus. I have found myself hard-pressed to recommend a better neighborhood restaurant with more local color than this seven-table spot near the Bon Marché department store. The interior, like the food, is simple. It consists of ochre-yellow walls, hanging green plants, and some strange, anthropomorphic pictures of vegetables and fruits.

The tables, which are shared, are waited on by two clucking-hen type waitresses, who shout the orders to the chef through a window in the kitchen door. From Monday through Saturday, the timeless dishes bring diners back for their own special favorites of thick soups, pâtés, kidneys in cream, roast beef, salmon, and *petit salé* (salt pork) with carrots or lentils. The warm *pomme clafoutis* with thick cream or the homemade chocolate cake swimming in *crème anglaise* are enough to keep me coming back every night. Weight Watchers it is not! It *is*, however, *the* destination if you are looking for something truly authentic . . . and cheap.

TELEPHONE
01-42-73-28-34

MÉTRO
Vaneau

OPEN
Mon–Fri lunch and dinner, Sat lunch only

CLOSED
Sat dinner, Sun, holidays, Aug

HOURS
Lunch noon–2:30 P.M., dinner 7–9:30 P.M.

RESERVATIONS
Recommended for dinner

CREDIT CARDS
None

À LA CARTE
80–100F, BNC

PRIX FIXE
Lunch only, *formule rapide* (only between noon–12:30 P.M.), 45F, 3 courses, BNC; lunch and dinner, 65F, 3 courses, BC

ENGLISH SPOKEN
Yes

MISCELLANEOUS
No smoking allowed

(25) RESTAURANT DU PALAIS D'ORSAY
1, rue de Bellechasse (museum entrance) (7th)

TELEPHONE
01-45-49-42-03

MÉTRO
Solférino

OPEN
Tues–Wed, Fri–Sun lunch and tea; Thur lunch and dinner

CLOSED
Mon; Thur for tea; any holiday the museum is closed; NAC

HOURS
Lunch Tues–Sun 11:30 A.M.–2:30 P.M.; tea Tues–Wed, Fri–Sun 4–5:50 P.M.; dinner Thur 7–9:30 P.M.

RESERVATIONS
For large groups

CREDIT CARDS
MC, V

À LA CARTE
100–160F, BNC

PRIX FIXE
Lunch and dinner: 100F and 120F, 2 courses, 140F, 3 courses, all BNC; *le formule buffet:* 90F, BC; children (under ten): 55F, 2 courses, BC; tea: 50F, tea and pastry

ENGLISH SPOKEN
Yes, with English menu

MISCELLANEOUS
Nonsmoking section

As everyone knows, cuisine and culture are uppermost in life to the French, so it is not surprising that most major museums in Paris have some sort of restaurant. The best of these by far is the Palais d'Orsay, situated in the Musée d'Orsay. Here diners sit in wide wicker armchairs in a massive Belle Epoque dining room with magnificent frescoed ceilings by the nineteenth-century painter Gabriel Ferrier. Marble statues, gilt-framed mirrors, sparkling chandeliers, and sprays of fresh flowers complete the spectacular room.

Fortunately, the food is as impressive as the decor. At first glance, you might think the prices would be, too, but they are not, especially *le formule buffet.* This bargain meal features a beautiful lunch buffet with a variety of salads, vegetables, cold meats, and fish followed by a choice of desserts and a pitcher of wine. Also available are two other prix fixe menu possibilities and a children's menu, as well as the à la carte. Tea is served in the afternoons, but not on Thursday. That is the only night of the week the restaurant stays open for dinner, since the museum is also open late.

Eighth Arrondissement

RIGHT BANK
American Embassy, Arc de Triomphe and l'Étoile, Champs-Élysées, elegant shopping, Madeleine Church, Petit and Grand Palais (built for the 1900 World Exhibition), Place de la Concorde

This is an area of splendor, elegance, money, and classic Parisian images, especially the sweeping view of the Champs-Élysées from the Arc de Triomphe to the Place de la Concorde. Shoppers with impressive bank balances ply the *haute couture* luxury shops along the avenues Marceau and Montaigne and on the rue de Faubourg St-Honoré. Gourmet and gourmands make pilgrimages to Fauchon, the world's most famous grocery store, and tourists dine at Maxim's, the one-time shrine where the beautiful people were seen in Paris. The area is alive and bustling during the weekdays, but on holidays and weekends, it is deserted.

NOTE: The most famous boulevard in the world, with its myriad of sidewalk cafés filled with pretty young men and women, is very deceptive. No true Parisian would ever seriously dine on the Champs-Élysées, anymore than any true New Yorker would head to Times Square for a fine meal. Of course, walking along the boulevard and stopping at a café for a drink *is* part of being in Paris. But, for a real increase in value and quality of food, walk one or two blocks on either side of the boulevard. A final word: Watch for pickpockets. This is fertile picking grounds for them, and they can do a number on you faster than you can say, "Stop thief!"

EIGHTH ARRONDISSEMENT RESTAURANTS

* Restaurants marked with an asterisk (*) are considered Big Splurges.

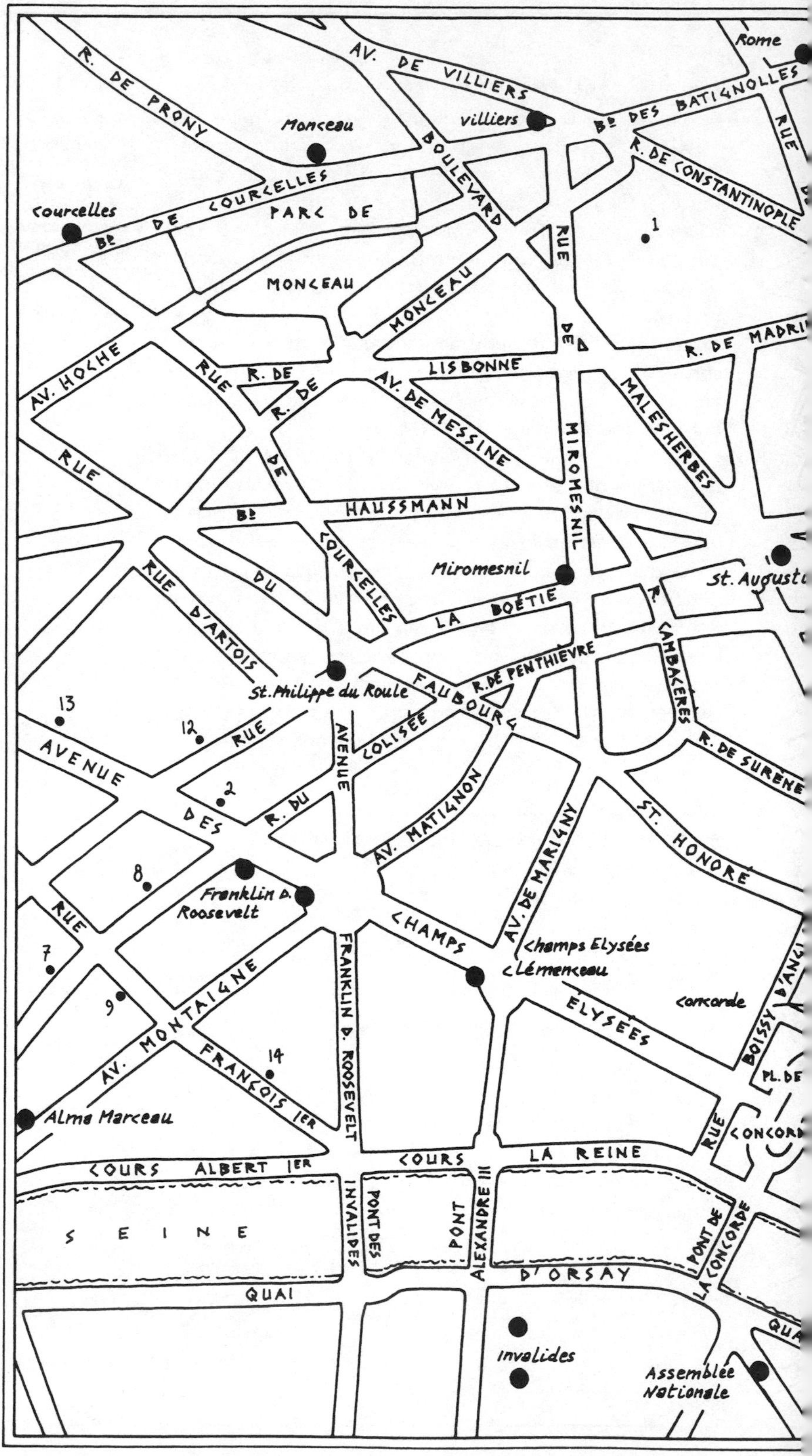

R. DE PRONY
AV. DE VILLIERS
Rome
Bd DES BATIGNOLLES
Monceau
villiers
R. DE CONSTANTINOPLE
BOULEVARD
Courcelles
Bd DE COURCELLES
PARC DE
MONCEAU
RUE
DE
1
MONCEAU
R. DE MADRID
AV. HOCHE
LISBONNE
RUE
R. DE
R. DE
AV. DE MESSINE
MALESHERBES
MIROMESNIL
RUE
DE
HAUSSMANN
Bd
DU
COURCELLES
Miromesnil
St. Augustin
RUE D'ARTOIS
LA BOÉTIE
R.
St. Philippe du Roule
R. DE PENTHIÈVRE
CAMBACÉRÈS
FAUBOURG
13
12
RUE
COLISÉE
AVENUE
R. DE SURÈNE
AVENUE
2
R. DU
DES
AV. MATIGNON
ST. HONORÉ
AV. DE MARIGNY
8
Franklin D. Roosevelt
RUE
CHAMPS
Champs Elysées Clémenceau
7
FRANKLIN D. ROOSEVELT
9
AV. MONTAIGNE
ÉLYSÉES
concorde
BOISSY D'ANGLAS
FRANÇOIS 1ER
14
PL. DE
Alma Marceau
RUE
CONCORDE
COURS ALBERT 1ER
COURS
LA REINE
SEINE
INVALIDES
PONT DES
PONT
ALEXANDRE III
PONT DE
LA CONCORDE
QUAI
D'ORSAY
QUAI
Invalides
Assemblée Nationale

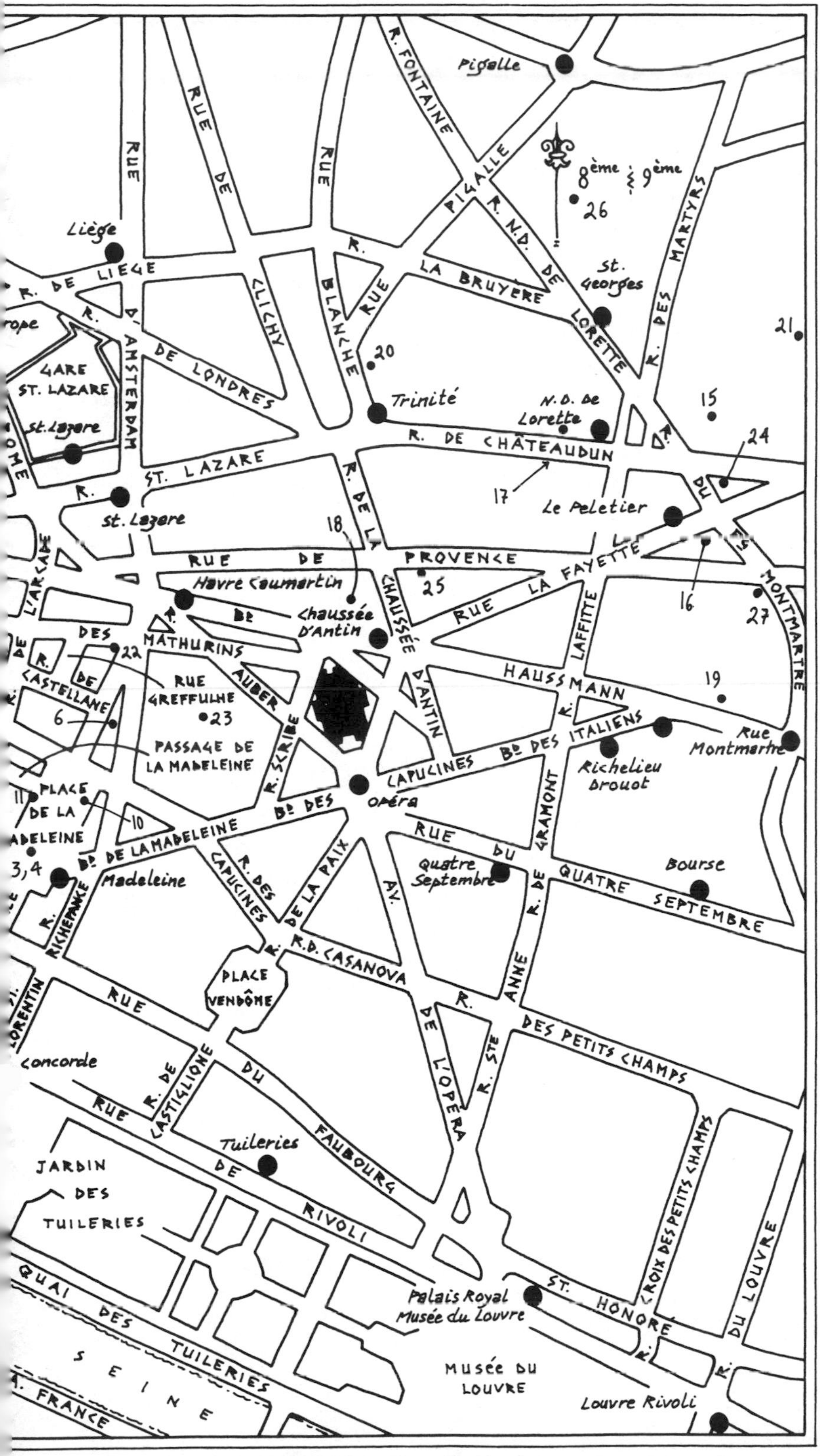

Pigalle
R. FONTAINE
PIGALLE
R. N.D. DE LORETTE
8ème & 9ème
26
RUE DE LONDRES
RUE
Liège
R. DE LIEGE
R. LA BRUYERE
St. Georges
R. DES MARTYRS
RUE DE CLICHY
RUE BLANCHE
R. D'AMSTERDAM
R. DE LONDRES
GARE ST. LAZARE
St. Lazare
20
21
Trinité
N.D. de Lorette
15
24
R. DE CHÂTEAUDUN
R. ST. LAZARE
St. Lazare
17
Le Peletier
18
R. DE LA CHAUSSÉE D'ANTIN
RUE DE PROVENCE
25
RUE LA FAYETTE
Havre Caumartin
Chaussée d'Antin
LAFFITTE
16
MONTMARTRE
27
Bd HAUSSMANN
R. DES MATHURINS
22
19
RUE GREFFULHE
AUBER
R. DE CASTELLANE
23
6
R. SCRIBE
Bd DES ITALIENS
Rue Montmartre
PASSAGE DE LA MADELEINE
Richelieu Drouot
Bd DES CAPUCINES
Opéra
PLACE DE LA MADELEINE
11
10
Bd DE LA MADELEINE
R. DE GRAMONT
3,4
Madeleine
RUE DU QUATRE SEPTEMBRE
Quatre Septembre
Bourse
R. DES CAPUCINES
R. DE LA PAIX
AV. DE L'OPÉRA
R. RICHEPANCE
R.D. CASANOVA
R. STE ANNE
PLACE VENDÔME
R. DES PETITS CHAMPS
RUE DU FAUBOURG ST. HONORE
Concorde
R. DE CASTIGLIONE
RUE DE RIVOLI
Tuileries
JARDIN DES TUILERIES
R. CROIX DES PETITS CHAMPS
R. DU LOUVRE
Palais Royal Musée du Louvre
MUSÉE DU LOUVRE
QUAI DES TUILERIES
SEINE
Louvre Rivoli

(1) BERRY'S
46, rue de Naples (8th)

TELEPHONE
01-40-75-01-56
MÉTRO
Villiers
OPEN
Mon–Fri lunch and dinner, Sat dinner only
CLOSED
Sat lunch, Sun, July 14–17, Aug 15–20
HOURS
Lunch noon–4 P.M.; dinner 7 P.M.–1 A.M.
RESERVATIONS
Advised
CREDIT CARDS
V
À LA CARTE
150F, BNC
PRIX FIXE
Lunch and dinner, 100F, 2 courses, BNC
ENGLISH SPOKEN
Limited

Berry's is owned by chef Patrick Cirotte, who also runs Le Grenadin, the successful, expensive restaurant next door. The atmosphere at Berry's is laid-back and casual, with eleven red-and-white tables downstairs and a few more upstairs on the mezzanine. Pictures of sport teams and their jerseys hang about and an antique Adidas football sits in the window facing the street. The menu is limited, featuring dishes from Cirotte's native Berry region in France. You will find *andouillette* and macaroni, *jambon de sancerre,* and for dessert, either *chanciau aux pommes* (a thick apple fritter in light egg custard) or a *poirat berrichon,* which is a new twist on a chocolate pear *tarte.*

(2) CAFÉ DI ROMA
35, Champs-Élysées (8th)

TELEPHONE
01-53-89-65-60
MÉTRO
Franklin-D-Roosevelt
OPEN
Daily
CLOSED
Never, NAC
HOURS
11 A.M.–1:30 A.M., continuous service
RESERVATIONS
Not necessary
CREDIT CARDS
AE, MC, V
À LA CARTE
80–110F, BNC
PRIX FIXE
Lunch and dinner: 55F, pasta and wine; 82F, 2 courses, BNC; 105F, 3 courses, BNC; children under twelve, 49F, 2 courses, BC
ENGLISH SPOKEN
Limited

Where to eat before or after seeing a film or just cruising along the Champs-Élysées? Finding an acceptable place along this famous avenue has always been a discouraging up-hill project. No longer, not if you know about Café di Roma, which is on the corner of rue de Marignan and the Champs-Élysées. I will admit that I have walked right by it for years, never giving it a second thought. It took a Paris pal to point it out to me after a movie one night and insist that we try it. While certainly not destination dining, it is a port in a storm with decent Italian staples served at Cheap Eater prices. The later you go, the more authentic it gets as it fills up with Italians of various ages in assorted garbs and guises. If you go for a pizza or a bowl of pasta, you will be happy. Scratch the desserts . . . instead walk a block or two toward place de la Concorde and duck into Häagen-Dazs for a double or triple scoop of their super ice cream.

(3) FAUCHON
26, place de la Madeleine (8th)

In 1886 August Fauchon opened his *épicerie fine* on place de la Madeleine. The rest is history. Today, a visit to Fauchon, the most famous gourmet grocery store in the world, is one of the must-dos in Paris. With its magnificent museum-quality window displays and its mind-boggling selection of more than thirty thousand gastronomic goodies, Fauchon is the ultimate gourmet mecca.

Its image has been polished even further by the addition of a three-level building next door containing an expensive rooftop garden restaurant and piano bar and an expanded grocery section, which carries a line of Fauchon china, crystal, and tableware. The Cheap Eater destination among all of these riches is the basement dining area, which is a cafeteria and rotisserie by day and a brasserie by night. In between it is open for morning coffee and afternoon teas. They don't miss a trick! Here, cafeteria dining is given new meaning with specials and rotisseried meats all prepared using the finest ingredients from Fauchon. All the food is reasonable, when you consider its source, and the service is fast, a real bonus for the Cheap Eater on the run. Keep in mind that the cafeteria is packed solid during the lunch hour, so early arrivals always have the best selection.

TELEPHONE
01-47-42-60-11

MÉTRO
Madeleine

OPEN
Mon–Sat

CLOSED
Sun, major holidays, NAC

HOURS
Store 8 A.M.–6:30 P.M., food 8:15 A.M.–2 A.M., continuous service; pastry counter 8:15 A.M.–6:30 P.M.; lunch 11:15 A.M.–2:30 P.M.; dinner (brasserie only) 7 P.M.–2 A.M.

RESERVATIONS
For dinner only

CREDIT CARDS
AE, DC, MC, V

À LA CARTE
Cafeteria/rotisserie 10–125F, BNC

PRIX FIXE
Dinner (brasserie only) 120–130F, 2 courses, 150F, 3 courses, both with coffee

ENGLISH SPOKEN
Yes

(4) FAUCHON—LA TRATTORIA AND BISTROT DE LA MER
26, place de la Madeleine (8th)

If Fauchon cafeteria and brasserie dining does not appeal to you, perhaps the smart La Trattoria or shiny Bistrot de la Mer will.

The Bistrot highlights three seafood menus (with no à la carte) plus platters piled high with shellfish and oysters. The food at La Trattoria is strictly à la carte Italian (with no prix fixe menu), with pastas capturing most of the attention. Of the two, I like La Trattoria the best thanks to its second-floor location and its window tables overlooking place de la Madeleine. In contrast, the ground-floor seafood bistro is in back of the produce section and feels squeezed in and cramped.

TELEPHONE
01-47-42-60-11

MÉTRO
Madeleine

OPEN
Mon–Sat

CLOSED
Sun, major holidays, NAC

HOURS
Lunch noon–3 P.M., dinner 7–11 P.M.

RESERVATIONS
Advised

CREDIT CARDS
AE, DC, MC, V

À LA CARTE
La Trattoria only, 80–180F, BNC

PRIX FIXE
Bistrot de la Mer only: lunch and dinner, 140F and 150F, 2 courses, 175F, 3 courses, all with coffee

ENGLISH SPOKEN
Yes

(5) LADURÉE
16, rue Royale (8th)

TELEPHONE
01-42-60-21-79
MÉTRO
Madeleine, Concorde
OPEN
Daily
CLOSED
Holidays, Aug
HOURS
Mon–Sat 8:30 A.M.–7 P.M., Sun 10 A.M.–7 P.M., continuous service; lunch 11:30 A.M.–3 P.M.; brunch 11:30 A.M.–3:30 P.M.
RESERVATIONS
Recommended for lunch and Sunday brunch
CREDIT CARDS
AE,V
À LA CARTE
50–155F
PRIX FIXE
Brunch, 140–150F, 3 courses, BC
ENGLISH SPOKEN
Sometimes
MISCELLANEOUS
Nonsmoking section

Ladurée opened its doors in 1862 and rapidly became one of the best tearooms in Paris. Today, it continues to be a superb choice for a proper lunch, Sunday brunch, or a cup of the best *café au lait* or hot chocolate along with one of their famed pastries. Blue ribbons in the dessert category go to their *royals,* almond-flavored macaroon cookie sandwiches filled with chocolate, mocha, vanilla, lemon, pistachio, or vanilla cream. Do *not* miss treating yourself to one . . . if you can stop at just one, because once sampled, they are habit-forming and unforgettable. The downstairs seating is around postage-stamp-sized tables arranged under a pastel ceiling mural of chubby cherubs performing all sorts of heavenly baking duties. Here you can watch the hustle and bustle of the well-dressed crowds standing ten-deep at the pastry counter. For lunch or brunch it is much more comfortable to reserve a table upstairs, where the atmosphere is rather solemn, but the scene less hectic, and there is no smoking allowed.

NOTE: Other locations: 75, avenue des Champs Élysées (8th), and Franck et Fils, 80, rue de Passy (16th).

(6) LA FERME SAINT HUBERT
21, rue Vignon (8th)

TELEPHONE
01-47-42-79-20
MÉTRO
Madeleine
OPEN
Mon–Sat
CLOSED
Sun, major holidays, NAC
HOURS
Lunch noon–3:30 P.M., dinner 7–11 P.M.
RESERVATIONS
Essential for lunch, advised for dinner
CREDIT CARDS
AE, MC, V
À LA CARTE
95–175F, BNC
PRIX FIXE
None
ENGLISH SPOKEN
Yes, with Engish menu

The cheese shop next door, run by *maître fromager* Henry Voy, has been long recognized as one of the best *fromageries* in Paris. From this treasure-trove of cheeses comes the first-class ingredients for the fondues, *raclettes,* cheese platters, and other cheese-based dishes served in the restaurant. It is a small room with banquette seating, orange paper table covers and napkins, and a large wall covering depicting cows. The location is around the corner from Fauchon in an area of many offices and shops, so it is swamped at lunch, and if you don't have a reservation, forget it. One of the most popular orders is the *dégustation* platter of seven varieties of cheese. Salads, cheese-based tarts, and hot plates, along with evening meals of *raclette* and fondue, make up the rest of the menu. If you want something light, order *le croque St-Hubert,* a perfectly grilled cheese sandwich. Pots of white goat's milk butter are served with Poilâne bread.

NOTE: There is a second location near the Opéra at 17-19, rue d'Antin (2nd); see page 58. A second cheese shop is located at 14, rue des Sablons in the Galerie St-Didier (16th); telephone: 01-45-53-15-77.

(7) LA FERMETTE MARBEUF 1900*
5, rue Marbeuf (8th)

Of the many Art Nouveau restaurants flourishing in Paris today, this one is exceptional. For the best experience of it, reserve a table in the *jardin d'hiver,* a spectacular glass-roofed winter garden with Art Nouveau grillwork, five thousand elaborate faience tiles, and beautiful leaded-glass windows with intricate floral designs. The room was purchased in total from the Maisons-Lafitte and installed as the *premiére salle* at La Fermette Marbeuf. The restaurant was declared a national historic monument in 1983.

Fortunately, the breathtaking decor does not overshadow the food, where the culinary cornerstones of beef tournedos, leg of lamb, and innovative fish preparations, plus a host of artistic desserts, highlight the lengthy menu. The best dining value is the three-course lunch or dinner menu, with a choice of four starters, including a *terrine de foies de volaille* (chicken liver terrine), four *plats,* followed by either a cheese course or dessert with their *gâteau fondant à l'americain,* a decadently rich fudge cake and the odds-on favorite.

There is no music, and the rooms are too large and brightly lit to be ideal for an intimate dinner, but La Fermette is close to the Champs-Élysées and is a very pleasing formal dining experience, especially on Sunday when so many other restaurants are closed.

TELEPHONE
01-53-23-08-00
MÉTRO
Franklin-D-Roosevelt
OPEN
Daily
CLOSED
Dec 24, NAC
HOURS
Lunch noon–3 P.M., dinner 7:30–11:30 P.M.
RESERVATIONS
Recommended
CREDIT CARDS
AE, DC, MC, V
À LA CARTE
275–300F, BNC
PRIX FIXE
Lunch and dinner, 185F, 3 courses, BNC
ENGLISH SPOKEN
Yes

(8) L'ASSIETTE LYONNAISE
21, rue Marbeuf (8th)

The prices are too cheap to ignore, the red-and-white interior is adorable, and the restaurant has the advantage of being open on Sunday for both lunch and dinner and nightly until 11 P.M. However, the menu is limited to the Lyonnaise specialties of *andouillettes* (chitterling sausages), tripe, blood sausage, and *plats du jour* featuring heavy-duty pork, *bavettes,* and fish on Friday. It is heaven for the carnivores, but for the vegetarian or light eater, better luck next time. This is not to say that what they do at L'Assiette Lyonnaise is not delicious, because it is—just be geared for mountains of hearty meats. The desserts follow suit with rich selections of *tarte Tatin, gâteau au chocolate,* and *profiteroles.*

TELEPHONE
01-47-20-94-80
MÉTRO
George V, Franklin-D-Roosevelt
OPEN
Daily
CLOSED
Never, NAC
HOURS
Lunch noon–3 P.M., dinner 7–11 P.M.
RESERVATIONS
Not necessary
CREDIT CARDS
MC, V
À LA CARTE
125–140F, BNC
PRIX FIXE
None
ENGLISH SPOKEN
Yes

(9) L'ÉCLUSE FRANÇOIS 1ER
64, rue François 1er (8th)

See L'Écluse page 114. All other information is the same.

TELEPHONE: 01-47-20-77-09
MÉTRO: Franklin-D-Roosevelt

(10) L'ÉCLUSE MADELEINE
15, place de la Madeleine (8th)

See L'Écluse page 114. All other information is the same.

TELEPHONE: 01-42-65-34-69
MÉTRO: Madeleine

(11) LE PENY
3, place de la Madeleine (8th)

TELEPHONE
01-42-65-06-75
MÉTRO
Madeleine
OPEN
Daily
CLOSED
Christmas, NAC
HOURS
7:30 A.M.–10 P.M., continuous service for breakfast, hot and cold snacks; lunch noon–3 P.M.
RESERVATIONS
Not necessary
CREDIT CARDS
MC, V
À LA CARTE
50–150F, BC
PRIX FIXE
None
ENGLISH SPOKEN
Yes, with English menu

In a neighborhood known for restaurants serving 500F and 600F lunches, Le Peny is a plush but reasonable alternative. The food is reliable, provided you order correctly, and the interior is clean, comfortable, and filled every day with an attractively stylish crowd. The brightly upholstered chairs on the sidewalk terrace offer some of the best places for the serious people-watching in this corner of Paris.

A wide variety of café food is offered, and some is better than others. One long-standing favorite is the *poulet à la creme* (boned chicken breast on toast smothered with a delicate cream sauce). The *only* desert to consider is the *gâteau à la noix de coco* (a feathery light coconut cake).

If you have spent the morning hoofing it around the Tuileries Gardens, Jeu de Paume, and La Madeleine, or visiting the boutiques that line rue du Faubourg St-Honoré, this is a good place to freshen up and relax, either inside or outside under the shade of umbrellas and sycamore trees while enjoying a great view of Parisian life.

(12) LE ROI DU POT-AU-FEU
40, rue de Ponthieu (8th)

TELEPHONE
01-43-59-41-62
MÉTRO
Franklin-D-Roosevelt
OPEN
Mon–Sat

It is easy to imagine little French *grand-mères* cooking in the kitchens of the two Le Roi restaurants (the other location is on page 153), which are monuments to one of the tastiest French peasant dishes, *pot-au-feu.* Places are set at wooden tables with red-and-white checked tablecloths and napkins.

Regulars show up once a week and pay no attention to anything else on the short menu, concentrating only on the restaurant's timeless specialty. Much lighter than its Anglo-American cousin, beef stew, *pot-au-feu* is served at Le Roi in two courses. The first is an earthenware pot of steaming broth. The second consists of the meat, vegetables, and bone marrow flavored with herbs and sea salt, which have been slowly simmering in the broth for hours. This is served with pickles, sharp mustard, and fresh bread. Enjoy your *pot-au-feu* with a nice Gamay wine and have a good sticky piece of the *tarte Tatin* for dessert.

CLOSED
Sun, holidays, mid-July to mid-Aug

HOURS
Noon–10 P.M., continuous service

RESERVATIONS
Not taken

CREDIT CARDS
MC, V

À LA CARTE
100–160F, BNC

PRIX FIXE
Lunch and dinner, 160F, 3 courses, BC

ENGLISH SPOKEN
Yes

(13) LE VAL D'ISÈRE À PARIS
2, rue de Berri (8th)

Antique wooden skis on the wall, a bar made of skis, and terrific old photos of famous skiers from the Val d'Isère region of southeastern France dominate the interior of this rather large restaurant, located only a half block from the clip joints along the Champs-Élysées.

This is a lively spot, thanks to the affable host and staff. Neighborhood businesspeople and families can usually be found sitting by the open sidewalk windows, greeting friends as they pass by. Big and ugly, but oh, so comfortable, red-and-brown Naugahyde-covered chairs—looking like stage props from a fifties movie—make it crowded during peak hours, and some stepping over and shuffling are required to get everyone seated at the Formica-topped tables, but the effort is worth it.

The menu consistently delivers sound French food from noon until past midnight. This is a good place to bring children for family favorites of spaghetti, thick onion soup, a *croque-monsieur* or *madam,* or a plate of ham and fried eggs. These, along with roast chicken, lamb chops, steaks, ice cream creations worthy of Baskin Robbins, plus a full range of fresh oysters and Burgandy and Savoie fondues, are served in lumberjack portions.

NOTE: Fondues (two-person minimum) are served nightly from 6:30 P.M. until 12:30 A.M. and for Saturday and Sunday lunch from noon to 3 P.M.

TELEPHONE
01-43-59-12-66

MÉTRO
George-V

OPEN
Daily

CLOSED
Never, NAC

HOURS
Noon–12:30 A.M., continuous service

RESERVATIONS
Advised for lunch, no reservations accepted after 8 P.M.

CREDIT CARDS
MC, V

À LA CARTE
140–190F, BNC

PRIX FIXE
Lunch and dinner, 150F, 3 courses, BNC; 175F, 3 courses, BC

ENGLISH SPOKEN
Yes

(14) PÉPITA
21, rue Bayard (8th)

TELEPHONE
01-47-23-58-49
MÉTRO
Champs-Élysées
OPEN
Mon–Fri
CLOSED
Sat–Sun, holidays, July15–Aug 15
HOURS
Lunch noon–3 P.M., dinner 7–10 P.M., bar 8 A.M.–10 P.M.
RESERVATIONS
Advised for lunch
CREDIT CARDS
None
À LA CARTE
180F, BNC
PRIX FIXE
None
ENGLISH SPOKEN
Yes

There *is* a Pépita, and she has been running this show for over forty years, along with her son, who handles the business side, and her daughter-in-law, who cashiers and runs the bar. Some of the help has been here for thirty years, and certain regulars are into their second decade of dining. Pépita has the formula for success down pat.

This unpretentious bistro comes complete with bentwood hat and coat racks and the original ice box, floor tiles, and zinc bar still in place. Tables are placed end to end and covered with red-and-white cloths and red paper napkins. The atmosphere is like a theater vignette with a constantly changing cast of characters. VIPs, svelte fashion models, and clusters of ladies in identical Chanel suits carrying Yorkshire terriers arrive for lunch. Free tables pop up once in a blue moon, if you forget to book at this busy time. Things mellow out in the evening, with professionals and *couturière*-clad, middle-aged couples who know how to eat well while spending less.

The food can be described as good and heavy. You will see serious servings of *chèvre chaude sur toast* (warm chèvre on toast), snails in buttery garlic sauce, and *oeufs en gelée* (jellied eggs) followed by pork and rice, veal kidneys spooned over egg-noodles paella, and pepper steak with Pépita's own homemade *frites.* A simple chocolate mousse or a floating island will be about all you can do for dessert. Inexpensive carafe house wines are good, so ordering anything else is not at all necessary.

Ninth Arrondissement

(See map on pages 140–141.)

The ninth is predominantly a business area, with many banks, corporate headquarters, law firms, and insurance companies. The Grands Boulevards, laid out by Baron Haussmann, are those wide thoroughfares that lead from the Opéra to place de la République. The smart end is at the Opéra, the center of Paris during the Belle Epoque, that period of elegance and gaiety characterizing Parisian life from the mid-nineteenth century to World War I.

RIGHT BANK
Grands Boulevards, *grand magazins* (Au Printemps and Galéries Lafayette), the Opéra

NINTH ARRONDISSEMENT RESTAURANTS

(†) indicates listing not shown on map

(15) CHEZ JEAN
52, rue Lamartine (9th)

Chez Jean is that intimate, romantic, off-the-beaten-path restaurant we all hope to find . . . where the owner, Didier Gaugan, speaks English, the chef is talented, the prices are right, and few other visitors to Paris have discovered it. It is located not too far from the honky-tonk world of Montmartre but it's worlds away in style, quality, and value. The wooden exterior looks like a mountain chalet, but there the similarity ends. Inside the tone is formal, with peach linens, lovely flowers, and nice china, all providing a delightful backdrop for the fine food prepared by chef Pierre Jay, who worked at La Tour d'Argent.

No doubt it is beginning to sound like a Big Splurge, but it's not when you consider the quality of the food

TELEPHONE
01-48-78-62-73

MÉTRO
Cadet

OPEN
Mon–Fri lunch and dinner, Sat dinner only

CLOSED
Sat lunch, Sun, holidays, May 1–10, first 3 weeks in Aug, Dec 24–Jan 2

HOURS
Lunch noon–2:30 P.M., dinner 7:30–10:30 P.M. (Sat till 11 P.M.)

RESERVATIONS
Advised

CREDIT CARDS
MC, V
À LA CARTE
60F for any *entrée* or dessert, 110F for any *plat*
PRIX FIXE
170F, 3 courses and cheese, BNC
ENGLISH SPOKEN
Yes

and the final bill. You can get a three-course meal of unusual and inventive dishes for 170F. Any appetizer or dessert selected from this prix fixe menu will be 60F; any main course will be 110F. The confirmed classics are here, but why not branch out and begin with their own smoked salmon, lightly grilled giant crabs with a watercress sauce, or sardines in a citrus vinaigrette. The honey-roasted duck, fresh cod, or the beef filet in red wine will have you asking for more. Indulgence wins over caution every time when presented with all the choices for the grand finale: pear *clafoutis,* sweet potato cake flavored with vanilla, or caramelized apple tart with an icy scoop of mango sorbet are only three of the temptations. All in all it will be a delightful meal that will be a dining highlight of your trip to Paris.

(16) FRUCTIDOR
67, rue de Provence (9th)

TELEPHONE
01-48-74-53-46
MÉTRO
Chausée-d'Antin, Trinité
OPEN
Mon–Sat lunch only
CLOSED
Sun, holidays, NAC
HOURS
11 A.M.–3 P.M.
RESERVATIONS
Not taken
CREDIT CARDS
None
À LA CARTE
50–100F, BNC
PRIX FIXE
None
ENGLISH SPOKEN
Yes

A dozen or more teas and some of the best sweet and savory tarts served anywhere are prepared here daily for a standing-room-only lunchtime crowd. If you are shopping at Galeries Lafayette, Au Printemps, or Marks & Spencer, try this little hole in the wall for a nutritious lunch that will leave plenty of money in your wallet for serious afternoon buying. Order a fresh vegetable cocktail with a tomato, carrot, or apple base by the glass or carafe. Try a savory tart, maybe the quiche lorraine, the *chèvre oseille* (goat cheese and sorrel), or the spicy *mexicaine* (corn, chorizo, and mushrooms), all of which come with a green salad. There are also large one-meal salads, and for dessert . . . more tarts. Choose from fresh fruit, cheese, or chocolate. If another tart is too much, they have ice cream and sorbets and *le dessert léger* (light dessert)—*fromage blanc* served with honey, nuts, raisins, and raspberry sauce.

At both locations, the tarts are available for take out, either whole or by the slice. On Thursday and Friday at the Chausée d'Antin location, chicken tandoori is the specialty prepared by the owner, Sathi, who is Indian.

(17) FRUCTIDOR
46, rue St-Georges (9th)

See entry above. All other information is the same.
TELEPHONE: 01-49-95-02-10

MÉTRO: St-Georges
OPEN: Mon–Fri lunch only
CLOSED: Sat–Sun, NAC

(18) LAFAYETTE GOURMET

48, boulevard Haussmann (1st floor) (9th)

It is Christmas Day and your birthday rolled into one at Lafayette Gourmet, the magnificent food department that is part of Galeries Lafayette on boulevard Haussmann.

Food lovers will feel they have hit the jackpot with the multitude of riches on display. Even if you are not shopping for food, you can come to eat at one of the food stations, where salads, fruits, cheeses, wines, coffees, Lenôtre pastries, pasta, grills, and sushi are served all day, every day but Sunday.

TELEPHONE
01-48-74-46-06
MÉTRO
Chausée d'Antin, Havre-Caumartin
OPEN
Mon–Sat
CLOSED
Sun, holidays, NAC
HOURS
9:30 A.M.–6:30 P.M., continuous service
RESERVATIONS
Not taken
CREDIT CARDS
AE, V
À LA CARTE
20F and up
PRIX FIXE
None
ENGLISH SPOKEN
Yes

(19) L'AMANGUIER

20, boulevard Montmartre (9th)

Trendy restaurants come and go every day in Paris, and the chains get weaker with each expansion. L'Amanguier, with four central Paris addresses, has lasted because it has developed a successful formula and stayed with it: efficient, pleasant service, reasonable prices, and good food served seven days a week in pretty garden settings. True, it is a chain, but there are very few restaurants in this price category that provide such consistent quality in both service and food, with a menu offering a wealth of appealing selections and an ever-changing list of seasonal specialties. The crowd depends on the location, but it generally includes a pastiche of cute young things in short dresses, grandes dames wrapped in furs, and successful businessmen wearing power suits.

NOTE: There are three other L'Amanguier restaurants in central Paris: 46, boulevard Montparnasse (15th), see page 193; 51, rue du Théâtre (15th), see page 193; 43, avenue des Ternes (17th), see page 208.

TELEPHONE
01-47-70-91-35
MÉTRO
Richelieu-Drouot
OPEN
Daily
CLOSED
NAC
HOURS
Lunch noon–2 P.M., dinner 7 P.M.–midnight
RESERVATIONS
Advised, especially weekends and holidays
CREDIT CARDS
AE, DC, MC, V
À LA CARTE
150–165F, BNC
PRIX FIXE
Lunch and dinner, 95F, 2 courses, 130F, 3 courses, both BNC
ENGLISH SPOKEN
Yes

(20) LE BISTRO DES DEUX THÉÂTRES
18, rue Blanche (9th)

TELEPHONE
01-45-26-41-43
MÉTRO
Trinité
OPEN
Daily
CLOSED
Never, NAC
HOURS
Lunch noon–2:30 P.M., dinner 7:15 P.M.–midnight
RESERVATIONS
Advised
CREDIT CARDS
AE, MC, V
À LA CARTE
None
PRIX FIXE
Lunch and dinner, 175F, 3 courses, BC
ENGLISH SPOKEN
Yes

Clichy and Pigalle are hardly bon-ton Paris neighborhoods. These infamous places, at the northern end of the ninth arrondissement, operate around the clock with peep shows, bordellos, and "ladies of the night" standing in doorways beckoning to passersby. Hidden in all this sleaze are little pockets and jewels of respectability. Le Bistro des Deux Théâtres is one such place, a fine *formule* restaurant with a single prix fixe menu. This solid bistro has preserved its good cooking and authenticity despite its setting. It manages to fill a variety of needs with its traditional charm, pressed linens, fresh flowers on each table, and food you would expect to find in a place charging twice as much.

The choices are excellent, at least ten for each course. Consider lobster ravioli, fresh asparagus in a buttery chervil sauce, artichoke hearts with smoked duck, or a dozen snails. Liver in a raspberry vinaigrette, thyme-flavored lamb, or *navarin de la mer printanier au safran* (a saffron fish stew with sea bass, salmon, and perch) are just a few of the possible main courses, which change frequently based on market availability and the season. This is a good place to save room for dessert—indulge in flaming Grand-Marnier crêpes, *croquant de pomme et banane sauce mandarine* (apples and bananas on a crisp crust base with mandarine orange sauce), or a dreamy crème brûlée shot with bourbon. Both an apéritif and wine are included in the price, and unlike most restaurants of this type, you have three choices for your red or white vintage. Dinner ends with a strong espresso.

(21) LE RELAIS SAVOYARD
13, rue Rodier (9th)

TELEPHONE
01-45-26-17-48
MÉTRO
Notre-Dame-de-Lorette, Anvers
OPEN
Mon–Sat
CLOSED
Sun, holidays, 10 days in winter, a few days in May, Aug
HOURS
Lunch noon–2:30 P.M., dinner 7:30–10 P.M., bar 8:30 A.M.–10 P.M.
RESERVATIONS
For 4 or more
CREDIT CARDS
V

Le Relais Savoyard is a good example of the traditional, family-run French bistro, where the middle-aged *patron* and his wife have run things from behind the bar forever and the loyal, long-term waitresses have no intention of leaving. Overall, it is not sophisticated, but for a blue-collar, working-class atmosphere and a Cheap Eat, it is just the ticket.

The timeless menu is a collection of homey dishes from the Savoy region of France. On a wintry evening it is nice to sit in the wood-paneled room in back, which is lined with the owners' collection of antique coffee and fondue pots, sauce dishes, and a stuffed boar's head.

Order the *côte de veau maison,* a rich combination of veal, ham, mushrooms, and cheese, topped with Mornay sauce and flambéed. If you go with a group, either of the fondue specialties makes a satisfying choice. Desserts tend to be an afterthought on the part of the chef, so it is better to concentrate on the rest of the meal.

À LA CARTE
130–150F, BNC
PRIX FIXE
Lunch and dinner, 80F and 120F, 3 courses, BC
ENGLISH SPOKEN
Limited

(22) LE ROI DU POT-AU-FEU
34, rue Vignon (9th)

See Le Roi du Pot-au-Feu page 146. All other information is the same.

TELEPHONE: 01-47-42-37-10
MÉTRO: Madeleine, Havre-Caumartin

(23) LES BACCHANTES
21, rue de Caumartin (9th)

You can't order a beer or a coke, and *l'eau municipale est sur demande* (tap water by request). You can, however, order fine wines by the glass or bottle at Raymond Pocous's popular wine bar. He stocks over forty different international vintages, along with the best France has to offer; he features different bottles weekly. Okay, the wine is good, but is there anything decent to eat? Absolutely . . . you can have plates of cheese or *charcuterie* (cold meats), *tartines* (open-faced sandwiches), their own foie gras and pâté, omelettes, daily specials, salads, and homemade desserts. Besides the good wine and food, the atmosphere is fun and friendly and the prices great for most Cheap Eaters in Paris

TELEPHONE
01-42-65-25-35
MÉTRO
Havre-Caumartin
OPEN
Mon–Sat
CLOSED
Sun, NAC
HOURS
11:30 A.M.–6 A.M., continuous service
RESERVATIONS
Not necessary
CREDIT CARDS
AE, MC, V
À LA CARTE
25–125F, BNC
PRIX FIXE
None
ENGLISH SPOKEN
Limited

LES DIABLES AU THYM
35, rue Bergère (9th)

If I could, I would return to Les Diables au Thym every night. Whenever you are fortunate enough to be in Paris, you can always come here for an exquisite meal and impeccable service, where you will feel you are in a friend's small, intimate dining room. Fresh flowers and hurricane candles grace the linen-covered tables, the china is Villeroy and Bosch, and the seating on banquettes and padded chairs is comfortable. One waiter serves the entire room, which has tables filled by 8:30 P.M. and people still arriving at 10:30 P.M. Every beautifully prepared and presented dish seems to be a winner, especially the foie gras and smoked duck salad garnished

TELEPHONE
01-47-70-77-09
MÉTRO
Rue Montmartre
OPEN
Oct–Mar: Mon–Fri lunch and dinner, Sat dinner only; April–Sept: Sun dinner also
CLOSED
Oct–Mar: Sat lunch, Sun; April–Sept: Sat–Sun lunch; major holidays; NAC
HOURS
Lunch noon 3 P.M., dinner 7–11 P.M.
RESERVATIONS
Essential

CREDIT CARDS
AE, MC, V
À LA CARTE
225–250F, BNC
PRIX FIXE
Lunch and dinner: 100F (Mon–Fri till 9 P.M.), 2 courses, BNC; 145F (daily), 3 courses, BNC
ENGLISH SPOKEN
Limited

with asparagus spears and the duck *à l'orange* surrounded by seven fresh vegetables and a potato *galette.* For dessert bliss, the *croquette au chocolate praline,* a voluptuous creation that oozes bittersweet chocolate with every bite, is required eating.

Coffee comes with a plate of homemade cookies and pieces of white and dark chocolate.

(24) RESTAURANT CHARTIER
7, rue de Faubourg Montmartre (9th)

TELEPHONE
01-47-70-86-29
MÉTRO
Montmartre
OPEN
Daily
CLOSED
Never, NAC
HOURS
Lunch 11 A.M.–3 P.M., dinner 6–9:30 P.M.
RESERVATIONS
Not necessary
CREDIT CARDS
MC, V (over 100F)
À LA CARTE
80–100F, BNC
PRIX FIXE
Lunch and dinner, 110F, 3 courses, BC
ENGLISH SPOKEN
Limited

You can trust the French to know a good food bargain when they smell it. For decades Restaurant Chartier (and its sister establishment Le Drouot, now closed) has been a major bargain destination for Cheap Eats. Not much has changed over the years in this authentic Parisian soup kitchen with its fin de siècle decor, squads of brusque white-aproned waiters, and basic "no parsley" food. There is no glamour or tinsel here. Big, noisy, barnlike, and always crowded, it is the blue-collar worker's Maxim's, and they and many others eat here in droves every day of the year.

The menu, which changes daily, is long, but if you select carefully, you will have a satisfying and cheap meal. Select the dishes that have to be made to order and save the fancier ones for another place. You could start with a beet or tomato salad, hard-boiled egg and mayonnaise, or a plate of ham. Order a jug of the house wine to go with your main coarse of roast chicken, fish, or grilled beef, along with potatoes that have been fried or boiled. All garnishes are extra, but not by much. The most reliable dessert is the daily fruit *tarte.*

(25) RESTAURANT LOU CANTOU
35, Cité d'Antin (at 61, rue de Provence) (9th)

TELEPHONE
01-48-74-75-15
MÉTRO
Chausée-d'Antin
OPEN
Mon–Sat lunch only
CLOSED
Sun, holidays, Aug
HOURS
Lunch 11 A.M.–3 P.M.
RESERVATIONS
Not necessary
CREDIT CARDS
None

It's *very* local, *very* cheap, and *very* good . . . just keep in mind where you are and don't expect hummingbird's tongues served under glass by stiff waiters in gilded surroundings. If you didn't know about this Cheap Eat beforehand, you would definitely miss it. Even though it is only a few minutes away from the Galeries Lafayette and Au Printemps shopping corridor, it is a hidden find known only to insiders. To find it, walk along rue de Provence until you come to the walkway Cité d'Antin, turn in, and you will recognize Lou Cantou by the blooming plants crowding the front window.

Fifty or more diners squeeze into a space that looks like a boardinghouse dining room (serving only lunch), with hard chairs, harsh lighting, and a few copper pots and farm tools thrown in for decoration. The unadorned prix fixe menu costs only 65F for three courses and a quarter liter of wine, mineral water, or beer. There is a choice of twelve starters, five main courses, and cheese or dessert. The owner, Mme. Bullat, is a gregarious hostess and seems to know everyone by name. Her husband is the jovial cook in the kitchen.

NOTE: Mme. Bullat will offer you a kir or coffee if you show or tell her about *Cheap Eats in Paris.*

À LA CARTE
None
PRIX FIXE
65F, 3 courses, BC
ENGLISH SPOKEN
Limited
MISCELLANEOUS
Nonsmoking section

(26) TEA FOLLIES
6, place Gustave Toudouze (9th)

Many first-time visitors to Paris do not stray far from the beaten track. This is too bad because they miss some of the most interesting places that way. Not too far from Montmartre, and near a number of small theaters, is Tea Follies, a welcome place to relax after looking through the antique shops and funky clothing boutiques around place St-Georges.

When I go, I order the tangy lemon-curd *tarte* or the *archedois,* a fattening delight made with chocolate and chestnuts, and spend a lazy hour leafing through the English and French periodicals stacked about. On warm afternoons, the cobblestone terrace is the place to sit and order a beautiful salad lunch or one of the specialties of the chef: either the chicken pie, the cheese ravioli, or the salmon tagliatelle. On Sunday, filling brunches are offered and include buttery scones, light soufflés, and a Bloody Mary to really get you going for the day.

Bonuses for many are the special nonsmoking section and the changing art exhibits featuring work by local artists.

TELEPHONE
01-42-80-08-44
MÉTRO
St-Georges
OPEN
Daily
CLOSED
Christmas and New Year's Day, NAC
HOURS
Winter: Mon–Sat 10 A.M.–8 P.M., Sun 10 A.M.–6 P.M.; summer: Mon–Sat 9 A.M.–9 P.M., Sun 9 A.M.–6 P.M.; continuous service: breakfast 9 A.M.–noon, lunch all day, tea 3 P.M.– closing, Sun brunch opening–4 P.M.
RESERVATIONS
Recommended for Sun brunch
CREDIT CARDS
AE, MC, V (over 100F)
À LA CARTE
90–150F, BNC
PRIX FIXE
Sun brunch, 90F and 150F, BC
ENGLISH SPOKEN
Yes
MISCELLANEOUS
Nonsmoking section

(27) VERDEAU DROUOT
25, passage Verdeau (across from 6, rue de la Grange Batelière) (9th)

Just because a French person goes to an office every day does not mean he or she is going to sacrifice having a proper lunch or, worse yet, brown-bag it. On the other hand, they usually have only an hour to eat, and they don't want to spend big francs on a wine-infused, expensive meal. Enter Verdeau Drouot, which brings a touch of class to *la cuisine rapide.* The restaurant is located in

TELEPHONE
01-45-23-15-96
MÉTRO
Richelieu-Drouot, Montmartre
OPEN
Mon–Fri lunch and tea only
CLOSED
Sat–Sun, holidays, Aug 15–30

HOURS
Lunch noon–3 P.M., tea 3–4 P.M.

RESERVATIONS
Advised

CREDIT CARDS
MC, V (over 100F)

À LA CARTE
85–125F, BNC

PRIX FIXE
La formule gourmande, 85–110F, 2 courses, BC; *verdeau express*, 75F, 2 courses, BNC

ENGLISH SPOKEN
Yes

the *passage* Verdeau Drouot, a nineteenth-century shopping arcade, which houses small shops selling old books, cameras, early rock-and-roll records, and other collectibles.

Verdeau Drouot offers full meals on a single plate, called *assiettes gourmandes froides* (cold) or *chaudes* (hot). Each has been given a catchy name, such as *Petrouchka* (smoked salmon, *tarama,* salad, dark bread, and fresh fruit), *Safari tartes* (assorted warm *tartes* with a green salad), *NémÈa* (chicken curry on basmati rice with a mixed salad), and *Winnipeg* (cold roast beef with fresh vegetables, potatoes, salad, and fruit). While these *assiettes gourmandes* are well priced, the best Cheap Eats here are the two prix fixe menus. For example, *la formule gourmande* includes any *assiette gourmande* and dessert, one glass of wine, and one coffee. *Le menu verdeau express* offers any *assiette gourmande* and a dessert or cheese of the day. All desserts are made here. The most popular are the Norwegian apple and cinnamon cake (adapted from a recipe of the owner's mother) and the house specialty, *gâteau noix* (nut cake). No matter how you order, it will be a filling meal that is much more interesting and French than a burger and fries someplace else.

Tenth Arrondissement

(No map for this arrondissment.)

Although most visitors to Paris only pass through the tenth when they take a train from either the Gare du Nord or the Gare de l'Est, there is another good reason to venture into this *quartier populaire,* or traditional working-class neighborhood: to shop for china and crystal along rue de Paradis and visit the famous Baccarat crystal museum and store about halfway down the same street. For bargains, if you consider anything in Baccarat to be that, look for the red dots on items displayed on the back tables.

RIGHT BANK
Canal St-Martin, Place de la République, Rue de Paradis, Gare du Nord, and Gare de l'Est

TENTH ARRONDISSEMENT RESTAURANTS

* Restaurants marked with an asterisk (*) are considered Big Splurges.

BRASSERIE FLO*
7, cour des Petites-Écuries (10th)

Brasserie Flo is another star in the crown of Jean-Paul Bucher's resurrected Art Nouveau brasseries, and if you are shopping along rue de Paradis (see *Cheap Sleeps in Paris,* "Cheap Chic"), this is a great lunch stop. To say that this one is not easy to find is an understatement if there ever was one. The first time I went, I was sure the taxi driver was taking me on a wild goose chase, and when he left me off at the opening of a dark alley in a questionable neighborhood, I was positive of it. Once inside, however, the approach was completely forgotten. Seated along a banquette in one of the two long rooms—with their dark wood walls, zinc bar, and waiters with long aprons serving a dressed-to-the-teeth crowd—you will feel truly Parisian.

Every day of the year Brasserie Flo is a great place to go for platters of oysters, Alsatian *choucroutes* (their specialty), onion soup, foie gras, and grilled meat. Late-nighters and lunch patrons have special menus in addition to the versatile à la carte.

NOTE: Cour des Petites-Écuries is a small alley between rue de Foubourg-St-Denis and passage des Petites-Écuries. Since the neighborhood is questionable, I would advise taking a taxi at night.

TELEPHONE
01-47-70-13-59

MÉTRO
Château d'Eau, Strasbourg St-Denis

OPEN
Daily

CLOSED
December 24, NAC

HOURS
Lunch noon–3 P.M., dinner 7 P.M.–1 A.M.

RESERVATIONS
Advised, definitely on weekends

CREDIT CARDS
AE, DC, MC, V

À LA CARTE
Lunch, 125–150F, BC; dinner, 190–250F, BC

PRIX FIXE
Lunch, 125F, 2 courses, BC; dinner: 175F, 3 courses, BC; 130F (after 10 P.M.), 2 courses, BC

ENGLISH SPOKEN
Yes

HÔTEL DU NORD
102, quai de Jemmapes (10th)

TELEPHONE
01-40-40-78-78

MÉTRO
Jacques-Bonsergent

OPEN
Tues–Sat lunch and dinner, Sun–Mon lunch only

CLOSED
Sun–Mon dinner, NAC

HOURS
Bar 10 A.M.–1 A.M., continuous service; lunch noon–2:30 P.M. (Sun till 4 P.M.); dinner 8–11:30 P.M.

RESERVATIONS
Not necessary

CREDIT CARDS
AE, DC, MC, V

À LA CARTE
100–150F, BC

PRIX FIXE
Lunch, 60F, 2 courses, 90F, 3 courses, both BNC; dinner, 120F and 170F, 3 courses, both BNC

ENGLISH SPOKEN
Limited

MISCELLANEOUS
Live music Thur–Sat from 9 P.M., Sun noon–4 P.M.

"Being here makes you feel you really know something about Paris," mused my friend as we sat outside overlooking the picturesque Canal Saint Martin and the footbridge crossing it. It was a lazy Sunday afternoon, the sun was shining, and spring was just brushing the trees with green. Along with the live music and good, basic café food, it added up to a wonderful Parisian experience. This romantic spot was the site of the 1938 French film classic of the same name, starring Louis Jovet and Arletty. The café has recently been rediscovered by an eclectic, almost trendy crowd featuring young couples holding hands and grannies peeking into prams. Any time of day, stop in and have a drink standing at the original thirties bar, or sit down and order the *plat du jour*, then walk along the length of the pretty canal. It all has great charm, a worthwhile stop in a part of Paris that has not lost its soul.

JULIEN*

16, rue du Faubourg St-Denis (10th)

Leave the shady red-light neighborhood behind as you pass through velvet curtains into this art deco wonderland, which encompasses one of the most beautiful brasserie dining rooms in Paris. The stunning decor is an amazing combination of magnificent stained-glass ceiling panels and Mucha-style molten glass, massive globe lights, huge floral displays, and a collection of vintage *chapeaux* hanging from brass hat racks. Even the tiled floor is remarkable. The menu is a standard list of brasserie favorites (without the oyster stand) accompanied by plenty of wine, good cheer, and a formally attired waitstaff serving an audience of fashionable French diners.

TELEPHONE
01-47-70-12-06

MÉTRO
Strasbourg St-Denis

OPEN
Daily

CLOSED
December 24, NAC

HOURS
Lunch noon–3 P.M., dinner 7 P.M.–1:30 A.M.

RESERVATIONS
Essential

CREDIT CARDS
AE, DC, MC, V

À LA CARTE
210–250F, BNC

PRIX FIXE
Lunch, 130F, 2 courses, DC, dinner: 190F, 3 courses, BC; 130F (after 10 P.M.), 2 courses, BC

ENGLISH SPOKEN
Yes

MISCELLANEOUS
A taxi is strongly suggested at night.

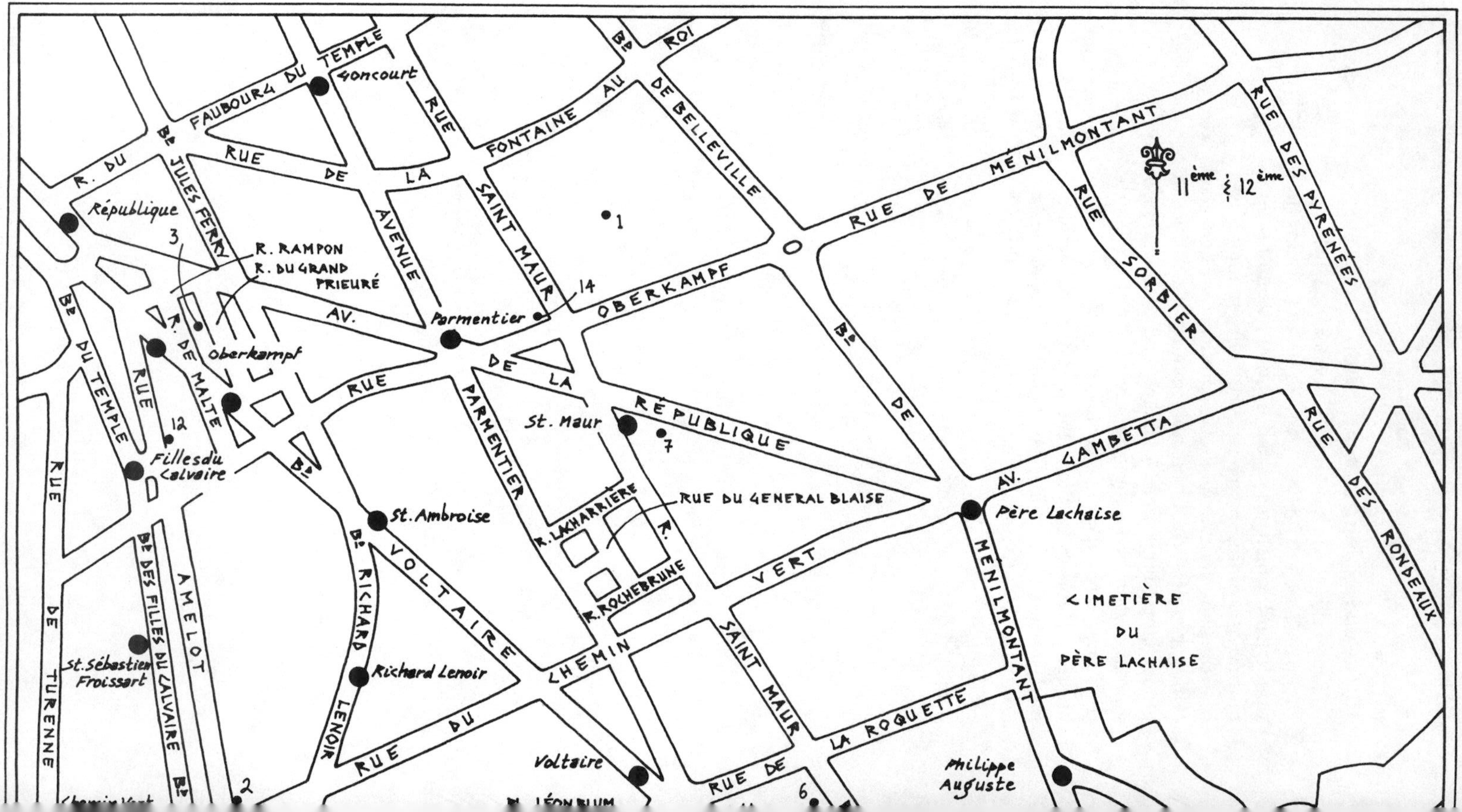

11ème & 12ème
R. DU FAUBOURG DU TEMPLE
Goncourt
RUE DE LA FONTAINE AU ROI
Bd DE BELLEVILLE
RUE DE MÉNILMONTANT
RUE DES PYRÉNÉES
RUE SORBIER
RUE DES RONDEAUX
Bd JULES FERRY
République
3
R. RAMPON
R. DU GRAND PRIEURÉ
AVENUE DE LA
RUE SAINT MAUR
1
14
Parmentier
AV. OBERKAMPF
Oberkampf
R. DE MALTE
RUE DE LA RÉPUBLIQUE
Bd DE
Bd DU TEMPLE
RUE
12
Filles du Calvaire
St. Maur
7
AV. GAMBETTA
Père Lachaise
PARMENTIER
RUE DU GENERAL BLAISE
R. LACHARRIÈRE
R.
R. ROCHEBRUNE
St. Ambroise
Bd VOLTAIRE
Bd RICHARD LENOIR
Richard Lenoir
VERT
CHEMIN
SAINT MAUR
MÉNILMONTANT
CIMETIÈRE DU PÈRE LACHAISE
RUE DE TURENNE
Bd DES FILLES DU CALVAIRE
AMELOT
St. Sébastien Froissart
RUE DU
Voltaire
RUE DE LA ROQUETTE
6
Philippe Auguste
2

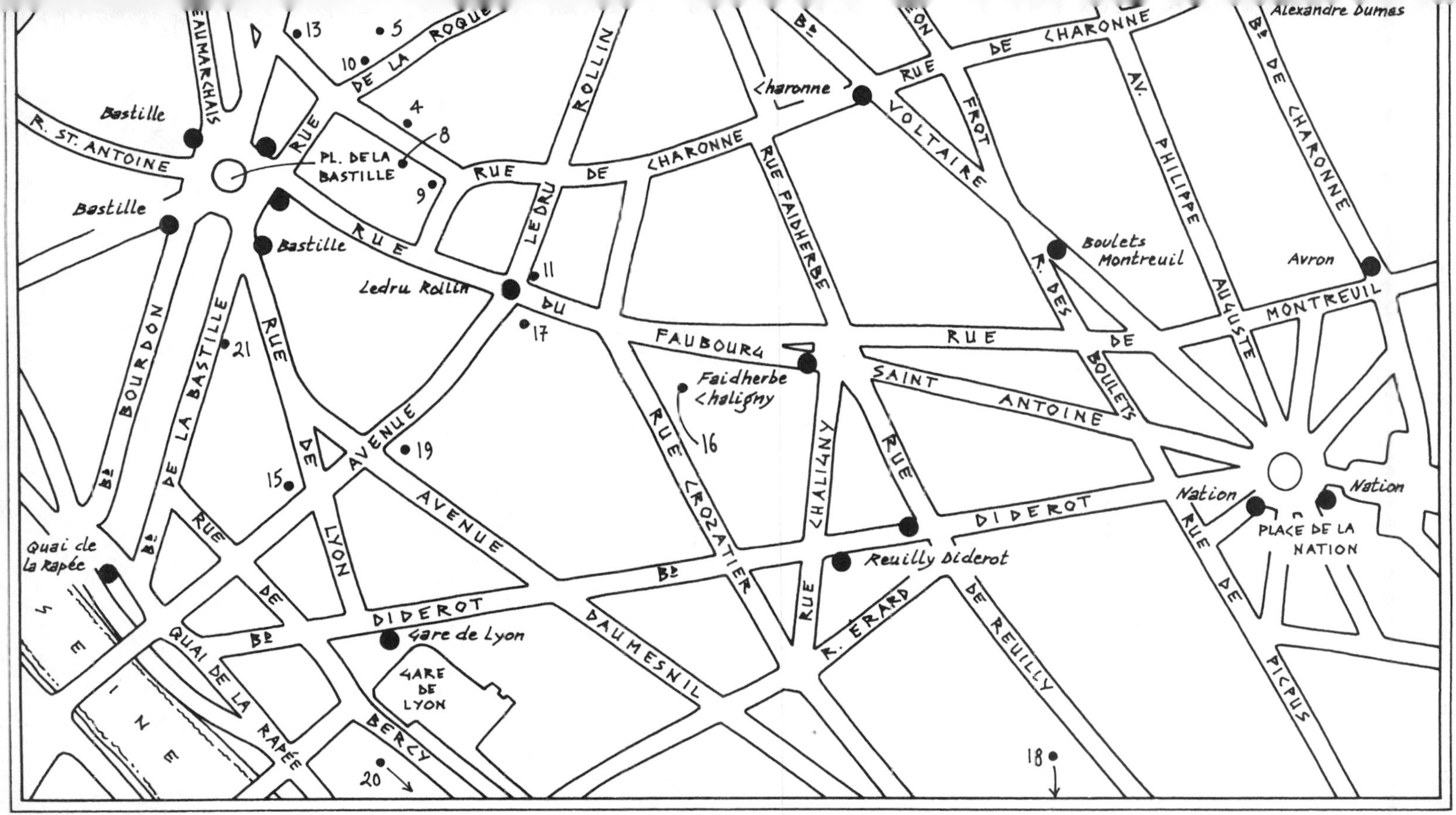
Alexandre Dumas
Bd DE CHARONNE
RUE DE CHARONNE
AV. PHILIPPE AUGUSTE
Avron
MONTREUIL
Boulets Montreuil
R. DES BOULETS
RUE FROT
VOLTAIRE
Charonne
RUE DE CHARONNE
RUE FAIDHERBE
R. DE LA ROQUE
RUE ROLLIN
RUE LEDRU
R. ST. ANTOINE
BEAUMARCHAIS
Bastille
PL. DE LA BASTILLE
RUE
Ledru Rollin
RUE DU FAUBOURG SAINT ANTOINE
RUE DE
Faidherbe Chaligny
RUE CROZATIER
RUE CHALIGNY
RUE DIDEROT
Nation
PLACE DE LA NATION
RUE DE PICPUS
Reuilly Diderot
R. ERARD
RUE DE REUILLY
AVENUE DAUMESNIL
Bd DIDEROT
Gare de Lyon
GARE DE LYON
AVENUE DE LYON
RUE DE LA BASTILLE
Bd BOURDON
Bd RUE DE BERCY
QUAI DE LA RAPÉE
Quai de la Rapée
SEINE
4
5
8
9
10
11
13
15
16
17
18
19
20
21

Eleventh Arrondissement

RIGHT BANK
Colonne de Juillet (July Column), Opéra Bastille

The Bastille was the site of France's most famous prison, overrun on July 14, 1789, marking the birth of the French Revolution. All that remains today of the Bastille is a faint outline traced in cobblestones. The latest revolution is the new Bastille opera house, which, upon completion, instantaneously turned this formerly "off limits" *quartier* into one of the most trendy, must-go, must-see, and must-try parts of Paris. By day it is not much. The area still mixes back-alley workers and workshops with hip new designers and their boutiques. Don't be surprised to see panhandlers, overflowing garbage cans, and some very seedy restaurants and bars all mixed in with the hot spots. Action in the eleventh begins around 10 P.M., when it becomes a meat market and cruising territory for the hipsters who prowl the streets, fill the restaurants, and drink in bars until the first rays of dawn.

ELEVENTH ARRONDISSEMENT RESTAURANTS

(1) ASTIER
44, rue Jean-Pierre Timbaud (11th)

If Astier did not exist, it would have to be invented because nowhere is everything you have ever heard about Paris dining more in evidence than in this noisy, hot, crowded bistro where everyone looks like a regular. The only thing to admire in the plain interior is the graceful staircase, which is almost lost behind the bar. The seating at the tightly packed, smaller-than-usual tables puts you practically on your neighbor's lap, and it causes some ducking if the casually clad waiters swing the plates too low. However, if you speak even a little French, your neighbor's conversations might provide some very thought-provoking eavesdropping.

Abundance is the name of the game for the kitchen and a warning is in order. The prix fixe meal, which is all that's available, includes four *enormous* courses that tend to grow as the meal progresses. Be careful when ordering because each course could comprise an entire meal, as my dining companion found out when he ordered the homemade pasta with basil as an *entrée.* When his plate arrived, we both gasped . . . it was enough for both of us and this was only the beginning. The handwritten (but legible) menu changes constantly, reflecting the seasonal changes at the market. A safe and sane beginning would be one of the salads, which should leave room to do justice to a *blanquette de porc, lapin à la moutard,* or any of the fresh fish dishes the chef loves to prepare. The cheese platter is magnificent and includes at least twenty choices. You are encouraged to help yourself to as much as you can eat. Desserts do not fall behind. There is an impressive array of fruit and sugar creations, which are all made here except for the sorbet. Those going for the calorie jackpot will want the chocolate fudge slice floating in a coffee cream sauce. Those hoping to walk out unassisted will probably go for the fresh fruit or the warm apple gratin.

The food at Astier more than makes up for the crowded conditions, scattered service, and uninspired decor. As my friend said, "You can't eat the decor or the service, but you can certainly pay for it." At Astier, you know that all you are paying for is the food, and it is worth *every* value-packed bite—as well as the diet you will swear to start tomorrow.

TELEPHONE
01-43-57-16-35

MÉTRO
Parmentier

OPEN
Mon–Fri

CLOSED
Sat–Sun, holidays, last 2 weeks in April, first 3 weeks of Aug

HOURS
Lunch noon–2 P.M., dinner 8–11 P.M.

RESERVATIONS
Essential as far in advance as possible

CREDIT CARDS
MC, V

À LA CARTE
None

PRIX FIXE
Lunch and dinner, 140F, 4 courses, BNC

ENGLISH SPOKEN

(2) AU C'AMELOT
50, rue Amelot (11th)

TELEPHONE
01-43-55-54-04
MÉTRO
Chemin-Vert
OPEN
Mon–Fri
CLOSED
Sat–Sun, holidays, Aug
HOURS
Lunch noon–2 P.M., dinner 7:30–10:30 P.M.
RESERVATIONS
Essential
CREDIT CARDS
MC, V
À LA CARTE
None
PRIX FIXE
Lunch, 130F, 4 courses, BNC; dinner, 150F, 4 courses, BNC
ENGLISH SPOKEN
Limited
MISCELLANEOUS
There is only one menu, with no choices and no substitutions.

No frills, no pomp, no choice . . . no kidding. This little bare bones bistro is sold out days in advance thanks to its straightforward, delicious food, which is complemented by a short list of wines. And no wonder it is so popular—it is the creation of Christian Constant, the famed two-star Michelin chef from the elegant Les Ambassadeurs dining room at the Hôtel de Crillon.

The narrow room at Au C'Amelot has a southern feel, with eleven tables covered with blue, white, and yellow Provinçal print cloths and napkins. Serving duties are handled by a plainly dressed waitress and bartender. A blackboard displays the list of modest wines . . . four or five red and only one white available by the glass or bottle. The food is homestyle, and there are no substitutions to the no-choice, four-course prix fixe menu. Everyone eats the same meal.

You start by helping yourself to soup and crunchy chunks of country bread. Next is a fish course, followed by a meat course—perhaps tender slices of veal roast on a bed of potatoes and surrounded by a light sauce and a sprinkling of salad greens. After a piece of perfectly ripe cheese comes dessert . . . maybe a sugar-dusted warm fruit *clafoutis* or a tangy lemon *tarte* will be served. Aside from being delicious, it is a tremendous Cheap Eat value in Paris.

(3) AU TROU NORMAND
9, rue Jean-Pierre Timbaud (11th)

TELEPHONE
01-48-05-80-23
MÉTRO
Oberkamph
OPEN
Mon–Fri lunch and dinner, Sat dinner only
CLOSED
Sun, holidays, Aug
HOURS
Lunch noon–2:30 P.M., dinner 7:30–10 P.M. (Sat till 11 P.M.)
RESERVATIONS
Not necessary
CREDIT CARDS
None
À LA CARTE
70–85F, BNC
PRIX FIXE
None
ENGLISH SPOKEN
None

Au Trou Normand is a good, old-time Cheap Eat that promises nothing fancy; it just delivers the basics to students, shirt-sleeved merchants, and backpacking tourists on budgets. Everyone sits at tables with red tablecloths and plastic overlays, and service is by a trio of matrons wearing comfortable shoes and housedresses. The menu hardly transcends the ordinary, but it will satisfy most hunger and budget pangs. A dozen or so *entrées* and *plats* feature crudités, anchovies and potatoes, and grated cabbage, carrot, or celery for *entrées,* and main courses include innards, grilled meats, and veal, lamb, or pork. To end, look only as far as the banana tart—it's not only the best desert, but the one nod to originality going.

(4) BISTROT LES SANS CULOTTES
27, rue de Lappe (11th)

Even though the dining establishments in and around the eleventh arrondissement near the new Opéra Bastille are considered *the* trendy places these days, some of them are old familiar fixtures that have been doing a brisk business for years. Such is Bistrot Les Sans Culottes on the well-trodden rue de Lappe, which cuts through the heart of the district. This is a place to eat and drink with friends. Seating is downstairs along wooden banquettes or upstairs in a mirrored room with aging yellow walls and an Art Deco mural of the Place Vendôme.

Concentrate on the prix fixe meals for either lunch or dinner and the final tab will be well within budget. For lunch you have a choice of any two courses, ranging from obligatory chicken liver terrine to the interesting bowl of mussels in a balsamic vinaigrette. Mouthwatering main dishes include *blanquette de veau,* chicken with thyme, and a tender *bavette* (skirt steak) smothered in shallots. A choice of substantial desserts—such as *tarte fine chaude aux pommes* (warm apple tart), pistacchio créme brûlée with cherries, or a bowl of fresh, seasonal berries—rounds out the meal.

NOTE: There is a hotel in connection with the restaurant, but it is not recommended.

TELEPHONE
01-48-05-42-92

MÉTRO
Bastille

OPEN
Tues–Sun

CLOSED
Mon, holidays, NAC

HOURS
Lunch noon–3 P.M., dinner 7:30 P.M.–midnight

RESERVATIONS
Advised

CREDIT CARDS
AE, DC, MC, V

À LA CARTE
185F, BNC

PRIX FIXE
Lunch, 90F, 2 courses, BC; dinner, 125F, 3 courses, BNC

ENGLISH SPOKEN
Yes

(5) CAFÉ DE L'INDUSTRIE
16, rue St-Sabin (11th)

The now-popular eleventh invites you to meander through narrow streets and *passages* to places like Café de l'Industrie, an old *café du coin* that has enjoyed a rebirth in this newly discovered part of Paris. Now considered one of the Bastille cool spots, it caters to an easy-going, young, plugged-in crowd, who keep it jumping night and day. Bear in mind that after 10 P.M., especially on the weekend, it becomes a good place to test your tolerance for crowds. However, if you go too early, you will miss the action and real flavor of it all. While the menu falls short of being an inspired bargain, the prices are affordable, and you can order as much or as little as you want. Hungry insiders tank up on bowls of the chili con carne. Couples share plates of *charcuterie* or a mixed cheese platter and a bottle of modest *vin rouge.* Frankly speaking, desserts don't warrant the guilt trip.

TELEPHONE
01-47-00-13-53

MÉTRO
Bréguet-Sabin

OPEN
Sun–Fri

CLOSED
Sat, NAC

HOURS
11 A.M.–1 A.M., continuous service

RESERVATIONS
Not taken

CREDIT CARDS
MC, V

À LA CARTE
75–110F, BNC

PRIX FIXE
None

ENGLISH SPOKEN
Limited

(6) JACQUES MÉLAC
42, rue Léon-Frot (11th)

TELEPHONE
01-43-70-59-27
MÉTRO
Charonne
OPEN
Mon–Fri (Mon lunch and bar only)
CLOSED
Mon dinner, Sat–Sun, holidays, Aug, one week at Christmas
HOURS
Lunch Mon–Fri noon–2:30 P.M., dinner Tues–Fri 7:30–10 P.M., bar Mon–Fri 9 A.M.–midnight
RESERVATIONS
Not taken
CREDIT CARDS
MC, V
À LA CARTE
60–85F, BNC
PRIX FIXE
None
ENGLISH SPOKEN
Usually

"L'eau est ici reservée pour faire cuire les pommes de terre!" (Water here is reserved for cooking potatoes), states the handwritten sign hanging in this wine bar not too far from the Bastille. Started by Jacques's father before World War II, Jacques Mélac is extremely popular, 100 percent authentic, and an absolute *must* for anyone who loves a good time and good wine. Jacques, with his handlebar mustache and infectious enthusiasm, broadcasts a message of welcome loud and clear to everyone who enters. Don't worry if your high school French is a little rusty; after raising a few glasses at the bar with the rambunctious crowd, your French will improve dramatically. Go with a group or alone and you are bound to be in good company, sampling wines and munching on platters of *charcuterie* or Auvergne cheeses and loaves of chewy Poilâne bread. On Tuesday to Friday nights, Jacques serves hot dishes and fantastic omelettes. For lunch there is always a selection of hot dishes.

Winner of the 1981 Meilleur Pot (best wine bar in Paris), the wine bar also sells its own wine by the bottle or the case. The wine, Domaine des Trois Filles, is a red named for Mélac's three daughters, Marie-Hèléne, Laura, and Sara. This is the only wine bar in Paris boasting its own vineyard, with the vines growing on the roof and climbing up the outside walls. In September the grapes are harvested, and usually there is enough for a single barrel of wine, which is always cause for great celebration. Celebration also ensues during the annual arrival of Beaujolais *nouveau* wine, which all but flows in the street in late November, as do the patrons. Don't worry, however, if you miss one of great parties, because as Jacques says, "Here we celebrate wine every day we're open."

NOTE: For a taste of Jacques Mélac in the United States, stop by Mélac's Restaurant in Pacific Grove, California, at 663 Lighthouse Avenue (408-375-1743).

(7) LA COURTILLE
16, rue Guillaume Bertrand (11th)

TELEPHONE
01-48-06-48-34
MÉTRO
St-Maur
OPEN
Mon–Fri lunch and dinner, Sat dinner only

Owners M. Pinson and M. Hillion serve good food at sensible prices to a growing band of repeat diners, including many *Cheap Eats in Paris* readers. The best dining Cheap Eat is either the lunch or dinner prix fixe menu, which is different for each meal and changes with the seasons. With this list of eight *entrées, plats,* and desserts, plus daily specials, no one ever goes away hungry or disappointed.

For a summer lunch, I like to start with the *salade nordique,* filled with fresh fish, lightly cooked, and served cold, and then have the *magret de canard* (duck) in blueberry sauce. For dessert, I absolutely never miss their specialty—*gâteau au chocolate amér,* a bitter chocolate cake surrounded by velvety custard sauce. The dinner prix fixe offers more inventive choices. Consider the tuna *basquaise* or the flambéed steak in a coarse pepper sauce. The wine list prices are in keeping with the spirit of the restaurant and offer many reasonable bottles, including several by the *pichet* (pitcher).

CLOSED
Sun, holidays, first 3 weeks in Aug

HOURS
Lunch noon–2 P.M., dinner 7:30–10:30 P.M.

RESERVATIONS
Advised

CREDIT CARDS
MC, V

À LA CARTE
150F, BNC

PRIX FIXE
Lunch, 80F, 3 courses, BNC; dinner, 125F, 3 courses, BNC

ENGLISH SPOKEN
Yes, with English menu

(8) LA GALOCHE D'AURILLAC
41, rue de Lappe (11th)

Regional hams and sausages are sold until the bewitching hour on the *charcuterie* side of this popular bistro . . . handy to know if someone wants a plate of wonderful sausage at midnight.

The two-level dining section is picturesque to say the least, all decked out with wooden Auvergne galoshes strung across the ceiling and walls along with hanging hams and sausages. The welcome from owners M. and Mme. Bonnet and their staff is warm. Even their dog holds court by the bar until the lunch crowd gets too thick; after that you will have to settle for looking at his photo.

The cooking plays tribute to the lusty foods of southwestern France and is nonchalantly indifferent to changing trends. The dishes are geared for those not paying attention to any sort of diet, but to those who just plain love to eat and relish a satisfying meal. To start, indulge in a plate of Auvergne ham or sausage, a salad filled with lentils, red beans, and goose liver, or a cheese soup whose number of calories could pass for a zip code. Respectable dishes of tripe, roast goose, *confit de canard,* and veal are served daily. On Saturday night, come for the *plate de resistance—chou farci* (baked, stuffed cabbage). Even though you will not be able to consume another bite, desserts do merit serious consideration, especially the cold Grand Marnier soufflé or the hot apple tart loaded with Calvados.

TELEPHONE
01-47-00-77-15

MÉTRO
Bastille

OPEN
Tues–Sat

CLOSED
Sun–Mon, holidays, Aug

HOURS
Lunch noon–2:30 P.M., dinner 7–11:30 P.M., *charcuterie* 10 A.M.–midnight

RESERVATIONS
Advised

CREDIT CARDS
None

À LA CARTE
190–200F, BNC

PRIX FIXE
Lunch and dinner, 150F, 3 courses, BNC

ENGLISH SPOKEN
Yes

(9) LE CAFÉ DU PASSAGE
12, rue de Charonne (11th)

TELEPHONE
01-49-29-97-64
MÉTRO
Ledru-Rollin
OPEN
Winter: Mon–Fri dinner only, Sat lunch and dinner; summer: daily lunch and dinner
CLOSED
Winter: Mon–Fri lunch, Sun; major holidays, NAC
HOURS
Winter: Mon–Fri 6 P.M.–2 A.M., Sat noon–2 A.M.; summer: daily noon–2 A.M., continuous service
RESERVATIONS
Not necessary
CREDIT CARDS
MC, V
À LA CARTE
50–90F, BNC
PRIX FIXE
None
ENGLISH SPOKEN
Yes

After opening the successful Le Passage around the corner (see below), Gerard Pantanacce turned the day-to-day operation over to his wife, and then he directed his attention to this sophisticated nocturnal wine bar, where he features an interesting selection of international wines and single-malt Scotch whiskeys. Seating options range from slat metal chairs on the sidewalk—where patrons have front-row viewing priviledges for the cast of characters strolling by—to overstuffed armchairs in the intimate, clubby back room, to a corner grouping of leopard cushioned wicker armchairs that overlook the garden.

Food plays second fiddle to the wine, but you can order sandwiches, *le hot dog* (with ketchup and mustard), three or four filling hot dishes, and the usual cheese and *charcuterie* platters.

(10) L'ÉCLUSE ROQUETTE
13, rue de la Roquette (11th)

For a description of this wine bar, see L'Écluse page 114.

TELEPHONE: 01-48-05-19-12
MÉTRO: Bastille
OPEN: Daily
CLOSED: Dec 24–25, Dec 31–Jan 1, NAC
HOURS: 11:30 A.M.–1 A.M., continuous service
RESERVATIONS: Not necessary
CREDIT CARDS: MC, V
À LA CARTE: 80–150F, BNC
PRIX FIXE: Lunch and dinner, 70F, 2 courses, BNC; 95F (until 8 P.M. only), 3 courses, BNC
ENGLISH SPOKEN: Yes

(11) LE PASSAGE
18, passage de Bonne-Graine (an alley off rue du Faubourg St-Antoine) (11th)

TELEPHONE
01-47-00-73-30
MÉTRO
Ledru-Rollin
OPEN
Mon–Fri lunch and dinner, Sat dinner only
CLOSED
Sat lunch, Sun, holidays, NAC

Le Passage is an established wine bar with a new outlook and renewed vigor. A few years ago, this area would never be considered for a smart wine bar . . . but no longer. Even though Le Passage is on a drab, dark street, it is well respected in terms of its fine wines and food.

For the cheapest Cheap Eat, consult the daily specials written on the blackboard. Every Thursday the boss makes the safari to Rungis and brings back the fixings for dishes of cold chèvre and spinach crêpes, chicken liver terrine with fresh herbs, rabbit liver served with lentils, and pork curry ragout. Don't overlook their A.A.A.A.A. *andouillettes,* either with creamed potatoes or fricaséed in a cream and bacon sauce. Pig's feet, pasta with smoked salmon, and *pain perdu* with red fruit or *fondant chocolat* for dessert keep everyone filled to contentment. So do the wines. There are more than three hundred possibilities listed, and the friendly crew will help you decide what to order to go best with your meal.

NOTE: See also Le Café du Passage (page 168), which is under the same ownership.

HOURS
Lunch noon–3:30 P.M., dinner 7:30 P.M.–midnight

RESERVATIONS
Advised

CREDIT CARDS
AE, MC, V

À LA CARTE
180F, BNC

PRIX FIXE
None

ENGLISH SPOKEN
Yes

(12) NICELIO
157, rue Amelot (11th)

If you have had it with foie gras and escargots and can't face another *boeuf bourguignon* or crème brûlée, head for Nicelio, a pint-size Italian hideaway near République. The dining room, with its red tablecloths and ladder-back chairs, won't win any prizes for interior design, but the prices should appeal to Cheap Eaters in Paris who have nearly emptied their wallets dining in more expensive French restaurants. The food here reflects the unpretentious atmosphere. Don't look for salads or fancy ways with fish. Do look for simple vegetable antipasti and homemade pastas of ravioli stuffed with spinach and ricotta cheese, lasagne loaded with cheese, and linguini simply dressed in tomato or gussied up with gorgonzola cheese and vodka. Top it all off with an order of *le delice Nicelio* (caramel and nougat ice cream) or the *gâteau à l'orange.*

TELEPHONE
01-43-38-26-48

MÉTRO
Filles-du-Calvaire

OPEN
Mon–Fri lunch and dinner, Sat dinner only

CLOSED
Sat lunch, Sun, holidays, NAC

HOURS
Lunch noon–2:30 P.M., dinner 7:30–11:30 P.M.

RESERVATIONS
Not necessary

CREDIT CARDS
MC, V

À LA CARTE
90–115F, BNC

PRIX FIXE
None

ENGLISH SPOKEN
Limited

MISCELLANEOUS
The pastas are available to take out.

(13) RELAIS DU MASSIF CENTRAL
16, rue Daval (11th)

Where do the neighborhood workers and local inhabitants go for a hearty feed and inexpensive wines? Right here, where the emphasis is on nutritionally incorrect, rib-sticking fare that is not recommended for defenders of moderation. Typical of the kitchen are such starters as frogs legs, snails, smoked salmon, and slabs of foie gras. Main courses feature steak with *frites* and duck preserved

TELEPHONE
01-47-00-46-35

MÉTRO
Bastille

OPEN
Mon–Sat lunch and dinner, Sun dinner only

CLOSED
Sun lunch, two weeks in Aug (dates vary)

HOURS
Lunch noon–3 P.M., dinner 7:30 P.M.–1 A.M.

RESERVATIONS
Not necessary

CREDIT CARDS
MC, V

À LA CARTE
125F, BNC

PRIX FIXE
Lunch and dinner: 65F, 2 courses, BNC; 90F and 115F, 3 courses, both BC (kir and wine)

ENGLISH SPOKEN
Enough to order

and cooked in its own fat. You can be conservative with only a two-course Cheap Eat, or go all out and for less than twenty-five dollars add a kir, dessert, and wine. Service is honest and kind, and if you need help with the menu, there is usually someone there with enough "menu English" to help.

(14) RESTAURANT OCCITANIE
96, rue Oberkampf (11th)

TELEPHONE
01-48-06-46-98

MÉTRO
St-Maur

OPEN
Mon–Fri lunch and dinner, Sat dinner only

CLOSED
Sat lunch, Sun, holidays, July 14–Aug 14

HOURS
Lunch noon–2 P.M., dinner 7:30–10:30 P.M.

RESERVATIONS
Essential for lunch

CREDIT CARDS
MC, V

À LA CARTE
165F, BNC

PRIX FIXE
Lunch only, 65F, 2 courses, BC; lunch and dinner: 85F and 135F, 3 courses, BNC; 198F, 4 courses, BC (kir and coffee)

ENGLISH SPOKEN
Yes

By 12:30 P.M., there is not a vacant chair at the rustic Occitanie. Home cooking without pretense sums up the style of the food. Homemade *confits, magrets, cassoulets,* Toulouse sausages, and most of the desserts are created right here in the busy kitchen. The faithful Cheap Eating franc pinchers don't worry about consulting the blackboard menu for lunch, scrawled by someone who did not win awards in penmanship. They know to order the 65F lunch menu that includes a choice of two courses—main course and an appetizer or dessert—with wine, beer, or orange juice included. Order this meal in a more tourist-heavy part of Paris and you would pay double. Other bargains include wooden platters heaped with steak, ground beef, chicken, sausage, or ham and served with a salad, a side of fries, and *fromage blanc.* There is an à la carte menu, but with the assortment of prix fixe bargains, who's looking?

Twelfth Arrondissement

(See map on pages 160–161.)

In the past, visitors seldom ventured into the untamed corners of the twelfth, which is situated between the Bastille and Gare de Lyon. A renaissance has taken place, and it is now very au courant. The grubby furniture makers have moved on, and people are now discovering its interesting hidden passages and courtyards, shopping at the multiethnic street markets at place d'Aligré and filling the new wave of *in* restaurants. The Viaduc des Arts, in a long section of abandoned railway, has had its arched space turned into artist workshops, boutiques, and restaurants. The Promenade Plantée, a walkway with benches, flowers, and a view to flat-fronted buildings that characterize the area, flows along the top.

RIGHT BANK
Bois de Vincennes, Musée des Arts d'Afrique et d'Océanie, Place d'Aligré, Viaduc des Arts

TWELFTH ARRONDISSEMENT RESTAURANTS

* Restaurants marked with an asterisk (*) are considered Big Splurges.

(15) À LA BICHE AU BOIS
45, avenue Ledru-Rollin (12th)

If you are looking for something real, go no further. À la Biche au Bois remains one of my all-purpose standbys: the place to take Great-Aunt Mabel or Cousin Bob to sample an untouristy meal on their first visit to Paris. Inside has about fifty *couverts* (place settings) crowded into a room surrounded by mirrors, live plants, starched linens, and contented diners enjoying full-dress fare that is in the medium price range. The outdoor terrace is nice if you are here in the evening, when the symphony of squealing tires and screeching brakes calms down.

Go with a big appetite and you will be satisfied. The menu lists a stampede of meats, features fish on Tuesday and Friday, and has wild game in season. From start to finish everything is good, reliable, well served, and enjoyable. The prix fixe, four-course menu is a virtual steal

TELEPHONE
01-43-43-34-38
MÉTRO
Bastille, Gare de Lyon
OPEN
Mon–Fri
CLOSED
Sat–Sun, major holidays, mid-July to mid-Aug
HOURS
Lunch noon–2 P.M., dinner 7:30–11 P.M.
RESERVATIONS
Highly recommended
CREDIT CARDS
AE, DC, MC, V
À LA CARTE
150–185F, BNC
PRIX FIXE
Lunch and dinner, 120F, 4 courses, BNC

ENGLISH SPOKEN
Yes

and includes all the favorite dishes. Wines are well priced.

(16) L'EBAUCHOIR
45, rue de Citeaux (12th)

TELEPHONE
01-43-42-49-31
MÉTRO
Faidherbe-Chaligny, Reuilly-Diderot
OPEN
Mon–Sat
CLOSED
Sun, lunch on holidays, NAC
HOURS
Lunch noon–2:30 P.M., dinner 8–10:30 P.M.
RESERVATIONS
Advised
CREDIT CARDS
MC, V
À LA CARTE
160–185F, BC
PRIX FIXE
Lunch only: 70F, 3 courses, BC; 90F, 3 courses, BNC
ENGLISH SPOKEN
Limited

Lunch is the serious Cheap Eater's pick at L'Ebauchoir, a noisy canteen just far enough away from the Bastille swarms to keep it honest. The cafeterialike room with wooden tables and chairs is devoid of a *soupçon* of decor, unless you count the messy bookcase by the door and the handful of flowers in a vase on the bar. There are two lunch menus, the cheaper of which is a good deal if you want wine and don't mind that your selection of main courses won't exceed fish, ofal, and one off-beat meat dish. The house star dessert, *gâteau de ris*, is part of the package.

At dinner only à la carte is available, but if you are a smart eater, you will get out for around 160F, including a taste of the house wine.

(17) LE SQUARE TROUSSEAU
1, rue Antoine Vollon (12th)

TELEPHONE
01-43-43-06-00
MÉTRO
Bastille, Ledru-Rollin
OPEN
Daily
CLOSED
Never, NAC
HOURS
Lunch noon–2:30 P.M., dinner 8–11:30 P.M.
RESERVATIONS
Essential
CREDIT CARDS
AE, MC, V
À LA CARTE
180–190F, BNC
PRIX FIXE
Lunch only, 100F, 2 courses, 155F, 3 courses, both BNC
ENGLISH SPOKEN
Yes

The appealingly energetic atmosphere surrounding the Bastille carries right to Le Square Trousseau, where the smart ambience possesses all the bustle you expect in a popular Belle Epoque bistro. Overlooking the leafy Square Trousseau, it has become the *rendezvous-obligé* for a distinctly chic Parisian crowd who wants to forget *nouvelle cuisine,* chichi settings, tiny portions, stuffy, snooty maître d's, and overbearing waiters. You know the minute you arrive and glance around the two ochre-colored rooms and the attractive sidewalk terrace, both of which are filled night and day, that this is a happening place.

Owner Phillipe Damas's commitment to quality is evident in the well-thoughtout menu, which carries the season's freshest offerings. The solid dishes are generous yet proportioned sensibly, allowing you to sample a full load of courses. You might start with a springtime *entrée* of asparagus lightly dressed in a créme fraîche chive sauce or the warming cauliflower soup topped with golden croutons and chervil. If you like fish, try any of the daily suggestions and hope one of them is the fresh perch served on a bed of spinach. Meat eaters will be happy with the veal liver cooked with balsamic vinegar and garnished with zucchini or the roasted chicken served with lentil fondu. Equally tempting desserts include a memorable caramelized apple crêpe with caramel ice cream and an almond-mango *tarte Tatin* with a tiny scoop of almond ice cream. If this isn't enough, you will be served sinfully rich bite-size brownies with your strong after-dinner espresso.

(18) LES ZYGOMATES
7, rue de Capri (12th)

Buried in the depths of the twelfth arrondissement near the Bois de Vincennes is this *quartier* choice that allows luxury dining for less with its two menus. The lunch prix fixe changes twice a week on Monday and Thursday; the dinner menu changes every Wednesday, with choices on both based on the seasonal market. The kitchen gives distinction to the most ordinary ingredients, and it is particularly adept with such starters as cannelloni stuffed with chèvre and a *niçoise* salad featuring smoked fish and tiny new potatoes. Adventurous eaters will like the pork tongue served with morille mushrooms or the beef cheeks in red wine sauce. Conservatives can rely on the roasted veal or the chicken cooked in parchment. Foodies of all persuasions will love the *assiette gourmande des Zygomates,* which gives tiny tastes of every dessert on the menu . . . including the bitter chocolate cake and the bread pudding with honey ice cream.

TELEPHONE
01-40-19-93-04

MÉTRO
Michel-Bizot, Daumesnil

OPEN
Mon–Fri lunch and dinner, Sat dinner only

CLOSED
Sat lunch, Sun, holidays, Aug

HOURS
Lunch noon–2 P.M., dinner 7:30–10:30 P.M.

RESERVATIONS
Advised

CREDIT CARDS
MC, V

À LA CARTE
170F, BNC

PRIX FIXE
Lunch, 80F, 3 courses, BNC; dinner, 135F, 3 courses, BNC

ENGLISH SPOKEN
Yes

(19) LE TRAVERSIÈRE*
40, rue Traversière, angle 72, rue de Charenton (12th)

Johny Bénaric is the *chef de cuisine,* and his attractive wife, Patricia, is the hostess. Her English is excellent and her welcome gracious. Be sure to tell her you read about them in *Cheap Eats in Paris*. Their restaurant is the kind of place you hope will be a block or two from where you are staying. Unfortunately for most, it is farther than that . . . but absolutely worth the trek. The timbered, stone-walled interior is properly arranged with well-spaced linen-covered tables and fresh flowers, and it continually draws a contented crowd of faithful diners with its emphasis on game in winter, wonderful, fresh fish, and a seasonal menu that always keeps its high quality intact.

TELEPHONE
01-43-44-02-10

MÉTRO
Ledro-Rollin, Gare de Lyon

OPEN
Tues–Sat lunch and dinner, Mon lunch only

CLOSED
Mon dinner, Sun, 3 weeks in Aug

HOURS
Lunch noon–2:30 P.M., dinner 7:30–10:30 P.M.

RESERVATIONS
Advised

CREDIT CARDS
AE, DC, MC, V

À LA CARTE
260–280F, BNC
PRIX FIXE
Lunch only (Mon–Fri), 125F, 3 courses, BNC; lunch and dinner, 165F, 3 courses, BNC
ENGLISH SPOKEN
Yes

Your meal might begin with the *salade gourmande au foie gras* or *le feuilleté d'escargot aux pleurotes*, which is an interesting mixture of snails and mushrooms in a very light pastry. The filet mignon with a macaroni gratin is a wonderful choice, as is the salmon cooked in Loire Valley wine. Fresh fruits star in the artistic desserts. Try the *vacherin maison*, a meringue topped with cherries and cream, or the delectable créme brûlée resting on Calvados soaked apples. Relax throughout this lovely meal with a bottle of well-priced wine, and be happy you have found this dining jewel in Paris.

(20) L'OULETTE*
15, place Lachambeaudie (12th)

TELEPHONE
01-40-02-02-12
MÉTRO
Dugommier
OPEN
Mon–Fri lunch and dinner, Sat dinner only
CLOSED
Sat lunch, Sun, Christmas Day, New Year's Day, NAC
HOURS
Lunch noon–2:15 P.M., dinner 8–10:15 P.M.
RESERVATIONS
Absolutely essential
CREDIT CARDS
AE, MC, V
À LA CARTE
300–335F, BNC
PRIX FIXE
Lunch and dinner: 160F, 3 courses, BNC; 240F, 4 courses, BC
ENGLISH SPOKEN
Yes

For a memorable place to celebrate a special occasion or just being with a special person in Paris, L'Oulette is on my very short list of recommendations. From the standpoint of cuisine, service, and ambiance, it is almost unbeatable . . . especially if you order the exceptionally good value *menu de saison,* which not only includes a cheese course but a very good bottle of wine.

A few years ago, Chef Marcel Baudis and his wife, Marie-Noëlle, opened a little bistro near place des Vosges—Baracane-Bistrot de l'Oulette (see page 74)—featuring dishes from Baudis's native Montauban in southwestern France. It was soon discovered by *toute le monde* and became the talk of the town. Now they have turned the day-to-day operations of the bistro over to trusted family members and moved to the Bercy district in the twelfth arrondissement. The new, less-than-central location has definitely not deterred savvy French diners. Neither has Baudis lost his inspired touch in the kitchen. Reservations as far in advance as possible are absolutely essential for both lunch and dinner.

The new L'Oulette combines understated elegance in a large room with banquette seating along one wall and floor-to-ceiling windows along another, which overlooks an umbrella-shaded dining terrace. Pots of jam and preserved fruits are whimsically arranged along with dried flowers, creating a southwestern feel that is further enhanced by sunny yellow linens and geometrically designed fabrics.

While the interior is modern and lean, the dazzling food is anything but. Chef Baudis spends hours preparing his seasonally inspired and meticulously arranged dishes, which are politely presented by a staff of knowledgeable waiters formally clad in black tuxedos. Meals like this cannot be rushed, so plan an evening of sitting back, enjoying a good bottle of wine, and savoring the truly outstanding food. Expect delicate perfection from the chef's talented hands: the innovative dishes include iced mussel soup flavored with saffron baked crab with tomato and artichokes and a very rich, cold vegetable torte encasing a softly poached egg. Old favorites have not been cast aside. The *escabèche de calamars*—squid cooked in olive oil and spices and served with warm potatoes—is still one of the most popular *entrées*. In the summer, miracles are performed with fresh fish. Wonderful lamb dishes, such as leg of lamb seasoned with garlic and rosemary, are served with assorted fresh vegetables, making dining decisions even more difficult.

For dessert, the *biscuit chocolat,* layers of rich chocolate filled with dark chocolate mousse in a cocoa sauce, is a required order for chocolate lovers. A lighter choice is a coffee ice cream soufflé served with a light cocoa sauce. Any fruit dessert creation is bound to be wonderful, especially the *tortière aux pommes et aux mendiants* (flaky apple tart flavored with almonds, figs, nuts, and raisins). There is really nothing more to say, except that if you love and appreciate fine dining, call L'Oulette for reservations the minute you know when you will be in Paris.

NOTE: Because the métro trip is a difficult one and the neighborhood not too populated at night, it is best to plan on using a taxi.

(21) SAINT AMARANTE
4, rue Biscornet (12th)

Saint Amarante looks like hundreds of other *cafés du quartier* in Paris, and you certainly would not be drawn to it by location or on esthetic grounds. The plain exterior and the easy-to-describe decor—there isn't any—belie the riches inside. The food is absolutely unbeatable in its category, and everyone who has eaten here over the years agrees. It is located a New York minute away from the new Opéra at the Bastille. By 12:15 P.M. it is full for lunch, and there is not an empty seat in the place for dinner at 9 P.M. Disciples bring their dogs, children, and mother-in-laws to feast on the uncomplicated fare, the type you want to go back for again and again.

The menu, which is written on an old blackboard with dull chalk, takes some doing to decode. The choices

TELEPHONE
01-43-43-00-08

MÉTRO
Bastille

OPEN
Mon–Tues lunch only, Wed–Fri lunch and dinner

CLOSED
Mon–Tues dinner, Sat–Sun, holidays, July 15–Aug 15

HOURS
Lunch Mon–Fri noon–2:45 P.M., dinner Wed–Fri 8–10:30 P.M.

RESERVATIONS
Absolutely essential

CREDIT CARDS
MC, V

À LA CARTE
165–180F, BNC

PRIX FIXE
None

ENGLISH SPOKEN
Limited

favor fish, but don't overlook the chef's light versions of lamb and veal standards, such as the melt-in-your-mouth *blanquette de veau,* adorned with a light cream sauce and fresh peas on the side. The flavorful kidneys are cooked with mushrooms and will convert you to this dish if you are not already a believer. Desserts are just as good as they look and sound. Cherries jubilee pours warm cherries over a delicate pistachio *fondant,* and the white chocolate cake with wild strawberries is a new twist on black forest cake.

A final note: There is just one thing you must never forget to do at Saint Amarante . . . make reservations. Without them you will be waiting a long time or, worse, not be seated at all.

Thirteenth Arrondissement

(No map for this arrondissement.)

The thirteenth is hardly impressive from a visitor's standpoint. One side is lined with railroad yards and tracks, and most of the rest seems to be a no-man's land. The one bright star is the area called Butte-aux-Cailles, a pocket of neighborhood charm where the clock stopped ticking fifty years ago.

LEFT BANK
Butte-aux-Cailles, Chinatown, Gare d'Austerlitz, Gobelins Tapestry Factory, Place d'Italie

THIRTEENTH ARRONDISSEMENT RESTAURANTS

* Restaurants marked with an asterisk (*) are considered Big Splurges.

L'AUBERGE ETCHEGORRY*
41, rue Croulebarbe (13th)

TELEPHONE
01-44-08-83-51

MÉTRO
Gobelins, Corvisart

OPEN
Mon–Sat

CLOSED
Sun, NAC

HOURS
Lunch noon–3 P.M., dinner 7:30–10:30 P.M.

RESERVATIONS
Advised

CREDIT CARDS
AE, MC, V

À LA CARTE
225–275F, BNC

PRIX FIXE
Lunch and dinner: 140F, 4 courses, BNC; 165F, 4 courses, BC

ENGLISH SPOKEN
Yes

Remember how we all loved to eat before fat grams and cholesterol counting became de riguer for diet-conscious health hippies? Well, the food at this bastion of Basque cuisine turns back the clock and tips the scales by serving earthy portions of regional dishes all flowing with delicious buttery fat; it will send your calorie count, if you keep count, off the charts. Despite the fact that it is two blocks beyond Mars for most Paris visitors, it is in a pretty neighborhood across the street from a lovely green park where *mamans* take their children to play and sweet old couples walk their dogs.

The restaurant resembles a regional country inn, loaded with charm and filled with a sense of happy camaraderie. It is the type of place sturdy French go to when they want to indulge in soul-warming comfort food. It is clearly a popular destination . . . every time I have been there it has been filled, while the dreary place next door stands almost empty. The interior is as robust as the food, with hanging hams and sausages, braids of garlic and onions, and a time-warped collection of knick-knacks telling you that nothing has changed, or will, for decades.

If you order à la carte, you will be in Big Splurge territory, but if you take one of the generous prix fixe meals, you will be fine. When ordering, remember to pace yourself. You will need plenty of room to do justice to the meat-inspired *entrées* and main courses, which are music to the ears of carnivores. Accompany your feast with plenty of red wine and finish it all off with a slice of *le gâteau Basque* for a culinary journey back to a time when we ate with abandon.

NOTE: The owner also runs a very nice hotel, Le Vert Galant, next door to this restaurant. See description in *Cheap Sleeps in Paris*.

LE JARDIN DES PÂTES
33, boulevard Arago (13th)

See description page 96. All other information is the same.

TELEPHONE: 01-45-35-93-67

MÉTRO: Gobelins

Fourteenth Arrondissement

LEFT BANK
Montparnasse

This artistic haven of the 1920s and 1930s is now modernized and for the most part ugly, the unfortunate victim of urban development without much taste or regard for history. The famous cafés—La Coupole, Le Select, Le Dôme, and La Rotunde—were once the center of literary and artistic life in Paris between the two World Wars. The area was also home to dancer Isadora Duncan, and singer Edith Piaf performed often at the Bobino Music Hall.

FOURTEENTH ARRONDISSEMENT RESTAURANTS

* Restaurants marked with an asterisk (*) are considered Big Splurges.

(1) AQUARIUS
40, rue de Gergovie (14th)

TELEPHONE
01-45-41-36-88

MÉTRO
Pernety

OPEN
Mon–Sat

CLOSED
Sun, holidays, Christmas through New Year's, NAC

HOURS
Lunch noon–2:30 P.M., dinner 7–10:30 P.M.

RESERVATIONS
Not necessary

CREDIT CARDS
AE, MC, V

À LA CARTE
100–125F, BNC

Aquarius has another location near the Marais in the fourth arrondissement (see page 72). While that one is more centrally located, this one has more zip in that the interior does not remind me of a utilitarian cafeteria. At this site in the fourteenth arrondissement, vegetarian food is served in three small rooms with either pine- or marble-topped tables sensibly set with red placemats and yellow napkins. There is also a shelf littered with yoga flyers, assorted announcements about New Age meetings and classes, and other notices about alternative lifestyles.

The politically and nutritionally aware patrons love the food, which is served on oversized white plates. The popular "mixed grill" pairs tofu and cereal sausages with

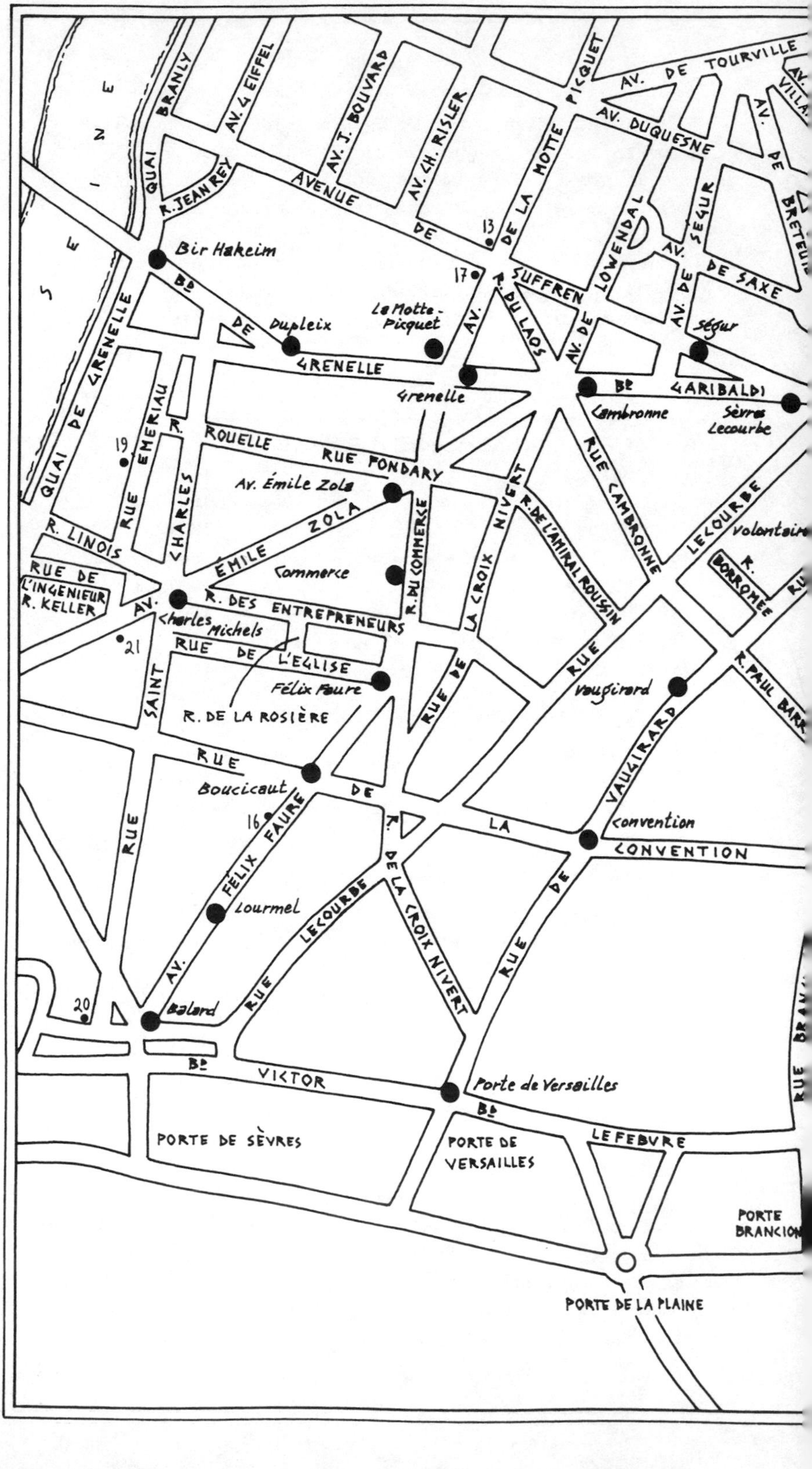
SEINE
QUAI BRANLY
AV. G. EIFFEL
AV. J. BOUVARD
AV. CH. RISLER
AV. DE LA MOTTE PICQUET
AV. DE TOURVILLE
AV. DUQUESNE
AV. DE BRETEUIL
R. JEAN REY
AVENUE DE SUFFREN
AV. LOWENDAL
AV. DE SÉGUR
AV. DE SAXE
13
17
Bir Hakeim
Bd DE GRENELLE
Dupleix
La Motte-Picquet
AV. DU LAOS
Grenelle
Bd GARIBALDI
Cambronne
Ségur
Sèvres Lecourbe
QUAI DE GRENELLE
RUE EMERIAU
19
R. ROUELLE
RUE FONDARY
Av. Émile Zola
AV. CHARLES
AV. ÉMILE ZOLA
R. LINOIS
RUE DE L'INGENIEUR R. KELLER
Commerce
R. DU COMMERCE
RUE DE LA CROIX NIVERT
R. DE L'AMIRAL ROUSSIN
RUE CAMBRONNE
LECOURBE
Volontaires
R. BORROMÉE
R. DES ENTREPRENEURS
Charles Michels
21
RUE DE L'EGLISE
Félix Faure
R. DE LA ROSIÈRE
RUE SAINT
Vaugirard
R. PAUL BARR
RUE DE VAUGIRARD
RUE DE LA CONVENTION
Boucicaut
16
7
convention
RUE
AV. FÉLIX FAURE
Lourmel
RUE LECOURBE
DE LA CROIX NIVERT
20
Balard
Bd VICTOR
Porte de Versailles
Bd LEFEBVRE
PORTE DE SÈVRES
PORTE DE VERSAILLES
PORTE BRANCION
PORTE DE LA PLAINE

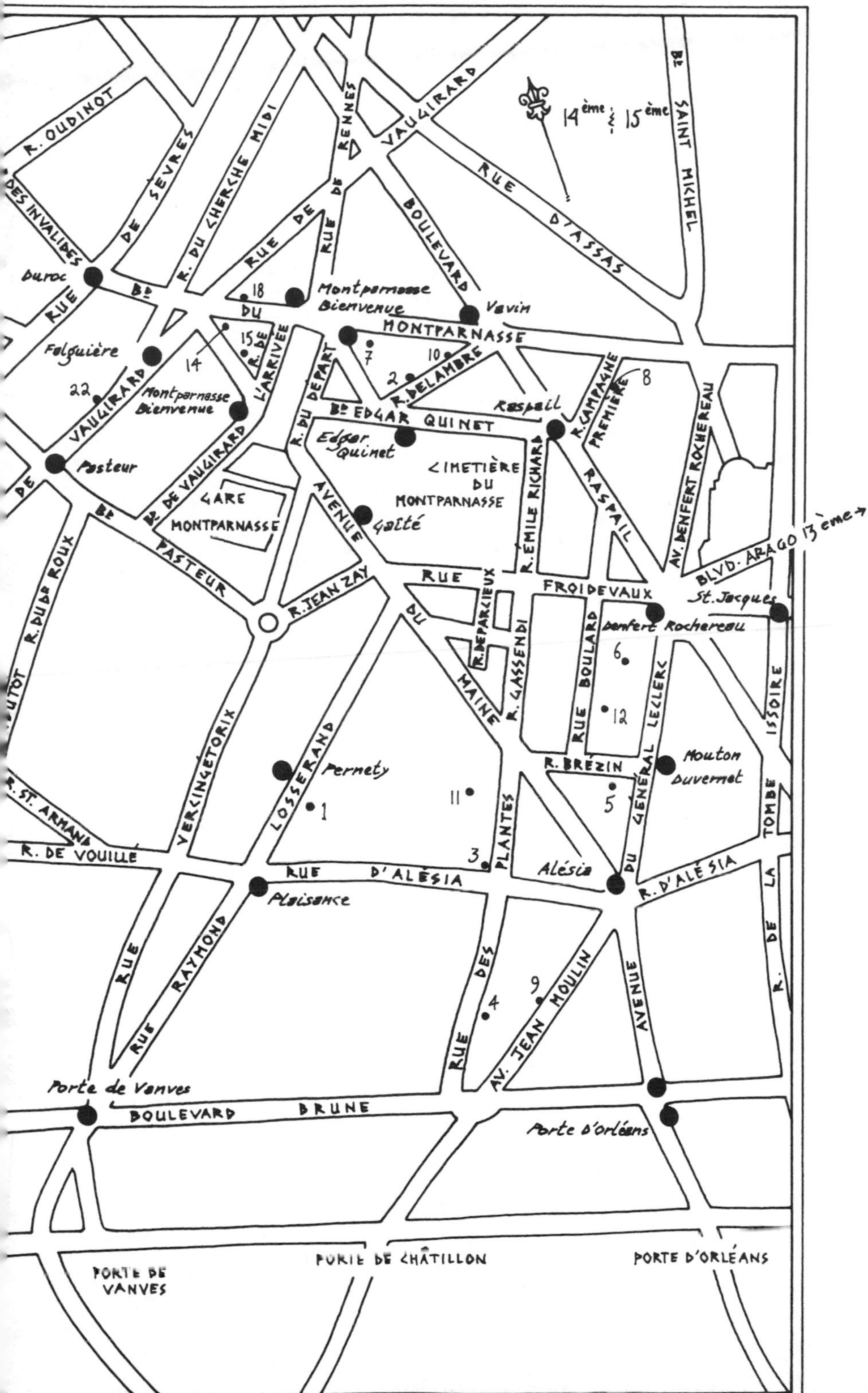
14ème & 15ème
R. OUDINOT
RUE DES INVALIDES
RUE DE SEVRES
R. DU CHERCHE MIDI
RUE DE RENNES
RUE DE RENNES
VAUGIRARD
RUE D'ASSAS
BOULEVARD
Bd SAINT MICHEL
Duroc
Montparnasse Bienvenue
Vavin
Bd DU MONTPARNASSE
R. DE L'ARRIVÉE
Falguière
Montparnasse Bienvenue
VAUGIRARD
R. DU DEPART
R. DELAMBRE
Raspail
R. CAMPAGNE PREMIÈRE
Bd EDGAR QUINET
Edgar Quinet
CIMETIÈRE DU MONTPARNASSE
Pasteur
R. DE VAUGIRARD
GARE MONTPARNASSE
AV. DENFERT ROCHEREAU
RASPAIL
R. EMILE RICHARD
Gaîté
AVENUE DU MAINE
Bd PASTEUR
R. DU ROUX
BLVD. ARAGO 13ème
RUE FROIDEVAUX
St. Jacques
Denfert Rochereau
R. JEAN ZAY
R. DEPARCIEUX
R. GASSENDI
RUE BOULARD
AV. DU GÉNÉRAL LECLERC
ISSOIRE
VERCINGETORIX
LOSSERAND
Pernety
R. BRÉZIN
Mouton Duvernet
R. ST. ARMAND
R. DE VOUILLÉ
RUE D'ALÉSIA
PLANTES
Alésia
R. D'ALÉSIA
R. DE LA TOMBE
Plaisance
RUE RAYMOND
RUE DES
AV. JEAN MOULIN
AVENUE
Porte de Vanves
BOULEVARD BRUNE
Porte d'Orléans
PORTE DE VANVES
PORTE DE CHÂTILLON
PORTE D'ORLÉANS
1
2
3
4
5
6
7
8
9
10
11
12
14
15
18
22

PRIX FIXE
Lunch only, 65F, 3 courses, BNC (not served on holidays)
ENGLISH SPOKEN
Yes

wheat pancakes, brown rice, and veggies in a mushroom sauce. There is also vegetarian chili, lasagna, and a soybean *choucroute.* Other healthy options are the salads, omelettes, and the *plat du jour.* Purists can always order the steamed vegetable plate; sinners will enjoy the chocolate brownie, the chocolate cake, or the cheesecake. Thirst-quenching juices, teas, *biologique* wines, and designer mineral water complete the menu. Admittedly you must have a certain mind-set to eat here, but if you do, you will be filled with well-executed, wholesome food that won't give you or your budget heartburn.

(2) AUBERGE DE VENISE
10, rue Delambre (14th)

TELEPHONE
01-43-35-43-09
MÉTRO
Vavin
OPEN
Daily
CLOSED
Some holidays, Aug (call to check)
HOURS
Lunch noon–2:30 P.M., dinner 7–11:30 P.M.
RESERVATIONS
Essential, especially for dinner
CREDIT CARDS
AE, MC, V
À LA CARTE
150–190F, BNC
PRIX FIXE
Lunch and dinner, 110F, 3 courses, BNC
ENGLISH SPOKEN
Yes, and Italian

Buon appetito and welcome to the Auberge de Venise, a taste of *bella Italia* in Paris. The restaurant has been in business almost since time began, and it has served such luminaries as Hemingway, Fitzgerald, and Picasso during their heydays in Paris. Today, it continues to fill to capacity with confirmed regulars, who come back not only for the outstanding food but for the comfortable, homey atmosphere and old-fashioned service.

There is a limited-choice prix fixe menu, but if you love Italian food, treat yourself and order à la carte—some of these wonderful dishes are in many ways better than most you will have in Italy. Any one of the beef carpaccios make a nice starter, and so does the simply dressed tomato and mozzarella salad. It is easy to get carried away and make a meal on the *entrée,* with several pieces of bread and a good Chianti, but save yourself, there is lots more to come. A rich *tagliatelle al salmone* is a filling main dish, as is the ravioli with either basil or mushrooms. The cream *tortelloni ai 4 fromaggi* throws fat gram counting into orbit, but just this once won't kill you. The pastas are not garnished, so if you are feeling really hungry, consider an order of green beans liberally tossed with garlic and sautéed in olive oil. Meat eaters will be pleased with the list of veal dishes; try one prepared with lemon, Marsala wine, and tomato sauce or the osso buco.

When it comes time for dessert, you might think it impossible . . . but wait a few minutes and then order the best tiramisu you will have in Paris. Or if you love *profiteroles,* their version of these filled cream puffs, seductively covered with a thick chocolate topping and served cold, are *bellissimo!*

(3) AU MOULIN VERT
34 bis, rue des Plantes (at rue du Moulin Vert) (14th)

If you want to treat yourself to a nice meal before or after pounding the pavement along rue d'Alésia in search of the ultimate Parisian bargain (see *Cheap Sleeps in Paris,* "Cheap Chic"), reserve a table at Au Moulin Vert. For my dining franc, it is the best in the area and definitely one of the prettiest dining choices in Paris. It is set in a building with a wraparound glass-walled dining terrace, giving you the feeling you are miles away from everything, surrounded by a serene garden of lush green and blooming plants. There has been a restaurant on this corner since 1842, and a black-and-white photo of the original hangs by the front door. Fellow diners will be from the neighborhood . . . maybe a large family of three generations celebrating a birthday, a young couple all dressed up on their first or second date, a middle-age couple reliving their first date—and you, watching the drama with pleasure. The later you go the better it gets, especially when the hurricane lights are glowing and the mood says *l'amour.*

The one-price-fits-all menu is far above the usual in terms of the sheer number of choices and the imaginative preparations. The large meal starts with a kir royale, includes a bottle of good wine, a choice of seasonally changing *entrées, plats,* and desserts, as well as after-dinner coffee. There are the chef's *suggestions du jour* for each course, and you should look here for the most creative choices.

TELEPHONE
01-45-39-31-31

MÉTRO
Alésia

OPEN
Daily

CLOSED
Never, NAC

HOURS
Lunch noon–2:30 P.M., dinner 6–11 P.M.

RESERVATIONS
Advised

CREDIT CARDS
AE, MC, V

À LA CARTE
None

PRIX FIXE
Lunch Mon–Fri, 100F, 2 courses, BNC; dinner daily and lunch Sat–Sun, 185F, 3 courses, BC

ENGLISH SPOKEN
Yes

(4) AU RENDEZ-VOUS DES CAMIONNEURS
34, rue des Plantes (14th)

If you only have a little bit to spend on lunch or dinner, and want to get away from most of the other tourists in the same boat, head for Monique and Claude's Cheap Eat concealed in the bottom of the fourteenth arrondissement, near the rue d'Alésia Cheap Chic shopping mecca. Au Rendez-vous des Camionneurs wins top honors as a classic that will be here *only* until the hardworking couple, who have labored here for thirty years, decides to hang up the chef's hat and spatula and retire to the south of France. This restaurant is a dying breed due to today's more sophisticated dining demands. What to expect? Think school lunchroom. Interior decor? Not a lot, with a bar along one side of the lime-

TELEPHONE
01-45-40-43-36

MÉTRO
Alésia

OPEN
Mon–Fri

CLOSED
Sat–Sun, holidays, Aug

HOURS
Lunch 11:30 A.M.–2:30 P.M., dinner 7:30–9:30 P.M.

RESERVATIONS
Required

CREDIT CARDS
None

À LA CARTE
100–120F, BNC
PRIX FIXE
Lunch and dinner, 75F, 3 courses, BNC
ENGLISH SPOKEN
None

green room, whose walls are punctuated by pictures and posters. Tables are accessorized by crocks of mustard, salt in the box it comes in, and a pepper grinder.

The cuisine is definitely Mom's kitchen. The typed menu is changed monthly and lists plates of cucumbers, beets, grated carrots, sardines, *saucisson sec,* or sliced terrine to start things off. Then comes the *bavette* (skirt steak), *cervelle de veau meunière* (veal brains), sautéed lamb with white beans, or fish. If you are ordering prix fixe, desserts don't get much fancier than a piece of fruit or a bowl of *fromage blanc.* À la carte diners may order the chocolate mousse. Wines by the *pichet* resemble the Thunderbird, screw-cap variety, so spring for a bottle or drink *eau naturel* (tap water) if your budget is extra tight. Though it's not as grim as it may sound, put away any thoughts of *gourmet.* Arrive desiring only filling and cheap, and you will leave satisfied.

(5) CHEZ CHARLES-VICTOR
8, rue Brézin (14th)

TELEPHONE
01-40-44-55-51
MÉTRO
Mounton-Duvernet
OPEN
Mon–Fri lunch and dinner, Sat dinner only
CLOSED
Sat lunch, Sun, holidays, NAC
HOURS
Lunch noon–2:30 P.M., dinner 7:30–11:30 P.M.
RESERVATIONS
Advised
CREDIT CARDS
MC, V
À LA CARTE
None
PRIX FIXE
Lunch and dinner: 70F, 2 courses, BNC; 95F, 3 courses, BNC
ENGLISH SPOKEN
Yes

If *Cheap Eats in Paris* gave awards, one would go to the two menus offered at this friendly Montparnasse enclave. It is a family affair, with an owner who is on site, loves Americans, and is beamingly proud of his two children, Clara and Grégoire, whose photos are displayed under glass at the cash register.

The handwritten (and readable) menu on green chalkboard entices with *canapés de grand-mère*, eggplant caviar, or baked eggs with smoked salmon. For your *plat,* steak tartare and lamb chops are acceptable but ultimately plebian choices when compared to the house Basque specialty—*axoa,* a *hot* and *spicy* affair with sliced chicken, chorizo, onions, and a mixture of red and green peppers. Desserts keep you going with the hot chocolate *profiteroles*, three-chocolate *fondant,* or a fruit crumble, all of which are made here.

(6) CHEZ PERET
6, rue Daguerre (14th)

TELEPHONE
01-43-22-57-05
MÉTRO
Denfert-Rocherau
OPEN
Daily

For a peek into the life of the average Parisian, look no further than rue Daguerre in the fourteenth arrondissement. This is a typical *quartier populaire* (middle-class, working area) and rue Daguerre is the principal market street, with shops selling everything the inhabitants need to keep body and soul together.

Chez Peret is located right in the middle of it all, and for years it has been an important local watering hole. A cross section of regulars comes daily—some to jump start their day with a shot of espresso; others to trade insults with the bartender later in the day; and most to sit around outdoor café tables into the evening discussing everything . . . and nothing.

Orders are placed for sandwiches on *pain Poilâne,* plates of warm Lyonaisse sausage and potatoes, daily specials, and both of the homemade desserts: apple crumble and fruit *tarte*. Beaujolais and Burgandy are the wines of choice, and the tables of choice are on the covered terrace, where you may have to resort to pantomine to communicate when it is full, but don't be stressed—instead, enjoy the charm and appeal of being part of the real Paris, even if it is only for an hour or two.

CLOSED
Major holidays, 2 weeks in Feb (school holidays)

HOURS
Food service 9 A.M.–11:30 P.M. (bar from 8 A.M.), continuous service

RESERVATIONS
Not necessary

CREDIT CARDS
V

À LA CARTE
50–110F, BNC

PRIX FIXE
None

ENGLISH SPOKEN
Yes

(7) CRÊPERIE DE JOSSELIN
67, rue du Montparnasse (14th)

Montparnasse is known for its Breton *crêperies,* and nowhere in the *quartier* is this more evident than along rue du Montparnasse, where they line both sides of the street. Let me eliminate the guesswork over which one to try: the top choice on the street is Crêperie de Josselin, which brings the best of Brittany to Paris with their spectacular crêpes. Plump Breton ladies make crêpes as fast as they can in the open kitchen, rosy-cheeked waitresses rush from table to table, and the happy crowd loves every bite, knowing the final tally will be reasonable. Lace-covered hanging lamps cast a romantic glow over the wooden booths and tables. Quimper faience plates line the high plate rail, and an old grandfather clock gently ticks in one corner.

Abundant fillings of egg, ham, cheese, vegetables, fish, meat, and fresh herbs are folded into mammoth whole-wheat crêpes. Dessert crêpes are equally as overwhelming, filled with wonderful mixtures of honey, nuts, chocolate, fruits, and ice cream and covered with flaming liqueurs. The most authentic drink to order to go with your crêpes is a pitcher of the Breton apple cider.

NOTE: Just down the street is Crêperie Le Petit Josselin, the family's second crêperie, which is run by a brother-in-law. The room is smaller, and the crêpes and the prices are about the same. The only advantage to going here is that it is open Monday for lunch and dinner, when the first store is closed. It's at 59, rue du

TELEPHONE
01-43-20-93-50

MÉTRO
Edgar Quinet, Vavin

OPEN
Tues–Sun

CLOSED
Mon, NAC

HOURS
Tues–Fri: lunch noon–3 P.M., dinner 7–11:30 P.M.; Sat–Sun: noon–midnight, continuous service

RESERVATIONS
Not necessary

CREDIT CARDS
None

À LA CARTE
95–140F, BNC

PRIX FIXE
None

ENGLISH SPOKEN
Yes, with English menu

Montparnasse (tel: 01-43-22-91-81), and it's open similar hours on Monday to Saturday, closed Sunday.

(8) LA MÈRE AGITÉE
21, rue Campagne-Première (14th)

TELEPHONE
01-43-35-56-64
MÉTRO
Raspail
OPEN
Mon–Sat
CLOSED
Sun, holidays, NAC
HOURS
Lunch noon–3 P.M., dinner 8–11 P.M.
RESERVATIONS
Advised
CREDIT CARDS
MC, V
À LA CARTE
Entrées 35F, *plats* 70–75F, cheese 30F, desserts 35F
PRIX FIXE
None
ENGLISH SPOKEN
Yes

La Mère Agitée is about as big as a minute, but the food packs a wallop. Valérie de la Haye and Dominque Decombat are the talented and imaginative cooks, and every day they prepare a different à la carte menu with two choices for each course. There are two things you will know for sure: you will always have fish on Friday, and sausage from Lyon is a main course option every day.

Other than that, it is pot luck, but what good luck you will have. One day you could start with a chilled gazpacho or a cucumber-and-mint soup, then enjoy a strapping duck stew cooked in red wine, followed by a dish of fresh seasonal berries sprinkled with sugar or a lime mousse. Another day, it could be a slice of pâté, followed by lemon chicken with fat prunes for the garnish, and for the grand finale, a fruit *tarte.* Before your meal, have the house apéritif, Muscat de Corse, and be sure to order one of the Tourene wines to accompany the rest of your meal. When you finish, after complimenting the cooks on a meal well done, you will be checking to see what they're cooking the rest of the time you are in Paris.

(9) LA RÉGALADE
49, avenue Jean Moulin (14th)

TELEPHONE
01-45-45-68-58
MÉTRO
Alésia
OPEN
Tues–Fri lunch and dinner, Sat dinner only
CLOSED
Sat lunch, Sun–Mon, holidays, Aug, one week at Christmas
HOURS
Lunch noon–3 P.M., dinner 7:30 P.M.–midnight
RESERVATIONS
Absolutely essential as far in advance as possible
CREDIT CARDS
MC, V

Today, lovers of French cuisine are tired of paying wallet-numbing prices, and they are in constant search of good value for their money. As a result, they are branching out and willing to go to the hinterlands, so to speak, if a talented chef is serving food that has flavor, character, and personality.

Parisian gourmets have found what they are looking for at Yves Camdeborde's La Régalade. Camdeborde, a former student of Christian Constant at the Hôtel de Crillon, took a leap of faith and, with his wife, opened this small restaurant in an unimpressive corner of the fourteenth, specializing in dishes from his native Béarn in southwestern France. His cooking has an authority that commands attention, and as a result, his are the hottest tables in Paris, making reservations mandatory at least two to three weeks in advance. His food also challenges the notion that good has to be expensive. His one-price seasonal menu covers all three courses. Wines are extra, but if you look at one of the monthly featured wines, or order by the glass, they are well within reason.

You begin your meal by tasting the complimentary terrines brought to your table. Spread a chunk of the spicy mixture on a piece of whole-meal or white bread while you decide what to order. One of my favorite appetizers is the *beignets de légumes* (assorted Provençal vegetables quickly deep fried), served piping hot in a basket with tartar sauce. Barely cooked slivers of fresh tuna served with pesto spaghetti and dusted with a handful of herbs is another star-studded beginning, as is the daring lamb sweetbreads tossed with sweet peppers. A new twist on the classic shepherd's pie is the blood sausage covered with a layer of mashed potatoes and topped with a béarnaise sauce. The roasted lamb rubbed with garlic is marvelous, and the *fricasée de ris de veau et joue de porcelet* (sweetbreads and tender pork cheeks) with wild mushrooms is a fragrant, rich, tasty choice. The half dozen or more desserts might include a baked Alaska, Grand Marnier soufflé, or warm apples lightly cooked on a bed of thin, flaky pastry, topped with Camdeborde's own prune-Armagnac ice cream.

The simple interior is stark and inexpensively accented with a few photos, and the service is somewhat rushed when tables are full. It is not a place to relax and think romantic thoughts. However, the wonderful food makes up for this tenfold. It is a place where you will eat very well, and for the price, it is perhaps one of the best meals you will have in Paris.

À LA CARTE
None

PRIX FIXE
Lunch and dinner, 175F, 3 courses, BNC

ENGLISH SPOKEN
Limited

(10) LE BISTROT DU DÔME*
1, rue Delambre (14th)

See Le Bistrot du Dôme page 78. All other information is the same.

TELEPHONE: 01-43-35-32-00
MÉTRO: Vavin, Edgar-Quinet

(11) LE BLAVET
52 bis, rue de la Sablière (14th)

In this tourist-free zone of working-class Paris, the food and prices at Le Blavet are as good as it gets. The old-fashioned façade has half curtains at the windows and closely placed tables inside, and the blue-walled room is decorated with globe lights and a few run-of-the-mill paintings—clearly, Martha Stewart disciples

TELEPHONE
01-40-44-53-28

MÉTRO
Pernety

OPEN
Mon–Sat

CLOSED
Sun, holidays, Aug

HOURS
Lunch noon–2:30 P.M., dinner 7–10 P.M.
RESERVATIONS
Not necessary, but preferred
CREDIT CARDS
MC, V (minimum 100F)
À LA CARTE
80–110F
PRIX FIXE
Mon–Sat lunch: 60F, 2 courses, BNC; Mon–Fri lunch and dinner, Sat lunch: 68F, 2 courses, BC; Sat dinner: 70F, 2 courses, BNC; Mon-Sat lunch and dinner: 85F, 3 courses, BC
ENGLISH SPOKEN
None, but English menu

do not run this show. Claude Ponti, his wife, and their German shephard Prince *do* run the show, and they have developed a real neighborhood following of portly diners who relish the basics and wouldn't be caught dead eating low fat anything. The simple dishes are less than gourmet, but Claude turns out the kind of basic fare the French subsist on everyday. And all but the most destitute Cheap Eater will be able to afford the prices. As with almost all restaurants in Paris, regardless of stature or price, you will be most satisfied if you stick to the blue-plate special and sip the house wine.

(12) LE QUERCY
5, rue Mouton-Duvernet (14th)

TELEPHONE
01-45-39-39-61
MÉTRO
Mouton-Duvernet
OPEN
Tues–Sat lunch and dinner, Sun lunch only
CLOSED
Sun dinner, Mon, some holidays, Aug (call to check)
HOURS
Lunch noon–2:30 P.M., dinner 7–10:30 P.M.
RESERVATIONS
Advised
CREDIT CARDS
MC, V
À LA CARTE
170–180F, BNC
PRIX FIXE
Lunch only, 75F, 2 courses, BNC; lunch and dinner, 160F, 3 courses, BNC
ENGLISH SPOKEN
Yes

No matter when you go or what you order, this exemplary neighborhood restaurant is well worth the trip from wherever you may be staying in Paris. Despite the excellent food and a faithful lunch business, Le Quercy is just far enough from the usual tourist haunts to keep it from being "discovered," and that is just the way local patrons like it. Pascal Champ trained at one of the temples of haute cuisine in Paris, like many of his young colleagues, before striking out on his own with his wife, Virginie, and one other helper. By virtue of hard work and talent, they have earned a respected place in the hearts and minds of their customers.

In the kitchen, Pascal employs a light modern touch while adding an inspired spin to his seasonal and weekly menus. The three-course lunch offers three choices for each, beginning perhaps with a warm smoked duck and lentil salad, followed by a fresh sea trout and a fondu of leeks, and ending with a selection of fruit sorbet or rich *profiteroles*. If you love beef, the dish that is always available and absolutely wonderful is Pascal's specialty—*papillotte de filet de boeuf à la moëlle,* filet mignon flavored with marrow and shallots, dramatically served in its own parchment wrapper, and placed on a bed of egg noodles that are the perfect foil for all the natural meat juices. If chocolate is your passion, the chocolate mousse floating on orange sauce dotted with strawberry hearts is your dish. When dining here, plan to enjoy a fine bottle of wine from their cellar, which includes bottles from the best producers in France.

Fifteenth Arrondissement

(See map on pages 180–181.)

This vast and generally untraveled region for most Paris visitors is exemplified by La Tour Montparnasse, which looms from the intersection of the sixth, fourteenth, and fifteenth arrondissements. It is the tallest, and by some standards the ugliest, building in Europe. In this basically middle-class residential area you will find corners of charm, specifically around the Village Suisse, an expensive complex of antique shops selling everything imaginable at prices reserved for Arab sheiks. Stretching along the River Seine are high-rise apartments and a new park with walking paths and benches for enjoying the views.

LEFT BANK
La Tour Montparnasse

FIFTEENTH ARRONDISSEMENT RESTAURANTS

(13) BRASSERIE LE SUFFREN
84, avenue de Suffren (15th)

Everyone in the neighborhood goes to Brasserie Le Suffren. You can, too, if you find yourself near Invalides, are wandering on boulevard de Grenelle—one of the best street *marchés* in Paris—on a Tuesday or Sunday morning, or are hungry before or after seeing a film down the street at Kinopanorama, the biggest movie house in the city. Sitting at one of the outside terrace tables provides terrific people-watching in this comfortable middle-class area.

Basic brasserie standbys of salads, *choucroutes*, beef tartare, roast chicken, oysters, and desserts are served nonstop by a rushed crew of black-clad waiters, whose tolerance for tourists is sometimes stretched quite thin.

TELEPHONE
01-45-66-97-86

MÉTRO
La Motte-Picquet

OPEN
Daily

CLOSED
Never, NAC

HOURS
7 A.M.–midnight, continuous service

RESERVATIONS
Advised

CREDIT CARDS
MC, V

À LA CARTE
150–175F, BNC

PRIX FIXE
Lunch and dinner: 86F, 2 fish courses, BC; 106F, 3 courses, BC; 175F, 3 courses, BC (wine and kir)

ENGLISH SPOKEN
Usually

But I only had sympathy for this overworked waitstaff, which is constantly on the run, each waiter handling more tables than unions in America would allow five or more waiters to serve. So long as you don't expect to develop a personal relationship, you won't find the service rude. The three good value menus are always available, but only if you eat inside. That shouldn't be a problem, but please avoid the stuffy upstairs area.

(14) CHEZ YVETTE
1, rue d'Alençon (at boulevard Montparnasse) (15th)

TELEPHONE
01-42-22-45-55

MÉTRO
Montparnasse

OPEN
Mon–Fri

CLOSED
Sat–Sun, holidays, Aug

HOURS
Lunch 12:15–3 P.M., dinner 7:15-10 P.M.

RESERVATIONS
Advised

CREDIT CARDS
MC, V

À LA CARTE
175F, BNC

PRIX FIXE
None

ENGLISH SPOKEN
Limited

The dining room is flanked by brown velvet banquettes and heavy drapes hiding most of the outside light. Starched white linens and attractive china dress each correctly set table. A serving table with a vase of flowers sits in the middle of the room, and a stuffed deer head peers over the serving counter. A two-thousand piece jigsaw puzzle, put together by the owner's son, hangs proudly over the bar and cash register. As you can tell, Chez Yvette is homey, vintage Paris with the sort of warm and fuzzy ambiance that makes guests want to settle in for a long midday meal or an evening of dining pleasure.

"The menu never changes—the regular customers won't allow it," said the jovial chef and owner, Christian Pineau, who along with his wife and son have been catering to the hearts and souls of Parisians for thirty years. Pineau takes great pride in making everything himself, from the terrines to the sorbets. His à la carte–only menu includes all the standbys of satisfying cooking. If you love liver, don't fail to treat yourself to the house *foie gras de canard* or the *terrine de foie de volailles* (chicken livers). No serious meat eater should miss the Boudin sausages, which are made here and irresistible. There is a nicely done rabbit with herbs, and for the shy, steaks and tender lamb *provençale.* Top off the abundant feast with a light *île flottante,* a dish of refreshing sorbet, or if you can, a fruit *tartelette.*

(15) HARDEL RESTAURANT
8, avenue du Maine (15th)

TELEPHONE
01-45-44-39-41

MÉTRO
Montparnasse

OPEN
Daily

Cheap Eats in elegant surroundings packed with French diners, reliable food, and lots of nice little extras . . . that is what dining at Pascal Hardel's restaurant is all about. Another appealing feature for Cheap Eaters is that you can tailor your prix fixe meal to fit not only your budget but the size of your appetite by mixing and matching *entrées, plats,* and desserts into whatever combination suits you.

The pretty pastel dining room is done in a light mauve. It has open seating along the street, with comfortable high-backed chairs around well-spaced tables. There are some banquettes, a potted palm for show, and a small bar as you enter. The lunch bunch is strictly French bourgeoisie; the dinner guests are a mixed bag who do not want one of the glitzy, quick Montparnasse meals that seems to be the rule, not the exception, in the *quartier.* In addition to the bargain prix fixe meals, Hardel pays attention to pleasing details: a bowl of peanuts on the table to accompany your apéritif, cookies and chocolates served with after-dinner coffee, and always courteous, prompt service.

The food consists of a varied repertoire of top-quality products served in generous portions. For a dependable appetizer, the salad topped with slices of smoked duck is interesting. A shrimp salad lightly tossed in a saffron vinaigrette or one topped with a chunk of chèvre are other good openers. The best main courses are the *poulet à la creme*—a Normandy specialty of chicken cooked in a cream sauce with potatoes and leeks—or the house specialty, *la Bouillabaisse de Marseille,* a Mediterranean fish stew combining five types of fish. All the dishes are garnished with a choice of *gratin dauphinois, frites,* spinach, carrot custard, or rice. If you are like I am and think a day is incomplete without something chocolate, try the *surprise pour chocophile* (a new twist on an old theme)—orange mousse with chocolate sauce. Any of the ice creams are good, especially the blockbuster Coupe Hardel—rum raisin ice cream smothered in caramel and hot chocolate sauces with whipped cream covering the whole thing.

CLOSED
Never, NAC

HOURS
Lunch noon–2:30 P.M., dinner 6–11 P.M.

RESERVATIONS
Preferred

CREDIT CARDS
MC, V

À LA CARTE
Not available

PRIX FIXE
All menus available for lunch and dinner: *menu salade,* 75F, salad and dessert, BNC; *menu rapide,* 79F, *entrée* and *plat,* BNC; children's menu, 76F, 3 courses, BNC; *menu gourmand,* 109F, 2 courses, 135F, 3 courses, both BNC

ENGLISH SPOKEN
Yes

(16) LA CHAUMIÈRE
54, avenue Félix-Faure (15th)

Oliver Amestoy is typical of many talented young Parisian chefs who own their own restaurants. He began by running the successful kitchen at his family's restaurant, La Table d'Eiffel (see page 130). Now he and his delightful Australian wife, Marie, have branched out on their own and reinvented La Chaumière, a dining landmark that had rested on its laurels too long and, as a

TELEPHONE
01-45-54-13-91

MÉTRO
Boucicaut

OPEN
Daily

CLOSED
Never, NAC

HOURS
Lunch noon–2:30 P.M., dinner 8–10 P.M.

RESERVATIONS
Advised

CREDIT CARDS
AE, MC, V

À LA CARTE
None

PRIX FIXE
Lunch and dinner, 120F, 2 courses, BNC, desserts extra (40–50F)

ENGLISH SPOKEN
Yes

result, had to close its doors. When the Amestoy's took over, they breathed new life into the food and offered a friendly dining alternative to the dreary past. Diners today want pleasant, casual surroundings and more choices for less money, and Amestoy has risen to the challenge, consistently giving his patrons more than their money's worth.

His top-quality fare, which nourishes with its solid portions and pleases with its presentation, begins with generous *entrées* of rounds of warm chèvre cheese resting on crispy potato pancakes. His fresh crab ravioli in a delicate roe sauce and his smoked Scottish salmon with blini on the side underscore his skill with fish preparations. Main courses also lean heavily on fish—imaginatively paired with interesting sauces and garnishes—such as salmon and langoustines flavored with a sweet pepper sauce and accented with onion fondu. Besides the fish, my favorite dish here is the tender lamb, roasted to pink perfection and served with baby green beans and creamy potatoes.

Desserts are positively wonderful, and most must be selected when you first place your meal order. With a repertoire that includes Grand Marnier soufflé, flaming crêpes suzettes, apple tart flambéed in Calvados, and *bombe Alaska,* it is almost impossible to choose. From a purely theatrical standpoint, the *bombe Alaska* (baked Alaska) receives top billing from me. In fact, the night I ordered it a group of proper Parisians were sitting at a table next to me. They had finished their meal, paid for it, and were getting up to leave when they saw my flaming *bombe* served. After one look, they promptly sat down and ordered three to split among themselves. There was not a bite left on any of our plates.

While the food clearly has hit its stride, at times the service feels not quite up to speed and could use some polishing. But remember, this is Paris, where dining is not meant to be dispatched on the way to something else, especially when spending the evening in a nice restaurant. Be patient—good things always come to those who order another bottle of excellent wine. Any wait will be worth it at La Chaumière, which, once tried, will go straight to the top of your list of Paris dining favorites.

(17) LA GITANE

53 bis, avenue de la Motte-Picquet (15th)

Capacity crowds arrive for both lunch and dinner in La Gitane's seventy-plus seat dining room and secluded, plant-bordered summer terrace. Located across from the antique dealers in the Village Suisse and only a métro stop from the Eiffel Tower, it has become an address dear to the hearts of bistro lovers.

When you step inside, you immediately understand what the French mean by a good *quartier* bistro. The menu, handwritten on hanging blackboards around the room, changes often, reflecting the freshest market ingredients and the chef's inspirations. Those with healthy appetites will appreciate the well-constructed repertoire of *pot-au-feu, cassoulet, boudin noir,* and simply poached fish with light sauces. In the cooler months look for stuffed cabbage, *petit salé aux lentilles,* and steaming *choucroutes.* Good wines are modestly priced, and the desserts, especially the apples spiked with Armagnac and the *baba au rhum,* are as rewarding as the rest of the meal.

TELEPHONE
01-47-34-62-92

MÉTRO
La Motte-Picquet

OPEN
Mon–Sat

CLOSED
Sun, major holidays, one week at Christmas

HOURS
Lunch noon–2:30 P.M., dinner 7–11 P.M.

RESERVATIONS
Advised

CREDIT CARDS
AE, MC, V

À LA CARTE
160–185F, BNC

PRIX FIXE
None

ENGLISH SPOKEN
Usually

(18) L'AMANGUIER

46, boulevard Montparnasse, at rue Alençon (15th)

See L'Amanguier page 151. All other information is the same.

TELEPHONE: 01-45-48-49-16

MÉTRO: Montparnasse, Falguière

(19) L'AMANGUIER

51, rue du Théâtre (15th)

See L'Amanguier page 151. All other information is the same.

TELEPHONE: 01-45-77-04-01

MÉTRO: Émile-Zola

(20) LE BISTROT D'ANDRÉ

232, rue St-Charles, at rue Leblanc (15th)

Hubert Gloaguen purchased this old, tired restaurant and restored it to its original status, as a canteen for workers from the Citröen factory that once dominated this arid corner of the fifteenth arrondissement. The simple, bright interior now honors automobile pioneer André Citröen with large photographs of Citröen and his factory as it was in the old days. True, the bistro is far from the thick of things, but sometimes it is interesting

TELEPHONE
01-45-57-89-14

MÉTRO
Lourmel

OPEN
Mon–Sat

CLOSED
Sun, holidays, NAC

HOURS
Lunch noon–2:30 P.M., dinner 7:30–10:30 P.M.

RESERVATIONS
Advised for lunch or for more than two persons
CREDIT CARDS
V
À LA CARTE
130F, BNC
PRIX FIXE
Lunch only, 65F, 3 courses, BNC; children's menu (lunch and dinner), 40F, 3 courses, BC
ENGLISH SPOKEN
Yes
MISCELLANEOUS
Nonsmoking section

to get away from all the tourist hoopla and see Paris from a Parisian's viewpoint.

The best time to come is at lunch, when the place is wall to wall with a good-looking *quartier* crowd, their jackets off and their sleeves rolled up. The rushed service is efficient, considering the number of tables each waiter must serve. Another reason Cheap Eaters will want to make this a lunch stop is the 65F, three-course prix fixe menu, served in addition to an à la carte menu. A recent sampling included cucumbers in cream or a salad topped with fried chicken livers; veal with sautéed potatoes or a fish brochet with hollandaise sauce and rice; and a choice of cheese, fruit salad, or the dessert of the day. In the evening the scene is much calmer, and there is no prix fixe menu, but the à la carte prices are reasonable and the food is always worth the safari. If you are a wine enthusiast, Gloaguen's changing wine list made up of little-known French wines at very attractive prices merits special attention.

NOTE: To avoid a long, dull métro ride, take the No. 42 bus, which will drop you off across the street from the restaurant.

(21) OH! DUO
54, avenue Émile-Zola (15th)

TELEPHONE
01-45-77-28-82
MÉTRO
Charles-Michels
OPEN
Mon–Fri lunch and dinner, Sat dinner only
CLOSED
Sat lunch, Sun, holidays, 1st week in May (call to check), 3 weeks in Aug
HOURS
Lunch noon–2 P.M., dinner 7–10:30 P.M.
RESERVATIONS
Recommended
CREDIT CARDS
MC, V
À LA CARTE
120–195F, BNC
PRIX FIXE
Lunch and dinner, 110F, 2 courses, 145F, 4 courses, both BNC
ENGLISH SPOKEN
Yes

A reader writes: "Dear Sandra: We wanted to write to you about Oh! Duo, . . . by far the best meal of the trip. The service was impeccable, the staff constantly smiling. The food was, as I told the *patronne, ne pas de la cuisine, c'est un rêve.* We seriously considered just returning to this one restaurant every night. Please rave about this in your next edition." Consider it done. I am happy to rave about Oh! Duo because there is so much to rave about.

I first found out about this hidden restaurant from a friend who lives nearby. Because I follow through on all tips, I went for dinner. Judging from reader letters such as the one above, many Cheap Eaters in Paris have also found this gem and applaud everything about it.

The four-course prix fixe menu is definitely the best value. The offerings are seasonal, but the popular foie gras is always listed as an *entrée*. In the late spring, look for a warm leek *tarte,* curried eggs scrambled with chunks of smokey bacon, or thin slices of raw salmon marinated in lemon and coriander. Rabbit in some form is always a main course possibility, and so is the *petit sale de canard aux lentilles*. Watch for fresh fish, lamb chops, the *choucroute maison,* and whatever the *plat du jour* is. All the main courses are liberally garnished with potato gratin or purée and fresh spinach or another vegetable, if you wish. *Profiteroles* with honey and chocolate, fruit gratins, and the homemade nougat ice cream are only a few of the pleasant finishing touches awaiting you.

Wines are fairly priced, and the chef/owner Joel Valéro does his own shopping at Rungis. The provincial setting is attractive, especially upstairs by the window, and the service and welcome from his wife, Françoise, is friendly. You see, there is plenty to rave about at Oh! Duo.

(22) TY BREIZ
52, boulevard de Vaugirard (15th)

The message on the restaurant's business card says, *Les délices de la Bretagne peuvent également s'apprécier à Paris.* Or, "The delicacies of Brittany can also be enjoyed in Paris." And, of course, they mean right at Ty Breiz, which is as cute and cozy as a Breton crêperie can be. The blue-and-white dining room is decorated with Quimper pottery and dominated by a carved wooden bar and an open kitchen, where you can watch the chefs adeptly turning out at least thirty variations of this popular comfort food. Savory buckwheat crêpes (*galettes*) are filled with mouthwatering combinations of eggs, meat, fish, cheese, and creamy sauces. The servings look huge but they are surprisingly light, and you will find yourself ordering a dessert crêpe . . . maybe a flambéed crêpes suzette or a fancy Berthillon ice cream creation with rum raisin ice cream and rum sauce hiding under a mountain of whipped cream. To keep the experience authentic, order a pitcher of cider to go with your meal, but be careful. If you are not used to this sort of apple drink, a little can go a long way.

TELEPHONE
01-43-20-83-72

MÉTRO
Pasteur, Montparnasse

OPEN
Mon–Sat

CLOSED
Sun, major holidays, 3 weeks in Aug

HOURS
Lunch 11:45 A.M.–2:45 P.M., dinner 7–10:45 P.M.

RESERVATIONS
Advised

CREDIT CARDS
MC, V

À LA CARTE
90–125F, BC

PRIX FIXE
Lunch and dinner, 60F, 2 courses, BC

ENGLISH SPOKEN
Yes, with English menu

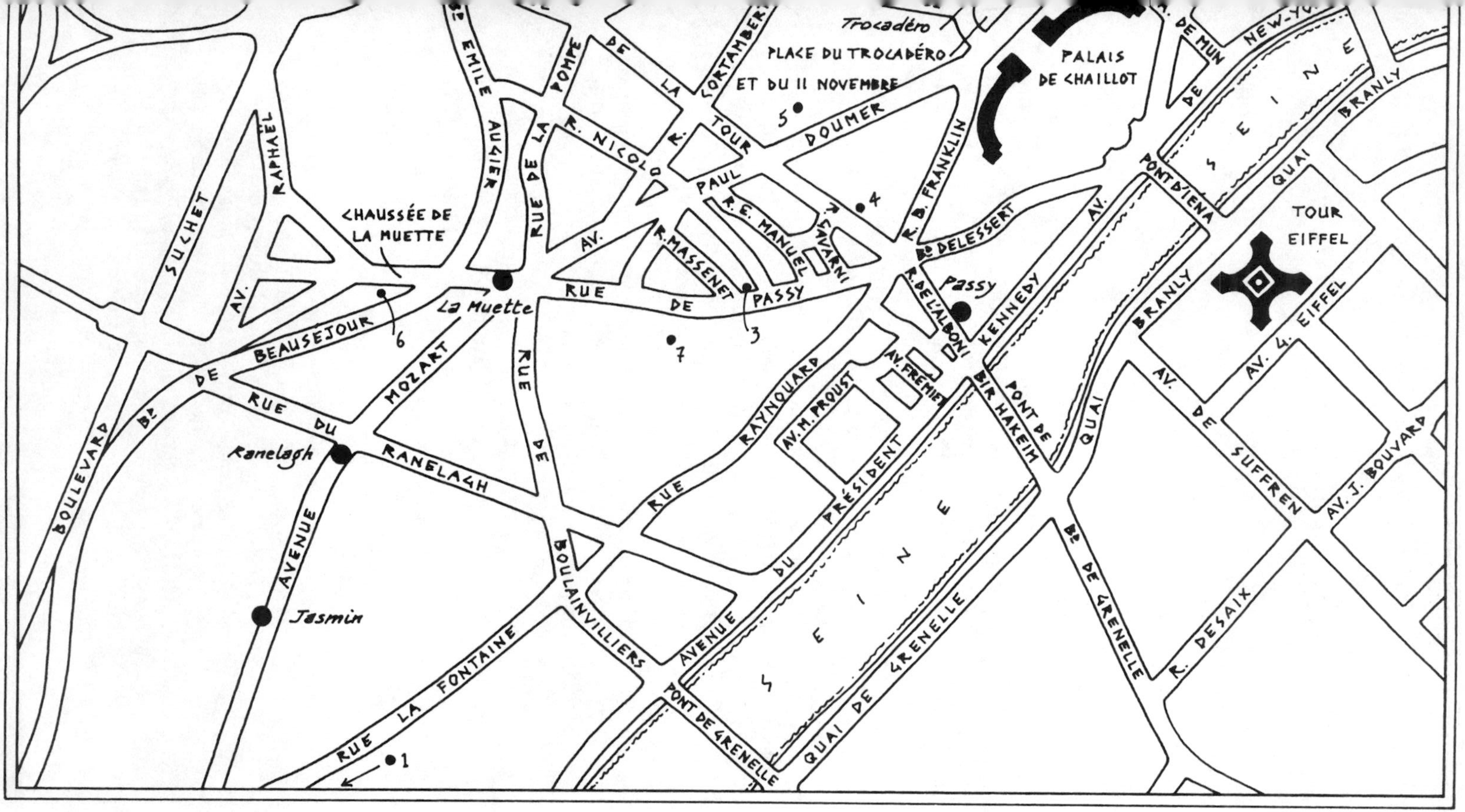

Trocadéro
PLACE DU TROCADÉRO
ET DU 11 NOVEMBRE
PALAIS
DE CHAILLOT
TOUR
EIFFEL
SEINE
SEINE
BOULEVARD
SUCHET
AV.
RAPHAËL
CHAUSSÉE DE
LA MUETTE
BD DE BEAUSÉJOUR
La Muette
RUE DU RANELAGH
Ranelagh
AVENUE
Jasmin
MOZART
RUE DE BOULAINVILLIERS
RUE LA FONTAINE
EMILE AUGIER
RUE DE LA POMPE
R. NICOLO
DE LA TOUR
CORTAMBERT
AV. PAUL DOUMER
R. MASSENET
R. E. MANUEL
GAVARNI
R. B. FRANKLIN
BD DELESSERT
RUE DE PASSY
Passy
RUE RAYNOUARD
AV. M. PROUST
AV. FREMIET
R. DE L'ALBONI
AV. KENNEDY
AVENUE DU PRÉSIDENT
PONT DE BIR HAKEIM
PONT DE GRENELLE
QUAI DE GRENELLE
BD DE GRENELLE
R. DESAIX
QUAI BRANLY
QUAI BRANLY
PONT D'IENA
AV. DE SUFFREN
AV. G. EIFFEL
AV. J. BOUVARD
DE MUN
NEW-YO
1
3
4
5
6
7

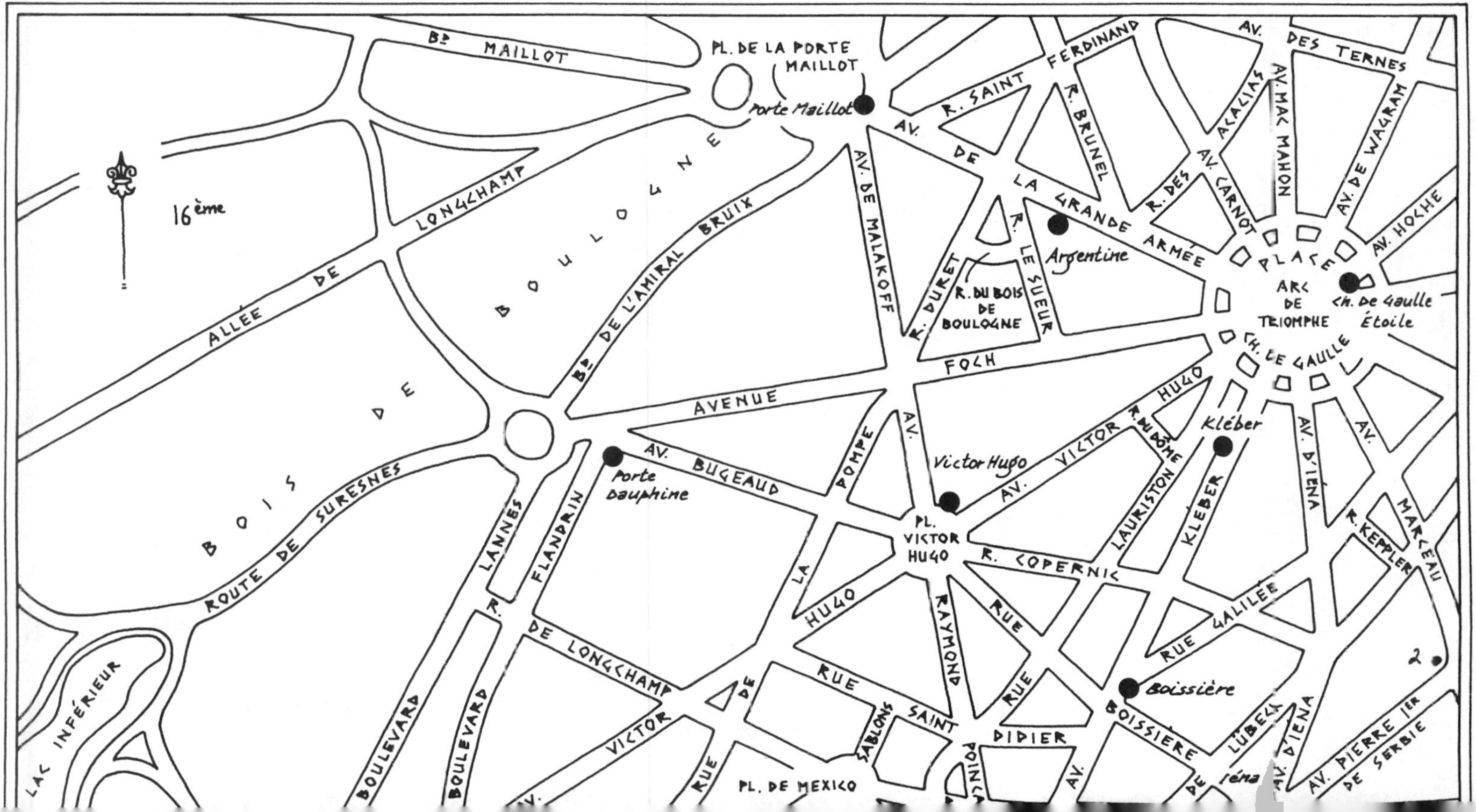

Bd MAILLOT
PL. DE LA PORTE MAILLOT
Porte Maillot
16ème
ALLÉE DE LONGCHAMP
BOIS DE BOULOGNE
Bd DE L'AMIRAL BRUIX
ROUTE DE SURESNES
LAC INFÉRIEUR
BOULEVARD
BOULEVARD
LANNES
R. FLANDRIN
AV. BUGEAUD
Porte Dauphine
AVENUE FOCH
AV. DE MALAKOFF
AV. DE LA GRANDE ARMÉE
R. SAINT FERDINAND
R. BRUNEL
R. DES ACACIAS
AV. CARNOT
AV. MAC MAHON
AV. DES TERNES
AV. DE WAGRAM
AV. HOCHE
Argentine
R. DURET
R. LE SUEUR
R. DU BOIS DE BOULOGNE
PLACE CH. DE GAULLE
ARC DE TRIOMPHE
Ch. De Gaulle Étoile
AV. VICTOR HUGO
Victor Hugo
R. DU DÔME
Kléber
KLEBER
LAURISTON
AV. D'IÉNA
AV. MARCEAU
R. KEPPLER
AV. DE LA POMPE
PL. VICTOR HUGO
R. COPERNIC
RUE HUGO
RAYMOND POINCA
RUE GALILÉE
Boissière
BOISSIÈRE
RUE DE LUBECK
Iéna
AV. D'IÉNA
AV. PIERRE IER DE SERBIE
2
R. DE LONGCHAMP
AV. VICTOR HUGO
RUE DE LA POMPE
RUE SAINT DIDIER
AV.
SABLONS
RUE DE
PL. DE MEXICO

Sixteenth Arrondissement

RIGHT BANK
Avenue Foche, Bois de Boulogne, Jardin d'Acclimitation, Musée Marmottan, Musée d'Art Moderne de la Ville de Paris, Musée de l'Homme, Palais de Chaillot, Passy, Trocadéro

The sixteenth, along with the seventh, is one of Paris' best addresses, especially around avenue Foche, where real estate prices are geared to oil moguls and multimillionaires. Elegant shopping can be found along avenue Victor Hugo and rue de Passy. The Trocadéro area, with its gardens, views of the Seine and Eiffel Tower, and complex of museums in the two wings of the Palais de Chaillot, forms the nucleus of tourist interest. At night the lighted fountains bring back the glamour of Art Deco Paris. Not to be overlooked is the Musée Marmottan, one of the hidden treasures of Paris museums. Bequests and gifts have enriched the collection so much that it rivals that of the Musée d'Orsay in Impressionist art, especially the collection of works by Monet.

SIXTEENTH ARRONDISSEMENT RESTAURANTS

* Restaurants marked with an asterisk (*) are considered Big Splurges.

(1) AU CLOCHER DU VILLAGE*
8 bis, rue Verderet (16th)

TELEPHONE
01-42-88-35-87

MÉTRO
Église-Auteuil, exit Chardon Lagache

OPEN
Winter: Mon–Fri lunch and dinner, Sat dinner only; summer: Mon–Fri lunch and dinner, Sat and Sun dinner only

CLOSED
Winter: Sat lunch, Sun; summer: Sat and Sun lunch; major holidays, NAC

Wine presses and old baskets hang from beams, posters plaster the ceiling and walls, a shining copper samovar graces the bar, a huge wooden four-door icebox dominates the small room off the kitchen, and enough trinkets and treasure to open a shop fill the restaurant—all of it creating a setting for provincial country dining at Au Clocher du Village. Reserve a table for a 1 P.M. lunch or a 9 P.M. dinner and you may be the only foreigner there, either in the main room or on the beautiful summer terrace in front. Admittedly it is close to nothing on the visitor's map, and the métro ride is long for most, but trust me, it is worth the extra effort and time it takes to get there.

The food is prepared in the traditional fashion and served by a staff who banter back and forth with long-time customers. When ordering, stick with the daily specials, the *tête de veau avec langue et cervelle* (calf's head with tongue and brains) or the grilled meats, and avoid the *haricots verts* (green beans). For starters, the mammoth plate of crudités or the artichoke hearts are good dishes. If you like apple tart, theirs is served warm with a tub of crème fraîche on the side to ladle over it. Or, if chocolate mousse is your downfall, here it is served in a big bowl *à volanté,* which means you can eat as much as you want.

HOURS
Lunch noon–2:30 P.M., dinner 7:30–11 P.M.
RESERVATIONS
Necessary
CREDIT CARDS
MC, V
À LA CARTE
225F, BNC
PRIX FIXE
None
ENGLISH SPOKEN
Yes

(2) DRIVER'S
6, rue Georges-Bizet (16th)

Framed uniforms, crash helmets, and autographed photos of famous race car drivers and their cars decorate the walls at Driver's, a classy little bistro owned by Stéphane Muller, the nephew of Michel Dubose, a well-known driver on the Formula I racing circuit.

But you don't have to know or care a thing about racing to appreciate the good food and excellent value offered by the three-course prix fixe lunch that includes both wine and coffee for under twenty dollars. The à la carte menu won't send your budget into overdrive and neither will a bottle of decent wine. The stick-to-your-ribs food kicks off with snails, lentil salad, or baked eggs with salmon. It picks up speed with rabbit, tripe, or *boudin noire* served with smooth mashed potatoes. Then you coast to the finish with rice pudding, *pain perdu,* or a winning chocolate cake—*le truffe Driver's au chocolat.*

TELEPHONE
01-47-23-61-15
MÉTRO
Alma-Marceau
OPEN
Mon–Fri lunch and dinner, Sat dinner only
CLOSED
Sat lunch, Sun, holidays, Aug (call to check)
HOURS
Lunch noon–2:30 P.M., dinner 7 P.M.–midnight
RESERVATIONS
Advised
CREDIT CARDS
AE, MC, V
À LA CARTE
175–180F, BC
PRIX FIXE
Lunch only, 100F, 3 courses, BC
ENGLISH SPOKEN
Yes

(3) LADURÉE—FRANCK ET FILS
80, rue de Passy (16th)

In September 1996, Ladurée opened its second tea-room on the top floor of this upscale Parisian clothing store in the heart of Passy, one of the most expensive *quartiers* of Paris.

Everything served is made by the Ladurée kitchens, even the ice cream and chocolates. It is a nice place to stop by for a refreshing cup of tea or coffee and some of their famous pastries or for a light lunch.

TELEPHONE
01-44-14-38-80
MÉTRO
La Muette
OPEN
Mon–Sat, lunch and tea only
CLOSED
Sun, holidays
HOURS
10 A.M.–6:30 P.M., continuous service; hot lunch 11:30 A.M.–4:30 P.M., tea 4:30–6:30 P.M.

RESERVATIONS
Advised for lunch
CREDIT CARDS
AE, MC, V
À LA CARTE
50–125F, BC
PRIX FIXE
Lunch, 110F, 2 courses, BNC
ENGLISH SPOKEN
Yes

The pretty setting displays paintings of beautiful cakes in addition to a table seductively displaying the real thing.

For more about Ladurée, please see page 144.

(4) LA PETITE TOUR*
11, rue de la Tour (16th)

TELEPHONE
01-45-20-09-31,
01-45-20-09-97
MÉTRO
Passy
OPEN
Mon–Sat
CLOSED
Sun, Aug
HOURS
Lunch noon–2:30 P.M., dinner 7:30–10:30 P.M.
RESERVATIONS
Essential
CREDIT CARDS
AE, DC, MC, V
À LA CARTE
350–385F, BNC
PRIX FIXE
None
ENGLISH SPOKEN
Yes

If only once during your stay in Paris you decide to have an exceptionally fine meal, you will not be disappointed by choosing Christiane and Freddy Israel's La Petite Tour in Passy. Offering marvelous food and service in a quiet, formal atmosphere, a meal here is a dining pleasure you will remember long after leaving Paris. The food, a blend of classic French with modern overtones, relies on first-class products, precise preparation, and elegant presentation. Even the house dog, a golden Lab named Foster, has a sense of grace and style as he lies contentedly by the doorway.

If you are here in the fall, order Israel's specialty: masterfully cooked wild game. One of the most outstanding dishes is the robust venison stew with whole baby vegetables. It is almost impossible to list all the other specialties, as the menu is long and changes with market availability and the seasons. Always on the menu, however, is the delicate lobster bisque and the *filets de sole aux mandarines.* The *caneton aux pêches* (duckling with peaches) is delicious, and so is the simple *fricassée de poulet au vinaigre* (stewed chicken in a vinegar sauce). The veal liver with raisins or bacon or the *filet de veau à la crème aux champignons* offers a wonderful new dimension on these French staples. No matter what your *entrée* and *plat* may be, you must save room for one of the picture-perfect desserts, especially the *pêches Pantagruel* or the blissfully light *île flottante.* In the spring and early summer, the *mille-feuilles aux fraises* (flaky pastry layered with cream and fresh strawberries) is spectacular.

Of course, all of this does not fall into the budget category, but while sipping an after-dinner cognac, I am sure you will agree with the many others who have been here that the delightful meal is well worth the extra francs.

(5) LE SCHEFFER
22, rue Scheffer (16th)

This is the part of Paris where the scarf is Hermès, the watch Cartier, the little outfit Chanel, and everyone has had a busy day at the boutique. That is why it is a bit of a surprise to discover Le Scheffer, a typical Left Bank bistro—right down to the turn-of-the-century posters and original tiled floors—where the kitchen dishes out generous and authentic food. A meal with a glass of the house vintage will ring in for around 175F, which is reasonable considering the price of real estate in this blue-blooded corner of Paris.

The well-heeled crowd—foreign as well as French—plan repeat visits for the familiar dishes supplemented with daily specials. The encyclopedia of bistro eats includes lentil salad topped with slices of rare duck, cold green beans quickly tossed with a vinaigrette dressing, slabs of pâté and terrine, grilled lamb and beef, the usual organ meats, a spicy *andouillette,* fresh fish, and conventional desserts featuring seasonal fruits, chocolate, whipped cream, and anything else to try to bend diners' willpower.

TELEPHONE
01-47-27-81-11

MÉTRO
Pompe

OPEN
Mon–Sat

CLOSED
Sun, major holidays, NAC

HOURS
Lunch noon–2:30 P.M., dinner 7:30–10:30 P.M.

RESERVATIONS
Advised

CREDIT CARDS
AE, MC, V

À LA CARTE
160–175F, BC

PRIX FIXE
None

ENGLISH SPOKEN
Yes, with English menu

(6) RESTAURANT DES CHAUFFEURS
8, Chaussée de la Muette (16th)

Famed chef Joël Robuchon selected this quarter-century-old, family-run café for a write-up in his newspaper column, praising it as one of the capital's last outposts of home cooking. Quite a tribute. If you want to experience the type of family-run operation that seems to be on its way out in today's Paris, you will find a good example at Restaurant des Chauffeurs, where the second generation of the Bertrand family is now in charge.

The restaurant has been collecting anecdotes and acquiring patina for years, and it is easy to imagine that the hard-core regulars leaning against the bar know all the stories. Another group of habitués sit at the sidewalk tables, assessing and evaluating what upscale Parisians in Passy are wearing *this* year.

The almost-readable, purple-inked menu features trucker-size portions of French comfort food. A typical selection might include a bowl of vegetable soup or marinated leeks, followed by sole *meunière* with steamed potatoes, roast chicken, fresh fish, or the house mainstay, liver with bacon and tomatoes. The desserts are simple versions of *clafoutis,* rice pudding, and fruit *tartes.* With a

TELEPHONE
01-42-88-50-05

MÉTRO
La Muette

OPEN
Daily

CLOSED
Dec 25, Jan 1, May 1, Aug 13–27

HOURS
5:30 A.M.–10 P.M., continuous service

RESERVATIONS
Suggested for lunch

CREDIT CARDS
MC, V

À LA CARTE
100–125F, BNC

PRIX FIXE
Lunch and dinner, 70F, 3 courses, BNC

ENGLISH SPOKEN
Yes

pitcher of house wine, a hundred francs or so will see you out the door.

(7) TANT QU'IL Y AURA DES HOMMES
1, rue Jean Bologne (16th)

TELEPHONE
01-45-27-76-64
MÉTRO
Passy
OPEN
Tues–Sat
CLOSED
Sun–Mon, major holidays, 1 week at Christmas, Aug
HOURS
Lunch noon–2 P.M., dinner 7:30–10 P.M.
RESERVATIONS
Advised
CREDIT CARDS
MC, V
À LA CARTE
165F, BNC
PRIX FIXE
Lunch only, 95F, 2 courses, BNC
ENGLISH SPOKEN
Yes

Food from the gardens of Avignon and Toulon whisks you to this sun-drenched corner of the south of France. Owners Jacques Dereux and Adrian La Fargue have not only looked south for inspiration but have avoided the mass production approach by using real country products purchased directly from the growers. They do the same with their wines, which you can try either by the glass or bottle.

The mood is set as you are seated in the bright yellow and blue provencial dining room. The menu promises good things ahead, with colorful salads of fresh vegetables, farm pies, sausage served with *aligot*, lusty *plats du jour,* and fresh fish. Reassuring desserts might include a plain bowl of *fromage blanc* dressed with fruit or a caramel nut *tarte* for those wanting more of a sugar fix to end their meal.

Seventeenth Arrondissement

The seventeenth is a sprawling area that includes leafy boulevards and upscale residences if you stay southwest of rue de Rome. The Palais des Congrès is here, a convention center with restaurants, several movie theaters, and the first stop in Paris for the Charles de Gaulle airport bus. The northeastern part of the arrondissement is scruffy as it merges with the eighteenth.

RIGHT BANK
Palais des Congrès, Parc Monceau

SEVENTEENTH ARRONDISSEMENT RESTAURANTS

* Restaurants marked with an asterisk (*) are considered Big Splurges.

(1) CHEZ FRED*
190 bis, boulevard Péreire (17th)

When old favorites change hands, it is always a cause for concern. Will the place lose its character, the food go downhill, and the prices rise? Fortunately, Alain Piazza has kept all the familiar elements at Chez Fred, including the rude waiters who serve to remind us just who is boss around here. The service shouldn't deter you from coming, however, because when the food awards are handed out, Chez Fred continues to be in the winner's circle. It is a colorful spot, known for its bistro-style cooking, which is meant to be eaten, not admired. The inside is 1930s *grand-mère,* with beveled mirrors, old pieces of china displayed here and there, tightly packed tables, and a hanging collection of umbrellas and Parisian street signs.

TELEPHONE
01-45-74-20-48

MÉTRO
Péreire (exit boulevard Péreire Nord), Port Maillot

OPEN
Mon–Sat

CLOSED
Sun, holidays, NAC

HOURS
Lunch noon–2 P.M., dinner 7–11 P.M.

RESERVATIONS
Advised

CREDIT CARDS
AE, DC, MC, V

À LA CARTE
235F, BNC

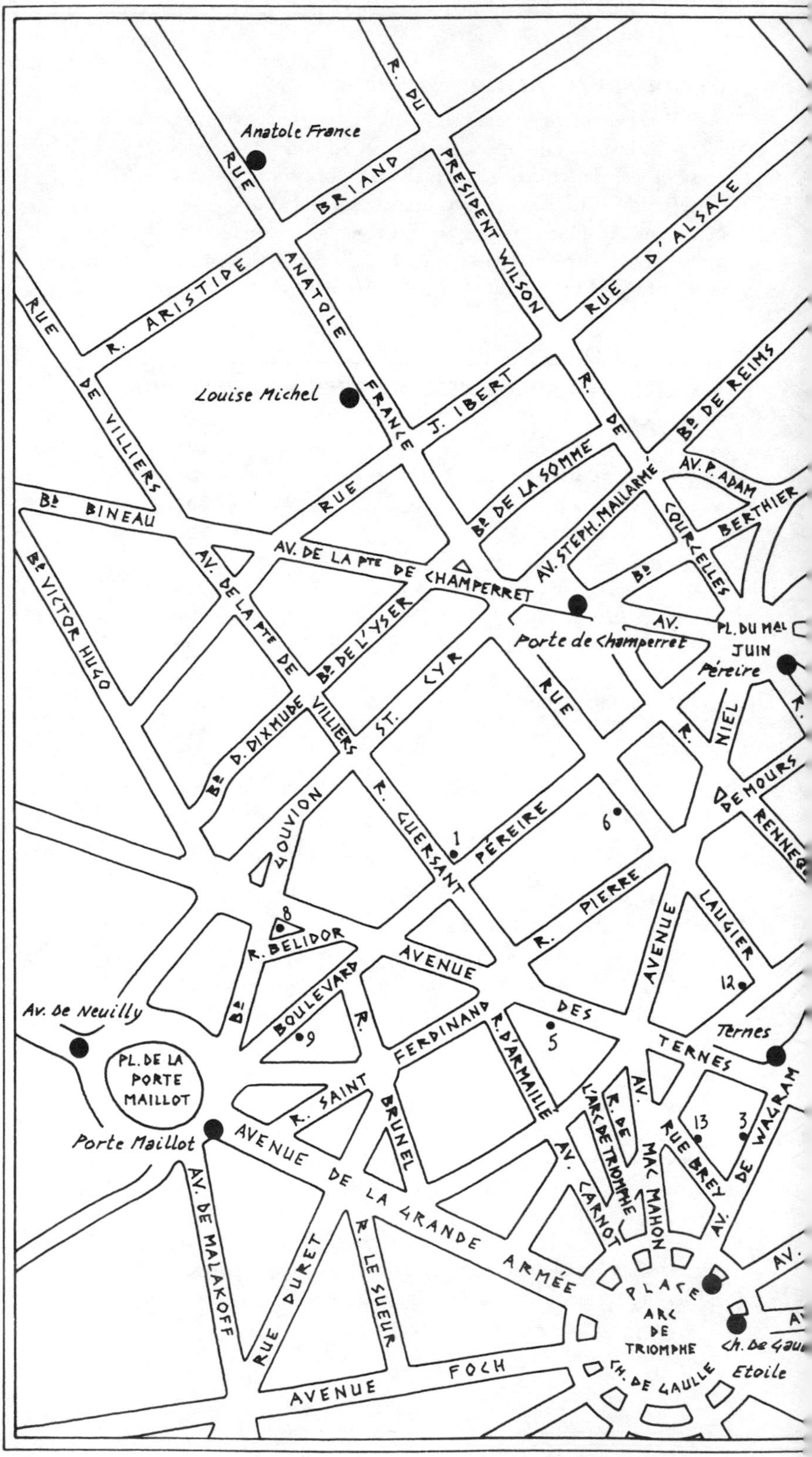
Anatole France
RUE
R. DU
PRESIDENT WILSON
BRIAND
R. ARISTIDE
RUE D'ALSACE
RUE
DE VILLIERS
ANATOLE
FRANCE
RUE
Louise Michel
J. IBERT
R.
DE
Bd DE REIMS
Bd DE LA SOMME
AV. STEPH. MALLARMÉ
AV. P. ADAM
BERTHIER
COURCELLES
Bd
Bd BINEAU
Bd VICTOR HUGO
AV. DE LA PTE DE CHAMPERRET
AV. DE LA PTE DE VILLIERS
Bd DE L'YSER
Porte de Champerret
AV.
PL. DU Mal JUIN
Péreire
ST. CYR
RUE
Bd D. DIXMUDE
R. NIEL
DEMOURS
RENNEQUIN
GOUVION
R. GUERSANT
1
PÉREIRE
6
R. PIERRE
8
R. BELIDOR
AVENUE
AVENUE
LAUGIER
12
Av. De Neuilly
Bd
BOULEVARD
R.
FERDINAND
R. D'ARMAILLE
DES
5
TERNES
Ternes
9
PL. DE LA PORTE MAILLOT
R. SAINT
BRUNEL
L'ARC DE TRIOMPHE
R. DE
AV.
MAC MAHON
RUE BREY
13
3
AV. DE WAGRAM
Porte Maillot
AVENUE DE LA GRANDE ARMÉE
AV. CARNOT
AV.
AV. DE MALAKOFF
RUE DURET
R. LE SUEUR
PLACE
ARC DE TRIOMPHE
CH. DE GAULLE
Ch. De Gaulle Etoile
AVENUE FOCH

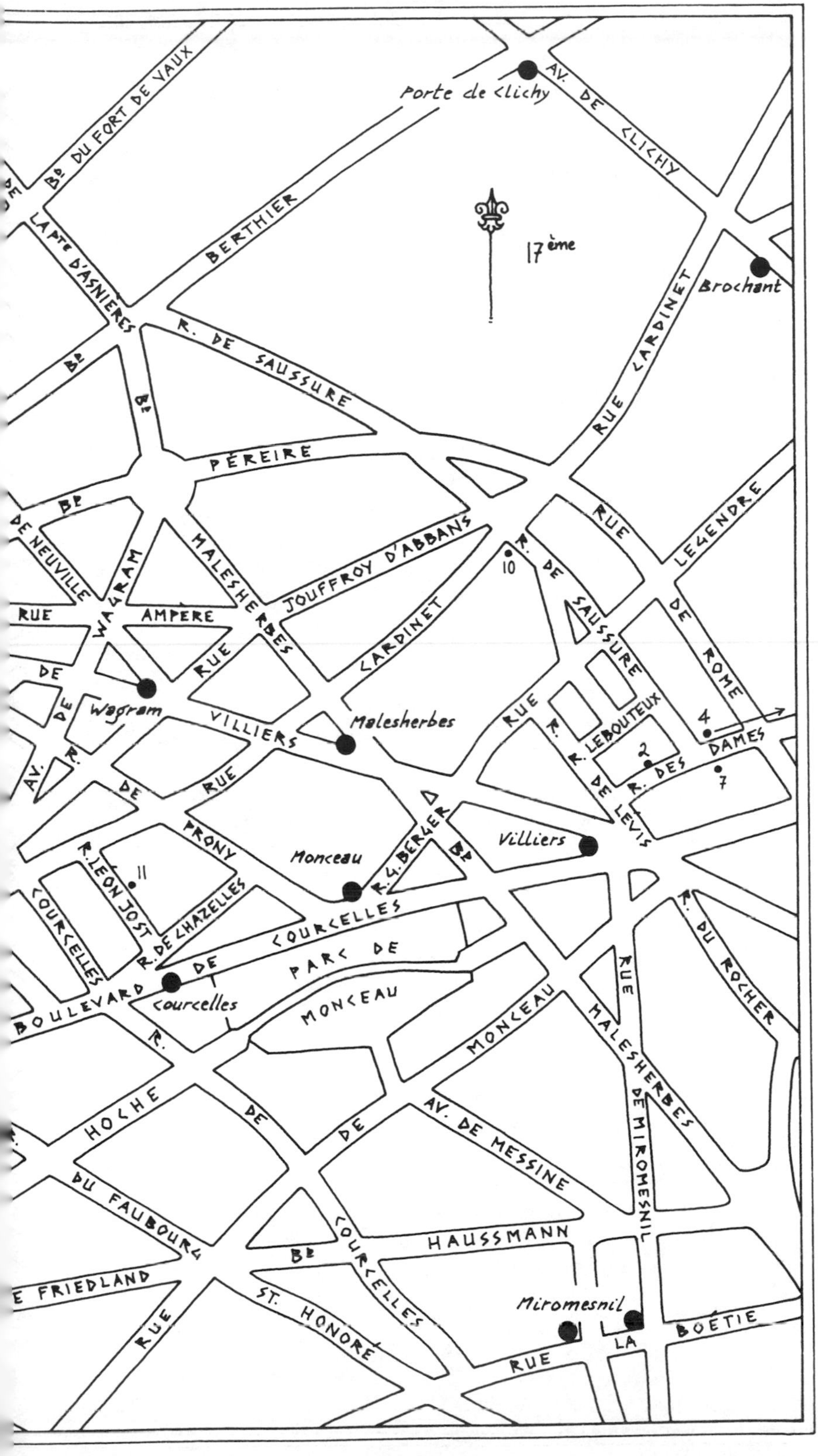

Porte de Clichy
AV. DE CLICHY
Bd. DU FORT DE VAUX
Bd. DE LA PTE D'ASNIERES
BERTHIER
17ème
Brochant
R. DE SAUSSURE
RUE CARDINET
Bd. PEREIRE
RUE LEGENDRE
Bd. DE NEUVILLE
Bd. MALESHERBES
JOUFFROY D'ABBANS
AV. DE WAGRAM
RUE AMPERE
10
R. DE SAUSSURE
DE ROME
CARDINET
RUE
Wagram
Malesherbes
VILLIERS
RUE
R. LEBOUTEUX
4
DAMES
2
R. DES
7
AV. DE
R. DE PRONY
RUE
R. DE LEVIS
R. 4. BERGER
Villiers
Bd.
Monceau
R. LEON JOST
11
R. DE CHAZELLES
COURCELLES
COURCELLES
R. DU ROCHER
RUE
PARC DE
BOULEVARD DE
Courcelles
MONCEAU
R.
MONCEAU
MALESHERBES
HOCHE
DE
DE
AV. DE MESSINE
DE MIROMESNIL
DU FAUBOURG
Bd.
COURCELLES
HAUSSMANN
E FRIEDLAND
ST. HONORE
Miromesnil
RUE
RUE
LA
BOETIE

PRIX FIXE
Lunch and dinner, 150F, 3 courses, BC
ENGLISH SPOKEN
Yes

At the entrance, a big table overflows with first-course temptations: marinated mushrooms, herring, *céleri rémoulade, museau de boeuf,* pâtés, terrines, and assorted salads. The *plat du jour* promises lamb on Monday, *petit salé* on Tuesday, and *tête de veau* on Wednesday; Thursday is *pot-au-feu,* Friday *boeuf à la mode,* and Saturday lamb again. In addition there is a full range of Lyonnaise offerings, truly wonderful if you love *saucisson* or *andouillette.* This is the place to ignore your diet and indulge in dessert. The chocolate cake with rich dark chocolate frosting is worth dieting for a week, as is the crème brûlée.

(2) CHOCOLAT VIENNOIS
118, rue des Dames (17th)

TELEPHONE
01-42-93-34-40
MÉTRO
Villiers, Rome
OPEN
Mon–Fri lunch and dinner, Sat lunch and tea only
CLOSED
Sat dinner, Sun, holidays, NAC
HOURS
10 A.M.–10:30 P.M., continuous service; salon de thé, boutique 10 A.M.–7 P.M.; lunch noon–2:30 P.M., dinner 7–10 P.M., drinks 3–10:30 P.M.
RESERVATIONS
Advised for lunch
CREDIT CARDS
MC, V (minimum 100F)
À LA CARTE
50–115F, BC
PRIX FIXE
Lunch, 95F, 2 courses, BNC; dinner, 140F, 3 courses and apértif, BNC
ENGLISH SPOKEN
Yes

If you are strolling along the colorful rue des Levis shopping street, this is a good place to stop in for lunch, dinner, a quick cup of chocolate topped with whipped cream, or a nice afternoon cup of tea and a pastry. The wood-paneled interior of this cozy restaurant looks like a mountain chalet. There are several seating areas in the tiny main room. Tables are tucked into corners, and special tables are reserved for nonsmokers, a real plus, even in Paris. If you see something you like, chances are it is for sale, from the painted wooden fruit and flower arrangements to chocolate and sugar tins on display.

The lineup of taste temptations ranges from huge salads, *raclette,* and fondue (both available for dinner and Saturday lunch) to quiches, savory tarts, and meat-based dishes. Desserts such as apple strudel, fruit crumble with cream, and an unpardonably rich chocolate cake served with vanilla ice cream and chocolate sauce will make most dieters wear a hair shirt for a week.

(3) EMPIRE STATE RESTAURANT BUFFET
41, avenue Wagram (17th)

TELEPHONE
01-43-80-14-39, 01-40-80-17-73
MÉTRO
Charles-de-Gaulle-Étoile, Ternes
OPEN
Mon–Sat lunch only
CLOSED
Sun, holidays, NAC

What! Forty-five francs for a three-course meal? In Paris? In the 1990s? Impossible, there *must* be a catch.

No, there isn't, not if you eat at the Empire State Restaurant Buffet not far from the Arc de Triomphe. From the street you will only see a signboard on the sidewalk touting the prix fixe meal. The restaurant is in the basement, and frankly, I expected to see *clochards* (bums) with plastic sacks and old ladies in fuzzy slippers occupying the tables. Well, *quelle surprise!* I found secretaries, middle-management types, and other smart Cheap Eaters enjoying a wide array of self-service food, all brightly displayed along a cafeteria line like something in an airport. Seating is on plastic-covered chairs around Formica tables in a room surrounded with posters of U.S. and French films. There is even a nonsmoking section. It is all quite nice and pleasant.

Even though you are in Paris, where the Cheapest Eat can be well done, and this one is, you still cannot expect to have delicate soufflés or subtle seasonings on wild game. What you see is what you get, and for the best choice and freshest food, get there early. The prix fixe meal changes daily and could include a yogurt with fruit, ground round steak garnished with fries, vegetables, and a roll. Aside from this incredible Cheap Eat, everything is priced individually, from the rolls and butter to the apple tart (whipped cream, extra).

HOURS
Lunch 11 A.M.–3 P.M.

RESERVATIONS
Not accepted

CREDIT CARDS
None

À LA CARTE
85F, BNC

PRIX FIXE
45F, 3 courses, BNC

ENGLISH SPOKEN
Very limited

MISCELLANEOUS
Nonsmoking section

(4) JOY IN FOOD
2, rue Truffaut, at rue des Dames (17th)

If you think *vegetarian* means only lentils and brown rice, you have not had a meal at Joy in Food, which I found a few years ago just walking by. The clean whitewashed interior caught my eye. The tempting aromas beckoned me; I had to try it and am glad I did. The imaginative vegetarian cuisine and the final bill, which matched the size of this tiny restaurant, made it a natural Cheap Eat.

The young, dynamic owner, Naema Aouad, puts on a virtual one-woman show as she cooks and serves from her compact, open kitchen. The room capacity is fourteen, and by 12:30 or 1 P.M., all seats are taken by diners who appreciate her health-conscious meals and no-smoking policy. Aouad works with organic products as much as possible, and she goes into the country to select her vegetables directly from growers. Everyday, patrons can depend on having a savory *tarte,* a *plate du jour,* and a choice of omelettes. Assorted crudités, crisp salads, vegetable pâté, and onion soup are the tempting starters. Even hard-core dieters succumb to the chocolate cake with pears or the apple cake filled with raisins, dried apricots, and cinnamon—order it warmed for best effect. Organic wine, beer, and cider are served in juice glasses along with banana milkshakes, fresh fruit and vegetable juices, and herb tea.

TELEPHONE
01-43-87-96-79

MÉTRO
Rome, Place de Clichy

OPEN
Mon–Sat lunch only; dinner for 10 or more by reservation only

CLOSED
Sun, major holidays, Aug

HOURS
Lunch noon–3 P.M.

RESERVATIONS
Advised; required for group dinner

CREDIT CARDS
None

À LA CARTE
50–100F, BNC

PRIX FIXE
60F, 2 courses, 75F, 3 courses, both BNC

ENGLISH SPOKEN
Yes

MISCELLANEOUS
No smoking allowed

(5) L'AMANGUIER
43, avenue des Ternes (17th)

See L'Amanguier page 151. All other information is the same.

TELEPHONE: 01-43-80-19-28

MÉTRO: Ternes

(6) LA PETITE AUBERGE*
38, rue Laugier (17th)

TELEPHONE
01-47-63-85-51

MÉTRO
Ternes, Péreire

OPEN
Tues–Sat lunch and dinner, Mon dinner only

CLOSED
Mon lunch, Sun, holidays (call to check), Aug

HOURS
Lunch noon–2 P.M., dinner 7:30–10 P.M.

RESERVATIONS
Advised

CREDIT CARDS
MC, V

À LA CARTE
225F, BNC

PRIX FIXE
Lunch and dinner, 170F, 3 courses, BNC

ENGLISH SPOKEN
Yes

Jöel Decloux and his gracious wife, Jackie, continue to build on their success, and each time I return to La Petite Auberge I find it better than the last. Decloux is a dedicated chef, always experimenting and improving his repertoire. He does it all, from making bread twice a day to creating the beautiful desserts. The polite, dignified service headed by Jackie fulfills the expectations of the most discriminating patrons, as she pays attention to the little details that make the difference between a mere meal and fine dining.

No matter what you order, you will be pleased. Star *entrées* are the *ravioles farcies au chèvre frais* (ravioli filled with chèvre) and the *salade gourmande au foie gras de canard*—a plate of assorted greens topped with a block of Decloux's foie gras and trimmed with fresh green beans, little apples, and a light vinaigrette. The main courses are all special, but if you like lamb, please order the roast lamb, served with an eggplant garnish and a potato *galette.* The sole and salmon dusted with herbs, the veal in a light parsley cream sauce, or the fillet of beef with shallots and potatoes *dauphine* are other equally marvelous choices. When you are seated, you will be asked if you want the Grand Marnier soufflé or the warm *mille-feuilles* for dessert. Yes, you do! Just hope you are not alone, that way you can share them. The light and flaky *mille-feuilles* (puff pastry filled with rum cream) are the best in Paris. In the spring and summer, treat yourself to the *feuilleté de fraise à la chantilly* (loaves of flaky pastry layered with fresh strawberries and whipped cream). After-dinner coffee is served with chocolates and *madeleines*.

La Petite Auberge continues to be my top choice for a special celebration meal. When you go, order a bottle of the featured wine of the month, sit back, savor the fine food, and toast to the fact that you are dining so well in Paris.

(7) LE PATIO PROVENÇAL
116, rue des Dames (17th)

The Patio Provençal, owned by Frederic and Stephan Poiri, the two brothers who run Chocolat Viennois next door (see page 206), is a charming slice of Provence deep in Paris. Bright yellow and greens mix with earth tones, lavenders, and oranges to create the feeling you are dining in the sunny south of France. The first room is appealing, with arbors over the tables and tiled and mirrored booths, but it gets noisy and congested, so you are better off asking for a table in the sky-lit garden next to the real Provençal fountain. Almost everything you see around you is for sale, except the lovely framed prints of Provence and the dried floral arrangements. The food is, of course, all about the south, featuring eggplant, squashes, fish, lots of garlic and onions, hearty soups, and seasonal fruit-based desserts. It is a delightful respite for a light lunch or dinner in a part of Paris few visitors ever go.

TELEPHONE
01-42-93-73-73

MÉTRO
Villiers, Rome

OPEN
Mon–Fri lunch and dinner, Sat lunch only

CLOSED
Sat dinner, Sun, major holidays, NAC

HOURS
Lunch noon–2:30 P.M., dinner 7–10:30 P.M.

RESERVATIONS
Advised for lunch

CREDIT CARDS
MC, V (100F minimum)

À LA CARTE
90–150F, BNC

PRIX FIXE
None

ENGLISH SPOKEN
Yes

(8) LE PETIT SALÉ
99, avenue des Ternes (17th)

Warning: This is not an affair for the timid eater!

At this little Cheap Eat, where heaping plates, good fellowship, and crowded tables are the rule, the substantial specialty is *petit salé*: salt pork cooked with vegetables and lentils and served with a big basket of crusty bread to mop up all the wonderful juices. If salt pork isn't your passion, there are other choices: house terrines, *cassoulet, andouillettes,* and a vegetarian plate with lentils, potato gratin, ratatouille, and salad. In the summer, cold meats, big salads, and light desserts are on the menu. Le Petit Salé has a good cheese selection, and the *tarte Tatin* is worth every filling bite. Order a bottle of Chinon or Gamay de Touraine to go with your *petit salé* or any other meat-inspired main course.

Lunchtime can be a madhouse, so schedule your arrival accordingly.

TELEPHONE
01-45-74-10-57

MÉTRO
Porte Maillot

OPEN
Mon–Sat

CLOSED
Sun, NAC

HOURS
Lunch noon–2:30 P.M., dinner 7–11:30 p.m

RESERVATIONS
Advised

CREDIT CARDS
AE, DC, MC, V

À LA CARTE
175–190F, BNC

PRIX FIXE
None

ENGLISH SPOKEN
Limited, with English menu

(9) LE RELAIS DE VENISE—LE RESTAURANT DE L'ENTRECÔTE
271, boulevard Péreire (17th)

It is on every Parisian's Cheap Eat map, and it should be on yours. You cannot call for reservations because

TELEPHONE
01-45-74-27-97

MÉTRO
Porte Maillot

OPEN
Daily
CLOSED
July, some holidays
HOURS
Lunch noon–2:30 P.M., dinner 7–11:45 P.M.
RESERVATIONS
Not accepted
CREDIT CARDS
MC, V
À LA CARTE
None
PRIX FIXE
Lunch and dinner, 115F, 2 courses, BNC
ENGLISH SPOKEN
Sometimes, depends on the mood of your waitress

they do not take them. As a result, you must go early or very late because there is almost always a line waiting outside Le Relais de Venise, better known as L'Entrecôte. The waitresses are something else: direct from hell, but they don't seem to deter the flock from coming back time and time again. The long-standing formula for success has been widely imitated but never improved on. They offer just a single meal: for 115F, you will be served a salad and an *entrecôte* steak with *pomme frites.* Desserts designed to make the finals at a Betty Crocker bake-off are extra and so is the wine. All this is served to an appreciative audience in a cheerful room with a mural of the Grand Canal in Venice along one side. In warm weather, tables are set on the sidewalk and are hotly contested.

(10) LE SCHEFFER
132, rue Cardinet, at rue de Saussure (17th)

For a description of Le Scheffer, see its listing in the sixteenth arrondissement, page 201.

TELEPHONE: 01-42-27-36-78
MÉTRO: Malesherves (10 minute walk)
OPEN: Mon–Sat
CLOSED: Sun, NAC
HOURS: Lunch noon–2:30 P.M., dinner 7–10:30 P.M.
RESERVATIONS: Advised
CREDIT CARDS: MC, V
À LA CARTE: 160–170F, BNC
PRIX FIXE: Lunch and dinner, 115F, 2 courses, BC
ENGLISH SPOKEN: Yes

(11) LES MESSUGUES*
8, rue Léon Jost (17th)

TELEPHONE
01-47-63-26-65
MÉTRO
Courcelles
OPEN
Mon–Fri
CLOSED
Sat–Sun, holidays, Aug
HOURS
Lunch noon–2:30 P.M., dinner 8–10:30 P.M.
RESERVATIONS
Advised
CREDIT CARDS
AE, DC, MC, V

Les Messugues is a prized gem well worth finding because once discovered, you will have one of the best meals of your trip to Paris. If you stray from the prix fixe menu, it could inch into the Big Splurge category, otherwise it will be an amazing value.

The setting is beautiful and so nicely arranged and appointed that I feel as though I am dining in someone's lovely home. The two rooms are small and intensely romantic, with hurricane candles, soft music, and masses of fresh flowers. It is the perfect place to dress for dinner and spend a marvelous evening enjoying a fine French meal with someone special. My friend's comment during our meal really sums up the feeling everyone has about Les Messugues: "Anyone cooking and running a restaurant with this much feeling and attention to detail deserves to be a great success."

The service by owner Alain Laforêt is flawless, and the cooking by Gérard Fontaine is nothing short of remarkable for its quality, variety, and presentation. In the evening, you start with the house apéritif, which is served with a plate of smoked salmon and chèvre cheese on toast. While fresh fish is the mainstay of the menu, it by no means overshadows the rest of the offerings. If you are ordering the prix fixe menu, you will have a choice of five or six *entrées* and *plats,* assorted cheeses, and dessert. As with the rest of the menu, the dishes change to reflect the seasons and inspiration of the chef. You might start with a salad of lightly poached vegetables, topped with a block of house foie gras. *Daurade* and *racasse* are grilled and served with a fresh tomato sauce, filets of perch rest on a bed of creamed sorrel. Tender *pot au feu de boeuf* is surrounded by colorful vegetables and perfectly prepared beef tournedos comes in a mustard sauce. If you order à la carte, the choices widen to include more fresh fish, lamb and beef grills, and *abats*—organ meats such as *ris de veau* or *rognon de veau,* both beautifully sauced with fresh mushrooms or wine. The desserts are works of art, especially the *fondant au chocolate sauce café* (dense chocolate cake with a coffee sauce) or the *gratin de fruits chaud,* which is a light, refined ending. Coffee arrives with a plate of Fontaine's truffles and candied citrus, ending a wonderful meal you will want to repeat as often as you are fortunate enough to visit Paris.

À LA CARTE
240–260F, BNC

PRIX FIXE
Lunch, 135F, 3 courses, BNC; dinner, 175F, 3 courses, BC (wine, kir, and coffee)

ENGLISH SPOKEN
Yes

(12) LE STÜBLI
11, rue Poncelet (17th)

Everyone who knows me well knows how much I like going to street markets, even in my own hometown. When I am traveling, it is the best way I know to see how people live day to day, not to mention discovering firsthand what to expect to be served wherever I am dining. One of my favorite markets in Paris is along rue Poncelet. I like to go early when it opens, then go to Le Stübli, the best German/Austrian bakery this side of the Rhine, and order a steaming coffee or hot chocolate and a slice of apple strudel. If I go later, I never miss a piece of *la véritable forêt-Noire,* a black forest cake that is heaven-sent.

TELEPHONE
Pâtisserie and tearoom 01-42-27-81-86; deli 01-48-88-98-07

MÉTRO
Ternes

OPEN
Tues–Sat; Sun and holidays half day only; deli daily

CLOSED
Mon, NAC

HOURS
Pâtisserie Tues–Sat 8:30 A.M.–7:30 P.M., Sun 9 A.M.–1 P.M.; tearoom Tues–Sat 9 A.M.–6:30 P.M., Sun 9 A.M.–12:30 P.M.; deli Mon 10:30 A.M.–7 P.M., Tues–Sat 9 A.M.–7:30 P.M., Sun 9 A.M.–1 P.M.

RESERVATIONS
Not necessary

CREDIT CARDS
MC, V

À LA CARTE
50–100F, BNC

PRIX FIXE
Breakfast, 55–145F, BC; lunch, 90F, 2 courses, BNC

ENGLISH SPOKEN
Limited

A nice thing about Le Stübli is that you are not limited to pastries. They also serve a full breakfast, a delightful lunch, and afternoon tea. Across the street is their deli, Le Stübli Delikatessen, where you can purchase ready-made salads and dishes to warm up later on . . . especially nice if you are staying in an apartment. If I am here for lunch, I stop by the painted cart in front and have the French equivalent of *le hot dog,* white sausage on a warm sesame or poppy seed bun, slathered in cooked onions. Be careful, the juice could drip to your elbows.

(13) L'ÉTOILE VERTE
13, rue Brey (17th)

TELEPHONE
01-43-80-69-34

MÉTRO
Charles-de-Gaulle-Étoile

OPEN
Daily

CLOSED
Never, NAC

HOURS
Lunch noon–3 P.M., dinner 6:30–11 P.M.

RESERVATIONS
Not necessary

CREDIT CARDS
AE, DC, MC, V

À LA CARTE
140F, BNC

PRIX FIXE
Lunch and dinner, 80F (until 9 P.M.) and 100–150F, 3 courses, BC

ENGLISH SPOKEN
Yes, with English menu

If you have been to any Denny's in the United States, or to Ken's House of Pancakes in Hilo, Hawaii, you have been to L'Étoile Verte, the Paris version of no-nonsense nourishment served daily to a nondemanding set of diners who are looking for a Cheap Eat bargain above all else. For years it has been known as a near miracle in Cheap Eating. This plain-Jane restaurant not far from the Arc de Triomphe and the Champs-Élysées is a good one to remember because it is open 365 days a year. The atmosphere and decor match the food: basic. The à la carte menu goes on forever, listing more than enough to please everyone from your picky five-year-old to Aunt Sally on a diet. In addition there are specials, a prix fixe, and a children's menu.

Eighteenth Arrondissement

Montmartre captivates visitors with its picturesque winding streets, magnificent view of Paris from the steps of the Sacré Coeur, and its history as the heart and soul of artistic Paris at the turn of the century, when the Moulin Rouge and Toulouse-Lautrec were at their peak. Today, Montmartre is more like a village: a jumble of secret squares and narrow alleyways make up the "Butte," or hill, where the white domed Sacré Coeur Basilica majestically sits. Montmartre is also a study in contrasts, as nostalgia mixes with the crass commercialism of Pigalle and the place du Tertre, a mecca for tourists and third-rate artists hawking their dubious wares.

RIGHT BANK
Montmartre, Sacré Coeur, Marché aux Puces St-Ouen (Paris' largest flea market)

EIGHTEENTH ARRONDISSEMENT RESTAURANTS

(1) CHEZ FRANCIS
122, rue Caulaincourt (18th)

Chez Francis is the type of restaurant I could come to every day and feel at home. Overseen by hardworking owner Felicité Erguy, its mood is perfect old-fashioned Paris: a bustling and cramped dining room with varnished paint, yellowing walls, smoky mirrors, and interesting Montmartre habitués sitting at their regular tables. On Sunday, the restaurant is alive with high-spirited family groups lingering on the covered terrace over a leisurely three-hour lunch.

The rich southwestern-inspired cuisine is from the old school and pays no attention to calorie watching. Serious followers of this type of cooking will adore the wide selection on the prix fixe menu. First-rate *entrées* include *terrine de Périgord, jambon de Bayonne,* and salade *landaise* filled with chunks of foie gras. The specialty is paella, and it's simply not to be missed if this is one of

TELEPHONE
01-42-64-60-62

MÉTRO
Lamarck-Caulaincourt (No. 80 bus stops at the door)

OPEN
Mon, Thur–Sun lunch and dinner, Wed dinner only

CLOSED
Tues; Wed lunch; Oct 1–8

HOURS
Lunch noon–2:30 P.M., dinner 7–10:30 P.M.

RESERVATIONS
For Sun lunch

CREDIT CARDS
AE, V

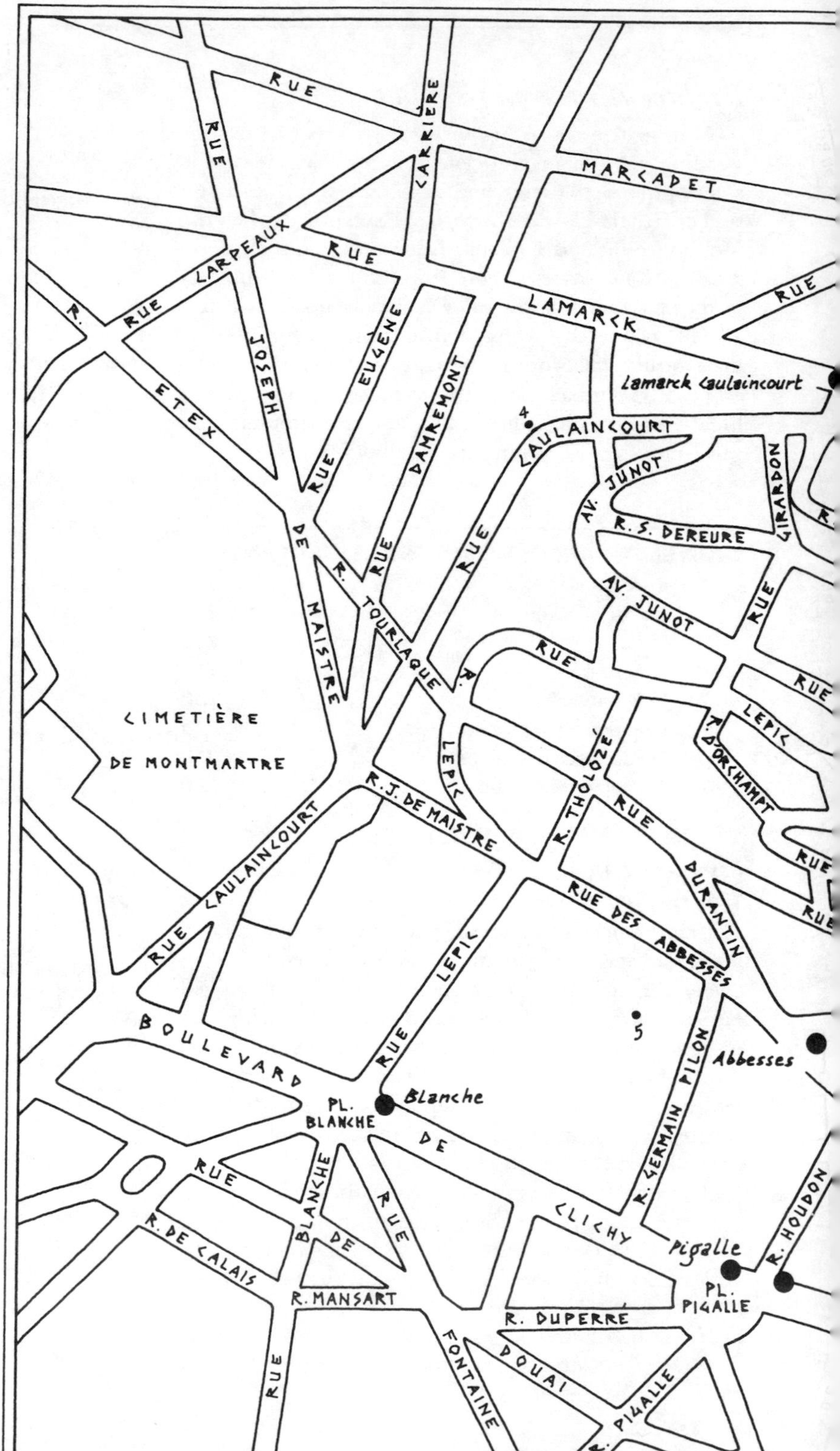
RUE CARRIÈRE
RUE MARCADET
RUE LARPEAUX
RUE LAMARCK
R. ETEX
RUE JOSEPH
RUE EUGÈNE
RUE DAMRÉMONT
Lamarck Caulaincourt
4
RUE CAULAINCOURT
AV. JUNOT
R. S. DEREURE
RUE GIRARDON
RUE DE MAISTRE
R. TOURLAQUE
RUE LEPIC
R. THOLOZÉ
R. D'ORCHAMPT
CIMETIÈRE DE MONTMARTRE
R. J. DE MAISTRE
RUE DURANTIN
RUE DES ABBESSES
5
Abbesses
BOULEVARD DE CLICHY
Blanche
PL. BLANCHE
R. GERMAIN PILON
RUE BLANCHE
R. DE CALAIS
R. MANSART
RUE FONTAINE
R. DUPERRE
RUE DE DOUAI
R. PIGALLE
Pigalle
PL. PIGALLE
R. HOUDON

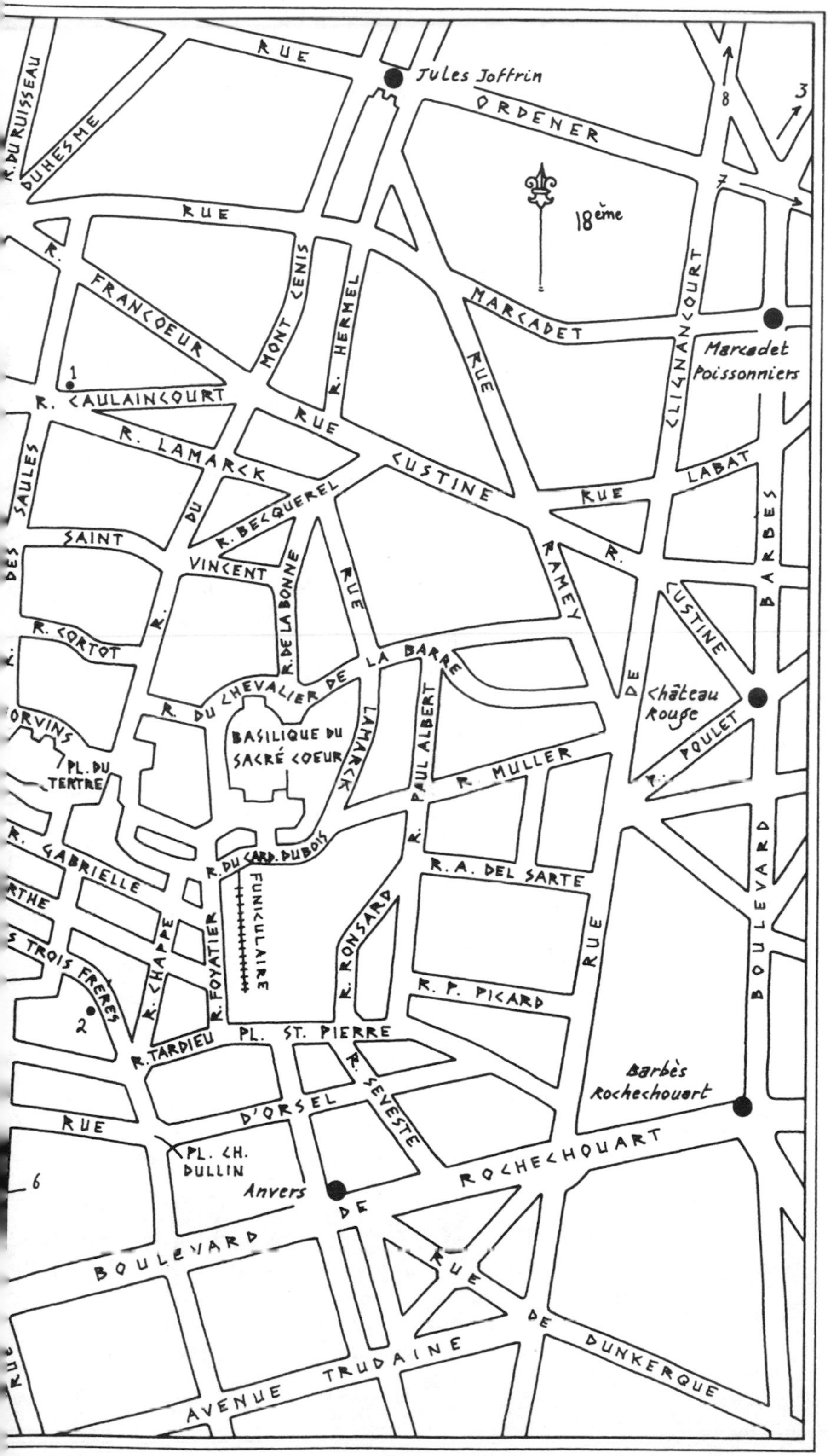
RUE
Jules Joffrin
ORDENER
8
3
7
R. DU RUISSEAU
DUHESME
RUE
18ème
R.
FRANCOEUR
MONT CENIS
R. HERMEL
MARCADET
Marcadet Poissonniers
CLIGNANCOURT
1
R. CAULAINCOURT
RUE
R. LAMARCK
CUSTINE
RUE
LABAT
RUE
SAULES
DES
DU
R. BECQUEREL
SAINT
VINCENT
R.
RAMEY
CUSTINE
BARBES
R. DE LA BONNE
RUE
R. CORTOT
R.
DE LA BARRE
R. DU CHEVALIER
R.
DE
Château Rouge
POULET
ORVINS
BASILIQUE DU SACRÉ COEUR
LAMARCK
PAUL ALBERT
R. MULLER
R.
PL. DU TERTRE
R. GABRIELLE
R. DU CARD. DUBOIS
R.
R. A. DEL SARTE
RTHE
FUNICULAIRE
R. FOYATIER
R. CHAPPE
R. RONSARD
RUE
BOULEVARD
S TROIS FRERES
2
R. P. PICARD
R. TARDIEU
PL. ST. PIERRE
R. SEVESTE
Barbès Rochechouart
RUE
D'ORSEL
PL. CH. DULLIN
6
Anvers
ROCHECHOUART
DE
BOULEVARD
RUE
DE
DUNKERQUE
AVENUE
TRUDAINE
RUE

À LA CARTE
150F, BNC
PRIX FIXE
Lunch and dinner, 130F, 3 courses, BNC
ENGLISH SPOKEN
Limited

your favorites. Other top choices are the *confit de porc,* the *escalope de veau aux pleurottes et crème* (veal with mushrooms and cream), and the *fricasée de poulet basquaise* (tender chicken in a tomato-based sauce). After a sumptuous meal it is hard to contemplate dessert, but if you can, try the *oeufs à la neige* or the *gateau basque.*

Later on, wander back up the hill to the top of Montmartre, stand on the steps of Sacré Coeur, and gaze over all of Paris lying at your feet. It is an experience you will not soon forget . . . I guarantee it.

(2) CLAUDE ET NICOLE
13, rue des Trois-Frères (18th)

TELEPHONE
01-46-06-12-48
MÉTRO
Abbesses
OPEN
Tues–Sat lunch and dinner, Sun lunch only
CLOSED
Sun dinner, Mon, NAC
HOURS
Lunch noon–2:15 P.M., dinner 7:30–10:30 P.M.
RESERVATIONS
Not necessary
CREDIT CARDS
MC, V
À LA CARTE
None
PRIX FIXE
Lunch, 68F, 3 courses, BNC; dinner, 85F, 3 courses, BNC
ENGLISH SPOKEN
Limited

The surroundings might lack elegance, but Claude et Nicole's Montmartre spot is bursting at the seams with eager Cheap Eaters seeking *les temps perdu* . . . and finding it.

The food offers no gourmet ruffles and flourishes, but the plentiful, good, filling fare is priced to please. A meal here starts with familiar dishes such as *oeuf dur mayonnaise*, homemade terrines, eggy-rich quiche, and *jambon persillé maison.* Rice, noodles, or homemade *frites* grace the three main course choices . . . two *plats du jour* and steak (10F extra). Cheese, crème caramel, fruit *tarte,* or their homemade yogurt wrap it all up. It's simple and successful because it never tries to be more than it is . . . a decent Cheap Eat in Paris.

(3) LA CASSEROLE
17, rue Boinod (18th)

TELEPHONE
01-42-54-50-97
MÉTRO
Simplon, Marcadet-Poissonniers
OPEN
Tues–Sat
CLOSED
Sun–Mon, holidays, mid-July–mid-Aug
HOURS
Lunch noon–2:30 P.M., dinner 7:30–10:30 P.M.
RESERVATIONS
Essential
CREDIT CARDS
MC, V

For a dining experience in an atmosphere found nowhere else on this planet, head for La Casserole. It was opened forty years ago by Bernard Dubois, who served as General Eisenhower's personal chef when the general was in Versailles. Dubois is still at the restaurant, but he has turned the day-to-day operation over to Daniel Darthial.

La Casserole is the type of restaurant where you can take spirited in-laws, your kids, your mom, and your spouse and everyone will love it. Located on the back side of Montmartre, it consists of several rooms festooned with an endless assortment of knickknacks, stuffed animals, plants, doo-dads, fishnets, seashells, cooing birds, pots, pans, fans, feathers, flags, banners, and badges, all hung on the beams, ceilings, and walls, in the windows and over the door. No space has been left unadorned, including the unisex toilet, which you absolutely *must* see to believe. When I asked how often the paraphernalia was dusted I was told, "Once a year, when we are closed in the summer. It takes us two days just to take it down, and another two to put it all back." Once you see it all, you will wonder how they do it in such a short time.

But what about the food and the service? They are both great. The portions are copious, the service friendly, and the diners fun to watch and be with. In the fall and winter, all sorts of wild game tops the list of favorite dishes to order. During the rest of the year, traditional preparations of robust French standards keep everyone well fed and happy. Look for goose, the most tender *blanquette de veau* in these parts, chicken, duck, and grilled steak, all liberally garnished with large servings of potatoes. The desserts are all made here, including the ice cream. Especially recommended is the *péché casserole. Péché* means "sin," and sinful this is, but oh, so good. It consists of chocolate cake with vanilla ice cream, chocolate sauce, and whipped cream, served in its own casserole. Less sinful, but still dangerous, is the homemade nougat ice cream with a honey, orange, and caramel topping.

À LA CARTE
185–200F, BNC

PRIX FIXE
Lunch only Tues–Fri, 70F, 3 courses, BC; lunch and dinner, 100F, 3 courses, BNC

ENGLISH SPOKEN
Absolutely

(4) LE MAQUIS
69, rue Caulaincourt (18th)

Montmartre is full of greasy spoons dedicated to scooping in the tourists and, in the process, turning off the locals. Well protected from this dining circus is Le Maquis, one of the increasingly hard-to-find *restaurants de quartier* with a loyal following for its sound food served at a consistently fair price. The fifty-five-seat dining room is rather formal, with pink linen tablecloths and waiters clad in black. In the summer, the tiny terrace along the front is a good vantage point for the Parisian hobby of people-watching.

The seasonal menus are dedicated to traditional dishes, beautifully prepared from the best ingredients. The *carte* changes four time a year, and the prix fixe lunch menu is different each day, so it is virtually impossible to describe all the possibilities. If I am here in the late spring, I look for chilled gazpacho, the house foie

TELEPHONE
01-42-59-76-07

MÉTRO
Lamark-Caulaincourt

OPEN
Mon–Sat lunch and dinner, Sun lunch only

CLOSED
Sun dinner, major holidays, NAC

HOURS
Lunch noon–2 P.M., dinner 7:30–10 P.M.

RESERVATIONS
Advised

CREDIT CARDS
MC, V

À LA CARTE
180F, BNC

PRIX FIXE
Lunch and dinner, 95F, 3 courses, BC; 160F, 3 courses, BC (wine, kir, and coffee)
ENGLISH SPOKEN
Yes

gras on a bed of chilled greens, *lotte* (monkfish) with pesto, or the leg of lamb with its trio of fresh vegetables. The desserts are all *à la maison* and may include raspberries on a cinnamon crust, *fromage blanc* with honey and fresh fruits, or peaches in champagne with fresh mint.

(5) LE RESTAURANT
32, rue Véron (18th)

TELEPHONE
01-42-23-06-22
MÉTRO
Abbesses, Blanche
OPEN
Tues–Fri lunch and dinner, Mon and Sat dinner only
CLOSED
Sun; Mon and Sat lunch; holidays, NAC
HOURS
Lunch noon–3:30 P.M., dinner 7:30–11:30 P.M.
RESERVATIONS
Advised
CREDIT CARDS
AE, DC, MC, V
À LA CARTE
140F, BNC
PRIX FIXE
Lunch, 80F, 2 courses, BNC; dinner, 130F, 2 courses, BNC; desserts extra 35–40F
ENGLISH SPOKEN
Yes

Chef and owner Yves Peladeau is a skilled cook from Cameroon who honed his talent at the renowned Lamazère and Le Grand Véfour. Now on his own, he has opened a simple corner restaurant a block away from rue Lepic and rue des Abbesses in Montmartre. It is a good place to get away from all the kitsch of the area and enjoy an original meal at prices almost as minimal as the restaurant itself. The simple, spacious room blends paver tiles with green plants and an amusing collection of chairs, which range from old bistro numbers to black wooden fold-ups.

The inventive cooking, which emphasizes exotic spices and light sauces, attracts a stylish young audience for the good value, two-course menu. Starters of tuna tartare, rabbit sausage, chicken livers with an eggplant sauce, and the vegetable terrine seasoned with basil are appetizing blends of *nouvelle* and traditional. The *plats* don't lag in style. Seasonal offerings of roast duckling, basted in a honey-coriander sauce and featuring a compote of figs on the side, pork with fruit chutney, and lamb with a lemon *fondant* are only three of the unusual spring dishes. Desserts are all made by Peladeau. Try his fruity sorbets, the chocolate *tarte,* slightly warmed and capped with his own vanilla ice cream, or the ultimate—a plate of his assorted sweet temptations. Wines of the month are value priced by the glass or bottle and selected to complement the changing menu.

(6) L'HOMME TRANQUILLE
81, rue des Martyrs (18th)

TELEPHONE
01-42-54-56-28
MÉTRO
Abbesses
OPEN
Tues–Sat dinner only
CLOSED
Sun–Mon, several days between Christmas and New Years, Aug

For almost fifteen years, Catherine Le Squer has been cooking here—with the help of her mother, who makes all the terrines, her son and one other helper, who do the serving, and her ten-year-old daughter, who adds a bright note of joy as she skips about in the afternoon after school. Casual observers might think this is just another Montmartre-Pigalle eatery dedicated to luring in tourists, plying them with cheap food and drink, and then charging anything but cheap prices. Not so. This family-owned restaurant is out of the mainstream of Pigalle grunge and just far enough from the tourist traps in Montmartre to maintain its character.

The funky interior has a design-by-garage-sale esthetic. Collections of coffee grinders, pitchers, and bottles sit in clusters around the room. Candles in teapots are lighted at night, aging posters are taped to equally aging yellow walls, and there is the usual bouquet of fresh flowers and a few green plants in need of a bit more TLC. Tables are set with paper maps and chunky wine glasses.

For your Cheap Eat, start with a pitcher of the drinkable house wine and order one of the terrines to spread on chunks of fresh bread. Save enough room for a healthy portion of roast pork, lamb chops, or veal smothered in mushrooms, followed by one of the dessert specialties: a fruit crumble or a slice of chocolate *fondant.* From start to finish you will have had a basic, fairly priced meal in a section of Paris where this is not an easy feat.

HOURS
Dinner 7–11:30 P.M.

RESERVATIONS
Preferred

CREDIT CARDS
MC, V

À LA CARTE
100–140F, BNC

PRIX FIXE
125F, 3 courses, BNC

ENGLISH SPOKEN
Limited

(7) RENDEZ-VOUS DES CHAUFFEURS
11, rue des Portes Blanches (18th)

If you are willing to go where most other mortal tourists fear to tread and want a lot of Cheap Eats for less, go to the Rendez-vous des Chauffeurs. This nostalgic throwback to the past is an honest-to-goodness neighborhood hangout where the decor has been given a minimum of attention and importance.

Nouvelle cuisine never caught on here, and neither will any other passing food fad, but the restaurant is always packed with a comfortable clientele eager to lap up the adored staples of bourgeois cooking. The bargain *du jour* is definitely the 70F, three-course meal, which includes wine. Starting with a plate of fresh crudités or *saucisson sec,* continuing on to the garnished *plat* of *escalope de veau, jambon de Paris, entrecôte,* and lamb chops, and down to the last bite of *pâtisserie,* a meal here is a very filling and satisfying experience that every Cheap Eater in Paris will appreciate.

Additionally, English is readily understood here, as the new owner, Janot Rocchi, has spent twenty-seven years in the United States in New York, Arizona, and Hawaii.

TELEPHONE
01-42-64-04-17

MÉTRO
Marcadet-Poissonniers

OPEN
Thur–Tues

CLOSED
Wed, NAC

HOURS
Lunch noon –2:30 P.M., dinner 7:30–11 P.M.

RESERVATIONS
Not necessary

CREDIT CARDS
MC, V

À LA CARTE
100–120F, BNC

PRIX FIXE
Lunch and dinner (until 8 P.M.), 70F, 3 courses, BC

ENGLISH SPOKEN
Yes

(8) RESTAURANT MARIE-LOUISE
52, rue Championnet (18th)

TELEPHONE
01-46-06-86-55

MÉTRO
Simplon

OPEN
Tues–Sat

CLOSED
Sun–Mon, holidays, Aug

HOURS
Lunch noon–2 P.M., dinner 7:30–10 P.M.

RESERVATIONS
Advised

CREDIT CARDS
DC, MC, V

À LA CARTE
185F, BNC

PRIX FIXE
Lunch or dinner, 135F, 3 courses, BNC

ENGLISH SPOKEN
Limited

Most people pass hurriedly through this part of Paris on their way to the flea market at Clignancourt. In so doing, they are missing a restaurant that has been serving wonderful food for three decades. From the street it looks like a thousand others and probably wouldn't catch your attention unless you knew about it. Inside, the two rooms are very proper, with thick white linens, shining crystal, fresh flowers, a sweet dog named Eva, and mature diners who are as hearty as the food. Marie-Louise is the type of restaurant where you must arrive hungry to best appreciate the beautifully cooked servings of classical French cooking.

Planning your meal requires a certain amount of careful thought because owner and chef Jean Coillot does not believe in letting anyone go away hungry, so his portions are large—no, make that enormous. I always order the *salade maison,* a mixture of finely sliced ham, mushrooms, celery, and lettuce in a light cream dressing. The pâté maison or the *rosette* (a pork sausage served in slices) also make nice appetizers, but they are more filling, and I need to save room for the house specialty, *poularde Marie-Louise*—a classic version of chicken cooked with tomatoes, tarragon, and chicken livers in a white wine sauce. After a seasonal dessert or a satiny crème caramel, you will have happily finished another respectable French meal.

Nineteenth Arrondissement

(No map for this arrondissement.)

The nineteenth arrondissement is largely a working-class area and home to many immigrants from Africa, India, and East Asia. Other than the large public Parc des Buttes-Chaumont and the redeveloped fifty-five-hectare Parc de la Villete, which houses a huge science museum and exhibit hall, there is not much to draw a visitor to this northeastern corner of Paris.

RIGHT BANK
La Villette, Parc des Buttes-Chaumont

NINETEENTH ARRONDISSEMENT RESTAURANTS

LA VERRIÈRE—LA RESTAURANT D'ÉRIC FRECHON

10, rue du Général-Brunet (19th)

Culinary habits are changing thanks to the new generation of chefs who, having trained with the culinary maestros, offer a simpler, more affordable cuisine in out-of-the-way bistros. Some thought Eric Frechon showed great daring by leaving the luxurious Hôtel de Crillon for this inexpensively appointed site in northeastern Paris, near the Buttes-Chaumont park. He proved doubters wrong, for in record time he has established a popular spot with a dedicated clientele drawn to his creative, yet very solid menu and the youthful staff who make everyone feel welcome. Tables are now so in demand that reservations are mandatory as far in advance as possible, even made before you arrive in Paris.

The four-course, weekly changing menu is nothing short of amazing. If asparagus is on, order it in any form and be rewarded with a cold *mousseline* of asparagus covered with a soft poached egg and surrounded by tomato coulis. Or, try the different green asparagus *clafoutis,* accented with a morelle mushroom cream sauce. Second courses delight with *osso bucco de lotte,* braised pork paired with *lentilles du Puy,* and roast pigeon served with bacon-flavored baby peas. The bread is delicious, especially when enjoyed with a sampling of the cheese board brought to your table for your third course. Desserts follow with an unusual mango and banana *tarte* with marscapone cream, and a *sablé* sugar wafer holding bright red strawberries and a puckery rhubarb compote. The *moëlleaux et craquant au chocolate légèrement safranés* is the epitome of chocolate desserts–it will make converts of even determined nonchocoholics. A bottle of good wine will round out your meal and make this a special event well worth traveling across Paris to enjoy.

TELEPHONE
01-40-40-03-30

MÉTRO
Botzaris

OPEN
Tues–Sat

CLOSED
Sun–Mon, major holidays, Aug

HOURS
Lunch noon–2:30 P.M., dinner 7:15–11 P.M.

RESERVATIONS
Essential as far in advance as possible and request a banquette

CREDIT CARDS
V

À LA CARTE
Not available

PRIX FIXE
Lunch and dinner, 190F, 4 courses, BNC

ENGLISH SPOKEN
Yes

Twentieth Arrondissement

(No map for this arrondissement.)

RIGHT BANK
Cimètiere Père Lachaise

The twentieth arrondissement is proletarian, intensely ethnic, and at times, radical. The northern section, Belleville, is a cultural melting pot. Ménilmontant, in the south part, is where you will find the Cimètiere Père Lachaise. Within its winding maze of paths you can visit the graves of Balzac, Colette, Moliere, Jim Morrison (lead singer of the Doors), Gertude, Stein, Edith Piaf, and Oscar Wilde, to name only a few of the famous folks and Parisians who rest here.

TWENTIETH ARRONDISSEMENT RESTAURANTS

* Restaurants marked with an asterisk (*) are considered Big Splurges.

LES ALLOBROGES*
71, rue des Grands-Champs (20th)

TELEPHONE
01-43-73-40-00

MÉTRO
Maraîchers (see directions)

OPEN
Tues–Sat

CLOSED
Sun–Mon, major holidays, Aug 3-27

HOURS
Lunch noon–2 P.M., dinner 7:30–10 P.M.

RESERVATIONS
Essential as far in advance as possible

CREDIT CARDS
AE, MC, V

À LA CARTE
230–260F, BNC

PRIX FIXE
Lunch and dinner, 95F and 164F, 4 courses, both BNC

ENGLISH SPOKEN
Yes

If you didn't know about Les Allobroges, you wouldn't come here, but judging by the filled tables night after night, it has caught on in a big way. Paris' smart set has found it; they have been happily traveling to this outpost neighborhood since Chef Olivier Pateyron and his wife, Annette, opened the doors. The two small dining rooms display pictures and posters of farm animals on the walls, and there are big pots of daisies in the windows. Seating is at comfortably spaced, properly set, linen-covered tables.

By reflecting a cooking style that respects the classics, Pateyron's dishes represent all that is modern and refreshing about Paris dining. Everything he prepares tastes clean, unmasked, and satisfying. The two sensational value-priced menus are definitely the way to go. The cheaper one allows a choice of *entrées,* only the *plat du jour* for the main course, plus cheese and dessert. The more expensive option offers six or eight choices for every course and includes most of the best from the à la carte side.

An ideal meaty starter is the *gallete de pommes de terre au lard et fois gras*, a crisp potato pancake holding the house foie gras. The *salade d'oignons blancs et roquette avec ragoûts d'asperges aux morilles* is a springtime palate pleaser with its perfect blending of vegetables and a warm morille sauce. If you love lamb, please consider the *souris d'agneau braisée et ail confit,* a melt-in-your-mouth tender lamb served with roasted garlic cloves. Otherwise, have the succulent, golden roast chicken—a divine preparation you must order when booking your table. Inspired desserts will beguile you with a bread pudding accented with a *fromage blanc sorbet* and a pear meringue with pistachio sauce.

NOTE: Admittedly, Les Allobroges is off—way off—the beaten track. You might be tempted to take a taxi, but the ride could cost more than the dinner. The best way to go is the métro. Get off at the Maraîchers stop, walk down rue des Pyrénées to rue des Grands-Champs and turn right, then walk until you come to the restaurant, which is at 71, rue des Grands-Champs.

University Restaurants

Institutional food, even in Paris, is nothing to write home about, but it *is* cheap. CROUS (Centre Régional des Oeuvres Universitaires et Scolaires) runs university restaurants known as Restos-U that offer so-so food at unbeatable prices. Anyone with an international student ID can buy meal tickets (cash only) either at the main office or at any of the sites listed below. The following list of CROUS Restos-U includes those that are most convenient, but it is by no means exhaustive. For a complete list, consult the main office.

It is important to know that a visit to the CROUS main office will get you more than a Cheap Eat in Paris. The office is also a place to book a bed in a student residence, arrange a cheap trip, or buy a discounted ticket for sports or cultural events. Of course, you must be a student and present your international ID card to qualify for any of the bargains.

CROUS RESTAURANTS IN PARIS

MAIN OFFICE: 39, avenue Georges Bernanos (5th)
TELEPHONE: 01-40-51-36-00, 37-10, or 37-14
MÉTRO: RER-Port Royal
OPEN: Mon–Fri 9 A.M.–5 P.M.
CLOSED: Sat–Sun, holidays, Aug

The following information is good for all the CROUS Restos-U listed:
LUNCH: 11:30 A.M.–1:30 P.M.
DINNER: 6–8 P.M.
CREDIT CARDS: None, cash only
SINGLE-MEAL TICKETS: 15F, *carnet* of ten: 125F
ENGLISH SPOKEN: Usually

Assas, 92, rue d'Assas (6th), 01-46-33-61-25 **MÉTRO:** Notre-Dame-des-Champs
Bullier, 29, avenue Georges-Bernanos (5th), 01-44-41-33-44 **MÉTRO:** Porte Royal
Censier, 31, rue Geoffroy-St-Hilaire (5th), 01-45-35-41-24 **MÉTRO:** Censier-Daubenton
Chatelet, 10, rue Jean Calvin (5th), 01-43-31-51-66 **MÉTRO:** Censier-Daubenton
Citeaux, 45, boulevard Diderot (12th), 01-49-28-59-40 or 41 **MÉTRO:** Gare de Lyon
Cuvier, 8, rue Cuvier (5th), 01-43-25-46-65 **MÉTRO:** Jussieu
Dareau, 13–17, rue Dareau (14th), 01-45-65-25-25 **MÉTRO:** St-Jacques
Grand Palais, Cours la Reine (8th), 01-43-59-88-70 **MÉTRO:** Champs-Élysées
I.U.T., 143, avenue de Versailles (16th), 01-42-88-85-59 **MÉTRO:** Exelmans
Mabillon, 3, rue Mabillon (6th), 01-43-25-66-23 **MÉTRO:** Mabillon

Quick-Reference Lists

These quick-reference lists contain the restaurants that fall into the Big Splurge category, those that are completely nonsmoking or that have specific nonsmoking sections, those specializing in non-French food and in vegetarian fare, and finally, boulangeries, pâtisseries, tearooms, and wine bars.

BIG SPLURGES

These restaurants are for those with more flexible budgets, or for special occasion dining to celebrate a birthday, anniversary, or just being in Paris. An asterisk (*) indicates a Big Splurge in the list of restaurants for each arrondissement and in the text.

RESTAURANTS THAT ARE NONSMOKING OR WITH NONSMOKING SECTIONS

BOULANGERIES AND *PÂTISSERIES*

RESTAURANTS SERVING NON-FRENCH FOOD

AMERICAN

Chicago Meatpackers (1st)	**42**

ITALIAN

Auberge de Venise (14th)	**182**
Café di Roma (8th)	**142**
Chez Enzo (6th)	**107**
La Castafiore (4th)	**77**
Nicelio (11th)	**169**

RESTAURANTS SERVING VEGETARIAN FOOD

Aquarius (4th, 14th)	**72, 179**
Country Life (2nd)	**57**
Entre Ciel et Terre (1st)	**43**
Guenmaï (6th)	**109**
Joy In Food (17th)	**207**
La Petite Légume (5th)	**93**
Le Grenier de Notre-Dame (5th)	**95**
Les Quatre et Une Saveurs (5th)	**99**

TEAROOMS

À la Cour de Rohan (6th)	**104**
Au Lys d'Argent (4th)	**71**
Chocolat Viennois (17th)	**206**
La Charlotte de l'Île (4th)	**77**
Ladurée (8th, 16th)	**144, 199**
La Mule du Pape (3rd)	**68**
La Nuit des Thés (7th)	**129**
Le Stübli (17th)	**211**
Mariage Frères (4th, 6th)	**83, 118**
Marie-Thé (6th)	**118**
Rose Thé (1st)	**53**
Tea Follies (9th)	**155**
Thé Au Fil (2nd)	**62**

WINE BARS

Aux Bons Crus (1st)	**42**
Jacques Mélac (11th)	**166**
Juveniles (1st)	**43**
Le Bar du Caveau (1st)	**46**
Le Café du Passage (11th)	**168**

Glossary of Menu and Food Terms

Eating out should be pleasurable, but negotiating an incomprehensible menu can ruin a meal. This glossary of French menu terms used in *Cheap Eats in Paris,* as well as many other words you may encounter, is designed to help you make sure there will not be a difference between what you want to eat and what you actually order.

A

abricot	apricot
addition	restaurant bill
agneau	lamb
aiguillettes	thin slices, usually of duck breast
ail	garlic, or wing
aïoli	garlicky blend of eggs and oil
à la carte	from the menu, not part of the prix fixe or *formule*
à la reine	with chicken
à la vapeur	steamed
à l'étouffée	stewed
aligot	puréed potatoes with melted Cantal cheese and garlic
allummettes	fried matchstick potatoes
aloyau	beef loin
amandes	almonds
amér	bitter
amuse bouche (or amuse gueule)	small nibbles eaten before food is ordered
ananas	pineapple
anchoïade	puree of anchovies, olive oil, and vinegar
andouille, andouillette	chitterlings (chitlins) sausage
aneth	dill
anguille	eel
apéritif	before-meal drink
à point	medium rare
artichaut	artichoke
asperge	asparagus
assiette (de)	plate (of)

aubergine	eggplant
au four	baked
avocat	avocado

B

baba (au rhum)	yeast cake (with rum sauce)
baguette	long thin loaf of bread
baies roses	pink peppercorns
ballotine	"small bundle," usually meat or fish, boned, stuffed, and rolled
banane	banana
bar	sea bass
barbue	brill
basilic	basil
basquaise	Basque style, with ham, sausage, tomatoes, and red pepper
bavarois	custard made with cream and gelatin
bavette	skirt steak
beignet	fritter, usually batter-fried fruit
Belon	flat-shelled oyster
betterave	beet
beurre	butter
bien cuit	well done
bifteck	steak (can be tough)
biologique	organic foods and wines
bisque	shellfish soup
blanc (de volaille)	breast (of chicken)
blanquette	stewed meat in rich white sauce
blanquette de veau	veal stew with onions, mushrooms, and cream
blette	Swiss chard
bleu	blood-rare (meat)
boeuf à la mode	beef marinated and braised in red wine
boeuf au gros sel	boiled beef with vegetables and coarse salt
boeuf bourguignon	beef cooked with red wine, onions, and mushrooms
boeuf en daube	beef cooked with red wine and vegetables
boissons (compris ou non-compris)	drinks (included or not included)
bombe	molded, layered ice cream dessert
boudin blanc	white sausage made with chicken or veal
boudin noir	pork sausage made with blood

bouillabaisse	Mediterranean fish and shellfish soup
bouilli	boiled
bourride	like bouillabaisse, but without shellfish
bouteille de	bottle of
brandade de moru	creamed salt cod
brouillé	scrambled
bourride	fish stew
braisé	braised
brochette	meat on a skewer
brûle	dark caramelization

C

cabillard	fresh cod
cacahouètes	peanuts
caille	quail
calamar	squid
Calvados	apple brandy
campagne	country style
canard	duck
caneton	young male duck
canette	young female duck
cannelle	cinnamon
carafe d'eau	pitcher of tap water
carbonnade	beef stew with onions and beer
carotte	carrot
carpaccio	thinly sliced, raw meat or fish
carré d'agneau	rack of lamb
carte	menu
carte (des vins)	wine list
cassis	black currants
cassoulet	casserole of white beans with combinations of pork, duck, lamb, goose and sausage
céleri rémoulade	shredded celery root salad with herbs and mayonnaise
cèpe	wild mushroom
cerfeuil	chervil
cerise	cherry
cervelas	pork sausage with garlic; can also be fish or seafood sausage
cervelles	brains
champignon	mushrooms
chanterelle	wild mushroom

chantilly	sweetened whipped cream
charcuterie	cold cuts; terrines, pâtés, sausages; also a shop selling these and other deli items
charlotte	molded dessert, usually lined with ladyfingers
chasseur	sauce cooked with mushrooms, shallots, white wine and tomatoes
châtaigne	chestnut
chaud	hot
chausson	filled turnover
châvignin	sharp goat cheese
cheval (à cheval)	horse (with a fried egg on top of food, not the horse)
chèvre	goat cheese
chevreuil	venison
chicorée	curly endive
chiffonnade	thin strips, usually vegetables
chiperon	Basque word for squid
choix	choice
chou (rouge)	cabbage (red)
chou frisée	kale
choucroute	sauerkraut served with smoked meats
chou farci	stuffed cabbage
chou-fleur	cauliflower
choux	cream puff
choux de Bruxelles	Brussels sprouts
ciboulette	chive
cidre	apple cider
citron	lemon
citron vert	lime
civet de lièvre	stewed hare, thickened with blood
clafoutis	tart of crêpe batter filled with fruit and baked; served warm
claires	oysters
clementine	small Spanish tangerine
cochon	pig
cochonnailles	assortment of pork sausages and pâtés served as a first course
coeur	heart
coeur de filet	best part of beef fillet; chateaubriand
compote	stewed fruit
concombre	cucumber
confit	meat cooked and preserved in its own fat

confit d'oie	preserved goose
confiture	jam
contre-filet	cut of sirloin steak
coq-au-vin	mature chicken stewed in red wine
coquelet	young male chicken
coquillages	shellfish
coquilles St-Jacques	sea scallops
cornichon	tart pickle
côte	rib, chop
côte d'agneau	lamb chop
côte de boeuf	beef rib
côte de veau	veal chop
coulis	puree of raw or cooked vegetables or fruit
courge	squash
courgette	zucchini
couscous	granules of semolina; a spicy North African dish with semolina, various meats, and vegetables
couteau	knife
couvert	place setting
crème anglaise	custard sauce
crème brûlée	custard with a brown-sugar glaze
crème caramel	custard with caramel flavoring
crème fraîche	fresh thick cream with the consistency of yogurt
crêpe	thin pancake
crêpe suzette	thin pancake flambéed with Grand Marnier liqueur
crêpinette	small, flat grilled sausage
cresson	watercress
crevette grise	shrimp
crevette rose	prawn
croque-madame	toasted ham and cheese sandwich with an egg on top
croque-monsieur	toasted ham and cheese sandwich, no egg
croustade	bread or pastry case, deep fried
(en) croûte	in a pastry case
cru	raw
cruditées	raw vegetables
crustacés	shellfish
cruillère	spoon
cuisse de poulet	chicken leg
cuit	cooked

D

darne de saumon	salmon steak
datte	date
daube	meat stew
daphinois	scalloped potatoes
daurade	sea bream (or white fish)
dégustation	taste or sample
déjeuner	lunch
diable	reduced sauce with cayenne pepper, shallots, and white wine
digestif	after-dinner drink (liqueur)
dinde	turkey
dîner	dinner
dorade	red sea bream (not as good as *daurade*)
duxelles	chopped mushrooms and shallots sautéed in butter and mixed with cream

E

eau (minérale)	water (mineral)
eaux-de-vie	fruit brandies
échalote	shallot
écréme	skim milk
ecrevisse	crayfish
émincé	thin slice of meat
endive	chicory
entrecôte	beef rib steak
entrée	first course
épaule	shoulder of lamb, pork, etc.
épices	spices
épinard	spinach
escalope	thinly sliced meat or fish
escargot	snail
escarole	slightly bitter salad leaves
estouffade	slowly stewed dish
estragon	tarragon

F

façon	way of preparing a dish
faisan	pheasant
farci	stuffed
faux-filet	sirloin steak

fenouil	fennel
ferme	farm fresh
fermé	closed
(en) feuilleté	(in) puff pastry
fèves	broad beans
figue	fig
fines de claire	crinkle-shelled oysters
fines herbes	mixture of parsley, chives, and tarragon
flageolet	small, pale green kidney bean
flambé	flamed
flan	custard tart
flétan	halibut
fleur	flower
florentine	with spinach
foie	liver
foie de veau	calf's liver
foie de volaille	chicken liver
foie gras d'oie (canard)	fattened goose liver (duck)
fondant	chocolate dessert
fond d'artichaut	heart and base of artichoke
fondue (du fromage)	melted (cheese)
fondue (bourguignonne)	pieces of beef dipped and cooked in hot oil
forestière	garnish of wild mushrooms, bacon, and potatoes
formule	set-price menu, also known as prix fixe or *menu*
(au) four	baked
fourchette	fork
fraîche, frais	fresh or chilled
fraise	strawberry
fraise de bois	wild strawberry
framboise	raspberry
fricassée	stewed or sautéed fish or meat
frisée	curly endive
frites (pommes)	French fries
froide	cold
fromage	cheese
fromage blanc	creamy cheese served for dessert with sugar
fruits de mer	seafood
fumé	smoked

G

galantine	boned meat, stuffed and glazed
galette	pancake, cake, or flat pastry
gambas	large prawns
garni	garnished
gâteau	cake
gâteau de riz	rice pudding
gaufre	waffle
gelée	aspic
génoise	sponge cake
gésier	gizzard
gibier	game
gigot (d'agneau)	leg (of lamb)
girofle	clove
girolles	wild mushrooms
glace	ice cream
glacé	iced, crystallized, or glazed
glaçons	ice cubes
goujons	small catfish, breaded and fried
goût	taste
graine de moutard	mustard seed
graisse	fat, grease
grand cru	best quality wine
grasse double	ox tripe
gratin	crusty-topped dish or casserole
gratin dauphinois	scalloped potatoes
gratiné	browned with breadcrumbs or cheese
gratuit	free
(à la) grecque	cold vegetables cooked in a seasoned mixture of olive oil and lemon juice
grenouille (cuisses de)	frog (legs)
grillade	grilled
groseille	red currant
gros sel	rock salt
Gruyère	hard swiss cheese

H

hachis (parmentier)	minced or chopped meat or fish (shepherd's pie: minced beef covered with mashed potatoes)
hareng	herring
haricot de mouton	mutton stew with white beans

haricot vert	green bean
homard	lobster
hors-d'oeuvre	appetizer
huile	oil
huître	oyster

I

île flottante	floating island, poached meringue in custard sauce topped with caramel; used interchangeably with *oeufs à la neige*
infusion	herb tea

J

jambon	ham
jambon cru	salt-cured or smoked ham, aged but not cooked
jambonneau	pork knuckle
jambon persillé	chunks of ham in a molded parsley aspic
jardinière	garnish of fresh or cooked vegetables
jarret	shin
jeune	young
joue (dé boeuf)	beef (cheek, jowl)
julienne	slivered vegetables
jus	juice

K

kir	aperitif made with crème de cassis and white wine
kir royale	kir made from champagne instead of wine

L

lait	milk
laitue	lettuce
landaise	cooked in goose fat with garlic, onion, ham
langouste	small freshwater lobster (sometimes called cray-fish)
langoustine	smaller than *langouste*—scampi
langue (de boeuf)	tongue (beef)
lapereau	young rabbit
lapin	rabbit
lardon	cubed, thick bacon
léger	light
légume	vegetable
liégois	with juniper berries or gin

liégoise	ice cream sundae made with coffee and chocolate
lièvre	wild hare
lotte	large, firm-fleshed saltwater fish
loup de mer	similar to striped bass
Lyonnaise (à la)	Lyon-style, usually with onions and/or sautéed potatoes

M

mâche	lamb's lettuce
madeleine	small tea cake
magret de canard (oie)	breast of fattened duck (goose)
maigre	thin, no fat
maison (de la)	house (in the style of, or made there)
mandarine	tangerine
mange-tout	snow pea
mangue	mango
maquereau	mackerel
marchand de vin	sauce with red wine, stock, and shallots
marché	market
marinée	marinated
*marquise au chocola*t	rich chocolate mousse cake
marron	chestnut
médaillon	round piece of slice
mélange	mixture
méli-mélo	assortment of fish served in a salad
menthe	mint
menu	set price selection, also called prix fixe or *formule*
menu du marché	a *menu* using fresh produce from that day's market
mer	sea
merguez	very spicy sausage
mesclun	mixture of seven types of baby salad greens
mets selon de la saison	according to the season
meunière	rolled in flour and cooked in butter
meurette	red wine sauce made with mushrooms, onions, bacon, and carrots
miel	honey
mignonette	small cubes of beef; coarsely ground white or black peppercorns
mille feuille	pastry with many layers, filled with pastry cream
mimosa	garnish of chopped hard-boiled egg

mirabelle	yellow plum
möelle	beef bone marrow
morceau	piece
morille	wild mushroom
morue	salted or dried cod fish
moule	mussel
moules marinères	mussels cooked in white wine with shallots
mousse	light whipped mixture containing eggs and cream
mousseline	ingredients whipped with cream and eggs
moutard	mustard
mouton	mutton
mûres	blackberries
museau de boeuf, (de porc)	vinegared beef (or pork) muzzle
myrtille	European blueberry
mystère	ice cream dessert; also meringue filled with ice cream and covered in chocolate sauce

N

nappé	covered with a sauce
nature	simple, plain, no sauce
navarin	lamb or mutton stew with root vegetables
navet	turnip
niçoise, à la	in the style of Nice; made with tomatoes, onions, anchovies, and olives
noisette	hazelnut; center out of lamb chop; small rounds of potato
noix (de coco)	nuts (coconut)
Normande	Normandy style, with cream and mushrooms or cooked in cider or Calvados
nouilles	noodles
nouvelle (cuisine)	new; describes foods in style of *nouvelle cuisine*

O

oeuf	egg
oeuf à la coque	soft-cooked egg
oeuf brouillé	scrambled egg
oeuf dur	hard-boiled egg
oeuf en meurette	egg poached in red wine sauce
oeuf poché	poached egg
oeufs à la neige	whipped egg whites poached in milk; served in a custard sauce (used interchangeably with *île flottante*)

oeufs au jambon	ham and eggs
offert	free
oie	goose
oignon	onion
omelette nature	plain omelet
onglet	beef cut similar to flank steak; can be strong tasting and tough
os	bone
oseille	sorrel
oursin	sea urchin
ouvert	open

P

pain (complete) (grille)	bread (whole meal) (toasted)
pain perdu	French toast
pain Poilâne	round loaves of dark bread baked in wood-fired ovens
pamplemousse	grapefruit
panaché	denotes any mixture
pané	breaded
papillote	cooked in parchment paper
parfum	flavor
parmentier	dish with potatoes, usually mashed
pastis	anise liqueur
pâté	finely minced and seasoned meat, baked and served cold as a rich spread
pâté à choux	cream puff
pâtes (fraîche)	pasta (fresh)
paupiette	slice of meat or fish rolled up and tied, usually stuffed
pâtisserie	pastry
pavé	thick slice of meat
(à la) paysan	country style, with vegetables and bacon
pêche	peach
pêche Melba	peach with vanilla ice cream and raspberries
pêcheur	refers to fish preparations
perche	perch
perdrix	partridge
persil	parsley
petit déjeuner	breakfast
petit gris	small snails
petit pain	roll

petit-pois	peas
petit salé (aux lentilles)	salted pork (with lentils)
pétoncle	scallop
pièce	a piece of something
pied (du porc)	foot (of pork)
pignon	pine nut
piment	red pepper
pintade	guinea fowl
pipérade	Basque dish of scrambled eggs, pepper, ham, tomatoes, and onions
pistache	pistachio
pistou	sauce of basil, garlic, cheese, olive oil; sometimes stirred into fish soups
plat	dish
plat du jour	dish of the day
plateau de fruits de mer	platter of seafood
pleurotte	oyster mushroom
poché	poached
poêlé	pan-fried
poire	pear
poireau	leek
poire belle Hélène	poached pears with vanilla ice cream and hot chocolate sauce
poisson	fish
poitrine	breast of meat or poultry
poivre	pepper
poivron (rouge, vert)	sweet pepper (red, green)
pomme	apple
pomme au four	baked potato
pomme de terre	potato
pommes dauphine	mashed potatoes, shaped into balls and fried
pommes frites	French fries
pommes Parisienne	fried potatoes tossed in meat glaze
porc (carré de, côte de)	pork (loin, chop)
potage	soup
pot-au-feu	beef simmered with vegetables
pot-de-crème	individual custard dessert
potée	rich soup with cabbage and pork
potiron	winter squash, often called pumpkin
poularde	fatted hen
poulet (rôti)	chicken (roasted)

poulpe	octopus
prairie	small clam
pressé	squeezed
prix fixe	set menu price
profiterole	pastry puff filled with ice cream and covered with chocolate sauce
provençal(e)	cooked and served with tomatoes, garlic, and onion and often with the addition of eggplant, anchovies, or olives
pruneaux	prunes
purée	mashed

Q

quenelle	dumpling, usually fish, veal, or poultry
quetsche	purple plum
queue (de boeuf)	tail (of beef)
quiche Lorraine	*tarte* made with eggs, cream, and ham or bacon

R

racasse	saltwater fish—scorpion fish
raclette	melted cheese on boiled potatoes, served with *cornichon* pickles and pickled onions
radis	radish
ragoût	stew
raie	skate fish (stingray)
raisin	grape
râpé	grated or shredded
ratatouille	eggplant, zucchini, onions, tomatoes, and peppers, cooked with garlic and olive oil
ravigote	thick vinaigrette
rémoulade	sauce of mayonnaise, capers, mustard, herbs, and pickles
repas	meal
rillette	coarsely minced spread of duck, pork, et cetera
rillons	pieces of crisp pork belly
ris (d'agneau, de veau)	sweetbreads (lamb, veal)
riz	rice
rognon	kidney
romarin	rosemary
rosbif	roast beef
rose	meat or poultry cooked rare
rosette	dry pork sausage from Lyon

rôti	roast
rouget	red mullet
rouille	cayenne-seasoned mayonnaise served with fish soups
roulade	rolled and stuffed meat or fish

S

sabayon	a thick, sweet, wine-based dessert sauce
sablé	shortbread-type cookie
safron	saffron
saignant	rare meat
St. Pierre	John Dory (fish)
saison (suivant la)	season (according to)
salade mixte	mixed salad
salade verte	green salad
salé	salted
sandre	pike or perch, a freshwater fish
sanglier	wild boar
sans alcool	without alcohol
sarrasin	buckwheat
saucisse	small fresh sausage
saucisson (sec)	small sausage (hard, dry sausage eaten cold)
sauge	sage
saumon (fumé)	salmon (smoked)
sauté	browned in fat
sauvage	wild
savoyarde	flavored with Gruyère cheese
sec, sèche	dry
sel	salt
selle	saddle of meat
selon le marché	according to market availability
service compris	service charge included
serviette	napkin
soja	soy
sorbet	sherbet
soubise	onion sauce
sucre	sugar
supplement, en sus	extra charge
suprême de volaille	chicken breast fillet
sur commande	made to order

T

tapenade	puree of black olives, anchovies, capers, olive oil, and lemon juice
tarama	mullet roe made into a spread
tartare	chopped raw beef served with raw egg
tarte	open-faced pie
tarte Tatin	caramelized upside-down apple pie; served warm
tartine	buttered bread, open sandwich
tasse	cup
terrine	baked minced meat or fish; served cold
tête de veau	calf's head
thé	tea
thon	tun
tiède	warm
tilleul	lime or linden blossom herb tea
tisane	herbal tea
tortue	turtle
toulouse	savory *tarte* or pie
traiteur	a delicatessan or caterer
tranche	slice
tripes à la mode de Caen	beef tripe, carrots, and onions cooked in cider and Calvados (apple brandy)
tripoux	Auvergne dish of sheep's tripe and feet
truffaude	fried mashed-potato cake with cheese, bacon, and garlic
truffe (blanche, noire)	underground fungus (white or black), very expensive delicacy
truite	trout

V

vacherin	dessert of baked meringue with ice cream and fresh cream
vapeur	steamed
veau	veal
velouté	veal or chicken cream sauce
verdure	salad greens, green vegetables or herbs
verre	glass
viande	meat
viennoiserie	catch-all term for croissants and various other pastries

volaille	poultry, fowl
vol au vent	flaky pastry shell
volonté (à)	at the customer's discretion

X

xérès	sherry

Y

yaourt	yogurt

Index of Restaurants

M, N

O, P

R

S, T

U, V

Readers' Comments

The listings in *Cheap Eats in Paris* are described as they were when the book went to press, and as I hope they will stay, but as seasoned travelers know, there are no guarantees. With the passage of time, things will change: prices will increase, special menu deals will no longer be offered, chefs and owners will move on. While every effort has been made to assure the accuracy of all the information in this book, neither the author nor the publisher can accept responsibility for any changes that occur.

Cheap Eats in Paris is revised on a regular basis. If you find a change before I do, or make an important food discovery you want to pass along, please send me a note stating the name and address of the restaurant, the date of your visit, and a description of your finding. Your comments are *very* important to me. I follow up on every letter received.

Please send your information to Sandra A. Gustafson, *Cheap Eats in Paris,* c/o Chronicle Books, 85 Second Street, Sixth Floor, San Francisco, CA 94105.